Improving the Effectiveness of the Helping Professions

An Evidence-Based Approach to Practice

This book is dedicated to the clients who suffer unspeakable traumas and still manage to enrich us with their contributions, and to the tenacious and often underappreciated helping professionals who work with hopelessness and despair, and yet provide sunshine, guidance, and affirmation. God bless each and every one of you!

Improving the Effectiveness of the Helping Professions

An Evidence-Based Approach to Practice

Morley D. Glicken

SAGE Publications
Thousand Oaks ■ London ■ New Delhi

For information:

Sage Publications, Inc.
2455 Teller Road
Thousand Oaks, California 91320
E-mail: order@sagepub.com

Sage Publications Ltd.
1 Oliver's Yard
55 City Road
London, EC1Y 1SP
United Kingdom

Sage Publications India Pvt. Ltd.
B-42, Panchsheel Enclave
Post Box 4109
New Delhi 110 017 India

Library of Congress Cataloging-in-Publication Data

Glicken, Morley D.
Improving the effectiveness of the helping professions: an evidence-based approach to practice/by Morley D. Glicken.
    p. cm.
The Big Sky Institute for Personal Growth: A Research, Training, and Treatment Cooperative.
Includes bibliographical references and index.
ISBN 0-7619-3025-6 (cloth)
    1. Mental health counseling. 2. Psychiatric social work. 3. Evidence-based medicine. I. Title.
RC466.G56 2005
616.89—dc22   20040057033

Printed on acid-free paper in the United States of America.

04   05   06   07   08   09   10   9   8   7   6   5   4   3   2   1

Acquisitions Editor:	Arthur T. Pomponio
Editorial Assistant:	Veronica Novak
Production Editor:	Tracy Alpern
Copy Editor:	Brenda Weight
Typesetter:	C&M Digitals (P) Ltd.
Indexer:	Cristina Haley
Cover Designer:	Edgar Abarca

Contents

Acknowledgments

I want to thank Eileen Gambrill, professor of Social Welfare at the University of California, Berkeley, for her pioneering work in evidence-based practice. She has been a strong advocate of research-guided practice and critical thinking in the helping professions. Her work has influenced the writing of this book immeasurably. Thanks, Eileen!

I also want to acknowledge my editor at Sage Publications, Arthur Pomponio, who epitomizes all the positive attributes one would hope for in an editor. He supported the writing of this book for Sage Publications, and I thank him for helping to get many ideas I've had about practice into print. Thanks, Art!

Les Kong, my friend, tennis partner, and the head of Public Services at the John M. Pfau Library, California State University, San Bernardino, has been very helpful in suggesting many sources of information used in this book and in other books I've written. He listened patiently to my sometimes rambling ideas during tennis breaks and coffee sessions and offered calm, assuring, and supportive feedback. Thanks, Les!

Many people allowed me to discuss half-developed ideas for this book. My sister and friend, Gladys Smith; my cousin and surrogate brother, David Naiditch; and my daughter and wise woman, Amy Glicken, listened above and beyond the call of duty and gave me critical, helpful, and loving feedback. Thanks, Gladys, David, and Amy!

Finally, my parents, Rose and Sam Glicken, provided a challenging and provocative home environment where having and defending ideas were encouraged, even when those ideas were in conflict with their own. The immigrant Jewish tradition of encouraging children to read, question, assert themselves, and follow ideas wherever they might lead was always alive and well in my home. Thanks, Mom and Dad!

Sage Publications gratefully acknowledges the contributions of the following individuals: Eleanor Castillo, EQM Children and Family Services; Randall E. Basham, the University of Texas at Arlington; and Kristin Cotter Mena, University of Houston-Downtown.

The DSM-IV quotes used throughout this book are taken from *Diagnostic and Statistical Manual of Mental Disorders, 4th Edition.* Copyright © 1994 American Psychiatric Association. Reprinted with permission of the American Psychiatric Association.

Preface

This book on evidence-based practice (EBP) is about the use of research and critical thinking in assisting practitioners to determine the most appropriate and helpful ways of treating clients with social and emotional problems. The use of EBP comes at a time when managed care and concerns over health care costs coincide with growing evidence that psychotherapy, casemanagement, and counseling may not be sufficiently effective ways of helping people in social and emotional difficulty. In a review of the effectiveness of psychotherapy over a 40-year period, Bergin (1971) writes, "Psychotherapy has had an average effect that is modestly positive. It is clear, however, that this conclusion . . . obscures the existence of a multiplicity of processes occurring in therapy, some of which are now known to be unproductive or actually harmful" (p. 263).

In providing a reason for the lack of good evidence that psychotherapy works, Flaherty (2001) believes that there is a "murky mythology" behind certain treatment approaches that causes them to persist and that "unfounded beliefs of uncertain provenance may be passed down as a kind of clinical lore from professors to students" (p. 1).

As a response to subjective and sometimes incorrect practice approaches, EBP believes that we should consult the research and involve clients in decisions about their treatment. This requires a cooperative relationship with clients where helping professionals act in facilitative ways to encourage their clients to gather information and to rationally and critically analyze it. EBP differs from authoritarian approaches that assume the worker knows more about the client than the client does and that the worker is the sole judge of what is to be done in the helping process.

Without a shift to more effective practice, past American Psychological Association President Nick Cummings predicts that half of today's therapists will be out of work in the next 10 years and that most treatment will be intermittent, with clients coming back for treatment only as needed. He also believes that treatment provided over a single long-lasting period of time will not be the norm, and that most practice will consist of psychoeducational and group treatments with only a fourth of the time spent in individual therapy.

Krauth (1996) believes that the next decade will be an agonizing one for the helping professions because of the continuing mental health care "revolution." She thinks that the shift to EBP might lead to "transforming new approaches" in the way treatment is offered but that there will be anxiety, in the meantime, as therapists find their ways in the new mental health care environment. Reynolds and Richardson (2000) suggest that the future of psychotherapy will be similar to that of medicine, with more resources placed into research efforts that will ultimately lead to increased and improved services to clients. Managers, they believe, will have a basis for making better judgments about the use of resources and effectiveness research will be significantly increased.

This book on EBP is a simple guide for students and practitioners in the helping professions. It includes definitions of EBP, information about where to find best evidence of practice effectiveness, ways of analyzing and evaluating best evidence, and suggestions about how best to read research. The book also contains a number of chapters on how to apply EBP to common practice situations. Best evidence is provided in these chapters with case studies added to show how EBP can be used in actual clinical situations. Many of the studies provided in each chapter as best evidence are critically examined using "falsification" as an antidote to authoritarian research that tells us to believe the findings because, well, because we should. Falsification offers practitioners a way to challenge best evidence, and if a study doesn't measure up, to reject it and to go on to other more helpful studies. Just as we ask our physicians to provide treatments that have been scientifically proven to be effective, so should we in the helping professions do the same for our clients.

I want to thank Eileen Gambrill, PhD, for her work on EBP. I heard her give a lecture on EBP at a Dean and Directors of Schools of Social Work meeting and was so impressed that I invited her to the Worden School of Social Service in San Antonio, where I was dean, to talk about EBP to more than 150 field instructors. It was certainly a thought-provoking, exciting, and challenging experience for everyone attending. Her work has influenced this book in many important ways. I also want to acknowledge the work of a number of British scholars. EBP began in England and, thus far, England has constituted its most articulate and energetic supporters.

Although the book says some negative things about current practice in the helping professions, it is written as an aid to practice and not to denigrate the importance of our work. We all want to do the very best we can for our clients. This book is written with that goal in mind.

—Morley D. Glicken, DSW

Part 1

The Core Beliefs of Evidence-Based Practice

Part 1 of the book contains an explanation (Chapter 1) of evidence-based practice (EBP) and includes the core beliefs that guide the approach. Those core beliefs include the ability to read research as a sophisticated consumer (Chapters 1 and 2), the ability to think critically (Chapter 3), and the ability to understand the sources of information that help practitioners locate and critically analyze practice research (Chapter 4).

Because EBP is a research-guided approach to practice, the reader will be given some basic ideas that explain both the philosophy and the application of the scientific method for problem solving. Much of what practitioners do in treatment, although imaginative and often brilliantly creative, is also unproven. Hopefully, these four chapters will make a strong case for practitioners to understand and apply well-done practice research in their work with clients. Because many therapists argue that clinical practice is highly intuitive and artistic, a counterargument is made that without guidance from existing and developing research, clinical practice can also be harmful. Although practice research often lacks the scientific evidence looked for in research in the hard sciences, it's a beginning. If enough new research is undertaken, it may be possible to create new approaches to treatment that are not only innovative and exciting, but that also provide better assurance that clients will benefit from our help.

Just as we ask our physicians to know the best evidence for the treatment of our medical problems, these four chapters argue that we in the helping professions must also know the best evidence for treatment of social and emotional problems, and that our clients need to be involved in a cooperative relationship that permits them to search, with us, for best evidence. When that evidence is lacking, we need to be honest with clients and enlist them in additional attempts to seek information that will lead to the best treatment possible, given our level of knowledge. EBP is realistic about the need for practitioners to offer some type of help to clients who are in emotional pain when best evidence is lacking. However, although practice wisdom may be the usual direction clinicians take when best evidence is lacking, this section of the book argues that evidence *does* exist if we know where and how to find it.

An Explanation of Evidence-Based Practice

1

This book on evidence-based practice (EBP) is about the use of research and critical thinking in assisting practitioners to determine the most beneficial ways of helping clients with social and emotional problems. The current practice in psychotherapy, counseling, and in much of our work as helping professionals, too often relies on clinical wisdom with little evidence that what we do actually works. Clinical wisdom is often used as a justification for beliefs and values that bond us together as professionals but that often fail to serve clients. Many of those beliefs and values, although comforting, may also be inherently incorrect. O'Donnell (1997) likens this process to making the same mistakes, with growing confidence, over a number of years. Issacs (1999) calls practice wisdom "vehemence-based practice," where one substitutes volumes of clinical experience for evidence that is "an effective technique for brow beating your more timorous colleagues and for convincing relatives of your ability" (p. 1).

Flaherty (2001) believes that there is a "murky mythology" behind certain treatment approaches that causes them to persist and that "unfounded beliefs of uncertain provenance may be passed down as a kind of clinical lore from professors to students. Clinical shibboleths can remain unexamined for decades because they stem from respected authorities, such as time-honored text-books, renowned experts, or well-publicized but flawed studies in major journals" (p. 1). Flaherty goes on to note that, even when sound countervailing information becomes available, clinicians still hold on to myths. And more onerous, Flaherty points out that we may perpetuate myths "by indulging the mistaken beliefs of patients or by making stereotypical assumptions about patients based on age, ethnicity, or gender" (p. 1), concerns that still worry those in the mental health field.

In a review of the effectiveness of psychotherapy over a 40-year period, Bergin (1971) calls for an EBP approach when he writes,

"It now seems apparent that psychotherapy has had an average effect that is modestly positive. It is clear, however, that the averaged group data on which this conclusion is based obscure the existence of a multiplicity of processes occurring in therapy, some of which are now known to be unproductive or actually harmful." (p. 263)

In a more recent evaluation of the effectiveness of psychotherapy, Kopta, Lueger, Saunders, and Howard (1999) report, "The traditional view that the different psychotherapies—similar to medication treatments—contain unique active ingredients resulting in specific effects, has not been validated [and] the aforementioned situations are evidence of a profession in turmoil" (p. 22). Kopta and colleagues go on to say that new research designs might help provide needed answers about the efficacy of one form of therapy over another with specific groups of clients; however, "The field is currently experiencing apparent turmoil in three areas: (a) theory development for psychotherapeutic effectiveness, (b) research designs, and (c) treatment techniques" (p. 1). Kopta and colleagues go on to indicate that "researchers have repeatedly failed to find convincing evidence that different psychotherapies are differentially effective" (p. 3), and, when differences are taken into consideration, the differences noted often have to do with "researcher allegiance [which is] influenced by the superiority of some treatment classes over others for depressed patients" (p. 3).

The clinical wisdom view of practice has frequently been based on what the American Medical Association (AMA) Evidence-Based Practice Working Group (1992) refers to as (a) unsystematic observations from clinical experience, (b) a belief in common sense, (c) a feeling that clinical training and experience are a way of maintaining a certain level of effective practice, and (d) an assumption that there are wiser and more experienced clinicians to whom we can go when we need help with clients. All of these assumptions are grounded in a paradigm that tends to be subjective and is often clinician rather than client focused. Aware of the subjective nature of social work practice, Rosen (1994) calls upon the social work profession to use a more systematic way of providing practice and writes, "Numerous studies indicate that guidelines [for clinical practice] can increase empirically based practice and improve clients' outcomes" (as cited in Howard and Jensen, 1999, p. 283). Howard and Jensen continue by suggesting that guidelines for social work practice would also produce better clinical training, more cooperative client decision making, improved clinical training in schools of social work, more cost-effective practice, and a compilation of knowledge about difficult-to-treat conditions, because "few of the practice decisions social workers make are empirically rationalized" (p. 283).

An argument is often made by helping professionals that what we do is intuitive, subjective, artful, and based upon our long years of experience. Psychotherapy, as this argument goes, is something one learns with practice. The responses made to clients and the approach used during treatment may be so spontaneous and inherently empathic that research paradigms and knowledge-guided practice are not useful in the moment when a response is required. This argument is, of course, a sound one. The moment-to-moment work of the clinical practitioner *is* often guided by experience. As Gambrill (1999) points out, however, we often overstep our boundaries as professionals when we make claims about our professional abilities that we cannot prove. She points to the following statement made in a professional social work newsletter, and then responds to it:

> **Statement:** Professional social workers possess the specialized knowledge necessary for an effective social services delivery system. Social work education provides a unique combination of knowledge, values, skills, and professional ethics which cannot be obtained through other degree programs or by on-the-job training. Further, social work education adequately equips its individuals with skills to help clients solve problems that bring them to social services departments and human services agencies. ("Proposed Public Policies of NASW," p. 14)

> **Response:** These claims all relate to knowledge. To my knowledge, there is no evidence for any of these claims. In fact, there is counterevidence. In Dawes' (1994) review of hundreds of studies, he concluded that there is no evidence that licenses, experience, and training are related to helping clients. If this applies to social work and, given the overlap in helping efforts among social workers, counselors, and psychologists, it is likely that it does, what are the implications? (Gambrill, 1999, p. 341)

The psychotherapy literature is replete with concepts and assumptions that seem unequivocally subjective and imprecise. Consider, for example, definitions of psychotherapy that suggest it is socially acceptable to receive help offered by a trained professional to alleviate emotional pain. One might use the same definition for faith healers, psychics, and others who all have social sanction and alleviate pain. Or consider this whimsical definition of psychotherapy: two people playing together. The vagueness of such definitions certainly cannot convey to clients what we do and makes it more than a little difficult for clinical researchers to evaluate the effectiveness of treatment.

As a response to subjective and sometimes incorrect approaches to practice, EBP advocates consulting the research and involving clients in decisions about the best therapeutic approaches to be used, the issues in clients lives that need to be resolved, and the need to form a positive alliance with clients to facilitate change. This requires a cooperative and equal relationship with clients. EBP also suggests that we act in a facilitative way to help clients gather information and rationally and critically process it. This differs from authoritarian approaches, which assume the worker knows more about the client than the client does, and that the worker is the sole judge of what is to be done in the helping process.

Definitions of Evidence-Based Practice

Sackett, Richardson, Rosenberg, and Haynes (1997) define EBP as "the conscientious, explicit, and judicious use of current best evidence in making decisions about the care of individuals" (p. 2). Gambrill (2000) defines EBP as a process involving self-directed learning that requires professionals to access information that permits us to (a) use our collected knowledge to provide questions we can answer; (b) find the best evidence with which to answer questions; (c) analyze the best evidence for its research validity as well as its applicability to the practice questions we have asked; (d) determine if the best evidence we've found can be used with a particular client; (e) consider the client's social and emotional background; (f) make the client a participant in decision making; and (g) evaluate the quality of practice with that specific client (p. 1).

Gambrill (1999) says that EBP "requires an atmosphere in which critical appraisal of practice-related claims flourishes, and clients are involved as informed participants" (p. 345). In describing the importance of EBP, the AMA EBP Working Group (1992) writes,

> A new paradigm for medical practice is emerging. Evidence-based medicine de-emphasizes intuition, unsystematic clinical experience, and patho-physiologic rationale as sufficient grounds for clinical decision-making, and stresses the examination of evidence from clinical research. Evidence-based medicine requires new skills of the physician, including efficient literature-searching, and the application of formal rules of evidence in evaluating the clinical literature. (p. 2420)

Timmermans and Angell (2001) indicate that evidence-based clinical judgment has five important features:

1. It is composed of both research evidence and clinical experience.

2. There is skill involved in reading the literature that requires an ability to synthesize the information and make judgments about the quality of the evidence available.

3. The way in which information is used is a function of the practitioner's level of authority in an organization and his or her level of confidence in the effectiveness of the applied information.

4. Part of the use of EBP is the ability to independently evaluate the information used and to test its validity in the context of one's own practice.

5. Evidence-based clinical judgments are grounded in Western notions of professional conduct and professional roles, and are ultimately guided by a common value system.

Gambrill (1999) points out that one of the most important aspects of EBP is the sharing of information with clients and the cooperative relationship that ensues. She notes that, in EBP, clinicians search for relevant research to help in practice decisions and share that information with clients. If no evidence is found to justify a specific treatment regimen, the client is informed and a discussion then takes place about how best to approach treatment. This discussion includes the risks and benefits of any treatment approach used. Clients are involved in all treatment decisions and are encouraged to independently search the literature. As Sackett et al. (1997) note, new information is constantly being added to our knowledge base, and informed clinicians and clients may often find elegant treatment approaches that help provide direction where none may have existed before.

Gambrill (1999) believes that the use of EBP can help us to "avoid fooling ourselves that we have knowledge when we do not" (p. 342). She indicates that a complete search for effectiveness research will provide the following information (p. 343), which is relevant for work with all clients (first suggested by Enkin, Keirse, Renfrew, and Neilson, 1995):

1. Beneficial forms of care demonstrated by clear evidence from controlled trials.

2. Forms of care likely to be beneficial. (The evidence in favor of these forms of care is not as clear as for those in category one.)

3. Forms of care with a trade-off between beneficial and adverse effects. (Effects must be weighed according to individual circumstances and priorities.)

4. Forms of care of unknown effectiveness. (There are insufficient or inadequate quality data upon which to base a recommendation for practice.)

5. Forms of care unlikely to be beneficial. (The evidence against these forms of care is not as clear as for those in category six.)

6. Forms of care likely to be ineffective or harmful. (Ineffectiveness or harm demonstrated by clear evidence.) (Gambrill, 1999, p. 343)

Hines (2000) suggests that the following fundamental steps are required by EBP to obtain usable information in a literature search: (a) developing a well-formulated clinical question; (b) finding the best possible answer to the question; (c) determining the validity and reliability of the data found; and (d) testing the information with the client. Hines also says that a well-formulated clinical question must accurately describe the problem you wish to look for, limit the interventions you think are feasible and acceptable to the client, search for alternative approaches, and indicate the outcomes you wish to achieve with the client. The advantage of EBP, according to Hines, is that it allows the practitioner to (a) develop quality practice guidelines that can be applied to the client, (b) identify appropriate literature that can be shared with the client, (c) communicate with other professionals from a knowledge-guided frame of reference, and (d) continue a process of self-learning that results in the best possible treatment for clients.

Haynes (1998) writes that the goal of EBP "is to provide the means by which current best evidence from research can be judiciously and conscientiously applied in the prevention, detection, and care of health disorders" (p. 273). Haynes believes that this goal is very ambitious, given "how resistant practitioners are to withdrawing established treatments from practice even once their utility has been disproved" (p. 273).

Denton, Walsh, and Daniel (2002) suggest that most of the therapies used to treat depression, among other conditions, have no empirical evidence to prove their effectiveness. The authors believe that before we select a treatment approach, we should consult empirically validated research studies that indicate the effectiveness of a particular therapeutic approach with a particular individual. The authors describe EBP as the use of treatments with some evidence of effectiveness. They note that EBP requires a complete literature search, the use of formal rules of proof in evaluating the relevant literature, and evidence that the selection of a practice approach is effective with a particular population.

In describing the ease with which EBP can be used, Bailes (2002) writes, "Evidence-based practice is not beyond your capability, even if you do not engage in research. You do not have to perform research; you can read the results of published studies [including] clinical research studies, meta-analyses, and systematic reviews" (p. 1). Bailes also indicates that the Internet permits access to various databases that allow searches to be done quickly and efficiently. Chapters 2, 3, and 4 in this book are devoted to ways of obtaining and analyzing information for use in making informed treatment decisions.

Finally, in clarifying the type of data EBP looks for in its attempt to find best practices, Sackett, Rosenberg, Muir Gray, Haynes, and Richardson (1996) write, "Evidence based practice . . . involves tracking down the best external evidence with which to answer our clinical questions" (p. 72). The authors note that nonexperimental approaches should be avoided because they often result in positive conclusions about treatment efficacy that are false. If randomized trials have not been done, "we must follow the trail to the next best external evidence and work from there" (p. 72).

Concerns About Evidence-Based Practice From the Practice Community

There are a number of concerns about EBP. One major concern is that EBP is a paradigm that was originally developed in medicine. Psychotherapy is a good deal less precise than medicine and cannot be held to the same scrutiny or the same standards as medicine since psychotherapy is often subjective in nature. Another concern is that EBP seems to ignore the importance of practice wisdom and the countless years of experience of effective and dedicated practitioners. Many clinicians believe that researchers have difficulty evaluating what we do in practice and that attempts to determine effectiveness usually result in inconclusive findings. According to Bergin (1971), psychotherapy effectiveness seems to relate to worker experience. Combining inexperienced workers with experienced workers in a research study often results in inconclusive and misleading findings. Witkin and Harrison (2001) provide another concern about EBP and the problems encountered in reviewing clinical research:

> Small alterations in the definitions of problems or "interventions" can lead to changes in what is considered best practice. A review of readily accessible online reports of EBP or evidence-based medicine studies (see, for example, Research Triangle Institute, 2000) shows that various types of 'psychosocial' treatments are sometimes aggregated across studies. (p. 293)

The authors suggest that finding the strongest evidence for a particular intervention may require a great deal of research sophistication at a level many clinicians do not posses and may never be interested in possessing. They are also concerned that "best evidence" may deny the fact that therapy is a joint effort and, although the therapist may have a certain treatment in mind that shows research promise, it may not be acceptable to the client, and ask, "But what if practice is viewed as a mutual activity in which what is best (not necessarily effective) is co-generated by clients and practitioners? What is the relative value of different sources and types of evidence in this scenario?" (Witkin and Harrison, 2000, p. 295).

In one of the more recent large-scale evaluations of the effectiveness of psychotherapy, Seligman (1995) found most clients generally well satisfied with the help they were receiving. Although Seligman found no difference in client satisfaction between short- and long-term treatment, one cannot deny that clients remain in treatment because of a need for ongoing support and encouragement. These two factors are not easy to reconcile with scientific notions of treatment effectiveness. Psychotherapy, unlike medicine, doesn't often result in a cure. Clients may have prolonged periods of relief followed by a return of symptoms and the need for additional treatment. Using that description of psychotherapy, however, few could deny that medical care often results in relief of symptoms followed by the need for additional treatment. Finally, clinicians are trained in a subjective form of help we incorrectly call treatment. It really isn't treatment, which implies a medical process, but a more didactic exercise in which two people focus on the client's hurts and try to provide relief. It is, necessarily, a softhearted and empathic approach to healing that exists outside of an objective framework. Findings in empirical studies of effectiveness are, therefore, likely to indicate vague and undramatic results.

Among the suggested benefits of EBP are practice guidelines that describe best practice with certain types of emotional problems. Commenting on the use of evidence-based guidelines for practice, Parry and Richardson (2000) believe that clinicians are often reluctant to use practice guidelines because they believe the research underlying many practice recommendations often incorrectly generalizes findings from a specific population of clients to all clients. The authors also believe that clinicians reject "the medical metaphor, that psychotherapies can be 'pre-scribed' in any 'dosage' in response to a 'diagnosis.' There is also a strong belief amongst psychotherapy practitioners, that clinical judgments cannot be reduced to algorithmic procedures" (p. 280).

Barker (2001) wonders if practitioners use best evidence in the form of manuals or standardized protocols, and says that the answer is, "Rarely, if ever. Rather, the successful therapist tailors therapy to suit the individual needs of the person, or the contextual factors" (p. 22). He defines tailoring therapy as meeting the needs of "often changing characteristics of clients" (p. 22), a description of therapy that makes effectiveness research improb-able. Baker goes on to say,

> The practice of psychotherapy is increasingly compromised by the pressures of economic rationalism and the demands for evidence-based practice. The diversity, which has characterized psychotherapy practice to date, risks being compromised by the narrow bandwidth of therapies which are deemed to fulfill the 'gold standard' validation criteria of the randomized controlled trials. (p. 11)

Chambless and Ollendick (2001) confirm that attempts to use EBP in manuals and in other disseminated ways often meet with rejection by practitioners for some of the following reasons:

1. Concerns about effectiveness studies suggest that nonempirically based research may be rejected as unscientific, but,

> "No matter how large or consistent the body of evidence found for identi-fied empirically supported treatments (EST's), findings will be dismissed as irrelevant by those with fundamentally different views, and such views char-acterize a number of practitioners and theorists in the psychotherapy area." (Chambless and Ollendick, 2001, p. 699)

2. Presenting evidence-based information about treatment effective-ness can be problematic because it is difficult to design a manual or report that meets the specific needs of all therapists. Therapists are often unlikely to use such reports or manuals even when provided.

3. ESTs are effective in clinical settings and with a diverse group of clients; however, the studies found to support evidence-based treatment were high in external validity but low in internal validity. Consequently,

although the authors found no compelling evidence why ESTs could not be used in agencies by trained clinicians, more research on their use was suggested.

4. Economic problems facing many social agencies suggest that manuals prescribing treatments for specific social and emotional problems will be more of an issue as the economy softens and services for social and emotional problems are curtailed. The authors write: "Whatever the reluctance of some to embrace ESTs, we expect that the economic and societal pressures on practitioners for accountability will encourage continued attention to these treatments" (Chambless and Ollendick, 2001, p. 700).

In discussing the effectiveness of psychotherapy, Kopta et al. (1999) raise the issue of whether research evidence even exists to support the use of EBP, and note that researchers have been unable to find evidence of the superiority of one type of therapy over another. They also worry that the belief system of the researcher, as Robinson, Berman, and Neimeyer (1990) discovered, might actually influence the outcomes of effectiveness studies.

Witkin and Harrison (2001) discuss social work and EBP and conclude that what social workers do may not be open to the same level or type of evaluation as that typically used in medicine. Social workers act as cultural bridges between systems, individualize the client and his or her problem in ways that may defy classification, and work with oppressed people; therefore, what social workers do may not fit neatly into organize theories of practice. In response to the use of EBP, the authors write:

> Sometimes this involves using the logic of EBP with clients when there is credible evidence of some relevant knowledge available. Other times, however, the most important work is in educating decision makers or those who have control of resources about how irrelevant the best scientific evidence is to the world of people whose experiences brought them into contact with the professionals. (p. 295)

Witkin and Harrison (2001) also raise the issue of whether the helping professions should be placed in the same precarious position as medicine when it relates to issues of managed care. The authors write, "Is it a coincidence that EBP is favored by managed care providers pushing practice toward an emphasis on specificity in problem identification and rapid responses to the identified conditions?" (p. 246). The AMA EBP Working Group (1992) reinforces this concern when it states,

> Economic constraints and counter-productive incentives may compete with the dictates of evidence as determinants of clinical decisions. The relevant literature may not be readily accessible. Time may be insufficient to carefully review the evidence (which may be voluminous) relevant to a pressing clinical problem (p. 2423).

Additional Criticisms of Evidence-Based Practice With Responses

In response to concerns that managed care may use EBP to lower costs, Sackett et al. (1996) write,

> Some fear that evidence based medicine will be hijacked by purchasers and managers to cut the costs of health care. Doctors practicing evidence based medicine will identify and apply the most efficacious interventions to maximize the quality and quantity of life for individual patients; this may raise rather than lower the cost of their care. (p. 71)

An editorial in *Mental Health Weekly* (2001) challenges the idea that EBP is being pushed by the health care crisis. The editorial argues that EBP is an expensive approach to implement, particularly during times when budgets are tight. And while the approach might be implemented, the ability to force practitioners to us best evidence is still unproven.

The AMA EBP Working Group (1992) identifies three misinterpretations about EBP that create barriers to its use, and then responds to those misinterpretations as follows:

1. Evidence-based practice ignores clinical experience and clinical intuition.

> On the contrary, it is important to expose learners to exceptional clinicians who have a gift for intuitive diagnosis, a talent for precise observation, and excellent judgment in making difficult management decisions. Untested signs and symptoms should not be rejected out of hand. They may prove extremely useful, and ultimately be proved valid through rigorous testing. The more experienced clinicians can dissect the process they use in diagnosis, and clearly present it to learners, the greater the benefit. (p. 2423)

2. Understanding of basic investigation and pathology plays no part in evidence-based medicine.

> The dearth of adequate evidence demands that clinical problem-solving must rely on an understanding of underlying pathology. Moreover, a good understanding of pathology is necessary for interpreting clinical observations and for appropriate interpretation of evidence (especially in deciding on its generalizability). (p. 2423)

3. Evidence-based practice ignores standard aspects of clinical training such as history taking.

A careful history and physical examination provides much, and often the best, evidence for diagnosis and directs treatment decisions. The clinical teacher of evidence-based medicine must give considerable attention to teaching the methods of history and diagnosis, with particular attention to which items have demonstrated validity and to strategies to enhance observer agreement. (p. 2423)

In a review of the most effective practices in psychotherapy, Chambless and Ollendick (2001) note that one argument used against EBP is that there is no difference in the effectiveness of various forms of psychotherapy and that identifying best practices is therefore unnecessary. However, Chambless and Ollendick found considerable evidence that, in the treatment of anxiety disorders and childhood depression, cognitive and behavioral methods were fairly clearly defined and that positive results often ensued from the treatment.

The British Medical Association raises other issues with EBP in an editorial appearing in the July 1998 *British Medical Journal*. The editorial calls into question the implied ease with which good evidence is available in medicine and, by implication, whether it is readily available to the helping professional. The editorial notes that most published research in medical journals is too poorly done or not relevant enough to be useful to physicians. In surveys, more than 95% of the published articles in medical journals did not achieve minimum standards of quality or relevance. Clinical practice guidelines are costly and slow to produce, difficult to update, and have poor quality ("Getting Evidence Into Practice," p. 6).

By way of response, Straus and Sackett (1998) report that EBP has been quite successful in general medical and psychiatric settings and that practitioners read the research accurately and make correct decisions. They write, "A general medicine service at a district general hospital affiliated with a university found that 53% of patients admitted to the service received primary treatments that had been validated in randomized controlled trials" (p. 341). The authors also go on to note that three quarters of the evidence used in the treatment of clients was immediately available through empirically evaluated topic summaries, and the remaining quarter was "identified and applied by asking answerable questions at the time of admission, rapidly finding good evidence, quickly determining its validity and usefulness, swiftly integrating it with clinical expertise and each patient's unique features, and offering it to the patients" (p. 341). Similar results, according to Straus and Sackett, have been found in studies of a psychiatric hospital (p. 341).

Is Evidence-Based Practice
Applicable to the Helping Professions?

Reynolds and Richardson (2000) argue that, despite concerns among clinicians that EBP may impede their freedom, new opportunities in practice research suggest that clinician freedom will be enhanced because more options will be available as creative research methodologies suggest new forms of treatment. As new research opportunities develop, the profile of psychotherapy will rise. And although EBP has been called "cookbook practice" and a "new type of authority" that threatens the autonomy of professionals, the possibility exists that research in psychotherapy effectiveness will have the same positive effect that medical research has had on the practice of medicine. In discussing the benefits of practice guidelines, Parry and Richardson (2000) believe that well-done practice guidelines will help clinicians crystallize their thinking about treatment. Published guidelines will also give clients more information and consequently give them additional power to decide on their own treatment. High-quality guidelines help in training new professionals and influence the writing of textbooks that must increasingly contain evidence of best practices. Parry and Richardson (p. 279) provide the following examples of well-done guidelines for professional practice:

1. The American Psychiatric Association has published practice guidelines for eating disorders (APA, 1993a) and for major depressive disorder in adults (APA, 1993b).

2. The Australian and New Zealand College of Psychiatrists ran a quality assurance project that has produced several treatment outlines for agoraphobia (Quality Assurance Project, 1982a), for depressive disorders (1982b), for borderline, narcissistic and histrionic personality disorders (1991b), and for antisocial personality disorders (1991a).

3. The U.S. Agency for Health Care Policy and Research has been influential. For example, their depression in primary care guideline (Agency for Health Care Policy and Research, 1993a, 1993b) was widely discussed (Munoz et al., 1994; Persons et al., 1996). More recently, Schulberg et al. (1998) reviewed research published between 1992 and 1998 to update this guideline. Other guidelines worth exploring include those on the treatment of bipolar disorder (Frances et al., 1996), choice of antidepressants in primary care (North of England Evidence-Based Guideline Development Project, 1997) and treatment of obsessive-compulsive disorder (March et al., 1997).

Whether we care to admit it or not, we are in the midst of a health care crisis in America. Although it's easy enough to blame managed care for the part of the crisis that relates to the helping professions, we, the helping professionals, must share the responsibility. As Witkin and Harrison (2000) and others have repeatedly noted, the helping professions have not embraced the concept of best practice or the need to function from a knowledge-guided frame of reference. The result is a growing suspicion among health care analysts and providers that what we do is expendable. In a warning to mental health professionals to begin close cooperative relationships with self-help groups, Humphreys and Ribisl (1999) give a prophetic view of what the current thinking is regarding the health of the helping professions by asking, "Why should public health and medical professionals be interested in collaborating with a grassroots movement of untrained citizens?"(p. 326). The reasons the authors provide are that money for health care is contracting and is likely to continue doing so, and that self-help groups often provide "benefits that the best health care often does not: identification with other sufferers, long-term support and companionship, and a sense of competence and empowerment" (p. 326).

Professions have a body of knowledge that shouldn't be based on practice wisdom or practice experience, but on the evidence that we are collecting from empirical data that support our interventions. Without such a body of knowledge, we begin to lose our status as professionals and the future of psychotherapy in the United States seems clear: less therapy provided, irrespective of client need; therapy provided by the least highly trained worker with heavy reliance on self-help groups; psychoeducational materials in the form of reading for clients and in lieu of therapy; and the hope that clients will be resilient and wise enough to get better, essentially, by themselves.

SUMMARY

This chapter discusses the definitions of EBP and some of the criticisms to the approach found in the literature. Among the strongest criticisms of EBP is that we fail to have a well-defined literature at present, and what we do have is not only difficult to read and comprehend, but it's far too time-consuming for most practitioners. There is also a strong suspicion that clinicians do not use manuals that contain best evidence on practice effectiveness. On the positive side, it is recognized that there is a need to organize best practices and to ensure clients and third-party providers that what we do works. EBP is an approach that tries to organize a way of providing the best possible service to clients by using a knowledge-guided approach to the research literature and substantial involvement of clients in decision making to ensure that the client-worker relationship is cooperative.

Integrative Questions

1. Do you think it's possible to organize best practice in ways that capture the individual nature of the client? Isn't this the problem with EBP, that it cannot individualize what's actually best for specific clients and their unique needs?

2. Why do you think training manuals are so unpopular with clinicians?

3. There is evidence in this chapter that we lack conclusive data to suggest best evidence for effective work with most client problems. Doesn't this suggest that EBP cannot function adequately until we have considerably more practice research available?

4. EBP originated in medicine. Do you think that medicine and therapy are similar enough to utilize an approach initially developed for medical practice?

5. Because therapy requires a more highly involved participation by the client than does medicine, do you accept Gambrill's criticism that we make statements in the helping professions about what we do and its effectiveness that are unsupported by the data and that create false impressions?

References

Agency for Health Care Policy and Research. (1993a). *Depression in primary care: Detection and diagnosis.* Washington, DC: U.S. Department of Health and Human Services.

Agency for Health Care Policy and Research. (1993b). *Depression in primary care: Treatment of major depression.* Washington, DC: U.S. Department of Health & Human Services.

American Medical Association Evidence-Based Practice Working Group. (1992). Evidence-based medicine: A new approach to teaching the practice of medicine. *Journal of the American Medical Association, 268,* 2420–2425.

American Psychiatric Association. (1993a). Practice guideline for eating disorders. *American Journal of Psychiatry, 150,* 207–228.

American Psychiatric Association. (1993b). Practice guideline for major depressive disorder in adults. *American Journal of Psychiatry Supplement, 150*(Suppl. 4).

Bailes, B. K. (2002, June). Evidence-based practice guidelines: One way to enhance clinical practice. *AORN Journal, 12*(6), 1–8.

Barker, P. (2001). The ripples of knowledge and the boundaries of practice: The problem of evidence in psychotherapy research. *International Journal of Psychotherapy, 6*(1), 11–24.

Bergin, A. E. (1971). The evaluation of therapeutic outcomes. In A. E. Bergin & S. Garfield (Eds.), *Handbook of psychotherapy and behavior change* (pp. 217–270). New York: Wiley.

Chambless, D. L., & Ollendick, T. H. (2001). Empirically supported psychological interventions: Controversies and evidence [Electronic version]. *Annual Review of Psychology, 52,* 685–716.

Dawes, R. M. (1994). *House of cards: Psychology and psychotherapy built on myth.* New York: Free Press.

Denton, W. H., Walsh, S. R., & Daniel, S. S. (2002). Evidence-based practice in family therapy: Adolescent depression as an example. *Journal of Marital and Family Therapy, 28*(1), 39–45.

Enkin, M., Keirse, M. J. N., Renfrew, M., & Neilson, J. (1995). *A guide to effective care in pregnancy and childbirth* (2nd ed.). New York: Oxford University Press.

Flaherty, R. J. (2001, September 15). Medical myths: Today's perspectives [Electronic version]. *Patient Care, 61*(9), 1–14. Retrieved December 2002 from www.patientcareonline.com/be_core/content/journals/p/data/2001/0915/09a01myths.html

Frances, A., Docherty, J. P., & Kahn, D. A. (1996). Treatment of bipolar disorder. *Journal of Clinical Psychiatry, 57*(Suppl. 12a).

Gambrill, E. (1999). Evidence-based practice: An alternative to authority-based practice. *Journal of Contemporary Human Services, 80*(4), 341–350.

Gambrill, E. (2000, October). Evidence-based practice. Handout to the deans and directors of schools of social work, Huntington Beach, CA.

Getting evidence into practice [Editorial]. (1998, July 4). *British Medical Journal, 317,* 6.

Haynes, B. (1998, July 25). Getting research findings into practice: Part 4. Barriers and bridges to evidence based clinical practice. *British Medical Journal, 317,* 273–276.

Hines, S. E. (2000, February 29). Enhance your practice with evidence-based medicine. *Patient Care, 60*(2), 36–45.

Howard, M. O., & Jenson, J. M. (1999). Clinical practice guidelines: Should social work develop them? *Research on Social Work Practice, 9*(3), 283–301.

Humphreys, K., & Ribisl, K. M. (1999). The case for partnership with self-help groups. *Public Health Reports, 114*(4), 322–329.

Isaacs, D., & Fitzgerald, D. (1999, December 18). Seven alternatives to evidence based medicine. *British Medical Journal, 319,* 1619.

Kopta, M. S., Lueger, R. J., Saunders, S. M., & Howard, K. I. (1999). Individual psychotherapy outcome and process research: Challenges leading to greater turmoil or a positive transition [Electronic version]? *Annual Review of Psychology, 50,* 441–469.

March, J. S., Frances, A., Carpenter, D., & Kahn, D. A. (Eds.). (1997). Treatment of obsessive-compulsive disorder. The expert consensus guideline series. *Journal of Clinical Psychiatry, 58*(Suppl. 4).

Munoz, R., Hollon, S., McGrath, E., Rehm, L., & VandenBos, G. (1994). On the AHCPR guidelines: Further considerations for practitioners. *American Psychologist, 49,* 42–61.

North of England Evidence Based Guideline Development Project. (1997). *Evidence based clinical practice guideline: The choice of antidepressants for depression in primary care.* Newcastle upon Tyne, UK: Centre for Health Services Research.

O'Donnell, M. (1997). *A skeptic's medical dictionary.* London: BMJ Books.

Parry, G., & Richardson, P. (2000). Developing treatment choice guidelines in psychotherapy. *Journal of Mental Health, 9*(3), 273–282.

Persons, J. B., Thase, M. E., & Crits-Christoph, P. (1996). The role of psychotherapy in the treatment of depression: Review of two practice guidelines. *Archives of General Psychiatry, 53,* 283–290.

Project to bring evidence-based treatment into real world. (2001, August 20) [Editorial; electronic version]. *Mental Health Weekly, 11*(32), 1, 4–5.

Proposed public policies of NASW. (1999, January). *NASW News, 44*(3), 12–17.

Quality Assurance Project. (1982a). A treatment outline for agoraphobia. *Australian and New Zealand Journal of Psychiatry, 16,* 25–33.

Quality Assurance Project. (1982b). A treatment outline for depressive disorders. *Australian and New Zealand Journal of Psychiatry, 17,* 129–148.

Quality Assurance Project. (1991a). Treatment outlines for antisocial personality disorders. *Australian and New Zealand Journal of Psychiatry, 25,* 541–547.

Quality Assurance Project. (1991b). Treatment outlines for borderline, narcissistic and histrionic personality disorders. *Australian and New Zealand Journal of Psychiatry, 25,* 392–403.

Research Triangle Institute. (2000). Assessing "best evidence": Grading the quality of articles and rating the strength of evidence. Retrieved December 17, 2002, from www.rti.org/epc/grading_article.html

Reynolds, R., & Richardson, P. (2000). Evidence based practice and psychotherapy research. *Journal of Mental Health, 9*(3) 257–267.

Robinson, L. A., Berman, J. S., & Neimeyer, R. A. (1990). Psychotherapy for the treatment of depression: A comprehensive review of controlled outcome research. *Psychological Bulletin, 108,* 30–49.

Rosen, A. (1994). Knowledge use in direct practice. *Social Service Review, 68,* 561–577.

Sackett, D. L., Richardson, W. S., Rosenberg, W., & Haynes, R. B. (1997). *Evidence-based medicine: How to practice and teach EBM.* New York: Churchill Livingstone.

Sackett, D. L., Rosenberg, W. M. C., Muir Gray, J. A., Haynes, R. B., & Richardson, W. S. (1996, January 13). Evidence based medicine: What it is and what it isn't [Electronic version]. *British Medical Journal, 312,* 71–72. Retrieved December 17, 2002, from www.bmj.com/cgi/content/full/312/7023/71?ijkey=JflK2VHy VI2F6

Schulberg, H. C., Katon, W., Simon, G. E., & Rush, A. J. (1998). Treating major depression in primary care practice: An update of the Agency for Health Care Policy and Research Practice Guidelines. *Archives of General Psychiatry, 55,* 1121–1127.

Seligman, M. E. P. (1995). The effectiveness of psychotherapy: The *Consumer Reports* study. *American Psychologist, 50*(12), 965–974.

Straus, S. E., & Sackett, D. L. (1998, August 1). Using research findings in clinical practice [Electronic version]. *British Medical Journal, 317,* 339–342. Retrieved December 17, 2002, from www.bmj.com/cgi/content/full/317/7154/339

Timmermans, S., & Angell, A. (2001). Evidence-based medicine, clinical uncertainty, and learning to doctor. *Journal of Health & Social Behavior, 42*(4), 342.

Witkin, S. L., & Harrison, W. D. (2001, October). Editorial: Whose evidence and for what purpose? *Social Work, 46*(4), 293–296.

A Simple Guide to Reading and Understanding Practice Research

2

Practitioners in the applied helping professions sometimes argue that being able to help others is something we are born with and that research and knowledge-guided paradigms like EBP can only serve to shape our innate helping abilities and give us some minor direction. The reality is that even those with a long history (perhaps since childhood) of being sought out because of their listening and advice-giving abilities may still not really be helping people. Like any method, effective therapy comes from objective knowledge. If we practitioners are not consulting the research literature about the clients we work with, how can we (or anyone else, for that matter) know that what we've provided is the best help possible?

And the answer is that clients, many of them poor and very needy, can never be certain that the help they are getting is going to make a difference if all we do is intuitively provide help that may, in the final analysis, do the client more harm than good. One way to remedy this situation is to actively read the research literature, evaluate it for any evidence of best practices, and share that evidence with clients so that together we can make the most informed decisions possible regarding the best interventions.

Understanding the Scientific Method

When reading a research study, it's important to remember that research is an objective way of discovering knowledge. Consequently, there are rules that researchers try to follow in social research and that you, as a sophisticated consumer, should keep in mind when evaluating any research study for best evidence. Some of the more important rules to keep in mind when reviewing research for best evidence are the following:

1. The study should truthfully describe what was done. All research has a mandatory expectation that researchers clearly and truthfully explain the way a study was conducted and the procedures used. The more objective the study and the more the rules of the scientific method were followed, the more we, as consumers, are inclined to accept the findings. The admission of any deviation from a predetermined plan by the researcher is very important because it may affect our willingness to accept the findings. The scientific method demands that researchers inform us of any problems encountered in the study, including changes in the procedures used, the research design, or the sampling procedure used to identify a group of subjects. If other researchers can't *replicate* an original study (do the study over again in the same way it was originally done) and obtain similar results, we should question the original findings. For the study to be replicated by another researcher, the original researcher must share every piece of data and information available with other researchers and with you, the consumer. If a study is repeated and the findings vary from the original study, we might ask whether the original findings were justified. We might also wonder if the replicated study used the same procedures and methods used in the first study. If not, another study might need to be done. By sharing information, we usually have a way of judging the accuracy of social research.

2. The study should be protected from the incorrect collection of data and distorted results. There are many examples of researchers failing to inform consumers of conflicts of interest or shortcuts taken in a study that might affect findings. For instance, when researchers who are paid by drug companies to test medications publish their research results in journals without disclosing who funded the research, it stretches their credibility and increases our cynicism. We suspect that being paid by someone with a clear self-interest in the outcome of the research may bias the study.

To avoid conflicts of interest, one safeguard researchers have agreed to use is seeking approval for their research from an institutional review board (IRB), which decides if the research violates the civil rights of subjects, if it is ethically conducted, and whether it ensures protection of the research subjects. The IRB also recommends sanctions against researchers who violate ethical standards. Although not a perfect solution and violations of ethical procedure may still continue, IRBs serve a cautionary function and usually keep researchers ethical. We can assume, for the most part, that research approved by an IRB is research we can trust.

3. The limitations of a study must be noted. The scientific method permits us, as researchers, to report only what we have found. We can speculate, of course, but we can't make more of our findings than are warranted by suggesting cause-effect relationships when none exists. Neither can we generalize the findings to other people, places, or events when this isn't the case. The scientific method doesn't promise complete answers but leaves the door open to new findings and new studies. All research encourages new research and a continuation of the scientific effort. If a study implies that truth is now evident as a result of a study, be very suspicious. This is what some researchers view as "mythology," not science.

A Few Important Issues to Consider When Reading Research

Some of the following material may be found in much greater detail in a prior book I wrote titled *A Simple Guide to Social Research* (Glicken, 2003). That book was written for students and practitioners who sometimes find research difficult to understand, and it may prove beneficial for readers who are unfamiliar with some research concepts.

STATING A HYPOTHESIS

At the beginning of any research report, the researchers should provide a hypothesis, which is a research-driven prediction of what the study will find and is based on what similar studies have found in the past. If enough research isn't available to state a hypothesis, researchers may ask a research question or they may provide research objectives to the study. A hypothesis can be stated in a neutral direction (also called a null hypothesis), or in a positive or a negative direction. Most researchers use a neutral hypothesis to show objectivity and to tell readers that the outcome of the study is in doubt. Here is an example using a study of disclosure of heart conditions to family members based on whether men older than 50 have traditional or nontraditional socialization.

1. Null Hypothesis: "The disclosure rate of heart problems to family members by traditional men over 50 will be no different than that of nontraditional men."

2. Alternative Hypothesis (Negative Prediction): "The disclosure rate of heart problems to family members by traditional men over 50 will be lower than that of nontraditional men." (This may also be called a one-tailed hypothesis.)

3. Alternative Hypothesis (Positive Prediction): "The disclosure rate of heart problems to family members by traditional men over 50 will be higher than that of nontraditional men." (This may also be called a one-tailed hypothesis.)

4. Alternative Hypothesis (A Relationship but No Direction): "The disclosure rate of heart problems by traditional men over 50 to family members will be significant." (This is also called a two-tailed hypothesis because the researcher predicts a relationship but doesn't indicate whether it will be positive or negative.)

5. Research Question: "What is the disclosure rate of heart problems to family members among traditional men over 50?"

6. Research Objective: "The purpose of this study is to determine the disclosure rate of heart problems by traditional men over 50 to family members."

TYPE-ONE AND TYPE-TWO ERRORS

Researchers sometimes incorrectly predict the outcome of a study and whether it proves or disproves a hypothesis. A type-one error occurs when researchers reject the null hypothesis and believe that a relationship exists between variables when, in fact, none exists. A type-two error occurs when researchers accept the null hypothesis and predict that no relationship will exist when, in fact, one does. Type-one and -two errors aren't clearly understood until the study has been completed. They often occur because researchers use their own bias in the selection of the data on which to base a hypothesis. This concern about the use of biased data in providing predictions of the outcomes of studies strengthens the argument that research requires an unbiased approach with a mission to find truth rather than justifiy preexisting beliefs.

The Types of Research Studies

EMPIRICAL (QUANTITATIVE) STUDIES

Empirical, or quantitative, research is based on the idea that a problem can be studied in a way that approximates the hard (physical) sciences. The empirical approach uses such significant methodologies that a study may be able to show meaningful relationships between variables. An example, in determining best evidence, is a study that tries to show a relationship between elements of social functioning and treatment. Social functioning indicators, such as work records, grades, DWIs (traffic citations for driving while intoxicated), or police reports in domestic violence and child abuse cases, can be compared before and after treatment. This stringent process gives us an objective comparison between a group of people receiving treatment and a group of people not receiving treatment. We might find that the treated people did better than the nontreated people, but we may not know why. Therefore, a limitation of empirical research is that, although it may show that a relationship exists, it may not give us enough data to understand the reasons. It is hoped that, with additional analysis, the reason may become clear.

NONEMPIRICAL (QUALITATIVE) STUDIES

Controlling for complex variables that relate to client improvement in treatment can be very difficult. Although qualitative research is limited by the fact that many important variables can't be controlled, it is based on the belief that even nonempirical findings can lead to a better understanding of treatment effectiveness. Although qualitative research cannot show cause-effect relationships between treatment and improved functioning, it may suggest trends, implied relationships, and weak associations among variables. If studies are repeated enough times by enough researchers, qualitative studies can provide compelling information. Some examples of qualitative research include single subject studies, client satisfaction studies, observations of clients interacting with coworkers or family members, and other indirect techniques that use the judgment of the researcher and that are not completely objective.

Quantitative (Empirical) Designs

The following are just a few very basic quantitative designs that might be commonly found in practice research.

COMPARISONS BETWEEN AN EXPERIMENTAL GROUP AND A CONTROL GROUP

This is a very basic quantitative design in which the control and the experimental groups are chosen at random. The experimental group is given some form of treatment while the control group goes without that treatment. Pretests are given before treatment begins to determine the baseline functioning of clients in both the control and the experimental groups. If done correctly, pretest scores should be the same for both groups. If they aren't, there may be a problem with the sampling procedures. After a specific period of time, both groups are given the same test again and the two groups are compared against one another to see which group did best. If the control group did better than the experimental group, it may tell us that the treatment is unhelpful. If the opposite is true, it may tell us that the treatment is helpful. Only statistical analysis can help us understand how much of the difference between the two groups is caused by chance.

ELIMINATING THE ISSUE OF TEST-WISENESS: THE SOLOMON FOUR-GROUP DESIGN

Giving the same test more than once often makes subjects test-wise. The Solomon four-group design eliminates this problem by using two experimental and two control groups. One control group and one experimental group are given both the pretest and posttest, while the other two groups are given only the posttest. In this way, problems related to subjects being test-wise might be determined.

Subjects who are test-wise are always a problem in research. Most people know that questions on psychological tests are measures of dysfunction and answer them the first time in the most positive and healthy way possible. Giving subjects the opportunity to take a test twice ensures that most subjects will know enough about the test to give the most socially correct answers the next time the test is given. This is particularly true of unsophisticated test takers, who answer truthfully the first time but figure out the purpose of the test the second time and thus give an incorrect but socially desirable response. "Am I afraid that my nightmares will actually occur? Yes, I am," responds the unsophisticated test taker the first time the test is taken. By the second time the test is given, though, he or she knows better than to answer truthfully. Another way to eliminate the issue of test-wiseness would be to give a different test for the posttest, but then we wouldn't be able to compare the pretest with the posttest. The use of a different test might also confuse the results of the first and second tests, because different tests often subtly measure different things.

QUASI-EXPERIMENTAL DESIGNS

Although quasi-experimental designs are not as objective as experimental designs, they are used when ethical or practical considerations limit our ability to use more precisely controlled studies. Denying someone help just to place them in a control group raises ethical problems with legal implications. If a control group subject injures someone or commits suicide because he or she has been denied treatment, for instance, the social agency involved in the study could be held liable. Yet research needs to be done to study the effectiveness of treatment, and quasi-experimental designs may be better than no research at all. It should be noted that, because a control group is missing, quasi-experimental designs are not able to show cause-effect relationships between treatment and client functioning, nor can the results be generalized to other settings or clients. Even with these limitations, some research controls can be developed that allow quasi-experimental research to generate very useful data. For example, we can compare treatment results in one agency with that of another agency serving similar clients. We can also do longitudinal studies to show the impact of services to clients over time. Quasi-experimental research is sometimes called "program evaluation" because it is often used to evaluate services provided by an agency rather than the effectiveness of single workers or of certain approaches to therapy.

Controlling for False Findings: Internal and External Validity

Internal validity refers to any aspects of a study that may interfere with identifying a cause-effect relationship between treatment and its impact on clients. The following common internal validity issues may limit our ability to show cause-effect relationships.

Internal Validity: Threats to Finding Cause-Effect Relationships

LIFE EVENTS

Events or life experiences quite apart from treatment may affect treatment outcomes. Inheriting a large amount of money while being treated for depression might be an example.

BIOLOGICAL CHANGES

People often undergo physical changes during treatment. The amount of physical change may be more significant than the treatment itself, particularly with clients undergoing rapid biological change, such as children, adolescents, the elderly, and anyone experiencing the early phases of a serious illness.

CHANCE OCCURRENCES

Events we can't control for may play a larger role in our research findings than the actual treatment we provide. Press reports of child abuse may substantially reduce abuse for a short period of time and we may believe that it was our treatment efforts rather than the media reports that led to reductions in abuse.

TEST-WISENESS

Taking a psychological test over a period of time may make a subject test-wise. The results of the study may be influenced more by familiarity with the test than by any actual change in behavior.

KNOWING HOW TO TAKE A TEST

Most people know how to take psychological tests and respond to questions in a more positive way than may be justified by their actual behavior. To create some control over false answers, many test makers include reliability checks by asking the same question in a number of different ways. Test takers trying to manipulate the test often get tripped up and score badly on the reliability index of a test. Most researchers discard those people's test results because the data they provide are tainted.

TESTS CHANGE OVER TIME

Test instruments may change over time and researchers attempting to compare test results over a long period of time may be unable to do so. In addition to renorming the SAT and a number of state licensure examinations in the helping professions, researchers sometimes change tests used to measure psychosocial functioning to guard against bias. By making a test more culturally sensitive, however, the test may no longer reflect its original purpose. Making comparisons between an earlier instrument and a newer version may, therefore, be impossible. If a researcher doesn't explain that findings from a newer version of a test are being compared with findings from an older version, you probably should question the findings.

STATISTICAL ANOMALIES

Extreme scores tend to move toward the mean over time. Extraordinary indications of improvement in treatment may be a statistical anomaly.

Responsible researchers always mention this as a reason for improvement rates that are unusually positive.

SAMPLE SELECTION ERRORS

Errors in the selection of subjects affect the results of a study. Keeping certain people out of a study results in biased findings, particularly if the people kept out of the study might provide negative information that may suggest that treatment isn't working. Very difficult clients whose improvement rates are slightly positive to slightly negative may often be kept out of studies of treatment success. Beware of the study that doesn't mention who is included and excluded in a study, and the reasons.

DROPOUTS

Dropouts affect the outcome of studies. This is particularly true in the control group, where disparities in size between the experimental and the control group result in unequal sample sizes. Ideally, the control and experimental groups should end up with the same composition. When subjects drop out, the dropouts may be the very ones who are most important to the study. In a small sample, just a few important dropouts (by race/ethnicity or religion) can significantly alter the findings.

SOME PEOPLE ARE JUST MORE RESILIENT

Some people improve in treatment because of their ability to use treatment. They might be more cognitively competent, have better language skills, or be more intelligent. Consequently, some people are more physically and emotionally resilient than others and treatment may offer a very limited explanation of why these people improve.

External Validity: Problems in Research That Limit Our Ability to Generalize Our Findings to Other Similar People, Situations, or Events

External validity refers to applying our findings to other places, people or situations. Although we may have a cause-effect relationship between treatment and outcomes, mistakes may have been made in the study that limit our ability to generalize the findings to other places, people, or situations. The following problems with external validity issues are the usual reasons:

TESTING INTERFERENCE

Using an instrument to measure change in behavior as a result of treatment may affect the results. The instrument rather than the treatment may suggest to the respondent the areas that should have improved; thus, social desirability may affect responses, giving us a positive rate of improvement when there may have been none.

KNOWING YOU'RE IN A
STUDY MAKES YOU TRY HARDER

When subjects know that they are in a control or an experimental group, they may try harder to change because knowing you're being studied increases your desire to do better (or, if you have a rebellious nature, to do worse).

PROBLEMS WITH THE SAMPLE

Some researchers have problems finding settings that allow them to do a study. When they finally find a setting (for example, the 11th mental health clinic in a county after 10 others have turned them down), the sample of people in that setting may be quite different from those they'd originally wanted to study, and the findings may not apply to the other 10 mental health clinics.

A BIASED SAMPLE

Taking a small sample of people with certain skills, measuring those skills, and then using the findings to represent everyone in the larger population is a common way of using a biased sample. Researchers often do this by taking highly functioning people in a population and using their achievement levels to represent everyone in a population. Job-training programs are notorious for using this approach, as are many high schools, which have elaborate ways of weaning out poorly functioning students whenever achievement tests are given.

MULTIPLE TREATMENT INPUTS

This takes place when subjects in research have many possible treatment inputs. Narrowing down the exact reasons for change may be nearly impossible, such as in the case of residential treatment where many staff members contribute to a client's treatment.

MEANINGLESS RELATIONSHIPS

Instruments contain meaningless questions known as "fillers." Although responses to these meaningless questions suggest cause-effect relationships, they are, in reality, accidental and without validity.

TOO MANY REASONS TO KNOW WHY SOMETHING HAPPENED

If we consider the thousands of reasons people change their behavior, it's often extremely difficult to single out the most significant ones. A statistical test called regression analysis may show that only 20% of the reasons someone improved in treatment had to do with therapy, leaving 80% of the reasons unknown or linked to variables we've neglected to include in a study.

THE RESEARCHER'S BIAS

Sometimes a researcher's ego gets the better of him or her, and a study becomes unscientific because aspects of the study have been manipulated. Kopta, Lueger, Saunders, and Howard (1999) report that a researcher's belief is often the key to whether a type of treatment is found to be effective or ineffective.

Sampling: A General Discussion

Sampling is when we select a small group of subjects to help us understand what the larger population would tell us if we asked every member of the larger population the same questions. Although the art of sampling has become very sophisticated, egregious errors are sometimes made because important groups of respondents are left out of the sample. If a sample is poorly drawn or if it leaves people out by gender or race/ethnicity, the results of a study may be useless. This happened in the 2000 presidential election, where polls showed both candidates ahead by huge margins when the election was extremely close.

In sampling, we either know the population (called a probability sample) or the sample is unknown to us (called a nonprobability sample).

Sampling a Population Whose Members Are Known: Probability Sampling

In probability sampling, members of the larger population have the same chance of being selected. By selecting a sample at random, we hope that every variation among a population will be included and that what a sample may say about an issue is similar to what people in the larger population would also say. Selecting a sample is less time-consuming and less expensive than seeking information from everyone in a population. The more similar the members of a population are, the smaller and less sophisticated the sample size and selection process need to be. Based on information about a population, researchers decide the number of people needed in a sample to give the study an acceptable margin of error (how close they want to be to finding out how everyone in the entire population would respond). Once the sample size is established, the researcher uses one of the following approaches in selecting a sample:

SIMPLE RANDOM SAMPLE

In this approach, the researcher selects a certain number of people as his or her sample, such as 2% of the total names in a local phone book. This can be done by taking every 25th name in the phone book until the sample has been selected, or by putting names in a hat and drawing the sample that way. If we researchers choose enough people at random, we hope the sample will closely resemble the larger population. If some people are left out of the study whose sociodemographic characteristics are important, we might end up with a biased sample. This often occurs when our sample is too small or when certain people were not available when our sample was drawn. Both problems give us an unacceptably high margin of error. The margin of error is the difference between what everyone in a population would tell us and the error rate we get from using a sample to represent the entire population.

STRATIFIED RANDOM SAMPLING

Including all the elements of a larger population by race/ethnicity, gender, etc., requires us to break the population down into subgroups and then select a sample that is proportionately equal to the subgroups within a larger population. To draw a 10% sample from a population of 1,000 clients receiving services from a social agency that serves 40% Caucasian, 30% Latino, and 30% African American clients, we randomly select 40 Caucasian clients, 30 Latino clients, and 30 African American clients for our sample of 100. To be even more accurate, we can break down the subgroups by gender and age.

ALTERNATE SELECTIONS

To make up for dropouts and for people who return questionnaires only partially completed or who fail to return them at all, researchers usually randomly select a pool of alternates consisting of 3%–5% more participants than are actually needed.

Sampling a Population Whose Members Are Not Known: Nonprobability Sampling

We use the following nonprobability sampling approaches when we have no way of knowing the number or location of the people who comprise a population:

CONVENIENCE SAMPLING

When a population is very difficult to identify or locate, we often must use the cases we can actually find, even though they may give us inaccurate information and they may not represent the larger population.

SNOWBALL SAMPLING

In a difficult-to-find population, we might ask the subjects we've already identified to provide names of others who might join our study. If we start out with subjects providing self-serving responses, however, it's possible that the additional people suggested by our original subjects will also provide self-serving responses. Although this may be the only approach we can use, we shouldn't make too much of the findings.

PURPOSIVE SAMPLING

We use this sampling approach when we want to find subjects who have a special quality and a random sample may not be precise enough to select the subjects for our study.

QUOTA SAMPLING

Quota sampling is much like stratified random sampling without the scientific component. Let's assume that we want to find out the opinions of 1,000 subjects from a larger population of 50,000, and we decide to use a shopping mall to select our sample. We know that the total population of 50,000 consists of 40% Caucasian (60% female and 40% male), 40% Latino (55% female and 45% male), 10% Asian (60% male and 40% female), and 10% African American (60% female and 40% male). Using face recognition and directly asking people their ethnicity and gender, we could draw a sample from the shoppers at the mall that might come reasonably close to giving us a stratified sample, although the nonrandomness of selection makes our sampling approach less than scientific. As with all nonprobability approaches to sampling, researchers might argue that some information, even if less than scientific, is better than no information at all.

Incorrect Conclusions

To help the reader put the information presented thus far in perspective, the following summary of an article is included, which suggests that taking fatty acid supplements can curb violence in a prison population. The author (Arehart-Treichel, 2002) reports,

> Omega-6 and omega-3 essential fatty acids, which influence levels of the neurotransmitters serotonin and dopamine, have been found to be deficient among violent offenders. Thus, correcting this deficiency might help counter their antisocial behavior. [In a study involving] 231 young-adult prisoners aged 18 and over, half the subjects were randomized and received one vitamin-mineral supplement and four essential fatty acid supplements daily for an average of four or five months. The others were given placebos. Neither group knew what it was getting. The placebos looked like the supplements—opaque gelatin capsules—but contained vegetable oil instead.
>
> The number of disciplinary offenses committed by the supplement group at the end of the study was reduced 35 percent compared with the number it had committed by the start of the study—a highly statistically significant difference. In contrast, the placebo-group's number of disciplinary offenses was reduced only 7 percent during the study period, which was not a statistically significant difference. With regard to reduction in violent incidents from the start to the end of the study, the supplement group experienced a 37 percent decrease, which was highly statistically significant. In contrast, the placebo group experienced a 10 percent reduction, which was not statistically significant. When the number of disciplinary infractions of the supplement group at the end of the study was compared with that of the placebo group, there were 26 percent fewer in the former, a statistically significant difference.

It was concluded that the supplements reduced disciplinary offenses, especially those involving violence, among their subjects to a "remarkable degree," and their results suggest that "the effect of diet on antisocial behavior has been underestimated, and more attention should be paid to offenders' diets." (p. 26)

Can we accept this conclusion? Certainly not. Why not? Because although the reduction in violence may be statistically significant, it may also be slight. We don't know the level of violence to begin with and we don't know the definition of violence. Perhaps a new warden or a new disciplinary system reduced violence and not the fatty acids. And, as those who have worked in a prison know, everyone in a prison knows every secret there is to know. Research conducted in prisons isn't secret because prisoners work in the various departments that approve and run research studies. Finally, even though we have a randomly selected sample, we know too little about the randomization procedure to accept that the two groups were similar. Yet, this is a fabulous idea and any clinician working with violent clients would certainly want to find more studies about the relationship between fatty acids and a reduction in violence. That's really the key issue: the need for additional information before accepting the findings, intriguing though they may be.

Reviews of Research That Yield Best Evidence

Guyatt et al. (1995) suggest the following rank order of methods for evaluating best evidence of treatment effectiveness: (a) systematic reviews and meta-analyses, (b) randomized controlled trials with definitive (clear) results, (c) randomized controlled trials with nondefinitive (unclear) results, (d) cohort studies, (e) case-control or single-subject studies, (f) cross-sectional studies, and (g) narrative or case reviews.

The following discussion examines the best way to approach the task of finding best evidence for work with a specific client. Three types of review are included in this discussion: systematic reviews, meta-analyses, and narrative reviews. Concerns about using findings from a single study are also noted.

SYSTEMATIC REVIEWS

One way to gather a great deal of information about specific problems one might be encountering with clients is to do what Cook, Mulrow, and Haynes (1997) call a systematic review. The authors provide the following description:

Systematic reviews can help practitioners keep abreast of the literature by summarizing large bodies of evidence and helping to explain differences among studies on the same question. A systematic review involves the application of scientific strategies, in ways that limit bias, to the assembly, critical appraisal, and synthesis of all relevant studies that address a specific clinical question. (p. 376)

META-ANALYSES

In describing a meta-analysis, Cook et al. (1997) note, "A meta-analysis is a type of systematic review that uses statistical methods to combine and summarize the results of several primary studies" (p. 376). Egger and Smith (1997) write: "We believe that the term meta-analysis should be used to describe the statistical integration of separate studies, whereas 'systematic review' is most appropriate for denoting any review of a body of data that uses clearly defined methods and criteria" (p. 373). According to the authors, a well-done meta-analysis helps resolve uncertainty and disagreement, reduces the possibility of false-positive findings, allows us to note the heterogeneity of studies, promotes promising research questions, and suggests the size of future samples to explore the problem more adequately.

NARRATIVE REVIEWS

We usually think of traditional narrative reviews as the sharing of clinical experience. The typical narrative review is subjective and therefore may not be generalizable to other situations or problems, but rather is specific to the experience of the author. Egger and Smith (1997) point out one of the most common flaws in narrative reviews when they write, "Selective inclusion of studies that support the author's view is common: the frequency of citation of clinical trials is related to their outcome, with studies in line with the prevailing opinion being quoted more frequently than unsupportive studies" (p. 373). In psychotherapy, egregious errors may result from narrative reviews. An actual example from our clinical past is associating anorexia with child molestation on the basis of several clinical reports with very small samples. If we place poorly done studies into a narrative report, the findings can be misleading and may result in harmful treatments.

USING INFORMATION FROM SINGLE STUDIES

Obviously, a single study isn't enough to provide conclusive evidence of best practice. Replication of a single study may refute the original findings and research errors are often eliminated as more studies are done. One of the most common errors found in studies is the false-positive error, in which a positive result is found but problems in the study suggest that these findings are in error. Freiman, Chalmers, Smith, and Kuebler (1992) report that false positives were found 20% of the time when 136 studies of a specific medical treatment were evaluated. In psychotherapy, where research is limited and the findings of a single study may constitute all the information available, the practitioner must make judgments about a variety of factors in the study that influence research outcomes. Those judgments include concerns about the research design, sample size, the consistency of the treatment input, and whether the researcher included a discussion of potential problems that might have affected the findings.

To better use findings from a single study, many research articles include e-mail addresses for contacting researchers so that more complete information may be obtained. If a researcher isn't forthcoming with answers, or if the answers are evasive, there could be reason to doubt the findings of a study. Practitioners often think that researchers would rather not be bothered by e-mails or phone calls but, in fact, most researchers enjoy the contact and appreciate knowing that someone has read their research. Having supervised hundreds of student research projects, I can say that most researchers are kind and responsive to questions and they often aid practitioners by providing additional references and information. Being an informed consumer includes the right to ask relevant questions of the researcher, including information about data not included in a published report.

Applying Best Evidence to Practice

Sheldon, Guyatt, and Haines (1998) indicate, "Evidence of effectiveness alone does not imply that an intervention should be adopted; adoption of an intervention depends on whether the benefit is sufficiently large relative to the risks and costs" (p. 140). The authors go on to note that additional factors to consider, aside from the evidence of best practice, are the following:

1. Is the relative risk attributed to the intervention likely to be different in a specific case because of the client's physiological or psychological characteristics? This might be particularly relevant if we suspect underlying pathologies such as rage reactions or fugue states that might result in spontaneous and potentially dangerous behaviors.

2. What is the client's risk of aversive behavior without the intervention? This could be particularly important when suicide, homicide, or abusive behavior might occur without treatment.

3. Are there social or cultural factors that might suggest that a treatment intervention is inappropriate? This is obviously important when working with someone whose cultural background is unknown to us.

4. Even with the best practice identified, is it something the client and the family will accept? Keep in mind that one of the tenets of EBP is the cooperative involvement of clients in their treatment. Even though a particular treatment regimen is found to be the most effective way of resolving a client's problem, the client may find it intrusive, clearly incompatible with role and gender expectations, or so outside of their normal way of functioning that it causes them additional stress.

These four issues create a considerable problem for the practitioner who believes that simply finding best evidence will lead to a resolution of the problem. Practitioners hope this is the case, but sometimes clients have special needs that make the application of best evidence complex. In Chapter 13 on problems of depression and anxiety among older adults, the use of cognitive-behavioral therapies is often suggested as the most effective approach. Yet many older adults find cognitive therapy overly intrusive and prescriptive. As a result, not recognizing the unique qualities of clients often results in the misuse of best evidence. Culturally traditional Latino clients may be unwilling to use therapy approaches that are overly directive because this is an uncomfortable way for many Latino clients to communicate. Clients on the verge of harmful behavior to themselves or to others may be uncooperative, or they may find attempts to be supportive merely ways of placating or manipulating them, which may actually lead them to commit more dangerous behaviors. Consequently, finding the best evidence and individualizing it to a specific client is the task that makes EBP most interesting and useful. Helping professionals believe in the uniqueness of people, and EBP, in its cautionary stance on the use of best evidence, supports that belief.

SUMMARY

In this chapter, some very basic research concepts were presented to help the reader differentiate well done from less compelling research studies. Special attention was paid to empirical designs and to the responsibility of researchers to provide us with sufficient information on which to judge the quality of a study. Included in this chapter was a discussion of sampling, research designs, and the differences between quantitative and qualitative research. Caution was suggested in the way best evidence is applied by recognizing that EBP requires a cooperative relationship with clients in which decisions about the application of treatment are made jointly and cooperatively.

Integrative Questions

1. Of what benefit is best evidence when a client might reject treatment information and request interventions of minimal validity?

2. Basing treatment on the information provided in one study seems chancy. What are some ways that information from a single study might be used to help clients while making certain the information is worthwhile?

3. Asking very busy practitioners to find information on best evidence is asking quite a lot. Are there some shortcuts practitioners can use to search for best evidence in ways that are compatible with their workload?

4. Much of this chapter suggests the superiority of empirical research while also stating that empirical research is not only difficult to conduct but may provide limited findings. Wouldn't any research study, no matter how nonempirical, be better than no research at all?

5. This chapter seems to imply that much of what we do in the helping professions is subjective or based on prior experience. One could say the same thing about medical practice. Why should therapists who, after all, work in less objective fields of practice, be more competent as researchers than physicians?

References

Arehart-Treichel, J. (2002, October 4). Can taking supplements help curb prison violence? *American Psychiatric Association, 37*(19), 26.

Cook, D. J., Mulrow, C. D., & Haynes, R. B. (1997, March 1). Systematic reviews: Synthesis of best evidence for clinical decisions. *Annals of Internal Medicine, 126,* 376–380.

Egger, M. E., & Smith, G. D. (1997). Meta-analysis: Potentials and promise. *British Medical Journal, 315*(7119), 1371–1374.

Freiman, J. A., Chalmers, T. C., Smith, H., & Kuebler, R. R. (1992). The importance of beta, the type II error, and sample size in the design and interpretation of the randomized controlled trial. In J. C. Bailar & F. Mosteller (Eds.), *Medical uses of statistics* (p. 357). Boston: NEJM Books.

Glicken, M. D. (2003). *A simple guide to social research.* Boston: Allyn & Bacon/ Longman.

Guyatt, G. H, Sackett, D. L., Sinclair, J. C., Hayward, R., Cook, D. J., & Cook, R. J. (1995). Users' guides to the medical literature: IX. A method for grading health care recommendations. Evidence-based medicine working group. *Journal of the American Medical Association, 274,* 1800–1804.

Kopta, M. S., Lueger, R. J., Saunders, S. M., & Howard, K. I. (1999). Individual psychotherapy outcome and process research: Challenges leading to greater turmoil or a positive transition? *Annual Review of Psychology, 50,* 441–469.

Sheldon, T. A., Guyatt, G. H., & Haines, A. (1998, July 11). When to act on the evidence. *British Medical Journal, 317,* 139–142.

The Importance of Critical Thinking in Evidenced-Based Practice 3

One of the hallmarks of EBP is its focus on critical thinking. Astleitner (2002) defines critical thinking as

> a higher-order thinking skill which mainly consists of evaluating arguments. It is a purposeful, self-regulatory judgment which results in interpretation, analysis, evaluation, and inference, as well as explanations of the evidential, conceptual, methodological, or contextual considerations upon which the judgment is based (p. 53).

In describing what she calls "ways of knowing," Gambrill (1999), suggests, "Different ways of knowing differ in the extent to which they highlight uncertainty and are designed to weed out biases and distortions that may influence assumptions" (p. 341).

This chapter presents several alternative ways of knowing that should help the reader understand critical arguments about the functions and benefits of various approaches to clinical research. This discussion should help in determining how much we, as helping professionals, can depend on the findings of a given research study. As part of the evaluation of any study, the consumer of research should know the researcher's philosophy of science. Throughout this chapter, the opposing points of view of a number of authors are provided, as they discuss the value and limitations of various ways of gathering and viewing knowledge.

Many helping professionals believe that much of what we do is not open to the scientific method, and argue that our work isn't quantifiable because of its complexity. Some authors believe that overly controlling research methodologies severely limit inquiry and are responsible for the lack of practice research, while other authors argue that loose research designs have led the helping professions into beliefs that are better characterized as "pseudoscience" and are responsible for the lack of solid empirical research in the field. In this chapter, a discussion of several well-accepted beliefs in the helping professions will be challenged so that the use of critical thinking might be better understood. A progression of logical questions about a research article will also be offered to show the practical use of critical thinking in evaluating best evidence. I am indebted to Eileen Gambrill (1999) in this chapter for her work on critical thinking.

Ways of Knowing

THEORY BUILDING THROUGH OBSERVATION

The use of observation as an approach to gathering knowledge, also called "logical positivism," suggests that everything we need to know about a research issue can be learned through observation. It is a theory-free approach because observation precedes theory. One way logical positivism is applied in psychotherapy is the belief that, by working with a client over time, we can understand the client's behavior and then construct treatment interventions as our theory of the client evolves. Although this approach to problem solving sometimes results in breakthroughs of a major order (Freud's work, for example), it has many problems, not the least of which is the questionable objectivity of the observer. The inductive approach it utilizes can be highly subjective, illogical, and inaccurate (Freud's work, again, might be a good example).

As an indication of the bias that often develops when using logical positivism, it has been a firm belief in the helping professions that child abuse does long-lasting harm to people, and particularly to children. But what if this assumption is false and most people are able to cope with abusive behavior without professional help and without long-lasting harm? Rind and Tromovitch (1997) conducted a meta-analysis of the impact of child sexual abuse (CSA) on the emotional functioning of adult victims and concluded that the impact was limited. They write:

> Our goal in the current study was to examine whether, in the population of persons with a history of CSA, this experience causes pervasive, intense psychological harm for both genders. Most previous literature reviews have favored this viewpoint. However, their conclusions have generally been based on clinical and legal samples, which are not representative of the general population. To address this viewpoint, we examined studies that used national probability samples, because these samples provide the best available

estimate of population characteristics. Our review does not support the prevailing viewpoint. The self-reported effects data imply that only a small proportion of persons with CSA experiences are permanently harmed and that a substantially greater proportion of females than males perceive harm from these experiences. Results from psychological adjustment measures imply that, although CSA is related to poorer adjustment in the general population, the magnitude of this relation is small. Further, data on confounding variables imply that this small relation cannot safely be assumed to reflect causal effects of the CSA. (p. 253)

If the authors are correct, and their work has resulted in intense criticism from professionals, perhaps the assumption that early life traumas inevitably lead to emotional difficulties is incorrect. Much of the reason we believe that a relationship between abuse and emotional difficulty exists comes from Freud's initial work, which was based entirely on his observation of abused clients. Had he met with abused clients who were functioning well in spite of their abuse, he might have come to very different conclusions. Observation is a very intuitive approach, and although it may provide creative insights, it may also result in seriously flawed information.

POSTMODERNISM

Postmodernism, also know as relativism and postpositivism, believes that all forms of inquiry are equally valid. In showing the subjective nature of the relativist approach to inquiry, Gellner (1992) writes, "Those who propound it or defend it against its critics, continue, whenever facing any serious issue in which their real interests are engaged, to act on the non-relativistic assumption that one particular vision is cognitively much more effective than others" (p. 70). However, as a reaction against the tightly controlled methodologies of the empirical approach, Tyson (1992) believes that a significant occurrence in the applied social sciences is the "shift away from an outdated, unwarranted and overly restrictive approach to scientific social research which has long been unsatisfying to practitioners" (p. 541).

Gambrill (1999), however, sees a contradiction in the way many practitioners live their lives and the way the use of postmodernism affects their professional practice. She compares what social workers want from their personal physicians—an evidence- and knowledge-guided approach to their medical problems that is based on best evidence from controlled studies—with what they feel comfortable offering their own clients—treatment based on intuition, practice wisdom, folklore, mythology, and an occasionally badly done piece of research that validates their belief system.

In another work, I (Glicken, 2003) describe postmodernism as a way of thinking that concerns itself with social problems that have developed as a result of believing that there are rational explanations for most issues. Postmodernism comes from a core belief that it is this attempt to be rational that often causes us to passively accept gender bias, discrimination, inequitable distribution of wealth, war, poverty, conflicts among groups of people, and a range of other problems confronting us as a people. In many ways, postmodernism is a reaction against a world that still cannot control its more primitive instincts and stems from the disillusionment of many people after the Vietnam War. Postmodernism suggests that many current explanations of human behavior are incorrect and that the goal of all intellectual inquiry is to seek alternative explanations of people and events without the methodological limitations of empiricism. Those alternative explanations might include the importance of spirituality, the significance of intuition, and the relevance of non-Western approaches to health. For the postmodernist researcher, the purpose of research is to explore the world in a way that permits maximum flexibility in the use of research methodologies. In a sense, postmodernist researchers are atheoretical and value the flexibility of using a range of research methodologies to seek alternative explanations of events. They want little to do with empiricism because they believe it limits more creative and intuitive approaches while discounting the common experiences, observations, and insights we all have, which may not be supported by data or objective evaluations but which may, nonetheless, be true and which add to our knowledge base.

Gambrill (1999) worries that this freewheeling approach to research hides a more fundamental problem. Claims made by therapists that cannot be supported by hard evidence lead to claims supported by weak and limited research efforts that, over time, create a body of knowledge with a transparent lack of evidence. That body of knowledge is what Gambrill calls a psuedoscience. She believes that this weak body of knowledge has become so prevalent in the literature of social work because it looks like science, although it lacks its structure, methodology, and controls. Tanguay (2002) supports this point of view and writes,

> No matter how reassuring, no matter how exciting the finding, no matter what hope it holds out to clients, the results of anecdotal studies, single subject trials, nonrandomized designs, and noncontrolled investigations must be looked on with skepticism. Such studies may be helpful as pilot work but we are deceiving ourselves and our clients if we act on the results until they are proven. This applies to studies with negative as well as positive results. (p. 1323)

In two opposing articles about the use of the scientific method in psychiatry, Shea (2000) and McLaren (2000) express different thoughts about how well the scientific method can be used in a discipline focusing on the human condition. Shea believes that psychiatry is badly served by the scientific method and writes, "Any applications of that method to such essential human affairs as love, hate, religion, and the unconscious are bound to fail" (p. 227). In suggesting reasons for the lack of relevance of the scientific method to psychiatry, Shea argues that the scientific method assumes that everything is quantifiable and can be made rational, but that this is seldom the case in the helping professions. Many behaviors we deal with defy reason and are certainly not quantifiable. People often think that science is about the use of statistics, but, according to Shea, statistics "is for pedestrian science," (p. 228) because it doesn't suggest bold new theories but rather breaks information into minutiae. On the other hand, McLaren believes that Shea's arguments are spurious and that Shea has created a straw man out of the issue, which is meant to appeal to emotion rather than to reason. McLaren (2000) writes, "Science is mainly about bold and elegant theories which make sense of chaos, and the truly great advances in science have always vaulted far beyond the limited reach of statistics" (p. 374). McLaren goes on to say that in Shea's attempt to vilify the scientific method in psychiatry, he makes the mistake of suggesting that there is only one scientific method when, in reality, "there are lots of scientific methods, some of which are applicable across a broad range of fields and which, collectively, are directed at stripping prejudice and bias from our exploratory efforts" (p. 373).

THE SCIENTIFIC METHOD

The scientific method, also known as critical rationalism and positivism, is a way of "thinking about and investigating the accuracy of assumptions about the world. It is a process for solving problems in which we learn from our mistakes" (Gambrill, 1999, p. 342). The scientific method requires statements, findings, and conclusions to be tested so they can be accepted or rejected. In describing the scientific method, Munz (1985) writes, "Knowledge is not acquired by the pursuit of a 'correct' method; rather it is what is left standing when criticism has been exhausted" (p. 72). One of the key elements of the scientific approach is a willingness to critically evaluate and test knowledge and theories. By doing so, we are able to eliminate many of our mistakes and, in the process, advance knowledge.

Wuthnow (2003) says that the scientific method "involves thinking of ways in which our cherished assumptions about the world may prove to be wrong" (p. B10). He further notes that science expects "candidly disclosing what we have done so others can track our mistakes" (p. B10). In a statement not everyone will agree is representative of the scientific method, but one of importance to research on best evidence, Wuthnow goes on to say,

But the scientific method can equally pertain to studies involving qualitative information drawn from participant observation, interviews, and archival materials. Carefully sifting through letters and diaries in an archive, or through artifacts at an archaeological dig, is ever as much science as computing regression equations or life-expectancy tables. If science is understood in this broader way, then we can identify more clearly some of the challenges in which it may usefully be employed. (p. B10)

Tanguay (2002), however, calls for a more rigorous methodology and believes that we must be willing to maintain a "rigorous skepticism" concerning our personal beliefs about the effectiveness of our treatments and our cherished theories. "Professional ethics should preclude us waffling on the issues of scientific merit. A scientifically inadequate study will lead to unwarranted hope and lost incentives" (p. 1323). Shea (2000) goes even further and wonders if it's possible for the helping professions to use the scientific method at all. Shea writes, "No amount of wishful thinking about the scientific method is going to alter the fact that, in much of psychiatry, an indispensable element in the therapeutic process is what goes on between the therapist and the patient—the knowledge, understanding, rapport, trust and confidence that builds up over time" (p. 227). According to Shea, this subjective component of the therapeutic relationship is not open to measurement, and even if it were, the results would certainly be questionable. "Some feelings," Shea writes, "cannot be put into words that can communicate the exact nature of the experience let alone into words that can be adopted to either scientific use or logical analysis" (p. 227).

JUSTIFICATION AND FALSIFICATION

In approaches that use justification, researchers gather support to prove or justify their theories or hypotheses. In approaches that use falsification, researchers try to discover errors in their hypotheses or theories. The reader can readily see that falsification approaches require a much more thorough analysis than justification approaches because it takes a more concentrated effort to disprove something than to prove it. Proving a hypothesis or theory is weighted in the direction of the methodological information the researcher is willing to share with us and is often upheld by the authority the researcher derives from having done the research. Falsification requires no authority other than the logic of the critical analysis used to evaluate a researcher's methodology.

An example of justification and falsification can be found in a famous article written by Norman Cousins in the *New England Journal of Medicine* (1976). Some years ago, the well-known author was hospitalized with what was thought to be severe arthritis. In his article, Cousins contended that hospitals were bad for one's health because hospital personnel were often unsupportive, treatments tended to be uncreative, and focusing on illness rather than wellness discouraged patients from getting better.

Failing to improve over the course of many days, Cousins convinced his doctor to release him to a hotel room where friends entertained him, many of whom were famous comedians. Cousins also watched comedies because, he reasoned, laughter increased oxygen flow, which is related to better health. Gourmet meals were served on the assumption that good food improved the body's ability to heal itself. His doctor continued to see him, but large doses of aspirin, the common treatment for arthritis when the article was written, were discontinued and megadoses of vitamin C were substituted. Cousins believed that vitamin C, which was thought to be a curative by such well-known advocates as Nobel Prize–winning physicist Linus Pauling, would help in his recovery.

As a result of these alternative treatments, Cousins reported that his medical condition improved significantly. In the years 1976 and 1977, the *New England Journal of Medicine* received more than 3,000 letters from doctors supporting Cousin's claim that hospitals were terrible places for sick people and that we should avoid them if possible. As I noted in a previous work (Glicken, 2003), no one asked, until much later, whether Cousins would have experienced a spontaneous remission had he stayed in the hospital. Nor did anyone look at his past behavior (Cousins had a prior medical problem that made him deeply cynical about the medical establishment). Finally, no one sought to consider the validity of mega–vitamin C therapy (it has since been rejected and people now worry that large doses of vitamin C may cause kidney damage). The bias against doctors, hospitals, and the treatment of illness is so strong in American society, even among many doctors, that personal convictions caused many health care professionals to accept Cousins' findings without adequate supportive data.

To be sure, good came from the article because many people in the medical profession began to realize that hospitals needed to be more humane. Changes were made in food service, visiting hours were relaxed, and consideration of the wishes of the patient regarding treatment was improved. As a piece of research, however, the article was meant to appeal to our emotions and cannot be considered scientific. And, more to the point, had Cousins used falsification and given us the many reasons his experiences were idiosyncratic to him and thus should not be generalized to others, the material would have been more meaningful and truthful. However, this is a good example of justification used by a figure of authority to create the illusion of good science.

Mythologized Knowledge

Nickerson (1986) believes that knowledge serves to decrease uncertainty and that to make it usable to practitioners, it has to survive tests of its credibility that, in addition to evidence for the purpose of treating client problems, also keep us from making serious mistakes in our practice. One of the fundamental problems in the helping professions is the acceptance of knowledge that is not well-documented and has become mythologized through long acceptance without rigorous evaluation or debate. Gambrill (1999) points out the following characteristics of mythologized knowledge and the ways in which champions of mythologized knowledge maintain an incorrect and even harmful belief system:

1. They discourage scientific examination of claims, arguments, and beliefs.

2. They claim to be scientific but are not.

3. They rely on anecdotal evidence.

4. They are free of skepticism or discourage opposing points of view.

5. They confuse being open with being uncritical.

6. They fail to use falsification as a way of understanding information.

7. They use imprecise language.

8. They rely on appeals to faith.

9. They produce information that is not testable.

In the realm of the unscientific, here are a few mythologized beliefs we often see in the clinical literature without justifiable support:

1. **Belief:** A trained helping professional who has gone through a professional program and who is licensed to practice provides more effective help than an untrained and unlicensed professional. **Reality:** As Dawes (1994) reports, there is no relationship between training, licensure, and experience. Empathic nonprofessionals often provide more effective help than trained professionals (Gambrill, 1999). Consequently, a study using trained and licensed professionals to prove the effectiveness of any form of treatment would be remiss if it didn't compare professional help with nonprofessional help. Consumers of research need to know that other forms of help may be effective and that alternative approaches, such as self-help groups or informal therapy offered by indigenous helpers, may work as well—or better—than therapy provided by trained professionals. Using only trained people in a study limits the amount of information we can provide to consumers of research and may suggest unwarranted findings that confuse readers.

2. **Belief:** The longer a client is in therapy, the more likely important life questions will be uncovered that lead to enhanced social functioning. **Reality:** There is no relationship between length of treatment and better social functioning. In fact, Seligman (1995) found that clients with 6 months of therapy were doing as well, on self-reports, as clients with 2 years of

therapy. This belief is also used to suggest that longer therapy is more in-depth, but actually there is no evidence that this is true or that in-depth therapy is more effective than more superficial forms of therapy. Throughout this book, the reader will find evidence that, in many cases, short-term cognitive-behavioral therapies are more effective than therapies using insight over a longer period of time.

3. **Belief:** Early forms of trauma inevitably lead to problems later in life. This is one of the foundations of modern psychotherapy and it may be true of some people, but is it true of everyone? **Reality:** Research on resilience in traumatized children and adults suggests that three commonly held beliefs about human development may be incorrect: (a) that there are predictable stages of development that apply to all of us; (b) that childhood trauma inevitably leads to adult malfunctioning (Benard, 1994; Garmezy, 1994); and (c) that there are social and economic conditions, personal relationships, and institutional problems that are so problematic that they inevitably lead to problems in the social and emotional functioning of children, adults, families, and communities (Rutter, 1994).

Perhaps the best-known study of resilience in children as they grow into adulthood is the longitudinal research begun in 1955 by Werner and Smith (1982, 1992). In their initial report, Werner and Smith (1982) found that one out of every three children who were evaluated by several measures of early life functioning to be at significant risk for adolescent problems, actually developed into socially and emotionally well-functioning young adults by age 18. In their follow-up study, Werner and Smith (1992) report that two out of three of the remaining two thirds of children at risk had turned into caring and healthy adults by age 32. One of their primary theories was that people have "self-righting" capabilities, or what we would now call resilience. From their 30-year study, the authors concluded a significant factor for many children is the existence of a consistent and caring relationship with at least one adult. This adult (sometimes it was a peer) does not need to be a family member or to be physically present all of the time but in many cases is a teacher, a therapist, a relative, a minister, or a family friend. These relationships give the child a sense of protection and help develop the child's self-righting capacities. Werner and Smith believe that it is always possible to move from a lack of achievement and a feeling of hopelessness to a sense of achievement and fulfillment.

This finding is supported by similar findings of serious antisocial behavior in children. In summarizing the research on youth violence, the surgeon general (Satcher, 2001) reports, "Most highly aggressive children or children with behavioral disorders do not become violent offenders" (p. 9). Similarly, the surgeon general reports that most youth violence ends with the transition to adulthood. If people were indefinitely affected by childhood traumas, these early life behaviors would suggest that violence in youth would continue into adulthood. The report further suggests that the reasons for change in violent children relate to treatment programs, maturation, and biosocial factors (self-righting tendencies or, as it has more recently been termed, resilience) that influence the lives of many of the most violent youthful offenders. This and other research suggests that people *do* change, often on their own, and that learning from prior experience appears to be an important reason for change.

A person's positive view of life can have a significant impact on his or her physical and emotional health, a belief supported by a longitudinal study of a religious order of women in the Midwest (Danner, Snowdon, & Friesen, 2001). Longitudinal studies of the many aspects of life span and illness among this population suggest that the more positive and affirming the personal statements written when applicants were in their late teens and early twenties, the longer the life span, sometimes as long as 10 years beyond the mean length of life for the religious order and up to 20 years or more longer than the general population. Many of the women in the sample lived well into their nineties, and beyond. In a sample of 650, 6 members of the order were older than 100. Although some of the sample suffered serious physical problems, the numbers were much smaller than in the general population and the age of onset was usually later in life. Even though some of the members of the order had experienced severe childhood traumas, their life span and their level of health suggests that resilient people can overcome dysfunctional childhood experiences and live productive, successful, and fulfilling lives.

4. **Belief:** The therapeutic relationship is the key to successful psychotherapy and counseling. **Reality:** Noting the importance of the concept of the relationship in the professional literature, Gelso and Hayes (1998) wonder if we have a clear understanding of what is meant by the worker-client relationship, and write, "Because the therapy relationship has been given such a central place in our field for such a long period of time, one might expect that many definitions of the relationship have been put forth. In fact, there has been little definitional work" (p. 5).

In an attempt to determine the most effective approaches to treatment, Chambless and Ollendick (2001) reviewed the effectiveness of more than 75 approaches to therapy. The authors found little evidence that one approach worked better than another, although, in arguing for a more rational approach to treatment, they did find treatment protocols that seemed more effective with certain types of problems, but not with all clients, and not because of the quality of the therapeutic relationship. Chapter 7 considers issues related to the client-worker alliance in much more detail, but the reality is that helping professionals have limited evidence that the relationship is the key to client improvement even though many of us believe this to be the case, and have had experiences with our clients that lead us to believe the quality of the relationship is the key to positive client change.

Understanding the Logical Progressions in Research Ideas

One of my excellent students was having problems with an article on perpetrators of family violence. The article was a postmodernist observation of men who were abusive and their relationships with their wives. The researcher in the article sat in a courthouse waiting room and observed couples before the perpetrator was called into court for a hearing involving his spousal abuse. The researcher had a protocol to guide the observations that specified areas of behavior to observe and evaluate that had been developed from several research articles that discussed the behavior of perpetrators with their spouses in public places. The protocol, although untested and neither valid nor reliable, was the guide the researcher used to look for certain behaviors associated with abusive behavior. The researcher watched 34 couples over a 2-month period of time and spent an average of 20 minutes observing each couple. Most of the couples were non-Caucasian. The researcher concluded that the men were domineering, threatening, and exhibited potential for violence in the courthouse waiting room. Only two couples held hands or looked affectionate with one another.

My student wanted to use this article as the cornerstone of her study, which tried to predict the potential for violence in abusing men prior to supervised visitations with spouses and children living independently in shelters, certainly an important and worthwhile issue to study. We spoke about the research article the student wanted to use.

Instructor (I): This study makes me awfully uncomfortable.

Student (S): Why?

I: Let's look at the study critically. What did you think were the parts of the study worth using?

S: It's relevant to my research.

I: That's true, but does the methodology warrant your using the findings?

S: I wondered about the lack of Caucasian subjects. About sixty percent of the male perpetrators in California are Caucasian. This study only had 4 Caucasian subjects, way less than the usual number I'd see in my study.

I: Good point. Why would the researcher make such an obvious mistake?

S: Maybe she doesn't like certain racial groups.

I: Maybe.

S: Maybe she didn't have time to draw a better sample. But that doesn't make sense, does it?

I: No, it doesn't. Anything else?

S: I had some problems with the protocol she used. It hardly includes the possibility of any positive behaviors. She was just looking for potential for violence. I think people waiting to go to a court hearing are pretty uptight. I'd guess most of us would look upset.

I: Me, too. Anything else?

S: She doesn't say a word about how she selected her couples or what some of the problems might be with her research. I've noticed that most researchers have a pretty long section about the methodological problems in their studies. Also, she did the analysis of the data herself. It might have been a good idea to use another person or to have someone double-check her data, or maybe even have a second person using the protocol and making independent judgments about the perpetrators' behavior. Also, we don't know if her predictions were accurate. Did the men she saw as being potentially harmful become abusive at some point after the court hearing?

I: All very good points. Anything else?

S: Should I chuck the article and not use it for my study?

I: Ah, the eternal question. Maybe you should use it but point out the flaws and say that the article had relevance for your study but that the methodology makes the findings unreliable. That's always a wise approach in research when there are limited studies in the literature. Am I right? Are there limited studies?

S: Well, no. There are lots of them. I should go back and do a better literature review, huh?

I: Excellent idea. Better to use well-done studies than badly done studies. Basing your research on poorly done studies just weakens your work.

S: Why did I know you'd say that?

I: It's my job to help you see the flaws in research. When you see the mistakes other people make, then perhaps you won't repeat them.

S: No, I mean that I'd need to do more work.

I: Sorry, but better a little more work now than a lot more later when I read your research study.

S: There goes my weekend.

SUMMARY

This chapter on critical thinking presents several research philosophies that might help the reader understand that researchers have points of view about the value of various approaches to research. To help the reader understand the positive and negative views of each philosophy of research, conflicting points of view are provided. Critical thinking means that you should be able to logically evaluate all research, even the research you find most appealing. Knowing about methodologies and beliefs regarding the use of research can help you do this. A progression of ideas about the evaluation of a research study is also provided to show how one can approach a piece of research and, with some idea of how to evaluate a study, determine if the study is useful, well done, and a credible piece of work. Remember that the process of selecting best evidence is grounded in your desire to do what's best for the client, not in your desire to reinforce your personal belief system.

Integrative Questions

1. Because there is so little well-done research on treatment effectiveness, don't we run the risk of discounting everything we read?

2. Was the study of perpetrators in the courthouse waiting room so poorly done that we'd want to discount it completely?

3. How can practitioners be expected to use best evidence based on critical thinking when a client is in a life-threatening crisis? Don't we do what needs to be done at the moment and hope that it works? If we don't, we could have a suicide or a homicide on our hands. What do you think?

4. Many of the more subjective research philosophies provided in this chapter seem more likely to produce important information than empiricism. At least nonempirical studies give us hope and they challenge us. Empirical studies are cold and discouraging, or are they?

5. Everybody knows that therapeutic relationships are the key to good treatment, but the author includes arguments against that belief. What's his point? That we don't have enough evidence for the belief, or that we shouldn't accept the belief at all?

References

Astleitner, H. (2002). Teaching critical thinking online. *Journal of Instructional Psychology, 29*(2), 53–77.

Benard, B. (1994, December). Applications of resilience. Paper presented at a conference on the Role of Resilience in Drug Abuse, Alcohol Abuse, and Mental Illness, Washington, DC.

Chambless, D. L. (2001). Empirically supported psychological interventions: Controversies and evidence. *Annual Review of Psychology, 52,* 685–716.

Cousins, N. (1976, December 23). Anatomy of an illness. *New England Journal of Medicine, 295,* 1458–1463.

Danner, D. D., Snowdon, D. A., & Friesen, W. V. (2001). Positive emotions in early life and longevity: Findings from the nun study. *Journal of Personality and Social Psychology, 80*(5), 804–813.

Dawes, R. M. (1994). *House of cards: Psychology and psychotherapy built on myth.* New York: Free Press.

Gambrill, E. (1999, July). Evidence-based practice: An alternative to authority-based practice source. *Families in Society: The Journal of Contemporary Human Services, 80*(4), 341–350.

Garmezy, N. (1994). Reflections and commentary on risk, resilience, and development. In R. J. Haggerty, L. R. Sherrod, N. Garmezy, & M. Rutter (Eds.), *Stress, risk, and resilience in children and adolescents: Processes, mechanisms, and interventions* (pp. 1–18). Cambridge, UK: Cambridge University Press.

Gellner, E. (1992). *Postmodernism, reason, and religion.* London: Routledge.

Gelso, J., & Hayes, J. A. (1998). *The psychotherapy relationship: Theory, research and practice.* New York: Wiley.

Glicken, M. D. (2003). *A simple guide to social research.* Boston: Allyn & Bacon/Longman.

McLaren, M. (2000). Psychiatry and the scientific method. *Australian Psychiatry, 8*(4), 373–375.

Munz, P. (1985). *Our knowledge of the growth of knowledge.* London: Routledge & Kegan Paul.

Nickerson, R. S. (1986). *Reflections on reasoning.* Hillsdale, NJ: Lawrence Erlbaum.

Rind, B., & Tromovitch, P. (1997). A meta-analytic review of findings from national samples on psychological correlates of child sexual abuse. *Journal of Sex Research, 34*(3), 237–255.

Rutter, M. (1994). Stress research: Accomplishments and tasks ahead. In R. J. Haggerty, L. R. Sherrod, N. Garmezy, & M. Rutter (Eds.), *Stress, risk, and resilience in children and adolescents: Processes, mechanisms, and interventions* (pp. 354–385). Cambridge, UK: Cambridge University Press.

Satcher, D. (2001). *Youth violence: A report of the surgeon general.* U.S. Department of Health and Human Services, Office of the Surgeon General, Washington, DC. Available at http://surgeongeneral.gov/library/youthviolence/youvioreport.htm

Seligman, M. E. P. (1995). The effectiveness of psychotherapy: The *Consumer Reports* study. *American Psychologist, 50*(12), 965–974.

Shea, P. (2000). Psychiatry and the scientific method. *Australian Psychiatry, 8*(3), 226–229.

Tanguay, P. E. (2002). Commentary: The primacy of the scientific method. *Journal of the American Academy of Child and Adolescent Psychiatry, 4*(11), 1322–1323.

Tyson, K. B. (1992, November). A new approach to relevant scientific research for practitioners: The heuristic paradigm. *Social Work, 37*(6), 541–556.

Werner, E., & Smith, R. S. (1982). *Vulnerable but invincible.* New York: McGraw-Hill.

Werner, E., & Smith, R. S. (1992). *Overcoming the odds: High-risk children from birth to adulthood.* Ithaca, NY: Cornell University Press.

Wuthnow, R. (2003). Is there a place for "scientific" studies of religion? *Chronicle of Higher Education, 49*(20), B10–B12.

Locating Relevant Clinical Research 4

The search for best evidence must be done with a certain strategy in mind or the reader will find the process highly frustrating, time-consuming, and unproductive. I can say this with absolute conviction because a great deal of my time in writing books is spent chasing down sources that are often completely unusable. Titles may be misleading, abstracts are often unrelated to content, and I sometimes spend a good part of my day reading and discarding information that looks promising but actually isn't. I have learned to search for and review sources quickly by using a variety of methods. This chapter will, I hope, help the reader find clinical practice information and, having found the sources, decide whether they are usable. Here are some suggestions that will help you do a sophisticated search for best evidence and save time and effort in the process.

Useful and Not-So-Useful Sources

In a search for best clinical practices, sources have an order of quality. For additional discussion of this subject, the reader may want to look at Glicken (2003), where the subject is discussed in much more detail. I have found the following rank order to be most productive in finding high-quality material:

1. **Refereed Academic Journals.** Information from refereed scholarly journals is of the highest order when considering quality of findings in a literature search. A refereed scholarly journal informs the reader that other professional readers and an editorial board have reviewed and approved the article before publication. The review process may involve having the author do extensive revisions of the article that may include providing more detail regarding the methodology used. Universities

sometimes publish academic journals. Academic journals might also be the flagship journals for professional organizations such as the National Association of Social Workers, the American Sociological Association, the American Psychiatric Association, or the American Psychological Association.

Some professions have annual reviews that publish summary articles on important topics. *The Annual Review of Psychology* comes to mind. Two very useful articles for this book came from that publication: "Individual Psychotherapy Outcome and Process Research: Challenges Leading to Greater Turmoil or a Positive Transition?" by Kopta, Lueger, Saunders, and Howard (1999) and "Empirically Supported Psychological Interventions: Controversies and Evidence" by Chambless and Ollendick (2001). Both articles are excellent examples of very objective, clearly written, and highly useful pieces of scholarship.

The purpose of research is to share information with a broad audience. If you, the reader, can't make sense out of the language in an article, the author is either hiding something, the review panel is overly impressed with abstract language, or the material really is too technical to fully understand and perhaps you should ask for help in deciphering it. Asking for help is essential in becoming an informed consumer of research. Agency-based clinicians might benefit from having a research specialist available who can help them track down best practices and explain the findings when they are unclear.

2. Professional Journals. These journals are also refereed and have an editorial board, but the articles published in professional journals may be less empirical and may include theoretical articles that summarize existing research. Professional journals are often practitioner-oriented, use less technical language with fewer statistics, and are sometimes thought to be of a second level in quality.

3. Publisher Journals. Journals published by for-profit publishers are written to attract practitioners and are often more theoretical than empirical. Publisher journals may focus on specific topics such as child abuse, family violence, and women's issues, and may have a limited publication cycle of four to eight editions, or may devote an entire edition to one topic. Publisher journals have a review process and an editorial board, but the editorial board may be somewhat less demanding than those of the prior two types of journals. All journals have a lag time, from acceptance of the article to publication, of as much as 2 years. The wise reader should understand that a 2-year lag time may result in articles that are dated and obsolete by the time they reach the public.

4. Scholarly Books. Books are usually contracted out to authors after submission and acceptance of a book proposal and sample chapters. Book publishers have a fairly stringent review process, which includes sending the proposal to other academics in the writer's field for critical review. Once the reviews are in and the publisher is confident that the author will make the changes suggested by the reviewers, the author is sent a contract that only obligates the publisher to agree to consider the book for publication when it is done. The book can still be rejected if the publisher believes that it lacks sufficient quality. Once the book is submitted by the author and accepted by the publisher, the usual lag time is 9 months before it reaches the public. Although some books contain original research, many books in the clinical field are summaries of other research on a specific topic, which certainly makes it easier for the reader to review current research in one place without a lengthy search. But it also assumes that the author is compiling all the current research, or that the author's reporting of the research is accurate. For this reason, books should not be used as the sole method of finding best evidence.

Books come in two or more forms: scholarly and popular. This is a scholarly book because it is written for a limited readership: students and professionals in the helping professions. Popular books are written for a mass market, and even though they may be very good, there is always the concern that the author has written the book for mass consumption by reducing complex and sometimes contradictory material to the point where it lacks practical value to the reader. One can think of any number of books written about codependence, gender issues, sexuality, and love as examples.

5. **Highly Regarded Magazines and Newspapers.** Highly regarded magazines and newspapers sometimes suffer from quality problems because mental health–related stories are often written by nonprofessionals and therefore articles can be superficial and misleading. Going to the original source for the information is a much better idea and not very difficult with the use of the Internet. However, many professionals find out about interesting topics by first reading about them in the *New Yorker* or the *New York Times,* as two examples. An article in the *New Yorker* (Gladwell, 2002) on the Chicago heat wave and the more than 700 elderly or disabled people who died made many of us more aware that a similar problem could affect other cities in America and elsewhere. The more than 15,000 deaths of elderly and disabled people in France during a heat wave in the summer of 2003 was a confirmation that the Chicago experience had widespread implications. Professional articles may have been previously written on the subject, but professionals often first recognize a problem from reading about it in a well-regarded mass media periodical. The reader is encouraged to do additional research on subjects of interest by considering the more scholarly articles to confirm or reject stories in mass media periodicals and magazines.

6. The Popular Press. Hometown newspapers are generally less reliable sources of information because they often sensationalize or provide misleading information. How many of us have read about new cures for AIDS or radical new treatments for any number of emotional problems, only to find out that the promising studies reported were in the very early stages of development and, when completed, generally resulted in unusable treatments? For that reason, you should go to the original source for more complete information. Internet searches, to be discussed later in this chapter, can easily provide original data.

Evaluating the Quality of Articles Reviewed

When I review an article, I know almost immediately whether it will be of high or low value. This is determined by looking at the number of articles cited in the reference section, the abstract found at the beginning of the article, and the summary found at the end. The abstract indicates whether the title is misleading. Titles are often very misleading. Journals sometimes let this pass or use misleading titles because there is an absence of information on a subject and they want to grab the reader's attention.

Once having read the abstract, the reader should scan the article to see if it has anything new to say and to learn whether it has included other research already found on similar subjects. The conclusions section should also be read to see if the information included is justified. A section that uses falsification to show the reader possible problems with the research should also be read, if included in the article. Researchers who provide this information to the reader get high marks. To determine the breadth of the researcher's literature review, inclusion of literature from other fields and professions should also be looked for. A lack of material from other professions can be very disheartening. For example, articles on positive psychology almost never include material from what, in social work, is called the strengths perspective, a very similar approach. This suggests that authors have a narrow focus, haven't looked very hard for other material, have disdain for other professions, or are only using information from sources with which they are familiar. Whatever the reason, it amounts to poor scholarship.

The mood of the article should also be evaluated. Many of the articles I read for a book I wrote on violent children under the age of 12 (Glicken, 2004) were so negative and pessimistic that it was difficult to accept the conclusions reached by the authors. Similarly, highly optimistic articles make one wonder whether the author is being Pollyannaish. Research articles should have a neutral feel to them. The language should be controlled and objective while still being clear and precise. Having read many articles about the treatment of various emotional states, I find myself preferring articles with conclusions that are logical, well presented, and supported by the weight of a number of other research studies. A sudden breakthrough or an opinion divergent from that of most other researchers makes one wonder if the author is really justified in making these claims. If someone has something very new to say, and if it leads to a very different approach to treatment, one applauds the researcher while still being cautious about using the information generated by a study. For the most part, very divergent findings from the majority of articles in the literature can usually be explained by methodological differences. Looking carefully at the methodology in a study may quickly tell readers if the findings are useful. A study using a homogeneous group of clients will always differ from a study using a diverse group. For example, articles assuming that all clients experience depression in the same way make me nervous. Depression in older adults is very different from depression in young adults. When looking at two studies using different age groups, one wants to be careful not to overgeneralize the findings to everyone suffering from depression. Definitions can be misleading. What does the term "older adult" mean? Anyone older than 50, older than 60, or older than 70? The researcher must tell us. The reader can see that preciseness is fundamental in research.

When I read research, I am curious about the researcher's real purpose in conducting the study. Has the researcher made a career of studying depression? Is the article on depression the only one the author has written? The author's familiarity with a subject usually assures one that certain content will be included. Is the study funded by a government source, by private foundation money, or by a company? Every funding source puts some pressure on the researcher to write articles with a certain emphasis. As an example, the reader may be surprised by the differences of opinion in this book about the impact of antidepression medications. While I am not certain that the funding sources have anything to do with the difference of opinions, neither am I certain that antidepressants work. I should know, but after reading a number of studies, it's unclear. If I am uncertain, imagine the client's confusion when he or she tries to find out if antidepressants work.

Finally, there are authors who are quite reliable and who use very scholarly approaches. It may be wise to find those authors and to read them first to save time. The outcome is usually more beneficial than going on a fishing expedition (searching for sources without any idea of what you'll find in advance). Speaking of fishing expeditions, they're a waste of time. You can narrow your search to such specific parameters on an Internet search that you can be fairly certain you'll find exactly what you're looking for with a minimum of wasted effort.

Hunt and McKibbon (1997) provide some additional guidelines for assessing the quality of articles:

1. Assessment of the validity of a review article requires evaluation of each step in the review process before consideration of the results and how they might apply to our patient. [This is sometimes referred to as having an audit trail].

2. Did the reviewed article address a focused question? [In other words, did the article remain true to its initial problem formulation and follow that problem in a logical way?].

3. Is it likely that important, relevant studies were missed? Our confidence in the results of a review is greater when we are certain that no relevant and high-quality studies, either published or unpublished, were missed.

4. Were the criteria used to select articles [in the literature review] appropriate? These criteria may vary according to the population studied, interventions or exposures, outcomes, and methods of each study.

5. Was the validity of the included studies assessed? Although the conclusions we derive from a systematic review depend in large part on the rigor of the review methods, they obviously also depend on the quality of the included studies.

6. Were the assessments of studies reproducible [replicable]? Even when explicit criteria are used to include studies in a review and evaluate their methodological quality, the judgment of the review's authors is still required.

7. Were the results similar from study to study? If studies have different findings, pooling results may lead to meaningless or even misleading results.

8. What are the overall results and how precise are they?

9. Will the results help in caring for patients? Determining this involves asking several questions: Can I apply the results to my patients? Did the studies consider all the clinically important outcomes? Are the benefits worth any associated risks or costs? (Hunt and McKibbon, 1997, p. 535)

Locating Relevant Research

VIRTUAL LIBRARIES

In this era of the Internet and high-speed computers, most of what you need to know about clinical practice research can be located by accessing suitable Internet sites. Universities and colleges throughout the country have virtual libraries online, which allow you to access the most current clinical research articles directly from your home computer. To obtain access, you'll need to be a student or have an affiliation with the university, but it's such an easy way to do a significant literature search that you may want to contact your local college or university and arrange for whatever fees it may take to have computer access from your home or job. Some universities give alumni and associate or clinical faculty this privilege, and remember that you don't need to be in the same community as the university to access a virtual library. As an emeritus professor, I have library privileges at my California university even though I live in Idaho.

Does the Internet make libraries obsolete? Not really, because a serious problem with virtual libraries is that they don't have access to all the journals you'll need to do a review. Sometimes those journals require that you pay for articles, which can then be sent to you online or by mail.

If you're using your home computer to do an Internet literature search, you may want to consider using a cable modem rather than a dial-up modem. Although a cable hookup is more expensive, it's also much faster and often less affected by viruses and slowdowns or breakdowns in the Internet system. The Internet attracts hackers who run programs that affect the functioning of the Internet system and that may cause serious problems with your computer. You take a chance when you go online, but if you're willing to take the chance that a new virus might hit for which there is no protective program, it's a wonderful way to access information.

Another exciting virtual library development is that some universities can now send you an entire book by e-mail: You check out the book by e-mail, it is sent to you as a large attachment, you use it for the allotted time, and then you return it by e-mail. These systems often use a format that doesn't allow you to copy, save, or print the material. You should also be aware of the copyright laws and recognize that they apply to Internet material in the same way that they apply to printed material.

Care should be taken, when using the Internet, to make certain that the quality of the articles accessed is as high as those in first-tier scholarly journals. In a survey of Internet sources found to research the subject of depression, Griffiths and Christensen (2000) write:

> In our review of 21 popular websites containing information about treating depression, we found that the quality of this information was poor. This

finding reinforces concerns raised by other studies, which have found inadequate quality or poor coverage of important health issues on the web. There is a need to improve the accuracy and coverage of information about depression on the web with regard to the relative effectiveness of different treatments, the main indications for particular treatments, important management issues such as duration of treatment, reviewing and changing treatments, and the relevance of professional expertise and patient preferences. (p. 1514)

LIBRARIES

Many people think that libraries are obsolete because of advances in online searches. They're not. You won't find a number of very important sources on the Internet that may be available at your local university library or through interlibrary loan. Librarians can show you how to do a very sophisticated literature search online and can help you locate suitable material held in the library. And remember, even though the virtual library can send you books on clinical subjects, this is a new development and most virtual libraries have only a very small number of books available online.

Another reason to use libraries is that, although you may find much of what you're looking for on the Internet, some articles found on the Internet lack statistical tables or correct citations. You may find that Internet articles make it difficult to find correct names of authors or the exact references cited at the end of an article. Many academic Internet servers such as EbscoHost have articles dating back only 3–5 years on the Internet. To obtain earlier articles, you would need to contact the library and ask if the article you need is in the library's collection and, if not, whether they can get the article for you from another library. You can find out if the article is available by checking the library's catalog through their Web site. Many government documents are not available online, or a government Web site may contain only very recent documents. Again, you would need to contact your library to see whether the document is available there or if it has to be ordered from a government agency. Many libraries have journals that are available only on microfilm. You'll have to go to the library and read those directly. You can order back issues of a journal or the specific article from the publisher, but this can be expensive and time-consuming. Many journals are no longer published, but some libraries across the country may have the edition of the journal you need. You can find this out by entering the name of the journal in an Internet search and thus discover where the journal for a specific article might be held. It's a time-consuming and sometimes frustrating experience, but when in doubt, contact a reference librarian. They really are excellent resources.

NONACADEMIC SERVERS

Nonacademic servers such as Yahoo, Netscape, Lycos, Infoseek, and Google can also be used for literature searches, but much of what they provide is nonacademic, and it is sometimes unreliable because anyone who wants to create a Web site can do so and the content of those Web sites may be completely inaccurate.

RESEARCH ABSTRACTS

Paying to subscribe to research abstracts in clinical practice areas can be an excellent way of accessing important research. Most helping professions have research abstracts that contain short versions of the main findings in an article. If the abstract offers information that seems relevant, you can then find the article and delve into it more deeply. Don't be surprised and don't get discouraged if the abstract is just as informative as the complete article. Finding good information takes time, patience, and perseverance.

Locating Evidence-Based Material on the Internet

The following list of sources for finding EBP articles and research data is largely taken from Glanville and Haines (1998). Although some of these Internet sources are medical in nature, they often have reviews of clinical trials on a number of issues of interest to the helping professions, including substance abuse, psychotropic medications, comparisons between medication and therapy, short-term counseling in emergency rooms for substance abuse, mental health factors in physical illness and the use of adjunct mental health services in illness, death and dying, disabilities, and a number of other related issues. Many of the Web sites that follow are based in Great Britain, where EBP is highly regarded and widely practiced. I had no difficulty accessing Web sites based in Great Britain, although some Web site addresses change from time to time. If that's the case, a new address is usually given when the original Web site is accessed. Some of the Web sites are free and others require a subscription fee, which is usually nominal.

Common Internet Sources

1. The Cochrane Library. This Web site contains a collection of databases including the full text of the *Cochrane Database of Systematic Reviews*, which contains (a) critical commentaries on selected systematic

reviews that have been assessed for quality and (b) brief details of more than 170,000 randomized controlled trials. The Cochrane Library is available at www.medlib.com and www.hcn.net.au

2. Cochrane Database of Systematic Reviews. This Web site contains systematic reviews of the effects of health care using randomized controlled trials. Evidence is included or excluded on the basis of explicit quality criteria to minimize bias. Data are often combined statistically, with meta-analysis, to increase the power of the findings of numerous studies each too small to produce reliable results individually. Although the Cochrane Database of Systematic Reviews is available by subscription only, the Abstracts of Cochrane Reviews are available without charge and can be browsed or searched. www.cochrane.org/cochrane/revabstr/mainindex.htm

3. Cochrane Library [Abstracts]. This Web site allows the reader to search the abstracts of the Cochrane Database of Systematic Reviews. The full text of the reviews is only available through the Cochrane Library. www.cochrane.org/reviews/index.htm

4. Best Evidence. Here you'll find summaries of articles from the major medical journals. Details of subscriptions are found at the *British Medical Journal* Web site. www.bmjpg.com/template.cfm?name=specjou_be#best_evidence

5. Clinical Evidence. Hundreds of clinical questions cover the effects of treatments and interventions based on the best available research. Answers are the result of thorough research commissioned by the prestigious BMJ Publishing Group (*British Medical Journal*), employing premier medical resources, including the Cochrane Library, MEDLINE, EMBASE, and ACP Journal Club. www.ovid.com/products/clinical/clinicalevidence.cfm

6. ClinicalTrials.gov. The U.S. National Institutes of Health, through its National Library of Medicine, has developed ClinicalTrials.gov to provide patients, family members, and members of the public current information about clinical research studies. http://clinicaltrials.gov/

7. Database of Abstracts of Reviews of Effectiveness. This Web site contains a database of high-quality systematic research reviews of the effectiveness of health care interventions. http://agatha.york.ac.uk/darehp.htm

8. Evidence-based Medicine Resource Center Publications. This contains the latest articles on evidence-based health care provided by the Evidence-based Medicine Resource Center in New York. www.ebmny.org/pubs.html

9. Evidence-Based Medicine Reviews. This is a fully searchable database with links to MEDLINE and Ovid full-text journals produced by expert reviewers and information staff of the National Health Service's Center for

Reviews and Dissemination (NHS CRD). www.ovid.com/products/clinical/ebmr.cfm

10. Health Technology Advisory Committee Evaluation Reports. This Web site contains reports and issue briefs from the Health Technology Advisory Committee, a Minnesota Department of Health organization. www.health.state.mn.us/htac/techrpts.htm

11. Health Technology Assessment (HTA) Database. This Web site contains health-related abstracts. http://agatha.york.ac.uk/htahp.htm

12. InfoPOEMs Clinical Awareness System. This is a searchable database of POEMs (Patient-Oriented Evidence that Matters). www.infopoems.com

13. National Library of Medicine's Health Services/Technology Assessment Text (HSTAT). This Web site contains guidelines and technology assessments and reviews. http://hstat.nlm.nih.gov

14. National Research Register. At this Web site, you'll find ongoing and recently completed research projects funded by, or of interest to, the United Kingdom's National Health Service. www.update-software.com/National/

15. NHS Economic Evaluation Database (NHS EED). This Web site contains structured abstracts of economic evaluations of health care interventions. http://agatha.york.ac.uk/nhsdhp.htm

16. Primary Care Clinical Practice Guidelines. This Web site contains research protocols, primary articles, integrative studies, meta-analyses, critically appraised topics, and review articles. http://medicine.ucsf.edu/resources/guidelines/

17. RehabTrials.org. This Web site promotes, encourages, and supports clinical trials in medical rehabilitation. www.rehabtrials.org

18. SUMSearch. This Web site provides references to answer clinical questions about diagnosis, etiology, prognosis and therapy (plus physical findings, adverse treatment effects and screening/prevention). http://SUMSearch.UTHSCSA.edu/cgi-bin/SUMSearch.exe

19. Clinical Guidelines from the U.S. Agency for Healthcare Research and Quality (previously the Agency for Health Care Policy and Research). This Web site provides clinical guidelines based on thorough reviews of research evidence. http://text.nlm.nih.gov/

20. Effective Health Care Bulletins. Reports of systematic reviews are presented in a readable and accessible format. www.york.ac.uk/inst/crd/ehcb.htm

21. *Guide to Clinical Preventive Services, Second Edition.* This Web site provides evidence-based recommendations on preventive services. http://text.nlm.nih.gov/

22. Bandolier. This is a newsletter alerting readers to key evidence about the effectiveness of treatment in health care. This site has very good EBP material for helping professionals. www.jr2.ox.ac.uk/Bandolier

23. Effectiveness Matters. This Web site contains summaries of published research on single topics that provide clear messages on effectiveness. www.york.ac.uk/inst/crd/em.htm

24. Core Library for Evidence Based Practice. This Web site contains a number of links of direct relevance for helping professionals. Some of the articles are free but others require a fee and a subscription. www.shef.ac .uk/~scharr/ir/core.html

25. Find Articles. This is a free Web search for articles on the Internet. The following Web address will get you into articles on psychotherapy, but if you vary the subject (cognitive therapy, research on psychotherapy, the therapeutic relationship), you may find a wealth of downloadable and relevant articles. http://articles.findarticles.com/P/search?tb=art&qt= psychotherapy

26. American Journal of Psychiatry Collections. This Web site allows very specific searches for material relevant to helping professionals. http://ajp.psychiatryonline.org/collections/

ADDITIONAL SOURCES

Government Documents

If you know the title of a document and you think it may have been distributed as part of a Federal Depository Library Program (FDLP), you can use its monthly Internet catalog of documents from 1994 to present by entering its Web site, Catalog of U.S. Government Publications. This Web site is maintained by the U.S. Government Printing Office. Documents with earlier dates are available in paper form from any depository library. A depository library is one that has been designated as such by the U.S. Government.

If you think that the source you're looking for might be on a government agency Web site (the Department of Justice, for example), but not in the FDLP, you could search for it using a search engine like Hotbot (maintained by Lycos). If you use the Advanced Search option in Hotbot, it is possible to limit your search by entering location/domain. Limiting your search to Web sites ending with *.gov* (for government Web sites) or *.mil* (for military Web sites) is also a good way to find information published by agencies of the federal government.

If you believe that the source you're looking for may be a technical report and you know the name of the government agency that sponsored the report, you might want to look at that agency's Web site (for instance, the U.S. Department of Energy has an excellent report finder).

FULL-TEXT SOCIAL SCIENCE DATABASES

Britannica Online

EbscoHost

IDEAL/ScienceDirect

JSTOR

Lexis/Nexis Universe

Project MUSE

Wilson Web Social Science Index

CITATIONS AND ABSTRACTS

General

EbscoHost (selected full text)

Wilson OmniFile (selected full text)

Carl Uncover (citations)

Specialized

Social Work Abstracts (citations and abstracts in social work)

PsychInfo (citations and abstracts in psychology)

Sociological Abstracts (citations and abstracts in sociology)

Criminal Justice Abstracts (citations and abstracts in criminal justice)

Lexis/Nexis (full-text law reviews)

SOCIAL WORK

1. Institute for the Advancement of Social Work Research. The goal of this Web site is to increase the ability to do social work research by providing information on resources for funding technical assistance and career development in social work research. www.sc.edu/swan/iaswr/

2. National Association of Social Workers. This Web site includes the NASW publications catalog, the NASW code of ethics, accreditation information, links to job resources, and current issues in social work. www.naswdc.org

3. Social Work and Social Service Web Site. From the George Warren Brown School of Social Work, this Web site is broken down into 99 areas of interest. Gwbweb.wustl.edu/websites.html

4. World Wide Web Resources for Social Workers. This site organizes a huge number of links according to subject. www.nyu.edu/socialwork/wwwrsw

GENERAL SITES

1. Academic Writing: Reviews of Literature. University of Wisconsin, Madison. www.wisc.edu/writing/Handbook/Review of Literature .html

2. Writing a Psychology Literature Review. University of Washington. http://depts.washington.edu/psywc/handouts/pdf/litrev.pdf

3. Preparing for a Literature Review. Columbia University. www.columbia .edu/cu/ssw/write/handouts/review.html

4. Checklist of Sources for a Social Work Literature Review. California State University, Stanislaus. http://wwwlibrary.csustan.edu/lboyer/socwork/sw_checklist.htm

5. Resources for Graduate Student Writers. University of Michigan. www.lsa.umich.edu/swc/grad/resources.html

SUMMARY

This chapter discusses the best ways of conducting a search for best evidence. Suggestions are made regarding the best sources to use in a literature search and some guidelines are offered to help readers rank order the quality of sources. The use of the Internet in literature searches is also recommended and a number of Web sites of special interest to helping professionals are provided.

Integrative Questions

1. Doesn't the use of the Internet to find best evidence make libraries obsolete regardless of what the author says?

2. A novice to reading research will probably go directly to the findings section of a study and not read anything else. Why is this such a bad idea?

3. We trust the integrity of the researcher. Is there any reason to think that researchers will ever give us misleading, incorrect, or purposely false information?

4. Isn't it expecting a great deal of helping professionals to ask them to make sense out of the very arcane language used in research reports? What can clinicians do to make practice research more readable?

5. Isn't the quality of newspapers and magazines underestimated in this chapter? Aren't they two sources where most helping professionals learn about new treatments for a variety of medical and emotional problems?

References

Chambless, D. L., & Ollendick, T. H. (2001). Empirically supported psychological interventions: Controversies and evidence. *Annual Review of Psychology, 52*, 685–716.

Gladwell, M. (2002, August 12). Political heat. *New Yorker*, 76–80.

Glanville, J., & Haines, M. (1998, July 18). Finding information on clinical effectiveness. *British Medical Journal, 317*, 200–203.

Glicken, M. D. (2003). *A simple guide to social research.* Boston: Allyn & Bacon/Longman.

Glicken, M. D. (2004). *Violent young children.* Boston: Allyn & Bacon/Longman.

Griffiths, K. M., & Christensen, H. (2000, December 16). Quality of web based information on treatment of depression: Cross sectional survey. *British Medical Journal, 321*, 1511–1515.

Hunt, D. L., & McKibbon, K. A. (1997, April 1). Locating and appraising systematic reviews. *Annals of Internal Medicine, 126*, 532–538.

Kopta, M. S., Lueger, R. J., Saunders, S. M., & Howard, K. I. (1999, Febraury). Individual psychotherapy outcome and process research: Challenges leading to greater turmoil or a positive transition? *Annual Review of Psychology, 50*, 441–469.

Part 2

How Evidence-Based Practice Views Diagnosis, Assessment, and Worker-Client Relationships

Chapter 5 provides an EBP view of diagnosis. In this chapter, common errors made in diagnostic work are discussed and some critical suggestions are made regarding protocols that assure more accuracy in diagnostic work. This chapter also discusses the unfortunate existence of gender and racial bias in diagnosis and the harmful consequence of seeking information about clients to justify and reinforce incorrect perceptions of clients, which often leads to serious errors in treatment.

Chapter 6 provides a psychosocial assessment of a client using an EBP approach to collecting and interpreting data. The case used in the chapter is that of a child of survivors of genocide and the confusing messages given by his parents, which have affected the client's ability to form strong, intimate relationships with others. An outline is provided that summarizes the pertinent information we know about the client and integrates that with supportive evidence to justify conclusions about diagnosis and treatment.

Chapter 7 considers the importance of the client-worker relationship in the helping process and assesses the research on the attributes of an effective relationship. Like many of the beliefs we hold in the helping professions, compelling research does not necessarily support the belief that the relationship is the key ingredient to effective practice. This isn't to say that the alliance between the client and worker isn't important; it is. But as this chapter will point out, we know little about the specific attributes of a worker and a client that would lead to a positive fit that ensures more effective practice.

Using Evidence-Based Practice in Diagnosis 5

In an attempt to make diagnosis more objective, the profession has developed a series of diagnostic tools including the Diagnostic and Statistical Manual (DSM) series. The DSM provides clinicians with easy-to-follow guidelines for choosing a diagnostic category to fit a client's cumulative symptoms. If the guidelines are followed accurately, the diagnostic category should be consistent with the diagnosis most clinicians would give for a particular set of behaviors. However, the DSM has been criticized because it fails to provide an individual framework with which to fully understand many of the environmental and historical factors affecting clients. As a result, the DSM is often thought to be overly focused on pathology (Saleebey, 1996). The client's uniqueness is seldom represented by a DSM diagnosis, nor are the positive behaviors clients bring with them to treatment, which often determine whether the client will improve. As most clinicians know, it's not what's wrong with the client that helps in the change process; it's what is right. As Saleebey indicates,

> The DSM-IV (American Psychiatric Association, 1994), although only seven years removed from its predecessor, has twice the volume of text on disorders. Victimhood has become big business as many adults, prodded by a variety of therapists, gurus, and ministers, go on the hunt for wounded inner children and the poisonous ecology of their family background. These phenomena are not unlike a social movement or evangelism. (p. 296)

Concerns About the Diagnostic Process

Treatment paradigms, including the strengths perspective and EBP, individualize the client by looking in a hopeful and optimistic way at the client's culture, family life, support networks, coping abilities, past and current successes, and a number of other issues ignored in the DSM that often contribute to good mental health and can frequently be used in the helping process. Building on the strengths of a client seems much more likely to lead to change than focusing on the negatives. Cloud (2003) has even more fundamental concerns about a specific DSM manual, the DSM-IV, and writes,

> Can even a thousand Ph.D.s gathered at a dozen conferences ever really know the significance of such vague symptoms as "fatigue," "low self-esteem" and "feelings of hopelessness"? (You need only two of those, along with a couple of friends telling the doctor you seem depressed, to be a good candidate for something called dysthymic disorder.) Though it's fashionable these days to think of psychiatry as just another arm of medicine, there is no biological test for any of these disorders. (p. 105)

Other concerns noted by Cloud (2003) about the DSM-IV are that diagnostic categories were determined by ad hoc committee discussions that were often contentious, and were resolved only because of pleas for agreement and consensus. The lack of agreement and the contentious nature of the proceedings resulted in a manual that is little more than a checklist of symptoms used to justify an emotional condition. To improve the DSM-IV or diagnostic manuals like it, Cloud suggests the use of four categories of disorders: "Those arising from brain disease, those arising from problems controlling one's drive, those arising from problematic personal dispositions, and those arising from life circumstances" (p. 106).

Whaley (2001) is concerned that Caucasian clinicians often perceive African American clients as having paranoid symptoms when what they are displaying is really a cultural distrust of Caucasians because of historical experiences with racism. He believes that the diagnostic process with African American clients tends to discount the negative impact of racism, which leads to diagnostic judgments about black clients suggesting that they are more dysfunctional than they really are. This tendency to misdiagnose, or to diagnose a more serious condition than may be warranted, is what Whaley calls "pseudo-transference" and has its origins in cultural stereotyping by clinicians who fail to understand the impact of racism. Whaley believes that cultural stereotyping ultimately leads to "more severe diagnoses and restrictive interventions" (p. 558) with African American clients. Whaley's work suggests that clinicians may incorrectly use diagnostic labels with clients they either feel uncomfortable with or whose cultural differences create some degree of hostility. If this is true, it casts doubt on the accuracy of diagnostic labels with an entire range of clients who may differ educationally, racially and culturally from clinicians. These concerns reinforce the subjective nature of the diagnostic process in general and of the DSM-IV in particular.

In describing incorrect diagnoses, DeGrandpre (1999) found that a diagnosis of attention deficit hyperactivity disorder (ADHD), made solely from observation of children in a physician's office, was routinely a misdiagnosis. Sharp, Walter, and Marsh (1999) found that boys were diagnosed with ADHD at rates 3 and 4 times higher than girls even though ratios as low as 2-to-1 have been found in community studies. Wilke (1994) reports that women are underdiagnosed for alcoholism because of stereotypes of drinking that apply to men but not to women. Alcoholic women are less likely to drink publicly, become violent or aggressive, or have problems with the law because of their drinking. When these male behaviors that suggest alcoholism are applied to women and a similar pattern is not found, a diagnosis of alcoholism is not used with women when it should be.

As an additional indication of misdiagnoses in the mental health field,

> Morey and Ochoa (1989) asked 291 psychiatrists and psychologists to complete a checklist of symptoms for a client whom they had diagnosed with a personality disorder. When the checklists were later correlated with the DSM criteria, nearly three of four clinicians had made mistakes in applying the diagnostic criteria. (McLaughlin, 2002, p. 259)

In a sample of 42 psychologists and 17 psychiatrists, Davis, Blashfield, and McElroy (1993) had the clinicians read and diagnose case reports containing different symptoms of narcissistic personality disorder. Ninety-four percent of the sample of the clinicians made mistakes applying the diagnostic criteria, while 25% diagnosed narcissistic personality disorder when less than half of the DSM criteria were met.

In another example of incorrect diagnosis based upon first impressions, Robertson and Fitzgerald (1990) randomly assigned 47 counselors to watch videos of a depressed male portrayed by an actor. The only changes made in the videos were the client's type of employment (professional or blue collar) and the client's family of origin (traditional or nontraditional). The researcher found that counselors made more negative diagnostic judgments when the actor portrayed a blue-collar worker and came from a nontraditional family. The signs and symptoms of any specific emotional disorders were secondary to the worker's bias.

In an example of another type of bias, self-confirmatory bias, or a diagnosis based on only the information collected by the clinician that confirms his or her original diagnosis, Haverkamp (1993) had counseling and counseling psychology students watch a video of an initial counseling session and then write down the questions they wanted to ask in a follow-up session with the client. The results were that the majority of students (64%) wanted to ask questions that confirmed their original diagnostic impression of the client. A follow-up study by Pfeiffer, Whelan, and Martin (2000) came to a similar conclusion. In a related type of error, the error of using treatment approaches that confirm one's original diagnosis, Rosenhan (1973) had research associates admitted to a psychiatric hospital after complaining of auditory hallucinations. Although the researchers stopped complaining of the symptoms, the treatment staff continued using a diagnosis indicating a serious mental illness when none was present.

Reducing Errors in Diagnosis

McLaughlin (2000) suggests the following ways of reducing errors in diagnosing:

1. Don't make too much or too little of the evidence at hand.

2. Try to note the biasing effect of your workplace, which may routinely diagnose everyone in the same way.

3. Use falsification to try to disprove a diagnosis.

4. Consistently use all of the DSM diagnostic criteria and keep current about revisions.

5. Be aware of other disorders or a dual diagnosis, and delay making a diagnosis until you have more data.

6. Use symptom checklists to make certain your diagnosis adheres to DSM categories and follow a logical protocol to collect and evaluate data about the client before finalizing a diagnosis.

7. If you use psychological instruments in diagnosis, make certain they're valid and reliable with the type of client you're diagnosing (by age, gender, ethnicity, etc.).

8. Make absolutely certain your expectations of clients don't reflect racial, ethnic, gender, or religious bias, or self-fulfilling prophesies about certain categories of diagnosis.

9. Remember the importance of social factors in diagnosis and that the DSM may have a built-in bias against certain groups.

10. Consider other diagnostic possibilities and understand that the more time you take getting to know the client, the more likely you are to arrive at a correct diagnosis.

11. Consider the pros and the cons of a diagnosis before formally using it with a client.

12. Use multiple diagnostic instruments to determine a diagnosis, and accept a diagnosis only if those instruments are in agreement with one another.

13. Focus on what may be atypical about a client and follow those leads to help determine a diagnosis.

14. Follow ethical standards.

15. Use training to improve your diagnostic work, particularly with diverse ethnic and cultural groups.

The Adverse Impact of Labeling

One of the strong criticisms of diagnosis is the negative impact certain categories of dysfunction might have on the lives of clients. Markowitz (1998) believes that clients with diagnoses of any form of mental illness "may expect and experience rejection in part because they think less of themselves" (p. 343). The stigma often attached to mental illness may result in rejection in the workplace and may add to feelings of low self-worth and depression (Markowitz, 1998). Many employers view an initial diagnosis of mental illness, substance abuse, and personality disorders as life long, unchanging, and untreatable.

While labeling for diagnostic purposes may be relevant in medicine, diagnostic labels for mental health purposes are sometimes poorly defined and pejorative. Labels often harm people, and the most vulnerable among us—the poor, minority groups, women, immigrants, and the physically, emotionally, and socially disadvantaged, are those most harmed by labels. This may be particularly true of minority clients. Franklin (1992) says that African American men want to see themselves as "partners in treatment" and resent labels that suggest pathology because labels send negative signals to black clients who have had to deal with labels that subtly or overtly suggest racism. Franklin strongly suggests that African American men want to be recognized for their many strengths and that clinicians should take into consideration that African American men may be doing well in many aspects of their lives. According to Franklin, African American men are particularly sensitive to male bashing and other sexist notions that berate men or negatively stereotype men in general, and black men in particular. And while black workers are preferable when working with black men, Franklin urges all workers, regardless of color or gender, to be sensitive to the black experience and to approach black clients with respect and awareness of the many social behaviors that create tensions in the lives of African American men.

Case Study: A Culturally Sensitive Diagnosis

Jorge Rivera is a 19-year-old Mexican National who came to the United States under the sponsorship of his maternal uncle to attend a California university. Jorge had been in the country a year and was doing well until signs of emotional change became apparent to his loved ones. He was becoming increasingly aloof and secretive, had stopped attending school, and seemed to be a very different person from the happy, motivated young man he had been just a year earlier. Suspecting an emotional or physical problem, Jorge's uncle took him to see his family doctor, an American of Hispanic descent. The doctor was immediately struck by Jorge's aloofness, fearfulness, and social isolation. He did multiple tests and, unable to find anything physically wrong, urged the uncle to take Jorge to a Hispanic male social worker with whom the doctor had prior positive experiences.

The first interview was conducted in Spanish since this was Jorge's more proficient language and the one with which he could express his inner feelings with more accuracy than English. Jorge told the therapist that he was hearing voices at night when he tried to sleep and that the voices were telling him to do things that Jorge found repulsive and dangerous. The voices were new to Jorge and he feared that he was going insane. As Jorge began to talk about his fears that he was becoming psychotic and how this would place him in great jeopardy with his family, he said that being "muy loco" was what happened to people who were sinful, and that he would be punished by his family and friends with social isolation and ostracism.

It was clear to the therapist that Jorge was in great distress but, pending additional information, the therapist deferred making a diagnosis. Using the DSM-IV criteria, however, the therapist saw signs of schizophrenia. He decided to interview the uncle's family to determine the point of onset of his symptoms. Everyone confirmed that Jorge had previously been very outgoing, showing none of the signs of the mental illness he was now exhibiting. The onset was sudden, within the last 3 months, and the symptoms had been rapid and worsening. This didn't sound like the slow onset of mental illness the therapist had seen in other patients, nor was he convinced that he could use this diagnosis with someone so new to the country. He wondered if there were other factors involved.

In the next interview, he asked Jorge to tell him about his life in Mexico and to provide his theory about what was happening to him. It turned out that Jorge had been romantically involved with a young woman who came from a highly affluent family in Mexico. The couple was very much in love but the young woman's parents were strongly opposed to the marriage and had hired a *bruja* (literally a witch, but someone who can cast spells on others) to cast a spell on him so that he would become unattractive to the young woman and she would lose her feelings for Jorge. The bruja was sending Jorge little totems that represented evil and that were scaring him into social isolation and withdrawal. He was convinced the voices he heard were her doing and that, as a result of the spells she had cast, he would become insane, lose his beloved, and die a horrible death. He had known others who'd had similar fates in Mexico. Brujas were evil and they did immense harm, he told the therapist.

The therapist had grown up with stories of witches and spells, but wasn't a believer. Nonetheless, he contacted the uncle, told him what had happened, and asked if he knew of some way to deal with the effects of the bruja. The uncle said that he did and contacted a well-known *curandero* (the opposite of a bruja and someone who removes the harm done to people by brujas) he knew of in Mexico, paid his way to come to the

United States, and had the curandero remove the spell in a ritual that lasted 24 hours. When the ritual was over, the curandero gave Jorge an amulet to wear around his neck to ward off future spells and urged him to break off the relationship with the young woman as a way to stop the bruja's continued impact on Jorge's mental health. The uncle again intervened, spoke to the young woman's family in Mexico, promised that Jorge would no longer be in contact with the young woman, and urged them to cease any more witchcraft with Jorge. The family agreed, and a brokenhearted but functioning Jorge returned to school and, in time and with his family's support and an occasional visit to the therapist, is doing well in school, but mourns his lost relationship.

Practitioners in the helping professions would like to think that spells, witchcraft, and sorcery don't exist in the modern world, but for many people they do. The therapist spoke to the curandero, who told him,

"All of us have demons inside of us. When those demons collide with an outside force, and have no doubt but that brujas are very powerful outside forces, people often develop the problems we saw in Jorge. You can call this witchcraft, which most North Americans don't believe in, but I see the damage brujas do every day and myself have been a victim. I went through many of the same problems that Jorge has been having until my dear teacher came and cured me, but every day I live in fear of the bruja who cast this spell on me. I don't expect you to believe this, but it's true. In Mexico, these practices date back thousands of years and the bruja had generations of those before her to give her immense power.

"Whether Jorge believes in brujas and is susceptible to suggestion or whether their magic really exists, it isn't for me to prove. My job is to make spells go away as I did with Jorge. I think you would have called Jorge crazy, put him on strong medicines that would have done him harm, and then forgotten about him, believing that he was hopeless. A 24-hour ritual and he is now sad, but well again. He'll get over his lost love and he'll be protected for a while from the bruja if the family pays her off and tells her to leave Jorge alone. But brujas are cruel and you never know when she'll attack Jorge again just to prove she has power over him. Then I'll have to come back to Los Angeles, a place filled with evil, and do this again, only next time I may not be so lucky and Jorge may sink into mental illness. Believe what you'd like. The amulet will help him as will the little symbols I've urged Jorge to place around his bed at night, when brujas have the most power, but I offer no guarantee that the bruja won't come back to haunt Jorge again."

DISCUSSION

In a personal discussion I had in Mexico in 1994 with Pedro Guerrero, a University of California, Berkeley–trained cultural anthropologist and codirector of the Cemanahuac Educational Community in Cuernavaca,

Morelos, Mexico, Guerrero confirmed the importance of folk cures for a number of problems experienced by Mexicans. He assured me that, although the idea of brujas and curanderos was common in Mexico, it had a selective following. However, most Mexicans grow up with stories about the power of witches and black magic. He cautioned against taking that power literally because brujas have been known to take matters into their own hands, and told the story of a child molester in a small village whose political influence stopped the police from doing anything. The village hired a bruja known for her expertise in the use of poisons and, after observing the man over a period of weeks, noticed that he walked bare-footed to work every morning and that he used the same route. The bruja sprinkled poison across the path, and the man stepped in it, got very ill, and died.

Perhaps something similar happened to Jorge but wasn't detected by the laboratory tests run by his physician. In any event, a high degree of cultural awareness saved Jorge from an incorrect, stigmatizing, and probably harmful diagnosis of mental illness, a very good call by the therapist regardless of the cause of Jorge's symptoms.

Examples of Evidence-Based Practice Diagnostic Data

In EBP, diagnosis is based upon concrete evidence from the research literature. While clinical experience is still important in diagnostic work, the American Medical Association EBP Working Group (1992) notes that EBP places a reduced value on authority. Practitioners can, however, learn to make independent evaluations of the evidence and are therefore able to judge the opinions offered by experts. This doesn't imply that we can't learn from experienced colleagues; we should value their expertise in history taking and diagnostic strategies (p. 2422). However, the working group suggests caution in making more of clinical observation than may be warranted and writes, "In the absence of systematic observation, one must be cautious in the interpretation of information derived from clinical experience and intuition, for it may at times be misleading" (p. 2422). The working group goes on to note that a strong factor in making a correct diagnosis is the recognition of the client's discomfort and emotional distress. The working group believes that clinicians must be compassionate in their approach to clients and that the diagnostic process must directly involve the client. As Gambrill (2000) writes, "EBP begins and ends with clients" (p. 1).

To demonstrate the benefit of consulting the research evidence, the remainder of this chapter reports findings from the literature on several common emotional problems with a critical response to determine whether the research meets the standard of best practice.

ALCOHOLISM

Isaacson, Nielsen, Urbanic, and Challgren (1999) evaluated diagnostic markers to determine if alcoholism existed in a general medical population of patients who were being treated for nonalcoholic problems. They found, from responses to a lifestyle survey that included questions regarding social history, gastrointestinal complaints, anxiety and depression, and sexual dysfunction, and from responses to the Alcohol Use Disorders Identification Test, that the "overall prevalence of alcohol problems was 7.3%. Less than one-quarter of the patients in the study had chart documentation of an alcohol problem. Thirty percent of the alcoholic patients had a diagnosis of hypertension" (p. 141). Positive correlations with alcoholism were found in clients who failed to use seat belts ($p = 0.020$), had a history of heavy smoking ($p < 0.001$), used alcohol within 24 hours of the office visit ($p < 0.001$), and reported a family history of alcoholism ($p = 0.012$). There was no difference in somatic complaints between patients with and patients without alcohol problems. The authors write, "Despite the known relationship of excess alcohol use and elevations in blood pressure, we found no statistically significant correlation between these variables in our study. Symptomatic concerns of the patient appear to be too nonspecific to distinguish patients with and without alcohol problems" (p. 141).

WHAT DOES THIS STUDY TELL US?

A sample of 250 patients in one hospital facility can't be generalized to other similar facilities, but of significance in this study is the finding that alcoholic patients were no different in their medical problems than the general population of patients, and that a large number of patients were not known to be alcoholic prior to this study. Also, the 7.3% of the patients classified as alcoholic is much larger than the national alcoholism rate of 4.6% of the population, according to *Alcohol Alert*, a publication of the National Institute of Alcohol Abuse and Alcoholism (2000). This might be construed to tell us that alcoholism has a negative impact on physical health. Even though this study failed to show a relationship between alcoholism and hypertension, other studies suggest that hypertension and alcoholism are closely related. Perhaps there are additional physical problems that are even stronger diagnostic markers of alcoholism. It's good to keep in mind, however, that there are many biosocial differences among alcoholic clients that make a diagnosis of alcoholism very imprecise. And it's one thing to diagnose alcohol abuse and quite another to predict the long-term impact of the illness, or whether clients will make necessary changes to counteract their alcoholic behavior.

To show the vagaries of diagnosis with alcoholic clients, Lu and McGuire (2002) studied the effectiveness of outpatient treatment with substance-abusing clients and came to the following conclusions:

1. The more severe the drug use problem before treatment was initiated, the less likely clients were to discontinue drug use during treatment when compared to other users.

2. Clients reporting no substance abuse three months before admission were more likely to maintain abstinence than those who reported abstinence only in the past month.

3. Heroin users were very unlikely to sustain abstinence during treatment, and marijuana users were less likely to sustain abstinence during treatment than alcohol users.

4. Clients with "psychiatric problems" were more likely to use drugs during treatment than clients without psychiatric problems.

5. Clients with legal problems related to their substance abuse had reduced chances of improvement during their treatment.

6. Clients who had multiple prior treatments for substance abuse were less likely to remain abstinent during and after treatment.

7. Clients who were more educated were more likely to sustain abstinence after treatment.

8. Clients treated in urban agencies were less likely to maintain abstinence than those treated in rural agencies.

SCHIZOPHRENIA: FIRST WARNING SIGNS

Below is a list of warning signs that suggest the onset of schizophrenia. The list was developed by families that have a member with schizophrenia (World Fellowship for Schizophrenia and Allied Disorders, 2002, p. 1). While some of the behavior would be considered normal, family members noticed a subtle, yet obvious, awareness that the behavior they were witnessing was unusual. Everyone noted social withdrawal as an important early sign that something was wrong. Most respondents believed that their relative had been a "good person, never causing any trouble"; however, seldom had the person been socially "outgoing" during the formative years. The warning signs of schizophrenia noted by family members are the following:

Excessive fatigue and sleepiness or an inability to sleep

Social withdrawal, isolation and reclusiveness

Deterioration of social relationships

Inability to concentrate or cope with minor problems

Apparent indifference, even in highly important situations

Dropping out of activities (skipping classes)

Decline in academic and athletic performance

Deterioration of personal hygiene; eccentric dress

Frequent moves or trips or long walks leading nowhere

Drug or alcohol abuse

Undue preoccupation with spiritual or religious matters

Bizarre behavior

Inappropriate laughter

Strange posturing

Low tolerance to irritation

Excessive writing without apparent meaning

Inability to express emotion

Irrational statements

Peculiar use of words or language structure

Conversation that seems deep but is not logical or coherent

Staring; vagueness

Unusual sensitivity to stimuli (noise, light)

Forgetfulness

As a way of comparing the subjective reports of family members of clients with a diagnosis of schizophrenia, the National Institute for Mental Health (NIMH) indicates the following diagnostic signs of early onset schizophrenia:

> The first signs of schizophrenia often appear as confusing, or even shocking, changes in behavior. The sudden onset of severe psychotic symptoms is referred to as an "acute" phase of schizophrenia. "Psychosis," a common condition in schizophrenia, is a state of mental impairment marked by hallucinations, which are disturbances of sensory perception, and/or delusions, which are false yet strongly held personal beliefs that result from an inability to separate real from unreal experiences. Less obvious symptoms, such as social isolation or withdrawal, or unusual speech, thinking, or behavior, may precede, be seen along with, or follow the psychotic symptoms. (NIMH, 1999, p. 1)

As the reader can see, there are similarities in these two descriptions of the early signs of mental illness even though one report is fairly subjective (the observations of family members) and the other is more authority based (conclusions about the illness from the NIMH). This agreement in the findings, even though the research methods used were different, should give the clinician confidence that many of the diagnostic descriptors of early-onset schizophrenia noted in the two reports may be helpful in making an initial diagnosis. However, anyone familiar with mental illness knows that clinicians are often reluctant to make a diagnosis of any form of mental illness because of the strong stigmatizing factors involved. Markowitz (1998), for example, reports that people with mental illness are "more likely to be unemployed, have less income, experience a diminished sense of self, and have fewer social supports" (p. 335). Part of the reason for this finding may be a function of the stigma attached to mental illness. Markowitz also notes that the impact of anticipated rejection of mentally ill people is largely caused by "discriminatory experiences," in which the person observes an employer perceiving potential problems based solely on a diagnostic label rather than the person's actual behavior. This perception of rejection compounds feelings of low self-worth and depression (Markowitz, 1998). Consequently, even though the evidence is clear that a diagnosis is correct, many clinicians may prefer not to give a stigmatizing diagnosis.

To make the clinician's dilemma even more difficult, current studies suggest that an initial diagnosis of mental illness may not have long-term implications. Carpenter (2002) believes that mental health services have been developed with the belief that mental illness is a chronic disease requiring continual care and supervision. She notes that the DSM-IV (APA, 1994) still indicates that schizophrenia will result in progressive deterioration and cautions readers that complete remission of symptoms is rare. However, research studies fail to support the concept of long-term chronicity in patients diagnosed with mental illness. Carpenter (2002) reports that most people with an initial diagnosis of schizophrenia or other serious mental illnesses experience "either complete or significant remission of symptoms, and work, have relationships, and otherwise engage in a challenging and fulfilling life" (p. 89). In a study of more than 500 adults diagnosed with schizophrenia, Huber, Gross, and Schuttler (1975) found that over one fifth of the sample experienced complete remission and over two fifths experienced significant remission of symptoms. In a 40-year follow-up study, Tsuang, Woolson, and Fleming (1979) found that 46% of those initially diagnosed with schizophrenia had no symptoms or had only nonincapacitating symptoms later on. In a 20- to 25-year follow-up study of former state hospital patients, The Vermont Longitudinal Study, (Harding, Brooks, Ashikaga, Strauss, & Breier, 1986a, 1986b) found that 72% of the people diagnosed with schizophrenia had only slight or no psychiatric symptoms. Despite these very optimistic findings, Carpenter (2002) writes,

The premise of chronicity continues to be widely accepted in the mental health system, and dismal prognoses continue to be communicated to people with psychiatric disabilities (Kruger, 2000). These prognoses leave little room for a sense of hope on the part of those labeled with mental illness and, as such, may become a self-fulfilling prophecy (Jimenez, 1988). (p. 89)

Case Study: A Misdiagnosis

Barbara Wright is a 32-year-old social worker with a master's degree in social work and a clinical license. Barbara's behavior has become erratic of late and her supervisor, suspecting bipolar disorder, urged Barbara to seek medical help and severely curtail her workload or possibly lose her job. Barbara has missed a great deal of work in the past 2 months. She is gone from work at inappropriate times; seems to be losing weight rapidly; often has problems paying attention to clients; and is inappropriate with her clients, her colleagues, and her supervisor. Barbara openly talks about her sex life, which seems very dangerous and sometimes violent. She has come to work with bruises on her face and body, which she proudly shows everyone. She has begun having tattoos placed in noticeable areas of her body with messages that concern everyone: *Born to Lose, Wild Thing,* and *Miss Amazing* are a few of the tattoos visible on her arms and shoulders.

Barbara saw her family doctor, who was concerned that she might be having serious emotional problems and referred her to a psychiatrist. After a 30-minute examination, the psychiatrist diagnosed Barbara with bipolar disorder and placed her on very strong medication that she didn't use. In fact, Barbara is abusing drugs and alcohol. A careful interview and medical and laboratory workup would have confirmed the use of speed, cocaine, a variety of painkillers, and alcohol. Barbara's increasing drug and alcohol dependence has led to her current behavioral problems. Not wanting to believe that Barbara was drug and alcohol addicted, and having worked with her professionally, the psychiatrist failed to see the obvious symptoms, which could have been discovered had he used a behavioral checklist, done routine blood work, and taken a urine sample. The results of his misdiagnosis were that Barbara was fired from her job, was involved in a serious automobile accident where she badly injured a child, and now faces the possibility of going to prison.

A forensic psychiatrist who interviewed Barbara for a court report immediately diagnosed substance abuse and contacted the original psychiatrist to find out why such an obvious problem wasn't noticed. The original psychiatrist told him, "I guess I don't think most professionals are substance abusers. I knew Barbara from work and she's always been a highly capable person. This new behavior seemed consistent with DSM guidelines and so I used a treatable diagnosis of bipolar disorder. Substance abuse, had I used it, would have resulted in Barbara being fired, so I never use that diagnosis if something more treatable is available. I guess I really let my personal feelings interfere with my judgment."

The problem with Barbara's psychiatric diagnosis shows the subjectivity of diagnosis and the impact of personal bias. A professional with no prior knowledge of the client should have seen her initially. Using a psychiatrist she knew from work almost certainly assured bias in this case. One also wonders about the effectiveness of a 30-minute diagnostic interview. How can anyone diagnose bipolar disorder in 30 minutes? By the way, managed care often limits psychiatric interviews to 30 minutes, so this case isn't that unusual. A better approach might have been to have Barbara seen by a social worker for an in-depth psychosocial assessment, followed by a psychological evaluation using a battery of psychological tests, followed by lab and medical workups, and ending with the psychiatric interview and a staff meeting of all the professionals involved. This might have better assured a correct diagnosis and an accurate recommendation for treatment.

Highly Aggressive and Violent Young Children

The problem of long-term behavior and its relationship to a diagnosis is even more confusing when young children are the focus of a diagnosis by a clinician (Glicken, 2004b).

Although Moffitt (1994) believes that children who show early aggressive tendencies are more likely to move on to seriously violent behaviors than children who show no violent tendencies before adolescence, Werner and Smith (1982) found that one out of every three children thought to be at significant risk for adolescent problems actually developed into well-functioning young adults by age 18. In a follow-up study, Werner and Smith (1992) found that two out of three of the remaining two thirds of children at risk had turned into caring and healthy adults by age 32. Using Moffitt's (1994) work, however, early violence starters often show signs of disobedience, bullying, intimidation, and fighting as early as preschool and kindergarten. Sprague and Walker (2000) found, "Early starters are likely to experience antisocial behavior and its toxic effects throughout their lives. Late starters have a far more positive long-term outcome" (p. 370). Walker and Severson (1990) found that diagnostic signs of early violence starters included disobedience, property damage, conduct problems, theft, the need for a great deal of attention, threats and intimidation, and fighting.

The following childhood behaviors and diagnostic labels have correlated positively with violent behavior: (a) inattention and impulsivity (Lynam, 1996); (b) antisocial personality disorder; (c) conduct disorder;

(d) oppositional defiant disorder; and (e) serious emotional disturbance (APA, 1994). Mayer (1995) found that the following environmental factors may correlate with the potential for violent behavior: inconsistent and harsh parenting styles, disorganized or badly functioning schools, and the availability of drugs, alcohol, and weapons.

In considering the literature on early onset violence in very young children, Sprague and Walker (2000) note, "Well-developed antisocial behavior patterns and high levels of aggression evidenced early in a child's life are among the best predictors of delinquent and violent behavior years later" (p. 369). The authors go on to note that early violent behavior is a predictor of a number of serious problems throughout the life span, including "victimization of others, drug and alcohol use, violence, school failure and dropout, and delinquency. Over the developmental age span, these behavior patterns become more destructive, more aversive, and have much greater social impact as they become elaborated" (p. 369).

Dwyer, Osher, and Warger (1998) believe that we can diagnose the potential for violence as early as 5, but that few at-risk youth will commit serious violent acts throughout their life span. Many will, however, experience drug and alcohol abuse, domestic violence and child abuse, divorce or multiple relationships, employment problems, mental health problems, dependence on social services, and involvement in less serious crimes (Obiakor, Merhing, & Schwenn, 1997). But as Werner and Smith (1982, 1992) found in their longitudinal studies of children with markers for serious emotional problems including violence, early signs of violent behavior generally do not develop into more serious forms of violent behavior by the time a child is 18. A major reason for this is what the authors call self-correcting tendencies, which are often initiated by consistent and caring relationships with at least one adult. Werner and Smith believe that it is never too late to change feelings of hopelessness to a sense of achievement and fulfillment.

Even though signs of early aggression in children may lead to future aggression, I (Glicken, 2004b) believe that many factors affect the development of violent behavior in young children. While early diagnosis and intervention is helpful, we should be cautious about predicting a child's future behavior. The positive benefits of helping professionals, teachers, mentors, religious affiliations, parents, siblings, and extended family should never be discounted. Perhaps a more effective way to treat children with early signs of violent behavior would be an in-depth evaluation of why the violent behavior is beginning to appear so early in life. Violent behavior in children is often caused by early childhood physical and sexual abuse and neglect. Parental drug and alcohol abuse, learning difficulties, poor peer relationships, and a host of treatable conditions may also be factors in the child's behavior. Without care and flexibility, we may stigmatize these children with labels suggesting severe pathology and untreatability that may only exacerbate their anger and lead to even more serious problems.

SUMMARY

This chapter discusses the difficulty of making correct and accurate diagnoses in the mental health field. Unlike medicine, where a diagnosis serves to form a relationship between the specific medical problem and the best treatment, a diagnosis in the mental health field may be entirely too subjective initially for this purpose. Collecting sufficient data about the client's behavior over a period of time is suggested as one way to develop an accurate diagnosis. Much of the chapter deals with examples of why finding a correct diagnosis is so difficult and the changes people often make that suggest how an incorrect diagnosis can lead to social stereotyping, which affects jobs, education, and other important life factors. Perhaps what is needed are floating diagnoses, which change as the clients condition changes, or diagnostic terms that are less pejorative than those used at present.

Integrative Questions

1. Isn't it obvious that diagnoses in the mental health field are more likely to be incorrect than in the medical field? What are some of the reasons for the lack of accuracy in mental health diagnoses?

2. How can therapists possibly keep personal bias out of diagnoses? The entire therapeutic endeavor is based on subjective experiences between worker and client, or is it?

3. Just as medical diagnoses become more elaborate each year with the gain in new knowledge, shouldn't mental health diagnoses also become more elaborate?

4. What are the steps we can use to assure that clinicians, who may have little knowledge of diversity, don't use stereotypic or pejorative diagnoses with clients of color, women, and those out of the mainstream of American life?

5. A diagnosis may last forever. What can we do to help the public understand that a mental health diagnosis is just as likely to change with client improvement as a medical diagnosis?

References

American Medical Association Evidence-Based Practice Working Group. (1992). Evidence-based medicine: A new approach to teaching the practice of medicine. *Journal of the American Medical Association, 268*, 2420–2425.

American Psychiatric Association. (1994). *Diagnostic and statistical manual of mental disorders* (4th ed.). New York: Author.

Carpenter, J. (2002). Mental health recovery paradigm: Implications for social work. *Health & Social Work, 27*(2), 86–94.

Cloud, J. (2003, January 30). How we get labeled. *Time, 161*(3), 102–106.

Davis, R. T., Blashfield, R. K., & McElroy, R. A. (1993). Weighting criteria in the diagnosis of a personality disorder: A demonstration [Electronic version]. *Journal of Abnormal Psychology, 102,* 319–322.

DeGrandpre, R. (1999). *Ritalin nation: Rapid-fire culture and the transformation of human consciousness* [Electronic version]. New York: Norton.

Dwyer, K. P., Osher, D., & Warger, W. (1998). *Early warning, timely response: A guide to safe schools.* Washington, DC: U.S. Department of Education. (ERIC Document Reproduction Service No. ED418 372)

Franklin, A. J. (1992). Therapy with African American men: Families in society. *The Journal of Contemporary Human Services, 73,* 350–355.

Gambrill, E. (2000, October). Evidence based practice. Paper presented at a meeting of the dean and directors of schools of social work, Huntington Beach, CA.

Glicken, M. D. (2004). *Violent young children.* Boston: Allyn & Bacon/Longman.

Harding, C. M., Brooks, G. W., Ashikaga, T., Strauss, J. S., & Breier, A. (1986a). The Vermont longitudinal study of persons with severe mental illness: I. Methodology, study sample, and overall status 32 years later. *American Journal of Psychiatry, 144,* 718–725.

Harding, C. M., Brooks, G. W., Ashikaga, T., Strauss, J. S., & Breier, A. (1986b). The Vermont longitudinal study of persons with severe mental illness: II. Long-term outcome of subjects who retrospectively met DSM-II criteria for schizophrenia. *American Journal of Psychiatry, 144,* 727–735.

Haverkamp, B. (1993). Confirmatory bias in hypothesis testing for client-identified and counselor self-generated hypotheses. *Journal of Consulting Psychology, 40,* 305–315.

Huber, G., Gross, G., & Schuttler, R. (1975). A long-term follow up study of schizophrenia: Psychiatric course of illness and prognosis. *Acta Psychiatrica Scandinavica, 52,* 49–57.

Isaacson, J. H., Nielsen, C., Urbanic, R., & Challgren, E. (1999, September 20). Markers for patients with alcohol problems in an outpatient general medicine clinic. *Substance Abuse, 3,* 141–147.

Jimenez, M. A. (1988). Chronicity in mental disorders: Evolution of a concept. *Social Casework, 69,* 627–633.

Kruger, A. (2000). Schizophrenia: Recovery and hope. *Psychiatric Rehabilitation Journal, 24,* 29–37.

Lu, M., & McGuire, T. G. (2002). The productivity of outpatient treatment for substance abuse. *Journal of Human Resources, 37*(2), 309–335.

Lynam, D. (1996). Early identification of chronic offenders: Who is the fledgling psychopath? *Psychological Bulletin, 120,* 209–234.

Markowitz, F. E. (1998). The effects of stigma on the psychological well-being and life satisfaction of persons with mental illness. *Journal of Health & Social Behavior, 39*(4), 335–347.

Mayer, G. R. (1995). Preventing antisocial behavior in the schools. *Journal of Applied Behavior Analysis, 28,* 467–478.

McLaughlin, J. E. (2002). Reducing diagnostic bias. *Journal of Mental Health Counseling, 24*(3), 256–270.

Moffitt, T. E. (1994). Adolescence-limited and life-course persistent antisocial behavior: A developmental taxonomy. *Psychological Review, 100,* 674–701.

Morey, L. C., & Ochoa, E. S. (1989). An investigation of adherence to diagnostic criteria: Clinical diagnosis of the DSM-III personality disorders. *Journal of Personality Disorders, 3,* 180–192.

National Institute of Alcohol Abuse and Alcoholism. (2000). New advances in alcoholism treatment. (NIAAA Alcohol Alert Publication No. 49). Bethesda, MD: Author.

National Institute of Mental Health. (1999). Schizophrenia. Retrieved January 5, 2003, from www.nimh.nih.gov/publicat/schizoph.cfm

Obiakor, F. E., Merhing, T. A., & Schwenn, J. O. (1997). *Disruption, disaster, and death: Helping students deal with crises.* Reston, VA: The Council for Exceptional Children. (ERIC Document Reproduction Service No. ED403 709)

Pfeiffer, A. M., Whelan, J. P., & Martin, J. L. (2000). Decision-making in psychotherapy: Effects of hypothesis source and accountability. *Journal of Counseling Psychology, 47,* 429–436.

Robertson, J., & Fitzgerald, L. F. (1990). The (mis)treatment of men: Effects of client gender role and life-style on diagnosis and attribution of pathology. *Journal of Counseling Psychology, 37,* 3–9.

Rosenhan, D. L. (1973). On being sane in insane places. *Science, 179,* 250–258.

Saleebey, D. (1996, May). The strengths perspective in social work practice: Extensions and cautions. *Social Work, 41*(3), 296–305.

Sharp, W. S., Walter, J. M., & Marsh, W. L. (1999). ADHD in girls: Clinical comparability of a research sample [Electronic version]. *Journal of the American Academy of Child and Adolescent Psychiatry, 38,* 40–47.

Sprague, J. R., & Walker, H. M. (2000, Spring). Early identification and intervention for youth with antisocial and violent behavior. *Exceptional Children, 66*(3), 367–379.

Tsuang, M. T., Woolson, R. F., & Fleming, M. S. (1979). Long term outcome of major psychoses. *Archives of General Psychiatry, 36,* 1295–1301.

Walker, H. M., & Severson, H. H. (1990). *Systematic screening for behavior disorders.* Longmont, CO: Sopris West.

Werner, E., & Smith, R. S. (1982). *Vulnerable but invincible.* New York: McGraw-Hill.

Werner, E., & Smith, R. S. (1992). *Overcoming the odds: High-risk children from birth to adulthood.* Ithaca, NY: Cornell University Press.

Whaley, A. L. (2001). Cultural mistrust: An important psychological construct for diagnosis and treatment of African Americans. *Psychology: Research and Practice. 32*(6), 555–562.

Wilke, D. (1994). Women and alcoholism: How a male-as-norm bias affects research, assessment, and treatment [Electronic version]. *Health and Social Work, 19,* 29–35.

World Fellowship for Schizophrenia and Allied Disorders. Schizophrenia: First warning signs. Retrieved January 5, 2003, from www.world-schizophrenia.org/publications/20-warnings.html

Evidence-Based Practice and Psychosocial Assessments 6

R ather than using a diagnostic label that may fail to accurately describe a client's unique qualities or the historical reasons the client is having problems at critical points in time, a psychosocial assessment summarizes the relevant information we know about a client and organizes it into concise statements that allow other helping professionals to understand the client and the problem(s) as well as the clinician does. Psychosocial assessments differ from DSM-IV diagnostic labels because they provide brief historical information about the possible cause of the problem. While assessments are problem focused, they also provide an evaluation of the best evidence from the literature to support the assessment. The client's strengths are also included in an assessment, as are the problems that might interfere with the client's treatment. For those readers unfamiliar with the strengths perspective (also called positive psychology and the wellness approach), Van Wormer (1999) describes the elements of the strengths approach as follows:

> The first step in promoting the client's well-being is through assessing the client's strengths. A belief in human potential is tied to the notion that people have untapped resources—physically, emotionally, socially, and spiritually—that they can mobilize in times of need. This is where professional helping comes into play—in tapping into the possibilities, into what can be, not what is. (p. 51)

Case Study: Evidence-Based Practice and the Assessment Process

This case study is used to help show the way in which the EBP approach might be applied in assessing a client seeking help for depression. The outline used in the case is for illustrative purposes only. Under each heading is a description of the information one might include. The important thing to remember is that the assessment provides information to other professionals. It necessarily includes all the information relevant to the case. Some of that information might pertain to ongoing difficulties or prior life problems experienced by the client. Most important, however, it includes information from the research literature to support observations, impressions, initial diagnosis, and, ultimately, treatment. Some aspects of this case were first reported in Glicken (2004).

The Psychosocial Assessment Outline and the Relevant Information Pertaining to the Case

SECTION I: BRIEF DESCRIPTION OF THE CLIENT AND THE PROBLEM

In this section of the psychosocial assessment, practitioners should include relevant sociodemographic information about the client, including the client's age, marital status, the composition of the client's family of origin and their current level of interaction, what the client is wearing, the client's verbal and nonverbal communications, his affect, and anything of significance that took place during the interview, including the client's descriptions of the defined problem(s). Interpretations are normally not made in this section. The following is an example of how this section might be written from an EBP perspective:

Oscar Goldman is a successful 41-year-old Jewish businessman whose presenting problem is a mild but ongoing depression which developed in tandem with his divorce and with the death of his parents 2 years ago. The client believes that part of the reason for the depression relates to problems with his Holocaust-surviving parents and their unwillingness to accept his non-Jewish wife, who divorced him just prior to the death of his parents. He has little contact with an older brother and a younger sister and feels that he has been unsuccessful with close intimate relationships.

Mr. Goldman came to the appointment on time, was appropriately dressed, and says that he is 5 feet 10 inches and weighs 175 pounds. He wore no jewelry other than a gold watch. Initially, he moved about a great deal in his chair and his feet tapped on the floor. Midway through the interview, he slumped in his chair and wiped tears from his eyes. He seeks help resolving problems related to depression and feelings of guilt about his parents and his ex-wife.

Questions About This Initial Information

1. **Question:** Do depressed clients continue to do well at work, look fit and trim, and in other ways appear to be fairly normal? **Answer:** Yes, they do, but it's unusual for highly depressed clients to do exceptionally well, and often their psychosocial functioning deteriorates over time. One might think that Mr. Goldman is displaying early-onset depression, but neither dysthymic disorder (DSM-IV Code 300.4, APA, 1994, p. 349) nor depressive disorder not otherwise specified (DSM-IV Code 311, APA, 1994, p. 350) seem to be appropriate descriptors of his current functioning. Both suggest impairment in psychosocial functioning. Perhaps an alternative explanation for Mr. Goldman's depressed affect can be found in the answer to the following question.

2. **Question:** Has the lack of intimacy Mr. Goldman experienced with his parents and siblings led to depression? **Answer:** People who grow up in an environment with limited intimacy sometimes develop what Weiss (1961) calls an "existential crisis." An existential crisis usually develops after an important life event, such as the death of loved ones or health problems. It may also develop without any apparent reason and usually does not develop into a more severe clinical depression. Clients with an existential depression lose their sense of newness in life and often feel isolated and withdrawn. They may think of the world as a place of suffering and obsess about the unhappiness they see around them. If Mr. Goldman has an existential crisis, it may also be seen as a prolonged bereavement related to the death of the client's parents and the end of his marriage. As Weiss (1961) writes in paraphrasing Karen Horney, "It [an existential crisis] is a remoteness of the client in crisis from his own feelings, wishes, beliefs and energies. It is a loss of feeling of being an active, determining force in his own life [and results in] an alienation from the real self" (p. 464).

3. **Question:** Do the tears in his eyes, his slumping in his chair, and his feet tapping on the floor suggest any relevant emotional states? **Answer:** Mr. Goldman's behavior suggests a number of emotional states but not necessarily depression. One of the aspects of the DSM-IV to consider in understanding Mr. Goldman's behavior is the Global Assessment Functioning Scale, also known as the GAF score (APA, 1994, p. 32). The GAF score ranges from 100 ("superior functioning in a wide range of activities; life problems never seem to get out of hand; is sought after by others because of his or her many qualities; no symptoms" [p. 32]) to 10 and below ("danger to self and to others; inability to maintain hygiene and the possibility of suicidal acts" [p. 32]). In reviewing the GAF, an

appropriate score for Mr. Goldman might be in the 51–60 range: "moderate symptoms and moderate difficulty in social, occupational, or school functioning (few friends, conflicts with peers and co-workers" (p. 32). How serious is this score? It's serious enough to warrant treatment, and serious enough to worry about a more extreme depression, but basically, it's a hopeful and optimistic diagnosis. How do we know that the diagnosis is optimistic? We don't really know without more information. Let's see if we change our minds as we learn more about Mr. Goldman.

SECTION II: HISTORICAL ISSUES

This section includes any past issues of importance in understanding the client's current problems. The following might be relevant points to include in the historical section of our report:

Mr. Goldman went into business after his sophomore year at Northwestern University. He has not finished his degree and feels insecure about his intellectual abilities. However, he reads books recommended by people he respects as a way of compensating for his lack of formal education. Mr. Goldman has a brother who is 3 years older and a sister who is 4 years younger. His parents were very observant Jews who constantly complained about his lack of religious belief. His parents were also Holocaust survivors, and were serious, fearful, pessimistic, and emotionally aloof. When they died, they were not speaking to him because he had married a non-Jewish woman. He has a very limited relationship with his brother and sister and seldom sees or calls them. He has little other contact with members of a small extended family, who live in other parts of the country. More than 200 members of his extended family perished in Europe during the Holocaust.

Mr. Goldman and his ex-wife had serious marital problems, partially because his work took him away from home a great deal. The couple often fought and, on several occasions, hit one another. Mr. Goldman discovered that his wife was having an affair with one of his business rivals, which ended the 5-year marriage 2 years ago. The couple had no children.

Mr. Goldman has experienced a mild but persistent depression since his divorce. Both of his parents died soon after the divorce. He feels a great deal of animosity toward them because his parents disowned him after his marriage because his wife wasn't Jewish. He is proud to be Jewish but is angry that his parents would do something so cruel and pejorative in the name of Judaism. Mr. Goldman attends Jewish groups, reads about Jewish history and traditions, and has tried to understand and resolve his confused feelings about his religion, but isn't always successful.

He has always been very successful at work, although his relationships with people have usually been uncomfortable and he sees himself as being shy and withdrawn. He has no close friends and finds his business rivals mean-spirited because they often make bigoted remarks about Jews in his presence. He hasn't been in a relationship since his divorce and feels that his trust level for relationships is nonexistent.

He has no problem sleeping, his weight has been stable, and a recent physical examination found him to be healthy and in excellent physical condition. He has never been in therapy before but did take a tranquilizer prescribed by his family physician for anxiety after his divorce and the death of his parents. He found that the medication affected his work by making him sleepy, and he discontinued using it after 2 weeks. He is currently on no other medications.

Questions

1. **Question:** Is there a relationship between parents who survive genocide and emotional problems in their children? **Answer:** Sometimes. Baron, Eisman, Scuello, Veyzer, and Lieberman (1996) report that many clinicians who first saw survivors of the Holocaust believed that they would be very poor parents and that their children would suffer from a range of emotional difficulties. Children of survivors, however, have shown no pattern of maladjustment or psychopathology in most research. Last (1989) reviewed the research on Holocaust survivors and hypothesized that the effect of the Holocaust on parents "will be manifest in the offspring of those who suffered, more often in the form of specific character formations than in any psychopathological symptoms" (p. 87). Does this negate the possibility of a relationship between parental survival of genocide and depression in a child? No, but neither is it necessarily a strong indicator.

2. **Question:** Do perceived instances of bigotry lead to depression, anger, or other symptoms that might explain Mr. Goldman's current reason for seeking help? **Answer:** The persistence of anti-Semitism is demoralizing to many Jewish people. How does one rationally explain continued anti-Semitic behavior so many years after the discovery of German death camps and the attempt to exterminate all of the Jews in occupied Europe? In Mr. Goldman's case, it must reinforce what his parents told him about anti-Semitism in Europe and the need to be an observant Jew with a commitment to a strong Jewish lifestyle as one way of coping with anti-Semitism. The current rise of anti-Semitism in Europe is another reminder to Mr. Goldman of the accuracy of the messages his parents gave him. As Neaman (2002) writes,

> When Jews are attacked by right-wing thugs, as has happened all over Europe this spring, when editorials and cartoons in major European newspapers castigate Israel, and intellectuals pontificate about the actions of the Israeli army while remaining mute about Palestinian terrorism, when Jewish neighborhoods are defaced by graffiti and Jews become fearful for their lives, one cannot say that business is usual. (p. 5)

SECTION III: DIAGNOSTIC STATEMENT

The diagnostic statement is the clinician's best explanation of the reasons the client is experiencing problems now. The diagnostic statement combines material from the prior two sections and summarizes the most important information in a brief statement. Continuing on with Mr. Goldman, this might be an example of the diagnostic statement:

Mr. Goldman is a 41-year-old divorced Jewish businessman seeking help for a mild but ongoing depression since the death of his parents and his divorce 2 years ago from an unfaithful wife. He feels isolated, has no friends, and experiences anti-Semitism in his work.

Issues that need further discussion include a difficult and unsuccessful relationship with his deceased parents; problems of anti-Semitism in the workplace that reinforce his parents' experiences during the Holocaust; problems of intimacy, particularly with women; a lack of friends or support groups; ambivalent feelings about his religion; and a better understanding of the reasons for his persistent depression.

Mr. Goldman has many positive attributes. He is successful at work; has a very positive value system; has tried to be introspective and to understand the reasons for his current problems with depression; is concerned enough about his current emotional state to seek professional help; has tried to answer some of these questions by reading relevant literature; has some insight into the reasons for problems with his parents, siblings, and former wife; is motivated to change; and, even though he experiences a mild depression, is successful at work and has tried to improve his level of knowledge as a way of compensating for his lack of formal education. He understands that he has confused feelings about his religion and has tried to learn more about the history and the traditions of Judaism, something he strongly resisted earlier in his life.

A beginning diagnostic impression is that his persistent depression is a form of prolonged bereavement following the death of his parents and his divorce. That his parents rejected him for marrying out of his faith complicates the bereavement process. There is no evidence of any severe pathology that might lead to further depression or suicide, but continued observation and the weekly use of depression instruments, such as the CES-D (Radloff, 1977) and the Beck Depression Inventory (Beck, Ward, Mendelson, Mock, & Erbaugh, 1961), will help us determine this. He is motivated for change, is articulate and intelligent, is open about his problems, and seems to relate well. He continues to be successful at work and has tried to use the available literature to understand and resolve many of his problems, often effectively. At this point in time, the prognosis for improvement is very positive.

Questions

1. **Question:** Grief and unresolved issues related to the death of his parents seem to be one of the major contributing factors to Mr. Goldman's

current problems, according to the diagnostic statement. Is it possible for grief to be so prolonged after the death of his parents and to still play such a significant role in his current functioning? **Answer:** Balk (1999) believes that bereavement, which is the loss of a significant person in one's life, can result in physical and emotional problems, the most significant of which may include

> intense and long-lasting reactions such as fear, anger, and sorrow. Bereavement affects cognitive functioning (e.g., memory distortions, attention deficits, and ongoing vigilance for danger) and behavior (e.g., sleep disturbances, excessive drinking, increased cigarette smoking, and reckless risk taking). It impacts social relationships as outsiders to the grief become noticeably uncomfortable when around the bereaved. And bereavement affects spirituality by challenging the griever's very assumptions about the meaning of human existence. (p. 486)

Jacobs and Prigerson (2000) warn that bereavement sometimes develops into a complicated or prolonged grief lasting more than a year. The symptoms of complicated grief include intrusive thoughts about the deceased, numbness, disbelief that a loved one has passed away, feeling confused, and a diminished sense of security. Prolonged grief may be unresponsive to interpersonal therapy or to the use of antidepressants.

2. **Question:** Does the work Mr. Goldman needs to do to resolve many of his issues require a type of existential therapy? **Answer:** Possibly. Significant personal growth often takes place when people deal with bereavement. Kubler-Ross (1969/1997) believes that coping with the death of a loved one often leads to life-changing growth and new and more complex behaviors that focus on the meaning of life. One aspect of coping with loss is the development of spirituality. Finn (1999) writes that spirituality leads to "an unfolding consciousness about the meaning of human existence. Life crises influence this unfolding by stimulating questions about the meaning of existence" (p. 228). Balk (1999) suggests that three issues must be present for a life crisis to result in spiritual changes: "The situation must create a psychological imbalance or disequilibrium that resists readily being stabilized; there must be time for reflection; and the person's life must forever afterwards be colored by the crisis" (p. 485). All of these conditions exist in Mr. Goldman's life and suggest potential for significant life change if appropriately resolved.

SECTION IV. THE TREATMENT PLAN

The treatment plan describes the goals of treatment during a specific period of time and originates in the agreement made between the worker and the client in the contractual phase of treatment. In this example,

12 sessions are used over a 3-month period. The treatment plan for Mr. Goldman might be as follows:

1. Enlist Mr. Goldman in a cooperative effort to find the best treatment approaches for his current problems by reading the existing literature and discussing it with the worker.

2. Help him understand and resolve a prolonged grieving process that seems related to a troubled relationship with his parents and former wife, and that has resulted in a mild but persistent depression.

3. Discuss issues of intimacy that might help in promoting new and more satisfying relationships.

4. Evaluate the extent of his depression and to possibly ask for a psychiatric consultation to consider medication to relieve persistent symptoms of mild depression.

5. Help him develop better ways of coping with the anti-Semitism he experiences at work.

6. Explore the possibility of continuing his formal education.

7. Help him resolve confused feelings about his religion.

8. Encourage involvement in group activities, including self-help groups on bereavement and depression that might also help him develop relationship skills.

Questions

1. **Question:** Do we really have a diagnosis on which to base treatment? **Answer:** We don't know with certainty what Mr. Goldman's condition really is other than that he experiences a mild depression and has feelings of guilt and remorse. One way to determine his level of depression is to use an instrument such as the Beck Depression Inventory to evaluate the seriousness of the problem and to assess any risk for suicide. The Beck Depression Inventory has good reliability (.80 to .90) and good validity for measuring depression, according to Wilcox, Field, Prodromidis, and Scafidi (1998). Another depression inventory, the CES-D, is also a good instrument and has a high comparative correlation (.70) with the Beck Depression Inventory when the two instruments test the same people and the test results are compared (Wilcox, Field, Prodromidis, & Scafidi, 1998). A second professional opinion might also help. For the time being, let's consider the GAF score of 51–60 as an indication of his current social functioning and let's assume that Weiss's description of an existential crisis is applicable. How might this affect our treatment? In describing treatment for an existential crisis, Weiss (1961) writes, "To defrost, to open up,

to experience and to accept himself becomes possible for the patient only in a warm, mutually trusting relationship in which, often for the first time in his life, he feels truly accepted as he is, accepted with those aspects of himself which early in life he had felt compelled to reject or repress" (p. 474). Weiss also indicates that, as treatment progresses, the client who may appear so devoid of self-awareness and who seems emotionally lacking in feeling and introspection will "begin to reveal surprising aliveness and depth, passionate longings, and strong feelings of loss" (p. 475).

2. **Question:** Isn't it dangerous for therapists to begin helping clients reveal feelings about their religious and spiritual beliefs? Might this not reflect a therapist's personal bias and ultimately have a negative impact on the client? **Answer:** There is a growing belief that it's legitimate for therapists to allow clients to discuss religious and spiritual issues. In Mr. Goldman's case, his identity as a Jew and his ambivalence about his Jewishness are important issues to explore—if not in therapy, then at least with someone who understands the issues and can relate to them in a helpful way. Some beginning research suggests a relationship between religious and spiritual involvement and better mental health. For example, a study conducted by the National Institute of Health in 1998, as reported by Mitka (1998), found that people who attend religious services had consistently lower blood pressure than those who do so less frequently. Another study reported by Mitka found that the more religious patients were, the more quickly they recovered from depression. A study reported by Riley, Perna, and Tate (1998) examined religious, existential, and nonspiritual patients suffering from chronic illness or disability. The study considered the overall physical health, quality of life, and life satisfaction of the participants. Individuals in both the religious and existential groups experienced better quality of life than those in the nonspiritual and nonreligious groups. The benefits of religious and spiritual belief seem positive. If Mr. Goldman can resolve his confused feelings about Judaism, it may provide him with a belief system that helps him deal with meaning-of-life issues stemming from his complicated relationship with his parents and his divorce.

3. **Question:** Isn't there a good chance that using the right antidepressant might bring about behavioral changes without the need for therapy? **Answer:** This is a fundamental issue in treatment and not one to be taken lightly. The reason for a psychiatric consultation in the treatment plan is to make certain that Mr. Goldman's behavior doesn't have a biochemical origin. If it does, then certainly the correct psychotropic medication is in order. The issues he has identified might be effectively treated with a combination of drug therapy and psychotherapy. The research evidence seems to suggest that antidepressants alone are no more effective than therapy. However, antidepressants often have an impact on sexual functioning, which discourages many people from using them. Also, as therapists, we have no control over whether clients actually take the

prescribed antidepressants and no way to judge their functioning unless clients see us often. That's why therapy can be highly beneficial because it keeps close tabs on the client and can help identify depression that seems to be unresponsive to medication or to therapy.

To help answer the question of efficacy of medication for depression versus efficacy of therapy alone, several studies are provided that show the relationship between improvement in depression and the use of antidepressants and/or therapy:

Study 1: It is clear that antidepressant medications produce a 60% recovery rate when prescribed within proper dosages and for adequate duration. Depression-specific time-limited psychotherapies achieve similar outcomes, even with patients experiencing moderate to severe symptomatology. Two principles emerge from this body of work: (1) major depression should not be treated with anxiolytic medications alone or with long-term psychotherapy; and (2) patient preference for a particular guideline-based treatment should be considered when it is clinically and practically feasible. (Schulberg, 1998, p. 2)

Study 2: The most frequently cited results were reported by the National Institute of Mental Health Treatment of Depression Collaborative Research Program. Two hundred fifty unipolar depressed patients at three sites were randomly assigned to one of four conditions: cognitive-behavior therapy (CBT), interpersonal therapy (IPT), imipramine (a tricyclic antidepressant) plus clinical management (IMI-CM), and pill placebo with clinical management (PLA-CM). Results were generally as follows: (a) all four conditions resulted in significant improvement; (b) neither form of psychotherapy was superior to the other; (c) the only significant treatment difference for all patients occurred between IMI-CM and PLA-CM; (d) for the more severe cases, IMI-CM and IPT produced more improvement than PLA-CM whereas CBT did not; and (e) IMI-CM generally produced more rapid effects than the other conditions. (Kopta, 1999, p. 14)

Some Thoughts About Why Clients Change

Before we leave the treatment plan, perhaps a brief discussion about the literature pertaining to client change might be helpful. McConnaughy, Prochaska, and Velcer (1983) report that client change requires both worker and client to be at the same state of readiness in understanding the client's problems and the emotional commitment to change them. Howard, Lueger, Maling, and Martinovich (1993) believe that clients start therapy in a state of demoralization. Through the development of trust, the therapist helps them identify their primary problems, instills hope, and helps them develop a sense of well-being. As their sense of well-being increases, problems that seemed unsolvable to the client can be discussed and remedied. Remediation suggests that clients practice new behaviors that reinforce change through stages of treatment. Howard et al. (1993) add,

> From a psychotherapy practice point of view, the phase model suggests that different change processes will be appropriate for different phases of therapy and that certain tasks may have to be accomplished before others are undertaken. It also suggests that different therapeutic processes may characterize each phase. Therapeutic interventions are likely to be most effective when they focus on changing phase-specific problems when those problems are most accessible to change. (p. 684)

Howard, Moras, Brill, Martinovich, and Lutz (1996) add that, although these phases are distinct, they suggest different treatment goals and "thus the selection and assessment of different outcome variables to measure progress in each phase" (p. 1061). These are, of course, partially untested ideas from the literature, but they may help in better understanding the change process with a client like Mr. Goldman.

SECTION V. CONTRACT

The contract is an agreement between the worker and the client that specifies the problems to be worked on in treatment, the number of sessions agreed upon, rules related to being on time, the length of each session, the payment, and the cancellation policy. Many workers prepare the contract in written form and have both the client and worker sign it. A contract with Mr. Goldman might be as follows:

Mr. Goldman has agreed to attend 12 consecutive one-hour sessions. He agrees that more therapy might be required. The effectiveness of treatment and the progress made will be evaluated after each session and at the end of the 12 sessions using client feedback and a depression instrument. Mr. Goldman agrees to consult the research, to share the research he has read with his therapist, and to write summaries of what took place during each session and the future issues he would like to discuss. This summary will be provided to the therapist within 2 working days of each session. After 12 sessions, the client and worker will jointly determine whether additional sessions are needed. Mr. Goldman has agreed to other issues in the contract, including the need to be on time, prompt payment, and the cancellation policy.

Questions

1. **Question:** Can significant change take place in 12 sessions? **Answer:** Very often it can. Seligman (1995) found no difference in client satisfaction with treatment among clients who had been seen for an average of 6 months and those who had been seen for an average of 2 years. Kopta (1999) reports a study where clients with severe substance abuse problems were provided 12 sessions using three different types of treatment (12-step-based counseling, psychodynamic therapy, and cognitive-behavioral therapy) and that "significant and sustained improvements in drinking outcomes were observed for all three groups" (Kopta, 1999, p. 21). Fleming and Manwell (1998) report that people with alcohol-related problems, including persistent depressions, often receive counseling from primary care physicians or nursing staff in five or fewer standard office visits with very good results. Gentilello, Donovan, Dunn, and Rivara (1995) report that 25% to 40% of the trauma patients seen in emergency rooms may be alcohol dependent and depressed. The authors found that a single motivational interview at or near the time of discharge reduced drinking levels and readmission for trauma during 6 months of follow-up. Monti et al. (1999) conducted a similar study with 18- to 19-year-olds admitted to an emergency room with alcohol-related injuries. After 6 months, all participants had decreased their alcohol consumption; however, "the group receiving brief intervention had a significantly lower incidence of drinking and driving, traffic violations, alcohol-related injuries, and alcohol-related problems" (p. 993).

DISCUSSION OF THE CASE

While much of the current literature seems to suggest that a form of cognitive-behavioral therapy works best with depression, it's not entirely certain that it would work well with Mr. Goldman. The active and directive nature of cognitive-behavioral therapy could remind the client of similar communication patterns used by his domineering parents. One approach that might be worth considering is the strengths perspective, because it tries to view all of the participants in the client's current problem by framing them in the most positive and humane way possible. In a previous book, I (Glicken, 2004) defined the strengths perspective as

> a way of viewing the positive behaviors of all clients by helping them see that problem areas are secondary to areas of strength and that out of what they do well can come helping solutions based upon the successful strategies they use daily in their lives to cope with a variety of important issues. (p. 3)

One of the attributes of children who cope with abusive parents is their ability to define parental behavior in ways that "permits them to understand the reasons for their parent's behaviors and still feel a sense of loyalty and even love" (Glicken, 2004, p. 139). In that book, I also noted, "While clients need to understand any harm done to them by parental conduct and to understand its impact, they benefit from a more complete and potentially positive view of their parents" (p. 139). The ability to understand his parents as they might have explained and defended their own behavior is an important aspect of treatment with Mr. Goldman.

Survivors of genocide often see their families as their defense against the possibility of future harm. Accordingly, there is a sense that children must obey their parents or the terrible things that happened in the death camps could happen again. It's important to remember that Mr. Goldman's parents suffered from unimaginable terror and cruelty, which was dehumanizing to victims. Commenting on the impact of highly stressful experiences, including concentration camps, Sigal and Weinfeld (2001) write:

> Exposure to prolonged, excessive stress has been shown to have long-term negative effects on the psychological and physical health, as well as on the longevity of adult survivors. These effects have been demonstrated for American ex-POWs of the Japanese camps in World War II and the Korean War and for Jewish and non-Jewish survivors of the Nazi concentration camps. They suffer from anxiety, depression, and their somatic equivalents; sleep problems and social withdrawal; and many other symptoms. These are symptoms that are typically of psychological stress. (p. 69)

Mr. Goldman's parents may have believed that their lives were saved by their strong religious convictions and that those same beliefs were paramount to their continued safety. A nonobservant child could result in offending God and changing the family's luck. While this may sound illogical and superstitious, it's not a far-fetched belief when we consider the positive impact of religion and spirituality on the lives of people. To further upset the parents' concern about their relationship with God, Mr. Solomon married someone out of the faith, an act many traditional Jewish parents would see as a betrayal by their son of his family and their precious religious beliefs. It was not unusual for some parents in very traditional Jewish homes to perform the ancient ritual that considered their child to actually be dead for marrying out of the faith.

Trying to maintain religious beliefs in a child striving for independence must surely have alienated Mr. Goldman from his parents and them from him. To further confuse his relationship with his parents, Mr. Goldman may have thought that his success in business was a concrete way of protecting his family. Rather than being praised for his independence and good fortune at making a substantial living, he was criticized and denied the emotional support he needed to develop intimate relationships. This conflict in culture and generation must have been particularly troubling to everyone involved and might have set up barriers that were difficult to resolve. Not surprisingly, a confused Mr. Goldman now suffers from depression and guilt because what he thought would gain favor with his parents and provide protection for his family ended in alienating them. What further confuses him is that his preparation for life helped him to succeed in his career but at the expense of a limited ability to form and maintain intimate relationships. According to his parents, who experienced a terrible trauma and whose level of trust must have been very minimal, happiness and intimacy were secondary to hard work, determination, persistence, religious observance, and survival. And now the financially successful but unhappy client may actually believe that his parents were right all along, and that his life as an autonomous and unobservant man has become as unfulfilling as his parents predicted it would be.

While Mr. Goldman's values and behaviors are very positive and he has great determination to change, the one thing he lacks is an understanding of how one develops and maintains relationships that lead to intimacy. This is where the alliance between the worker and client becomes most significant. By involving Mr. Goldman in a cooperative relationship where he works closely with the worker in trying to resolve his current issues, Mr. Goldman may come to learn how one develops and maintains relationships. The experience of working closely with another person is filled with potential problems. Mr. Goldman is a highly successful man who has depended on few people in his life. Those he did depend on, including his parents, often failed him. The EBP model of involving the client at every juncture of treatment will hopefully help Mr. Goldman overcome his initial resistance and discomfort. His treatment also calls for a very empathic approach, one that Saleebey (2000) believes "obligates us to understand . . . to believe that everyone (no exceptions here) has external and internal assets, competencies and resources" (p. 128), and that these resources, regardless of how dormant or untested, are able to provide the wise helper with the ability to facilitate the relationship in a way that permits the client to work through relationship concerns and discomforts.

SUMMARY

In summary, the psychosocial assessment is a way of determining areas of difficulty and areas of strength. Used correctly, it can provide the practitioner with an understanding of the connecting elements that have created the current crisis in a client's life. The psychosocial assessment can also help the clinician develop strategies that may move the client in directions that create significant changes in the client. A key to the use of the psychosocial assessment is to remember to focus on positive client behaviors, while keeping in mind interfering negative behaviors that may affect client functioning. It is also very important to support client assumptions about the cause of a problem and the most efficacious treatment, with recognition of the best evidence available in the research literature.

Integrative Questions

1. We're assuming that Mr. Goldman is depressed because of the conflicts he had with his parents and his divorce. Are there alternative reasons for Mr. Goldman's depression?

2. We tend to assume that children of parents who have been traumatized will suffer negative consequences because parental traumas create problems in parenting. Do you believe that's necessarily true?

3. Many survivors of the Holocaust went on to live healthy, normal, and productive lives. Don't we make the mistake of assuming that most people aren't resilient enough to cope with severe traumas when, in fact, they are?

4. We often think of depression as an easily defined emotional state, but clearly people experience depression in unique ways. This makes one wonder if antidepressive medications will help Mr. Goldman. What do you think?

5. The GAF score of 51–60 seems a bit low for someone as successful as Mr. Goldman. He may be feeling depressed but his behavior doesn't necessarily show it. What might be a more accurate GAF score, in your opinion?

References

American Psychiatric Association. (1994). *Diagnostic and statistical manual of mental disorders* (4th ed.). New York: Author.

Balk, D. E. (1999). Bereavement and spiritual change. *Death Studies, 23*(6), 485–493.

Baron, L., Eisman, H., Scuello, M., Veyzer, A., Lieberman, M. (1996, September). Stress resilience, locus of control, and religion in children of Holocaust victims. *Journal of Psychology, 130*(5), 513–525.

Beck, A. T., Ward, C. H., Mendelson, M., Mock, J., & Erbaugh, J. (1961). An inventory for measuring depression. *Archives of General Psychiatry, 4,* 561–571.

Finn, J. (1999). An exploration of helping processes in an online self-help group focusing on issues of disability. *Health & Social Work, 24*(3), 220–231.

Fleming, M., & Manwell, L. B. (1998). Brief intervention in primary care settings: A primary treatment method for at-risk, problem, and dependent drinkers. *Alcohol Research and Health, 23*(2), 128–137.

Gentilello, L. M., Donovan, D. M., Dunn, C. W., & Rivara, F. P. (1995). Alcohol interventions in trauma centers: Current practice and future directions. *Journal of the American Medical Association, 274*(13), 1043–1048.

Glicken, M. D. (2004). *Using the strengths perspective in social work practice: A positive approach for the helping profession.* Boston: Allyn & Bacon/Longman.

Howard, K. I., Lueger, R. J., Mailing, M. S., & Martinovich, Z. (1993). A phase model of psychotherapy outcome: Causal mediation of change. *Journal of Consulting and Clinical Psychology, 61,* 678–685.

Howard, K. I., Moras, K., Brill, P. B., Martinovich, Z., & Lutz, W. (1996). Evaluation of psychotherapy: Efficacy, effectivenees, and client change. *American Psychologist, 51,* 1059–1064.

Jacobs, S., & Prigerson, H. (2000). Psychotherapy of traumatic grief: A review of evidence for psychotherapeutic treatments. *Death Studies, 24*(6), 479–496.

Kopta, S. M., Lueger, R. J., Saunders, S. M., & Howard, K. J. (1999). Individual psychotherapy outcome and process research: Challenges leading to greater turmoil or a positive transition? [Electronic version]. *Annual Review of Psychology, 50,* 441–469.

Kubler-Ross, E. (1997). *On death and dying.* New York: Scribner Classics. (Original work published 1969)

Last, U. (1989). The transgenerational impact of Holocaust trauma: Current state of the evidence. *International Journal of Mental Health, 17*(4), 72–89.

McConnaughy, E. A., Prochaska, J. O., & Velcer, W. F. (1983). Stages of change in psychotherapy: Measurement and sample profile. *Psychotherapy: Theory, Research and Practice, 20,* 388–375.

Mitka, M. (1998). Getting religion seen as help in being well. *Journal of the American Medical Association, 280*(22), 1896–1897.

Monti, P. M., Colby, S. M., Barnett, N. P., Spirito, A., Rohsenow, D. J., Myers, M., et al. (1999). Brief intervention for harm reduction with alcohol-positive older adolescents in a hospital emergency department. *Journal of Consulting and Clinical Psychology, 67*(6), 989–994.

Neaman, E. (2002, July 1). European right-wing populism and anti-Semitism [Electronic version]. *Tikkun, 17*(4), 53–55.

Radloff, L. S. (1977). The CES-D scale: A self-report depression scale for research in the general population. *Journal of Applied Psychological Measures, 1*(3), 385–401.

Riley, B. B., Perna, R., & Tate, D. G. (1998). Spiritual patients have a better quality of life than those who aren't. *Modern Medicine, 66*(5), 45–48.

Saleebey, D. (2000, Fall). Power to the people; strength and hope. *Advancements in Social Work, 1*(2), 127–136.

Schulberg, C. (2001, June 1). Treating depression in primary care practice: Applications of research findings [Electronic version]. *Journal of Family Practice, 50*(6), 535–537.

Seligman, M. E. P. (1995). The effectiveness of psychotherapy: The *Consumer Reports* study. *American Psychologist, 50*(12), 965–974.

Sigal, J. J., & Weinfeld, M. (2001, Spring). Do children cope better than adults with potentially traumatic stress? A 40-year follow-up of Holocaust survivors. *Psychiatry, 64*(1), 69–80.

Van Wormer, K. (1999, June). The strengths perspective: A paradigm for correctional counseling. *Federal Probation, 63*(1), 51–59.

Weiss, F. M. (1961). In E. Josephson & M. Josephson (Eds.), *Man Alone* (pp. 463–479). New York: Laurel.

Wilcox, H., Field, T., Prodromidis, M., & Scafidi, F. (1998, September 22). Correlations between Beck Depression Inventory and CES-D in a sample of adolescent mothers [Electronic version]. *Adolescence, 33*, 565–574.

Evidence-Based Practice and the Client-Worker Relationship 7

The Significance of the Therapeutic Relationship

This chapter considers the significance of the therapeutic relationship in effective counseling and psychotherapy. In recognizing the importance of the relationship in the counseling and psychotherapy literature, Warren (2001) indicates, "The relationship between the quality of the patient-therapist relationship and the outcome of treatment has been one of the most consistently cited findings in the empirical search for the basis of psychotherapeutic efficacy" (p. 357). Writing about the power of the therapeutic relationship, Saleebey (2000) says, "If healers are seen as non-judgmental, trustworthy, caring and expert, they have some influential tools at hand, whether they are addressing depression or the disappointments and pains of unemployment" (p. 131). In a review of EBP for psychotherapy, Kopta, Lueger, Saunders, and Howard (1999) conclude that the relationship is of key importance in the helping process, and Greenfield, Kaplan, and Ware (1985) note the beneficial effects of increasing a patient's involvement with his or her own care as a result of a positive client-worker relationship.

Defining the Therapeutic Relationship

Brent and Kolko (1998) define psychotherapy as a "modality of treatment in which therapists and patients work together to ameliorate psychopathological conditions and functional impairment by focusing on

(1) the therapeutic relationship; (2) the patient's attitudes, thoughts, affect, and behavior; and (3) social context and development" (p. 1). Entwistle, Sheldon, Sowden, and Watt (1998) suggest that clients are actively involved in decisions regarding their treatment in four ways:

1. through the care a patient will or will not receive,

2. through the research information indicating the effectiveness of certain interventions including their risks and benefits,

3. through the use of recommended approaches showing good research validity or doing nothing, and

4. through involvement in all decisions regarding treatment.

The American Medical Association EBP Working Group (1992) writes that all EBP practitioners must be sensitive to the emotional needs of clients and that "understanding patients' suffering and how that suffering can be ameliorated by the caring and compassionate practitioner are fundamental requirements for practice" (p. 2422). The working group also calls for much more research to better understand how the interactions between clients and practitioners affect the outcome of treatment.

In an assessment of a study done using *Consumer Reports* data on the effectiveness of psychotherapy, Seligman (1995) suggests that clients have the wisdom to "shop around" for therapists who meet their own particular needs and that the type of therapy they receive is less important than the intangible aspects of whether they like the therapist and believe that he or she will be able to help them. Seligman writes, "Patients in psychotherapy in the field often get there by active shopping, entering a kind of treatment they actively sought with a therapist they screened and chose" (p. 970).

Commenting on the importance of the therapeutic relationship in the change process and the hope that research will find evidence of the best fit between clients and the type of alliances that work best, Warren (2001) suggests that research on therapeutic relationships "make[s] possible the development of treatment protocols that can then increase [treatment] efficacy, influence the training of psychotherapists, and provide standard treatment protocols for the purposes of further treatment process research" (p. 357).

Orlinsky, Grawe, and Parks (1994) report that there are five variables that have consistently been demonstrated to positively affect the quality of both the therapeutic alliance and treatment effectiveness: (a) the overall quality of the therapeutic relationship; (b) the skill of the therapist; (c) patient cooperation versus resistance; (d) patient openness versus defensiveness; and (e) the duration of treatment.

Keith-Lucas (1972) defines the relationship as "the medium which is offered to people in trouble and through which they are given an opportunity to make choices, both about taking help and the use they will make of it" (p. 47). Keith-Lucas says that the key elements of the helping relationship are "mutuality, reality, feeling, knowledge, concern for the other person, purpose, the fact that it takes place in the here and now, its ability to offer something new and, its nonjudgmental nature" (p. 48).

In describing the significant elements of the relationship, Bisman (1994) says that therapeutic relationships are a form of "belief bonding" between the worker and the client, and that both parties need to believe that "the worker has something applicable for the client, the worker is competent, and that the client is worthwhile and has the capacities to change" (p. 77). Hamilton (1940) suggests that bonding takes place when the clinician and client work together and that "treatment starts only when mutual confidence is established, only when the client accepts your interest in him and conversely feels an interest in you" (pp. 189–190).

Weiss, Sampson, and O'Connor (1995) suggest that clients are highly motivated to resolve their problems, and that they actively work through-out their treatment to recall experiences and obtain knowledge that will help them so that they can "coach" their therapist about what needs to be done and the best way to do it. The effective therapist recognizes the significance of the client's coaching and, rather than seeing it as controlling or divisive, accepts it as an important part of the client's need for significant involvement in the process.

In a previous book about the importance of the relationship in a new practice paradigm, the strengths perspective, I (Glicken, 2004) wrote,

> The relationship is a bond between two strangers. It is formed by an essential trust in the process and a belief that it will lead to change. The worker's expertise is to facilitate communications, enter into a dialogue with the client about its meaning, and help the client decide the best ways of using the information accumulated in searches for best evidence. (p. 50)

Not all clients like a cooperative relationship. Some want advice and expect the clinician to be an expert in the issues that are troubling them, while other clients may want a prolonged analysis of the reasons for their current problems. What the client wants and needs is primary and the worker should be responsive to the needs and desires of clients while helping them develop skill in working cooperatively. As Saleebey (1996) suggests,

> How social workers encounter their fellow human beings is critical. They must engage individuals as equals. They must be willing to meet them eye-to-eye and to engage in dialogue and a mutual sharing of knowledge, tools, concerns, aspirations, and respect. The process of coming to know is a mutual and collaborative one. (p. 303)

The following is an EBP definition of the therapeutic relationship: It is the bond developed between two or more people for the purpose of helping clients resolve social and emotional difficulties. It derives its purpose from the belief that establishing a caring, facilitative, and change-oriented partnership, where power differences are eliminated and the worker and the client communicate in a way that is comfortable, sincere, and honest, will lead to positive change.

Evidence of the Importance of the Therapeutic Relationship to Treatment Outcomes

Noting the importance of the of the therapeutic alliance in the professional literature, Gelso and Hayes (1998) wonder if we have a clear understanding of what is meant by the worker-client relationship and write, "Because the therapy relationship has been given such a central place in our field for such a long period of time, one might expect that many definitions of the relationship have been put forth. In fact, there has been little definitional work" (p. 5). But in a review of EBP for psychotherapy, Kopta et al. (1999) say that the relationship is of key importance in the helping process. Horvath and Greenberg (1994) found research evidence of the central role of the relationship in successful therapies. Major advances, according to Horvath and Greenberg, have been made in

1. understanding the important role of relationships in the helping process,

2. having a better concept of how one operationalizes the relationship for research purposes,

3. having an increased awareness of variables prior to treatment that suggest potential for a successful therapeutic relationship, and

4. understanding the ways in which the relationship may change as treatment progresses, including "ruptures" in the relationship.

Krupnick et al. (1996) evaluated data from the large-scale National Institute of Mental Health Treatment of Depression Collaborative Research Program, which compared various treatments for depression. The authors found that a positive therapeutic relationship was predictive of treatment success for all levels of severity of depression. In another large study of diverse forms of therapy for alcoholism, the therapeutic relationship was also significantly predictive of success (Connors, Carroll, DiClemente, Longabaugh, & Donovan, 1997). Horvath and Symonds (1991) indicate that a positive relationship between scores on the quality of the initial (early) relationship and positive outcomes have been repeatedly found regardless of how the relationship is described by the practitioner. Kopta et al. (1999) write,

> Bordin (1994) argued that—regardless of the modality—the alliance always involves agreement on tasks and goals as well as a sense of compatibility or bonding. This latter viewpoint has been confirmed in the Working Alliance Inventory (Horvath 1994). Both Luborsky's and Bordin's programs have consistently found a predictive association between alliance [relationship] and outcome. (p. 8)

Commenting further on the importance of the relationship in outcome studies of therapy, Brent and Kolko (1998) report, "The contribution of therapeutic empathy and a good working alliance to positive clinical outcome has been demonstrated in several clinical trials of adult patients (Burns & Nolen-Hoeksema, 1992; Cooley & Lajoy, 1980; Luborsky, McLellan, Woody, O'Brien, & Auerbach, 1985; Murphy, Simons, Wetzel, & Lustman, 1984)" (p. 2). Brent and Kolko go on to say, "From the patients' points of view, provision of support, understanding, and advice have been reported as most critical to good outcome (Cooley & Lajoy, 1980; Murphy et al., 1984)" (p. 2). In further comments about the relationship between the treatment alliance and effective therapeutic outcomes, Brent and Kolko (1998) report, "The adult psychotherapy literature strongly supports the central role of the therapeutic relationship and therapeutic empathy in mediating the efficacy of treatment across many treatment models and psychopathological conditions" (p. 8). Finally, Brent and Kolko write,

> There appears to be a reciprocal relationship between therapist and patient behavior in both good and poor outcome psychotherapy. According to Henry, Schacht, and Strupp (1986), in "good outcome" therapy, the therapist is described as "helping and protecting, affirming and understanding," whereas the patient is seen as "disclosing and expressing." In "poor outcome" psychotherapy, the therapist tends to be "blaming and belittling," whereas the patient is depicted as "walling off and avoiding." Not surprisingly, therapists tend to attribute success to technique, whereas patients attribute a good outcome to the therapist's support and understanding (Feifel & Eells, 1963; Mathews, Johnson, Shaw, & Geller, 1974). (Brent & Kolko, 1998, p. 2)

Although it would appear that the relationship is of key importance in treatment outcomes, *Consumer Reports* magazine ("Mental Health: Does Therapy Help?" 1995) indicated that most of the readers responding to a survey about the benefits of psychotherapy were satisfied with the treatment they received and that no differences in treatment effectiveness were found between the various psychotherapy approaches, some of which emphasized the therapeutic relationship and others of which did not. There is ongoing criticism of this study, however. Only 4% of the original sample actually responded to the survey (2,900 readers). The results could be explained by the tendency of respondents to give positive feedback because of loyalty to their therapists or by regression to the mean. Since there was no control group used in the study, many of the people who said they improved as a result of therapy might have had the same improvement rate by talking to a friend. These and other similar studies suggest that readers of therapy research should be aware that generalized statements about any issue pertaining to therapy, including the importance of the client-worker relationship, must first be evaluated by determining the quality of the research.

Gender and the Therapeutic Relationship

Clinical wisdom usually suggests that gender is a neutral variable in clinical outcomes and that the quality of the help is more significant than issues related to the genders of the worker and the client. Studies by Gehart-Brooks and Lyle (1999) and Sells, Smith, Coe, Yoskioka, and Robbins (1994), however, suggest that therapist gender *is* an important factor affecting the client's therapy experience. Although clients specifically state that gender is important, parallel interviews with therapists suggest that it isn't important. Gehart-Brooks and Lyle (2001) believe that this "potential oversight has significant implications for the practice of ethical, gender-sensitive therapy and training" (p. 444) and go on to say, "Jones and Zoppel (1982) found that clients, regardless of gender, agreed that female therapists formed more effective therapeutic alliances than male therapists; however, both male and female clients of male therapists also reported significant improvements as a result of therapy" (p. 444).

Gehart-Brooks and Lyle (2001) report that further inquiry into the relationship between gender and therapeutic outcomes indicates that "male and female therapists interrupted females three times more often than male clients (Werner-Wilson et al., 1997)" (p. 444). Shields and McDaniel (1992) report that families made more directive statements to male therapists, but disagreed more openly with each other in front of females. They also found that male therapists explained issues more fully than female therapists and that male therapists provided more advice and direction than female therapists. Werner-Wilson, Zimmerman, and Price (1999) report that men were more successful at suggesting issues for discussion in family treatment, but women did better in marital therapy. Gehart-Brooks and Lyle (2001) believe that these "studies provide further evidence that gender may significantly affect the therapeutic process in ways in which therapists are currently unaware" (p. 444).

Gehart-Brooks and Lyle (2001) describe three possible types of gender-related connections made by clients:

1. The connection is stronger with a therapist of the same gender because it offers a common language and knowledge base.

2. The connection is stronger with a therapist of the opposite gender because gender differences may provide motivation to work harder in treatment.

3. The client develops a good relationship with a therapist of the same gender but often reports that therapists of the opposite gender are also effective.

In summarizing their work on gender, Gehart-Brooks and Lyle write,

> Perhaps the most striking pattern is that what one viewed as a therapist's strength, another viewed as a detriment. For example, clients described women as more feeling-focused, but only half found this helpful. Conversely, almost all clients described male therapists as more direct and problem-focused, yet only half found this approach helpful. What is consistent is that clients reported that they experienced a distinct and consistent difference between male and female therapists. (p. 452)

Racial and Ethnic Variables in Therapeutic Effectiveness

A number of studies have examined the relationship between racial bias and psychiatric diagnoses. Adebimpe (1981) found that a high number of African American patients were misdiagnosed as schizophrenic, a finding, according to Laszloffy and Hardy (2000), supported in subsequent studies that examined white, black, and Latino patients. Although the symptoms were the same, African American and Latino patients were often incorrectly diagnosed as schizophrenic, while white patients were almost always correctly diagnosed with emotional or affective disorders (Garretson, 1993; Lopez & Nunez, 1987; Loring & Powell, 1988; Malgady, Rogler, & Constantino, 1987; Pakov, Lewis & Lyons, 1989; Solomon, 1992). Laszloffy and Hardy (2000) believe that underlying the misdiagnosis is a "subtle, unintentional racism" (p. 35). In defining racism, the authors write that "all expressions of racism are rooted in an ideology of racial superiority/inferiority that assumes some racial groups are superior to others, and therefore deserve preferential treatment" (p. 35), a definition that makes unintentional or subtle racism difficult to accept.

Flaherty and Meagher (1980) found that, among African American and Caucasian male schizophrenic inpatients who had similar global pathology ratings, "African American patients spent less time in the hospital, obtained lower privilege levels, were given more p.r.n. medications, and were less likely to receive recreation therapy and occupational therapy. Seclusion and restraints were more likely to be used with black patients" (p. 679). While the authors avoid suggesting a direct relationship between racial bias and the treatment of minority patients, they conclude that it is an important intervening variable.

In a report on race and mental health, the U.S. surgeon general (Satcher, 2001) believes that the cultures of clinicians and the way services are provided influence the therapeutic alliance and, by extension, diagnosis and treatment. Service providers, according to the report, need to be able to build upon the cultural strengths of the people they serve. The surgeon general goes on to note that "while not the sole determinants, cultural and social influences do play important roles in mental health, mental illness and service use, when added to biological, psychological and environmental factors" (p. 1). In trying to understand barriers to treatment that affect ethnic and racial minorities, the surgeon general says that the mental health system often creates impediments that lead to distrust and fear of treatment, which ultimately deter racial and ethnic minorities from seeking and receiving needed services, and adds, "Mental health care disparities may also stem from minorities' historical and present day struggles with racism and discrimination, which affect their mental health and contribute to their lower economic, social, and political status" (Satcher, 2001, p. 1). In an earlier report on mental health, the surgeon general (Satcher, 1999) wrote that, although mental illness is at least as prevalent among racial and ethnic minorities as in the majority white population, "many racial and ethnic minority group members find the organized mental health system to be uninformed about cultural context and, thus, unresponsive and/or irrelevant" (p. 1) and may prefer clinicians who share their racial, ethnic, and socioeconomic backgrounds (Satcher, 1999, p. 4).

Laszloffy and Hardy (2000) believe that as long as racism occupies such a significant role in our everyday lives, it cannot be completely eliminated without carefully examining what we say to clients, what we do with clients, and, as a strong reminder of the importance of EBP, what we really believe. In validating the need for cultural and racial sensitivity, Pena, Bland, Shervington, Rice, and Foulks (2000) write,

> In work with African-American patients, the therapist's skill in recognizing when problems do or do not revolve around the condition of being black could have serious implications for the acceptability of treatment, the development of the treatment alliance, and in psychotherapy, the accuracy of interpretations. (p. 14)

The authors report that each of these variables has a significant impact on treatment outcomes and that therapists with limited awareness of the significance of race may experience problems in "listening empathically" and in actually understanding the client's conflicts.

Case Study: A Positive Therapeutic Relationship

Ana Krezney is a 43-year-old Russian immigrant who came to the United States with her family when she was 14 years old. She considers herself thoroughly assimilated and is married to an American man. Her family has had a difficult time in America and has been unable to resume the professional careers they had in Russia. Much of their interaction with Ana contains negative messages about all things American, including her husband. Ana considers herself to be a strong and competent woman, but her relationship with her family has become strained because her husband is beginning to disengage from Ana's family. Ana worries that the disengagement will ultimately include her. Like many clients new to therapy, Ana is looking for someone to give her advice. She expects that therapy will last just a few sessions and told the therapist she chose, "I just want some help with my family and my marriage. Just be honest with me and give me good information."

The therapist was very businesslike with Ana and helped her tell her story in a way that satisfied Ana's need for advice. He then suggested several articles she could find on the Internet that related to the issues with which she needed help and recommended that she carefully write down some concrete questions to ask in their next session. Ana left the interview feeling very satisfied with the therapist. She felt he was a no-nonsense person who was giving her exactly what she was looking for. Ana read the articles and found them very useful but had some questions she needed to ask the therapist about several parts of each article she found unclear. She e-mailed the therapist her questions and within a short period of time received clear answers. Once again, he urged her to carefully construct the questions she would like to discuss in their next session. Ana spent more than 2 hours writing down her questions but began to realize that she had more questions than the therapist could possibly answer in one session. She decided that perhaps the treatment might take several more sessions than she'd originally planned. The questions she wrote covered 3 pages, single-spaced.

Ana shared the questions with her therapist, who took a few minutes to read them. He noted that there was some similarity in several of them and asked if they could meld the questions together. Ana thought this was a good idea. He then said there were three fundamental areas covered by the questions and suggested that they focus on each area and the questions included to save time. Ana was delighted with the efficient way the therapist was responding. In one session, they covered two areas and all of the questions included. Once again, the therapist suggested that she read some additional articles, specifically articles on the immigrant experience, assimilation, and marriages where cultural differences existed. Ana found the articles very helpful and, having learned to use the Internet, was able to find other articles of a similar nature.

In the third session, the therapist answered all of the remaining questions Ana had and wondered if there were some other things Ana would like to discuss. Ana felt that, for the time being, she was very satisfied with the results of their work together and terminated treatment after three informative and useful sessions. Her evaluation of the treatment was highly positive and she referred two of her friends to the therapist. Both friends were surprised at how differently the therapist responded to them. When the three women compared the therapist's style, Ana said it was businesslike, one friend described it as very warm and supportive, and the second friend described the style as relaxed, slow, and intimate. Each client was looking for something different from the therapist and each received it. They agreed that it took a very competent person to relate to their stated needs and to the style of interaction they found most comfortable. All three women felt that the therapist had involved them at a very high level and that he had done exactly what each client had asked of him. He didn't argue that they needed more help or criticize their agendas. They all believed they had benefited significantly from the experience and that the presenting problems had been resolved. None felt the need for more treatment, and all felt that termination had occurred at just the right time.

In describing his work with the three clients, the therapist said that he believed clients should set the therapeutic agenda and, unless he felt the agenda was harmful, he usually believed that clients selected the correct issues to discuss. He also felt that it was important to enter the client's world and relate to it in ways clients felt would be most helpful. He always asked for client input in decisions about treatment, suggested additional reading, asked them to come with questions and, when asked a question, answered it. If he didn't know the answer, he said he would do some research and suggested that the client do the same. He encouraged e-mails and tried to answer them quickly. He always asked clients to e-mail him a summary of what they had learned in their prior session and to read as much as they could about the questions they intended asking him in the next session. He believed that being an informed client made for much faster and more effective therapy.

SUMMARY

This chapter covers some important issues related to the therapeutic relationship and its significance to treatment effectiveness. While some of the authors cited in this chapter believe that the relationship is a key element in treatment effectiveness, many also believe that much more research is needed to establish the specific aspects of the relationship that help or hinder client change. Issues of the significance of client-worker gender and race/ethnicity were also raised, with many authors believing that both issues have an impact on treatment efficacy and that much more time must be spent in training new workers for effective work with diverse client populations. It remains unclear whether the relationship is as central to client change as many helping professionals believe it to be because of the questionable quality of the research.

Integrative Questions

1. If you were seeking professional help, what might be the worker characteristics (style of relating, race, gender, religious background, etc.) that you believe would make the initial relationship easiest? Why?

2. Can you think of some instances when the therapeutic relationship might hinder client change or actually cause harm?

3. The author says the relationship is a bond between strangers. Isn't that overly dramatic? How can a bond develop between strangers?

4. The case study makes the therapist sound like a chameleon. Do you think it's possible for therapists to dramatically change their style of relating to meet the very different needs of clients?

5. In what ways might differences in the expectations of a relationship between the worker and the client result in conflict?

References

Adebimpe, V. R. (1981). Overview: White norms and psychiatric diagnosis of black patients. *American Journal of Psychiatry, 138*, 279–285.

American Medical Association Evidence-Based Medicine Working Group. (1992). Evidence-based medicine: A new approach to teaching the practice of medicine. *Journal of the American Medical Association, 268*, 2420–2425.

Bisman, C. (1994). *Social work practice: Cases and principles.* Belmont, CA: Brooks/Cole.

Brent, D. A., & Kolko, D. J. (1998, February). Psychotherapy: Definitions, mechanisms of action, and relationship to etiological models [Electronic version]. *Journal of Abnormal Child Psychology, 26*(1), 17–25. Retrieved December 17, 2002, from www.findarticles.com/cf_0/m0902/n1_v26/20565425/print.jhtml

Burns, D. D., & Nolen-Hoeksema, S. (1992). Therapeutic empathy and recovery from depression in cognitive-behavioral therapy: A structural equation model. *Journal Consulting and Clinical Psychology, 60,* 441–449.

Connors, G. J., Carroll, K. M., DiClemente, C. C., Longabaugh, R., & Donovan, D. M. (1997). The therapeutic alliance and its relationship to alcoholism treatment participation and outcome. *Journal of Consulting Clinical Psychology, 65,* 588–598.

Cooley, E. J., & Lajoy, R. (1980). Therapeutic relationship and improvement as perceived by clients and therapists. *Journal of Clinical Psychology, 36,* 562–570.

Entwistle, V. A., Sheldon, T. A., Sowden, A., & Watt, I. S. (1998). Evidence-informed patient choice. Practical issues of involving patients in decisions about health care technologies. *International Journal of Technology Assessment in Health Care, 14,* 212–225.

Feifel, H., & Eells, J. (1963). Patients and therapists assess the same psychotherapy. *Journal of Consulting Psychology, 27,* 310–318.

Flaherty, J. A., & Meagher, R. (1980). Measuring racial bias in inpatient treatment. *American Journal of Psychiatry, 137,* 679–682.

Garretson, D. J. (1993). Psychological misdiagnosis of African Americans. *Journal of Multicultural Counseling and Development, 21,* 119–126.

Gelso, J., & Hayes, J. A. (1998). *The psychotherapy relationship: Theory, research and practice.* New York: Wiley.

Gehart, D. R. & Lyle, R. D. (2001, December 22). Client experience of gender in therapeutic relationships: An interpretive ethnography. *Family Process, 40,* 443–458.

Gehart-Brooks, D. R., & Lyle, R. R. (1999). Client and therapist perspectives of change in collaborative language systems: An interpretive ethnography. *Journal of Systemic Therapies, 18*(4), 78–97.

Glicken, M. D. (2004). *Using the strengths perspective in social work practice: A positive approach for the helping professions.* Boston: Allyn & Bacon/Longman.

Greenfield, S., Kaplan, S., Ware, J. E., Jr. (1985, April). Expanding patient involvement in care: Effects on patient outcomes. *Annals of Internal Medicine, 102*(4), 520–528.

Hamilton, G. (1940). *Social casework.* New York: Columbia University Press.

Henry, W. P., Schacht, T. E., & Strupp, H. H. (1986). Structural analysis of social behavior: Application to a study of interpersonal process in differential psychotherapeutic outcome. *Journal of Consulting and Clinical Psychology, 54,* 27–31.

Horvath, A. O., & Greenberg, L. S. (Eds.). (1994). *The working alliance: Theory, research, and practice.* New York: Wiley.

Horvath, A. O., & Symonds, B. D. (1991). Relation between working alliance and outcome in psychotherapy: A meta-analysis. *Journal of Consulting Clinical Psychology, 38,* 139–149.

Jones, E. E., & Zoppel, C. L. (1982). Impact of client and therapist gender on psychotherapy process and outcome. *Journal of Consulting and Clinical Psychology, 50,* 259–272.

Keith-Lucas, A. (1972). *Giving and taking help.* Chapel Hill: University of North Carolina Press.

Kopta, M. S., Lueger, R. J., Saunders, S. M., & Howard, K. I. (1999). Individual psychotherapy outcome and process research: Challenges leading to greater turmoil or a positive transition? [Electronic version]. *Annual Review of Psychology, 50,* 441–469.

Krupnick, J. L., Sotsky, S. M., Simmens, S., Moyer, J., Elkin, I., Watkins, J., et al. (1996). The role of the therapeutic alliance in psychotherapy and pharmacotherapy outcome: Findings in the National Institute of Mental Health Treatment of Depression Collaborative Research Program. *Journal of Consulting Clinical Psychology, 64,* 532–539.

Laszloffy, T. A., & Hardy, K. V. (2000). Uncommon strategies for a common problem: Addressing racism in family therapy. *Family Process, 39,* 35–50.

Lopez, S., & Nunez, J. A. (1987). The consideration of cultural factors in selected diagnostic criteria and interview schedules. *Journal of Abnormal Psychology, 96,* 270–272.

Loring, M., & Powell, B. (1988). Gender, race, and DSM-III: A study of the objectivity of psychiatric diagnostic behavior. *Journal of Health and Social Behavior, 29,* 1–22.

Luborsky, L., McLellan, A. T., Woody, G. E., O'Brien, C. P., & Auerbach, A. (1985). Therapist success and its determinants. *Archives of General Psychiatry, 42,* 602–611.

Malgady, R. G., Rogler, L. H., & Constantino, G. (1987). Ethnocultural and linguistic bias in mental health evaluation of Hispanics. *American Psychologist, 42,* 228–234.

Mathews, A. M., Johnson, D. W., Shaw, P. M., & Geller, M. G. (1974). Process variables and the prediction of outcome in behavior therapy. *British Journal of Psychiatry, 125,* 256–264.

Mental health: Does therapy help? (1995, November). *Consumer Reports,* 734–739.

Murphy, G. E., Simons, A. D., Wetzel, R. D., & Lustman, P. J. (1984). Cognitive therapy and pharmacotherapy: Singly and together in the treatment of depression. *Archives of General Psychiatry, 41,* 33–41.

Orlinsky, D. E., Grawe, K., & Parks, B. K. (1994). Process and outcome in psychotherapy—Noch einmal. In A. E. Bergin & S. L. Garfield (Eds.), *Handbook of Psychotherapy and Behavior Change* (4th ed.). New York: Wiley. [See Bergin & Garfield, 1994a, pp. 270–378.]

Pakov, T. W., Lewis, D. A., & Lyons, J. S. (1989). Psychiatric diagnosis and racial bias: An empirical investigation. *Professional Psychology: Research and Practice, 20,* 364–368.

Pena, J. M., Bland, I. J., Shervinton, D., Rice, J. C., & Foulks, E. F. (2000, February 1). Racial identity and its assessment in a sample of African-American men in treatment for cocaine dependence [Electronic version]. *American Journal of Drug and Alcohol Abuse, 26,* 97–112.

Saleebey, D. (1996, May). The strengths perspective in social work practice: Extensions and cautions. *Social Work, 41*(3), 296–305.

Saleebey, D. (2000, Fall). Power to the people: Strength and hope. *Advancements in Social Work, 1*(2), 127–136.

Satcher, D. (1999). *Mental health: A report of the surgeon general* [Electronic version]. Washington, DC: U.S. Department of Health and Human Services, Office of the Surgeon General. Retrieved December 17, 2002, from http://www.surgeongeneral.gov/library/mentalhealth/home.html

Satcher, D. (2001). *Mental health: Culture, race, and ethnicity. A supplement to mental health: A report of the surgeon general* [Electronic version]. Washington, DC: U.S. Department of Health and Human Services, Office of the Surgeon General. Retrieved December 17, 2002, from http://www.surgeongeneral.gov/library/mentalhealth/cre/release.asp

Seligman, M. E. P. (1995). The effectiveness of psychotherapy: The *Consumer Reports* study. *American Psychologist, 50*(12), 965–974.

Sells, S. P., Smith, T. E., Coe, M. J., Yoshioka, M., & Robbins, J. (1994). An ethnography of couple and therapist experiences in reflecting team practice. *Journal of Marital and Family Therapy, 20*, 247–266.

Shields, C. G., & McDaniel, S. H. (1992). Process differences between male and female therapists in a first family interview. *Journal of Marital and Family Therapy, 18*, 143–151.

Solomon, A. (1992). Clinical diagnosis among diverse populations: A multicultural perspective. *Families in Society, 73*, 371–377.

Warren, C. S. (2001). Book review: *Negotiating the therapeutic alliance: A relational treatment guide. Psychotherapy Research, 11*(3), 357–359.

Weiss, W. D., Sampson, H., & O'Connor, L. (1995, Spring). How psychotherapy works: The findings of the San Francisco Psychotherapy Research Group. *Bulletin of the Psychoanalytic Research Society, 4(1)*. Retrieved December 17, 2002, from www.columbia.edu/~hc137/prs/v4n1/v4n1!.htm

Werner-Wilson, R. J., Price, S. J., Zimmerman, T. S., & Murphy, M. J. (1997). Client gender as a process variable in marriage and family therapy: Are women clients interrupted more than men clients? *Journal of Family Psychotherapy, 11*, 373–377.

Werner-Wilson, R. J., Zimmerman, T. S., & Price, S. J. (1999). Are goals and topics influenced by gender modality in the initial marriage and family therapy session? *Journal of Marital and Family Therapy, 25*, 253–262.

Part 3

Evidence-Based Practice With Special Client Populations

Part 3 applies EBP to a number of common and often complex client problems. Chapter 8 shows the way EBP would be used with "Cluster B" personality disorders, both in understanding the disorder using the research literature and in applying best practice. As in all the chapters in this section of the book, case studies are included to help the reader understand the way disorders affect clients and how the application of best evidence can have a positive effect on client functioning.

Chapter 9 shows the use of EBP with posttraumatic stress disorder (PTSD) resulting from acts of random violence and terrorism. Many of the concerns about large numbers of clients experiencing PTSD following terrorist acts such as 9/11 seem to ignore the self-righting tendencies of people who show great resilience in times of severely traumatic events. Still, the development of PTSD following traumas can cause long-term problems for clients that are often overlooked by medical and mental health personnel. Best evidence is provided for treating PTSD with one treatment approach, debriefing, which is identified as an approach that may cause more harm than good.

Chapter 10 considers best evidence in the treatment of substance abuse and includes a discussion of natural healing and nonprofessionally led self-help groups. Some people are able to walk away from their addictions without professional help or involvement in self-help groups and have a degree of resilience that clinicians need to consider in their assumptions about the diagnosis and treatment of alcohol and drug abuse.

Chapter 11 considers the best evidence used in diagnosing and treating mood disorders and mental illness. One of the important issues noted in this chapter is the tendency to see mental illness and mood disorders as chronic and nonchanging, even though many people significantly improve through treatment and natural healing. Yet the notion of chronicity remains and often leads to labeling that is stigmatizing and may do more long-term harm to clients than the illness.

Chapter 12 discusses best practice with clients who are terminally ill and the loved ones who experience prolonged grief as a result of their deaths. Prolonged grief occurs when a client is unable to cope with the death of a loved one and experiences severe grief for a much longer period of time than is thought to be normal or healthy.

Chapter 13 considers anxiety and depression in older adults and reviews best practice for working with a growing population of older adults, whose depressed or anxious symptoms are often ignored or avoided by medical and mental health personnel because of an incorrect belief that older adults are unable to benefit from treatment.

Evidence-Based Practice With Cluster B Personality Disorders

8

One of the most difficult problems facing clinicians is the treatment of clients diagnosed with a personality disorder. In the popular mind, personality disorders suggest major treatment problems. The DSM-IV (APA, 1994) doesn't help matters when it defines a personality disorder as

> an enduring pattern of inner experience and behavior that deviates markedly from the expectations of the individual's culture. This pattern is manifested in two (or more) of the following areas: 1) In ways of perceiving self, others and events; 2) in the range, intensity, lability and appropriateness of the response; 3) in interpersonal functioning and; 4) in impulse control. The enduring pattern is inflexibility and impairment in many important areas of functioning that can usually be traced back to early childhood and is of a long duration, and is not caused by a mental or physical disorder or brain trauma. (p. 633)

On a further discouraging note, the *Gale Encyclopedia of Psychology* ("Personality Disorders," 2001) says treatment of clients with antisocial personality disorders is very likely to fail and reports,

> Antisocial personality disorder is highly unresponsive to any form of treatment. Although there are medications available that could quell some of the symptoms of the disorder, noncompliance or abuse of the drugs prevents their widespread use. The most successful treatment programs are long-term, structured residential settings in which the patient systematically earns privileges as he or she modifies behavior. (p. 1)

This discouraging summary of treatment efficacy has generally made many therapists leery of working with clients who have what the DSM-IV calls "Cluster B" personality disorders. Personality disorders are placed into three clusters by the DSM-IV. Cluster A includes "Paranoid, Schizoid and Schizotypal Disorders. People with this disorder often appear odd or eccentric" (APA, 1994, p. 629). Clients with Cluster B personality disorders (also termed severe personality disorders) often appear dramatic, emotional, or erratic and have major difficulties in establishing and maintaining adequate social relationships because of their emotionally labile and impulsive behavior (APA, 1994, p. 630). Cluster B personality disorders includes individuals with "Borderline, Antisocial, Histrionic, and Narcissistic Personality Disorders" (APA, 1994, p. 630). Cluster C "includes Avoidant, Dependent and Obsessive Compulsive Personality Disorders. Individuals with this Disorder often appear anxious or fearful" (APA, 1994, p. 630). This chapter will focus on Cluster B personality disorders because they are clearly the most common and often the most difficult problems facing clinicians.

Establishing the number of people with severe personality disorders in the population is difficult because of the diversity of diagnostic criteria used (Stone, 1993). Drake and Vaillant (1985) estimate the prevalence of borderline personality disorders in the population as 1%, and an individual's lifetime risk of antisocial personality disorder as just under 3%, with a fourfold increase in risk among men (Robins, Tipp, & Przybeck, 1991).

The Four Types of Cluster B Personality Disorders

ANTISOCIAL PERSONALITY DISORDERS

Adult antisocial personality disorder (DSM-IV Code 301.7) is described in the DSM-IV as a pervasive disregard for others since the age of 15 with repeated unlawful behavior, evidence of a prior conduct disorder, lack of remorse, disregard for the safety of others, deceitfulness, irritability and aggressiveness, irresponsibility as noted in repeated failures at work or in honoring obligations to others, and impulsivity not specifically related to episodes of mental illness or mania (APA, 1994, p. 650).

Davison and Neale (1990) describe clients with an antisocial personality disorder as "disruptive individuals whose deep-seated ethical and moral maladjustments frequently bring them into serious conflict with their associates and with society" (p. 260). Messina, Wish, Hoffman, and Nemes (1990, p. 1) write that people with antisocial personality disorder are uninhibited about committing antisocial acts; have no fear of punishment; act without guilt or regret; fail to learn from prior experiences; are often impulsive and aggressive in their behavior toward others; and have increased numbers of additional psychosocial problems and dual diagnoses (antisocial personality disorder and substance abuse, for example).

The DSM-IV estimates that the prevalence in the population of antisocial personality disorder is about 3% for males and 1% for females. Prevalence in clinical settings varies from 3% to 30% (APA, 1994, p. 648). It is important to note that the diagnosis of antisocial personality disorder is usually not used with children under the age of 18, although the DSM-IV says that age 15 is the point at which a diagnosis of conduct disorder may be changed to one of antisocial personality disorder. The more common diagnostic category for children exhibiting severe behavioral problems is conduct disorder, which has many of the same features but is believed to take into consideration the changing behavior of children as they mature.

BORDERLINE PERSONALITY DISORDERS

Clients with borderline personality disorder (DSM-IV Code 301.83) have all of the elements of a personality disorder but have five or more of the following symptoms: (a) a pattern of unstable relationships; (b) an unstable self-image or identity; (c) self-destructive impulsivity; (d) suicidal behavior; (e) irritability, anxiety, and severe swings in mood; (f) chronic feelings of emptiness; (g) difficulty controlling anger; and (h) transient paranoid ideations or dissociative symptoms (APA, 1994, p. 654). Clients with borderline personality disorder may also experience numerous unfulfilling relationships, sexual acting out, behavior that sometimes appears to demonstrate signs of mental illness, and severe ongoing depression and/or anxiety. The rate of completed suicides in borderline personality disorder is 8–10% (APA, 1994, p. 651).

Craig (2001) believes that clients with borderline personality disorder can be distinguished from histrionic personality disorder and major depressive disorder by their "self-destructiveness, chronic emptiness and loneliness, and sensitivity to criticism and rejection" (p. 2). Patients with borderline personality disorder may have paranoia and delusions, although the episodes are usually transient and normally do not have the eccentric qualities associated with schizotypal personality disorder (Craig, 2001).

Frey (1999) describes clients with borderline personality disorder as unstable, prone to wide mood swings, experiencing frequent relationships that are very intense but troubled, impulsive, and experiencing confusion about important life issues. This sense of confusion about life issues may suggest severe confusion about self-identity. Frey notes that people with borderline personality disorder frequently cut or burn themselves and often threaten or actually attempt suicide. Many of these clients have experienced severe childhood abuse or neglect. Frey reports that roughly 2% of the general population has borderline personality disorder, and that 75% are female (Frey, 1999, p. 3).

In several quantitative studies, the origins of borderline personality disorder found in borderline children include physical and sexual child abuse and neglect, separation from parents (Bemporad, Smith, Hanson, & Cicchetti, 1982; Kestenbaum, 1983), and serious parental psychopathology, including depression, substance abuse, or antisocial personality disorder (Goldman, D'Angelo, & DeMaso, 1993). In a study of latency-aged children showing signs of borderline personality disorder, Guzder, Paris, Zelkowitz, and Feldman (1999) found that 34% of the children in their sample had actual reports of sexual abuse made by adults who had knowledge of the abuse. The authors suggest that, in seeing a relationship between sexual abuse and borderline personality disorder, it is also true that many abused children have little parental supervision and that lack of supervision could also relate to the development of borderline personality disorder. Children with the symptoms of borderline personality disorder go on to exhibit the same symptoms as adults at a very high rate (Guzder et al., 1999).

The prevalence of borderline personality disorder, according to the DSM-IV is "2% of the general population, 10% of those seen in mental health clinics, and about 20% of the psychiatric patients. Borderline Personality Disorder ranges from 30–60% of the clinical population with Personality Disorder" (APA, 1994, p. 652).

HISTRIONIC PERSONALITY DISORDER

Patients diagnosed with histrionic personality disorder (DSM-IV Code 301.50) often appear highly emotional, very dramatic, and badly in need of attention. They may be seductive as a way of gaining attention, and for those who know people with this disorder, they may also appear to be emotionally shallow, to live in a fantasy world, and to be easily bored with routine. About 2%–3% of the population is thought to have this disorder. Although the disorder has been associated largely with women, there may be a gender bias involved. The DSM-IV says clients diagnosed with histrionic personality disorder show a pattern of substantial attention seeking and five (or more) of the following symptoms beginning in early adulthood: (a) discomfort when they aren't the center of attention, (b) inappropriately sexually seductive behavior, (c) shallow and highly labile shifts in emotion, (d) overreliance on physical appearance as a way of getting the attention of others, (e) communication that is highly subjective and lacks detailed information, (f) exaggerated behavior and emotions, (g) easily influenced and manipulated by others, and (h) often seeing relationships as being more intimate and significant than they actually are (APA, 1994, p. 657).

NARCISSISTIC PERSONALITY DISORDER

Narcissistic clients are characterized by a feeling of self-importance, a craving for admiration, and exploitative attitudes toward others. They have unrealistically inflated views of their talents and accomplishments and may become very angry if they are criticized or outshone by others. Narcissists may be professionally successful but rarely have long-lasting intimate relationships. Less than 1% of the population has this disorder and about 75% of those diagnosed are male (Frey, 1999, p. 4). The DSM-IV says that clients diagnosed with narcissistic personality disorder (DSM-IV Code 301.81) have a pervasive pattern of grandiosity (in fantasy or behavior), a need for admiration, lack empathy and have, by early adulthood, five (or more) of the following symptoms of the disorder" (APA, 1994, p. 661): (a) exaggerated self-importance; (b) preoccupation with fantasies of limitless success, power, brilliance, and ideal love; (c) a belief they are so special that they should only associate with others they consider superior; (d) a need for excessive admiration; (e) a strong sense of entitlement; (f) a tendency to take advantage of others; (g) a lack of empathy; (h) a tendency to be envious or a belief that others are envious of them; and (i) a tendency to be arrogant and haughty (p. 661).

Developmental Theories
Explaining Cluster B Personality Disorders

In trying to understand the dynamics of children at risk for the development of Cluster B personality disorders, Bleiberg (2002) says these children share a striking incongruity: "paradoxically coexisting with remarkable self-centeredness and utter disregard for other people's feelings. One moment they can be engaging and appealing, the next moment, however, their capacity to manipulate others and their rage, demandingness, and self-destructiveness become overwhelming" (p. 2). Bleiberg notes that at the center of the developmental crisis children experience who exhibit Cluster B personality disorders as adults is the absence of a process called "mentalization," or in the their case, an inability to understand the behavior of other people and respond appropriately. When children achieve mentalization, the results are ownership of one's behavior, a capacity for social reciprocity and empathy, the ability to tolerate frustration, and the capacity to symbolize. Children with a predisposition for Cluster B personality disorders have none of these capacities. "Instead, their behavior becomes coercive, and aims at evoking stereotypical responses from others that fit children's expectations" (Bleiberg, 2002, p. 2).

Frey (1999) suggests that personality disorders result from a bad fit between a child's temperament and character on the one hand and his or her family environment on the other, and he defines temperament as a person's innate disposition. Just as infants vary in their sensitivity to light or noise, their level of physical activity, their adaptability to schedules, and to similar issues, they also vary in the way they react to their parents, the physical and psychological environments they live in, and the adaptations they must make to cope with external stimuli. Character, according to Frey, consists of the attitudes an individual develops over time. Character includes work and study habits, moral convictions, and concerns about others. "Since children must learn to adapt to their specific families, they may develop personality disorders in the course of struggling to survive psychologically in disturbed or stressful families" (Frey, 1999, p. 5). Frey also points out that a diagnosis of a personality disorder is made more difficult by the fact that patients often receive the diagnosis later in life as a result of work-related or marital difficulties. One common diagnostic clue that one is working with a personality disorder is the client's distorted view of a situation causing them difficulty, while another is that the impact of their behavior on others may be difficult for the client to empathize with or to understand. (Frey, 1999).

Messina et al. (1990) report a high correlation between a diagnosis of antisocial behavior and substance abuse. In two studies, the relationship between these two variables was as high as 90% (Forrest, 1991; Tims, De Leon, & Jainchill, 1986). Kasen, Cohen, Skodol, Johnson, and Brook (1999) believe that axis 1 problems in children, including anxiety and depression, may act as a catalyst for a variety of maladaptive behaviors that increase the risk for more persistent problems leading to personality disorders in young adulthood. They recommend early diagnosis and treatment for more severe pathology when symptoms begin to affect the child's functioning. Nakash-Eisikovits, Dutra, and Westen (2002) indicate the existence of a relationship between attachment theory and the development of personality disorders. Bowlby (1969, 1973, 1980) suggested that children form mental "representations" of relationships based on their interactions with, and adaptation to, their parental or care-giving environments. When the attachment between child and parents is weakened by dysfunctional parental behavior common in abusive, alcoholic, antisocial, and mentally ill parents, the result is often a personality disorder (Fonagy et al., 1996; Fonagy, Target, & Gergely, 2000). Brennan and Shaver (1998) studied a large nonclinical sample of adolescents and found a strong relationship between insecure attachments and self-reported behavior consistent with personality disorders. Noting the relationship between attachment disorders and personality disorders, Nakash-Eisikovits et al. (2002) write:

> Allen et al. (1996) investigated the relationship between severe psychopathology in adolescence (as indicated by a need for psychiatric hospitalization) and attachment classifications in young adulthood as assessed by the AAI. Across the sample, adolescents classified as insecure were more likely to abuse drugs, to be involved in criminal acts, and to have unresolved trauma histories. Rosenstein and Horowitz (1996) similarly found a high prevalence of insecure attachment styles in adolescent psychiatric inpatients. (p. 2)

Treating Cluster B Personality Disorders:
An Evidence-Based Practice Perspective

In a review of published articles on the treatment of Cluster B personality disorders, Kisley (1999) says most of the articles are descriptive or qualitative and that few of the studies reported use of empirical designs with randomized selection or control groups. Given the chronic nature of personality disorders, a follow-up period of at least 2 years is necessary to measure treatment outcomes. In most published studies, this period of time is lacking (Roth & Fonagy, 1996). Kisley (1999) indicates that, in initiatives in the United States, England, and Australia, the results of treatment of Cluster B symptoms has been contradictory, with some findings supporting the use of therapeutic community (Department of Health and Home Office, 1994), while other reports support behavioral therapies (NHS Executive, 1996).

In a review of studies providing effective approaches for the treatment of Cluster B personality disordered symptoms in children, Bleiberg (2002) reports that treatment requires a collaborative relationship between parents and clinicians that emphasizes

> the importance of interrupting the cycles of coercive behavior; of promoting parental competence, control and mentalization; and ultimately, of promoting a "mismatch" between the children's expectation of parental incompetence, insensitivity and abuse and parents' enhanced capacity to provide support and set limits. (p. 3)

Bleiberg also suggests that clinicians avoid confrontations with children, promote the child's ability to communicate feelings and thoughts, help parents gain control of situations in which children are manipulative or overly aggressive, improve the child's ability to understand situations, and place them in the proper emotional context by learning to respond in ways that help in the development of mentalization. Finally, Bleiberg says, "Children enter an advanced stage of therapy when they can tolerate their attachment to their therapist, as evidenced by their seeking help to find adaptive solutions to day-to-day problems" (p. 3).

Hoffman (2002) reports that clients with personality disorders do not improve as much as clients with non–personality-disordered psychiatric disorders. Hoffman also says clients with antisocial personality disorder generally do not have positive outcomes unless depression is also present. Depression increases the ability to form attachments and to develop a positive therapeutic alliance. Hoffman reports that dropout rates in treatment among clients with personality disorders vary from 10% to 30%, depending on the treatment length, with shorter treatments experiencing fewer dropouts. The empirical data, according to Hoffman, suggest that a good therapeutic alliance is associated with treatment effectiveness.

A type of treatment thought to be effective for personality disorders is therapeutic community. According to Kisley (1999), treatment in therapeutic community consists of scheduled daily group meetings, participation in the management of the community, and small group psychotherapy sessions involving 12–14 clients. Kisley says that there is disagreement about the effectiveness of therapeutic communities with Cluster B personality disorders. Although two controlled studies reported improvement rates of 40%–60% up to 5 years after admission, there were a number of methodological problems, including the loss of 70% of the control group in one study (Dolan, 1996), and all of the control group in another study (Dolan, Warren, & Norton, 1997). Because of the methodological problems in both studies, therapeutic community is still an unproven way to treat Cluster B personality disorders.

Several studies of the treatment of personality disorders note the effectiveness of cognitive-behavioral therapies. Dialectical behavioral therapy (DBT), for example, combines individual interventions and group therapy with behavioral skills training. Linehan, Armstrong, Suarez, Allmon, and Heard (1991) report that the use of DBT in groups and individual therapy, each meeting once a week, resulted in 1.5 acts of self-mutilation in a 12-month period compared with 9 in the control group. Episodes of self-mutilation were less severe, and there was a dramatic reduction in hospital days as a result of DBT, with the treatment group requiring 8.46 days of hospitalization in the entire year as compared with 38.86 days in the control group. An Australian study (Stevenson & Meares, 1992) using twice-weekly psychodynamic therapy resulted in the following improvements:

1. Absences from work declined from an average of 4.7 months per year to an average of 1.37 months per year.

2. Self-harm episodes fell by one fourth as a result of therapy.

3. Visits to medical professionals dropped to one seventh of the pretreatment rates after the psychotherapy.

4. Average time spent as an inpatient decreased by half.

5. Hospital admissions decreased by 59% after the therapy.

Stevenson and Meares (1995) confirmed that these changes were still in place after a 5-year follow-up assessment. In a study of the treatment of borderline personality disorder, Bateman and Fonagy (1999) studied 38 borderline patients in a psychoanalytically oriented partial hospital program with a similar group of controls. The researchers found a reduction in suicide attempts from 95% on admission to 5.3% after 18 months. Some promising results for patients with antisocial personality disorder emerged from a study of opiate addicts (Woody, McLellan, Luborsky, & O'Brien,

1985) in which 110 male patients with opiate addiction received either paraprofessional drug counseling alone or counseling plus professional psychotherapy (either supportive-expressive or cognitive-behavioral). Those in the study who had antisocial personality disorder with an axis 1 diagnosis of depression made significant improvement in both symptoms and employment. Clients with antisocial personality disorder without depression showed little improvement as a result of psychotherapy.

Lehmann (2003) believes, "Therapists often have intense, unproductive emotional reactions to patients with borderline personality disorder because borderline patients engage in self-injurious behavior and suicide attempts and perceive these acts as manipulative and attention seeking" (p. 29). These negative perceptions often result in stigmatizing clients with borderline personality disorder. To be effective, therapists must maintain a positive treatment alliance with clients and communicate often with other professionals involved with the client to prevent "splitting," a reaction that occurs when clients pit one therapist against another. Treatment approaches that seem best suited for effective work with the borderline clients are cognitive therapy and DBT with serotonin selective reuptake inhibitors and mood stabilizers added when drug therapy is recommended (Lehmann, 2003, p. 29).

In summarizing studies with positive outcomes for the treatment of Cluster B personality disorders, Kasen et al. (1999) report the following findings:

1. Many of the studies reviewed by the author show comorbidity for axis 1 and axis 2 conditions.

2. The research on treatment outcomes with personality disorders is at a very early stage of development.

3. Many of the studies evaluated lack good designs and randomized selection.

4. Depressed antisocial patients with substance addictions may be more treatable by psychotherapy than has been previously thought.

5. Psychodynamic psychotherapy appears to be very effective for borderline personality disorder when combined with an overall partial hospital program.

6. A psychodynamic approach appears to reduce feelings of depression in borderline clients.

7. Without adequate outpatient care, clients with personality disorders will need much more inpatient hospital care.

8. Extended outpatient care of a year or longer can lead to a significant reduction in hospital stays with a substantial cost savings.

Because much of the research suggests the negative results of treating personality disorders, particularly clients whose antisocial behavior involves the client in social and legal difficulty, some alternative ideas from the strengths perspective are presented that, although lacking research validity, are interesting and might provide the practitioner with some treatment philosophies at variance with the research presented thus far. In discussing the treatment of antisocial behavior, Van Wormer (1999) says, "At the heart of the strengths perspective is a belief in the basic goodness of humankind, a faith that individuals, however unfortunate their plight, can discover strengths in themselves that they never knew existed" (p. 51). Van Wormer goes on to suggest the use of the following techniques with clients experiencing legal problems because of antisocial behavior:

1. Seek the positive in terms of people's coping skills, and you will find it. Look beyond presenting symptoms and setbacks and encourage clients to identify their talents, dreams, insights, and fortitude.

2. Listen to the personal narrative. Through entering the world of the storyteller, the practitioner comes to grasp the client's reality, at the same time attending to signs of initiative, hope, and frustration with past counterproductive behavior that can help lead the client into a healthier outlook on life. The strengths therapist, by means of continual reinforcement of positives, seeks to help the client move away from what van den Bergh (1995, p. xix) calls "paralyzing narratives."

3. In contradistinction to the usual practice in interviewing known liars, con-artists, and thieves, which is to protect yourself from being used or manipulated, this approach would have the practitioner temporarily suspend skepticism or disbelief and enter the client's world as the client presents it. Showing a willingness to listen to the client's own explanations and perceptions ultimately encourages the emergence of the client's truth.

4. Validate the pain where pain exists. Reinforce persistent efforts to alleviate the pain and help people recover from the specific injuries of oppression, neglect, and domination.

5. Don't dictate: collaborate through an agreed upon, mutual discovery of solutions among helpers, families, and support networks. Validation and collaboration are integral steps in a consciousness-raising process that can lead to healing and empowerment (Bricker-Jenkins, 1991). (Van Wormer, 1999, pp. 54–56)

Case Study: Evidence-Based Practice
With a Borderline Personality–Disordered Client

Loni Morrison is a 28-year-old woman referred for residential treatment after her fourth suicide attempt and hospitalization in 4 months. Loni has been diagnosed with borderline personality disorder since age 16, when she began a long series of disastrous love relationships, alcohol and drug abuse, deep depressions often resulting in nearly fatal suicide attempts, and other symptoms of borderline personality disorder that have caused her a great deal of anguish. Loni is a well-respected artist and is just beginning to earn large commissions for her work. She is also brilliant. Superficial contact with her would indicate that this highly intelligent and creative person is much healthier than her history would suggest. Loni is currently on antidepressive medications and has been in therapy since age 16 with a number of therapists. She usually leaves therapy after a few sessions, believing that the therapists don't understand her well enough to help.

Her last four suicide attempts have been a response to a love interest who was unwilling to deal with her labile and irrational demands and expectations. He felt that Loni needed constant attention and reassurance and was troubled by her depressions and suicide attempts. Loni doesn't know what to do to get him back in her life and often feels that life is so hopeless that it isn't worth living. Her suicide attempts are increasingly serious and the last attempt would have been fatal had a friend not stopped by her house, found the doors locked, and—sensing something wrong—summoned the police.

Loni is highly depressed, often uncommunicative, and sits in the facility with a blank look on her face. After the initial 3 days of hospitalization, when she was placed on high levels of antidepressants to stabilize her and to reduce the threat of suicide, the medication dosage was reduced and her therapist was able to speak to her. Loni told her that she has little confidence in therapy, has had very poor experiences with therapists, recognizes that she has serious emotional problems, and doesn't feel optimistic that therapy will be helpful. Her depressions are worsening and the desire to end her life is becoming overwhelming. "I get up in the morning and I feel hopeless," she said. "I look at my paintings and I want to rip them up and throw them away. People say they're good but they seem artificial and dishonest to me. No one in my personal life can deal with my jealousy or my need to love and be loved. They think I'm oppressive. The therapists I've gone to give up on me right away. I can see it in the way they look at me. My parents don't talk to me anymore and neither do most of my friends. I feel alone and hopeless. The kind thing to do would be to let me get on with my plan to kill myself."

The therapist told Loni that these were serious problems that she didn't take lightly, but she felt there were many things that could be done to help Loni and urged her to go to the facility's library and do research on her condition using the available literature and the Internet. The therapist gave her a number of websites and said she thought that Loni might find other sources on the Internet reporting the best treatment for the symptoms Loni was experiencing. They would meet again the next day and discuss what Loni had found. While Loni thought the therapist was nice, she also wondered why she wasn't talking about the suicide attempt and the emotional pain Loni was in, and decided that the therapist was a "cold fish," but that she'd play along with her anyway.

Much to Loni's surprise, she found a number of very interesting studies that suggested treatments far different from the ones she'd had in the past. When she met with the therapist the next day, she brought the promising studies along and entered into a discussion of the best evidence for treating Loni's problems. The therapist urged Loni to continue searching for best evidence over the next few days and when she had at least 10 studies that seemed in agreement, they would establish a treatment regimen. Several days later, they did just that. The plan they agreed on was written and signed by Loni, the therapist, and the director of the facility, and was as follows:

1. Loni had to sign a "no suicide" contract. Once having signed it, she was committed to sharing suicidal feelings with the staff and to enter into emergency treatment to prevent any suicide attempts.

2. Loni had to keep a record of the relationship between highly labile emotions and events in her life. She was to use that record in discussions with her therapist so they could construct patterns that led to dangerous emotions that might then lead to destructive behaviors.

3. She was to stop self-medicating by using drugs and alcohol, and was to keep a record of her daily emotional life so that her medications could be monitored and evaluated. This also involved frequent use of psychological tests to evaluate her levels of depression and potential for suicide.

4. The focus on Loni's treatment was to contain dangerous behaviors and move toward stability in her life. This precluded love relationships until she was better prepared to handle them.

5. She was to write a letter to her parents asking if they might have contact with her, explaining that she was in residential treatment and that seeing them might hopefully lead to an improvement in her condition. In any event, she missed them and wanted to reestablish contact.

6. She was to be actively involved in group treatment and patient-management efforts. This meant establishing involvement with other patients in the facility.

7. She was to begin working on her art again and the facility would set up an area for her to continue painting. She was not to destroy any work but would get feedback from others she respected and use that feedback in the development of her artwork.

8. If she progressed in treatment, the facility had bungalows on the grounds where she could live more independently, although she would continue with the same treatment regimen that she presently had.

9. If treatment was successful and she no longer felt suicidal or worried about self-destructive or dangerous behaviors, plans would be made for her to live off the grounds but to be involved in the program on a daily basis. Therapy would continue.

10. Her progress would be continually evaluated and any concerns she had about treatment, including the relationship with her therapist, would be discussed. She would agree to individual and group treatment even though she had concerns about both. It was her responsibility to share those concerns and to be involved in making the needed changes to improve the effectiveness of her therapy.

11. The facility agreed to make Loni a full partner in her treatment.

Loni stayed in the facility for 6 months before returning to independent living. The last 2 months were spent in a bungalow on the grounds of the facility. After leaving the facility and establishing independent living, she has been attending the facility's day program for 8 months now. She hasn't attempted suicide since entering the facility, although she's had days when she has been highly depressed. She self-medicates occasionally but not to the same degree that she did before her treatment began. She has a good working relationship with the therapist and staff, can be difficult and manipulative at times, but always recognizes her behavior, apologizes, and tries to work on feelings and issues that may have led to the behavior. She is painting, enjoys moderate success, and has begun a romantic relationship quite unlike those she was involved in prior to treatment. The man in her life grew up with a borderline sister and understands and empathizes with Loni's emotional turmoil. He is supportive and encouraging but also knows when to confront Loni about aspects of her behavior that interfere with their relationship. They attend a couples group together and have found it helpful in resolving problems that would have ended a relationship for Loni in the past.

Loni understands that, just as people have medical conditions that need constant monitoring, she has an emotional condition that requires monitoring and treatment. Keeping a daily log, attending the day program, working in a stable therapeutic relationship, and maintaining close contact with a psychiatrist to make certain her medications are working have all been helpful. In evaluating her progress, Loni said, "I have no illusions. I'm a troubled person and I'll always be a troubled person. What the program did was to stabilize me and give me a sense of family. I love the people in the program as if they really were my family. I've been able to reestablish some contact with my real family, but years of trouble make it hard for us to get past a certain point. This program is expensive and it has allowed me to work, and paint, and try to pay back the facility all the money I owe it. I'll be doing that all my life, and it's worth it. I know that others like me without money wouldn't have had the chance to get such wonderful treatment, and I'm thankful I had the resources. I hate the label of being a borderline, but I am, and it's good that I can read the research and be involved in my treatment. Every day is a struggle for me and I don't know if I'd be honest to say that I'm over the hump. I feel better and I'm doing better. All I can do is to keep a watchful eye on myself and trust the people I work with to help me when I go off the deep end. You never know when that might happen and every day I pray that it won't."

In adding to Loni's evaluation of her situation, her therapist said, "Loni has come a long way, but she's absolutely right that every day is a challenge. This program seems to work for people with Loni's symptoms, but it's a terribly expensive program and it offers no short-term solutions. We keep up on the latest research, constantly evaluate the effectiveness of our work, believe that clients should be in a cooperative relationship when it comes to their treatment, and learn from our successes and our failures. We spend a great deal of time in staff meetings poring over the literature, and we take our responsibility seriously to use the best available evidence in treating our clients. The new research is exciting and hopeful, but we move cautiously. People with borderline personality disorder have very high rates of suicide. One suicide attempt throws the staff into a long period of self-evaluation about whether we're doing the best we can for our clients."

SUMMARY

This chapter on EBP and personality disorders focuses on Cluster B disorders and presents the cause and the best evidence of treatment effectiveness. A case study describes treatment with a client suffering from borderline personality disorder. Far from being untreatable as the literature tends to suggest, there are indications that Cluster B personality disorders are treatable with cognitive-behavioral approaches and with antidepressants when depression is noted. Concerns were noted that clinicians often dislike working with Cluster B personality disordered clients because they find the clients manipulative and unlikely to change as a result of treatment. This often leads to poor results that can only be improved by more positive clinician attitudes and a willingness to search for, and use, best evidence as it becomes available in the literature.

Integrative Questions

1. The diagnostic category of personality disorders is troubling since it suggests a character (personality) defect. Do you think the label of personality disorder can be off-putting to clinicians and, as a self-fulfilling prophecy, lead to the belief that personality disorders are untreatable?

2. The explanation that personality disorders often develop as the child adapts to highly dysfunctional families suggests that most children from dysfunctional families will become personality disordered. Since we know that's not true, what do you think happens in the lives of children that causes them to develop, or not develop, personality disorders as a response to highly dysfunctional families?

3. The case study of Loni proposes a treatment regimen out of most people's level of affordability. How might that same treatment be integrated into programs that are more affordable for many clients with borderline personality disorder?

4. Do you believe the use of labels with highly negative connotations such as those associated with personality disorders might assume a lifetime diagnosis with little likelihood of change? If that's the case, what might be some harmful outcomes of incorrectly assuming that an initial diagnosis will last throughout the life cycle?

5. Men are disproportionately associated with antisocial behavior while women represent the majority of those with borderline personality disorder. Do you think this may have to do with gender roles or could it be more genetic and bio-chemical in nature?

References

American Psychiatric Association. (1994). *Diagnostic and statistical manual of mental disorders* (4th ed.). Washington, DC: Author.

Bateman, A., & Fonagy, P. (1999). The effectiveness of partial hospitalization in the treatment of borderline personality disorder: A randomized controlled trial. *American Journal of Psychiatry, 156,* 1563–1569.

Bemporad, J. R., Smith, H. E., Hanson, G., & Cicchetti, D. (1982). Borderline syndromes in childhood: Criteria for diagnosis. *American Journal of Psychiatry, 139,* 596–601.

Bleiberg, E. (2002, June). How to help children at risk of developing a borderline or narcissistic personality disorder. *The Brown University Child and Adolescent Behavior Letter, 18*(6), 1, 3–4.

Bowlby, J. (1969). *Attachment and loss: I. Attachment.* New York: Basic Books.

Bowlby, J. (1973). *Attachment and loss: II. Separation, anxiety and anger.* New York: Basic Books.

Bowlby, J. (1980). *Attachment and loss: III. Loss.* New York: Basic Books.

Brennan, K. A., & Shaver, P. R. (1998). Attachment styles and personality disorders: Their connections to each other and to parental divorce, parental death, and perceptions of parental caregiving. *Journal of Personality, 66,* 835–878.

Bricker-Jenkins, M. (1991). The propositions and assumptions of feminist social work practice. In M. Bricker-Jenkins, N. R. Hooyman, & N. Gottlieb (Eds.),

Feminist social work practice in clinical settings (pp. 271–303). Newbury Park, CA: Sage.

Craig, D. Y. (2001, December 15). Managing borderline personality disorder. *Patient Care, 23,* 60–64.

Davison, G. C., & Neale, J. M. (1990). *Abnormal psychology* (5th ed.). New York: Wiley.

Department of Health and Home Office. (1994). *Report of the Department of Health and Home Office Working Group On Psychopathic Disorder.* London: HMSO.

Dolan, B. (1996). *Perspectives on Henderson Hospital.* Sutton, UK: Henderson Hospital.

Dolan, B., Warren, F., & Norton, K. (1997). Change in borderline symptoms one year after therapeutic community treatment for severe personality disorder. *British Journal of Psychiatry, 171,* 274–279.

Drake, R. E., & Vaillant, G. E. (1985). A validity study of axis II of DSM-III. *American Journal of Psychiatry, 142,* 553–558.

Fonagy, P., Leigh, T., Steele, M., Steele, H., Kennedy, R., Mattoon, G., et al. (1996). The relation of attachment status, psychiatric classification, and response to psychotherapy. *Journal of Consulting Clinical Psychology, 64,* 22–31.

Fonagy, P., Target, M., & Gergely, G. (2000). Attachment and borderline personality disorder: Theory and some evidence. *Psychiatric Clinician North America, 23,* 103–122.

Forrest, G. G. (1991). *Chemical dependency and antisocial personality disorder: Psychotherapy and assessment strategies.* New York: Hawthorne Press.

Frey, R. J. (1999). Personality disorders. *Gale encyclopedia of medicine: Vol. 5* [Electronic version]. Farmington Hills, MI: Gale Research.

Goldman, S. J., D'Angelo, E. J., & DeMaso, D. R. (1993). Psychopathology in the families of children and adolescents with borderline personality disorder. *American Journal of Psychiatry, 150,* 1832–1835.

Hoffman, L. (2002, March). Psychotherapy for personality disorders. *American Journal of Psychiatry, 159*(3), 504–507.

Guzder, J., Paris, J., Zelkowitz, P., & Feldman, R. (1999, February 1). Psychological risk factors for borderline pathology in school-age children. *Journal of the American Academy of Child and Adolescent Psychiatry, 38,* 206–212.

Kasen, S., Cohen, P., Skodol, A. E., Johnson, J. G., & Brook, J. S. (1999, October). Influence of child and adolescent psychiatric disorders on young adult personality disorder. *American Journal of Psychiatry, 156,* 1529–1535.

Kestenbaum, C. J. (1983). The borderline child at risk for major psychiatric disorder in adult life. In K. R. Robson (Ed.), *The borderline child* (pp. 49–82). New York: McGraw-Hill.

Kisley, S. (1999, May 22). Psychotherapy for severe personality disorder: Exploring the limits of evidence based purchasing. *British Medical Journal, 318,* 1410–1412.

Lehman, C. (2003, January 17). Clinicians strive to avert frustration with BPD patients. *Psychiatric News, 38*(2), 29.

Linehan, M. M., Armstrong, H. E., Suarez, A., Allmon, D., & Heard, H. L. (1991). Cognitive-behavioural treatment for chronically parasuicidal borderline patients. *Archives of General Psychiatry, 48,* 1060–1064.

Messina, N., Wish, E., Hoffman, J., & Nemes, S. (2001, November). Diagnosing antisocial personality disorder among substance abusers: The SCID versus the MCMI-II [Structured Clinical Interview for the DSM-III-R, Millon Clinical Multiaxial Inventory, 2nd ed.]. *American Journal of Drug and Alcohol Abuse, 27,* 699-717.

Nakash-Eisikovits, O., Dutra, L. & Westen, D. (2002). Relationship between attachment patterns and personality pathology in adolescents. *Journal of the American Academy of Child and Adolescent Psychiatry, 41(9),* 1111–1122.

NHS Executive. (1996). *NHS psychotherapy services in England: Review of strategic policy.* London: Department of Health.

Personality disorders. (2001). *Gale encyclopedia of psychology* (2nd ed.). Detroit, MI: Gale Group.

Robins, L. N., Tipp, J., & Przybeck, T. (1991). Antisocial personality. In L. N. Robins & D. A. Regier (Eds.), *Psychiatric disorders in America* (pp. 258–290). New York: Macmillan.

Roth, A. D., & Fonagy, E. (1996). *What works for whom? A critical review of psychotherapy research.* New York: Guilford Press.

Stevenson, J., & Meares, R. (1992). An outcome study of psychotherapy for patients with borderline personality disorder. *American Journal of Psychiatry, 149,* 358–362.

Stevenson, J., & Meares, R. (1995, May). Borderline patients at 5-year follow-up. Paper presented at the Annual Congress of the Royal Australia-New Zealand College of Psychiatrists, Cairns, Australia.

Stone, M. H. (1993). Long term outcome in personality disorders. *British Journal of Psychiatry, 162,* 299–313.

Tims, F. M., De Leon, G., & Jainchill, N. (Eds.). (1986). *Therapeutic community: Advances in research and application.* NIDA Research Monograph 144. Rockville, MD: U.S. Department of Health and Human Services, Public Health Service, National Institutes of Health, National Institute on Drug Abuse.

van den Bergh, N. (Ed.). (1995). *Feminist practice in the 21st century.* Washington, DC: NASW Press.

Van Wormer, K. (1999). The strengths perspective: A paradigm for correctional counseling. *Federal Probation, 63(1),* 51–58.

Woody, G. E., McLellan, T., Luborsky, L., & O'Brien, C. P. (1985). Sociopathy and psychotherapy outcome. *Archives of General Psychiatry, 42,* 1081–1086.

Evidence-Based Practice With Victims of Violence and Terrorism

9

W ith the threat of domestic and international terrorism increasing in America since the 1995 Oklahoma City bombing of a federal building and the September 11, 2001, terrorist attacks on the World Trade Centers and the Pentagon (hereafter referred to as 9/11), a condition related to reliving the trauma known as posttraumatic stress disorder (PTSD) has increasingly been thought to be a leading physical and emotional by-product of random violence. This chapter defines PTSD, shows its relationship to acts of violence, and discusses the primary treatment approaches demonstrating best evidence in working with those who develop PTSD symptoms following a serious trauma.

Unquestionably, there are many acts of random violence that affect Americans, including assaults, rapes, muggings, carjackings, and gang violence. Natural and man-made disasters also account for a certain amount of PTSD, but not in the numbers attributable to acts of random violence. Although disasters and other forms of violence are mentioned in this chapter, the primary emphasis of the chapter is on understanding the dynamics of PTSD, the probability of developing PTSD symptoms, the populations most at risk, and the most effective treatment approaches. Not everyone who experiences an act of violence develops PTSD, and the research on resilience may offer us direction in understanding why some people develop PTSD and others do not.

Understanding the Link Between Trauma and the Development of Posttraumatic Stress Disorder

DESCRIPTIONS OF PTSD

According to the DSM-IV (APA, 1994), the core criteria for PTSD include distressing symptoms of (a) reexperiencing a trauma through nightmares and intrusive thoughts; (b) numbing by avoiding reminders of the trauma, or feeling aloof or unable to express loving feelings for others; and (c) persistent symptoms of arousal as indicated by two or more of the following: sleep problems, irritability and angry outbursts, difficulty concentrating, hypervigilance, and exaggerated startle response with a duration of more than a month, causing problems at work, in social interactions, and in other important areas of life (APA, 1994, pp. 427–429). The DSM-IV judges the condition to be acute if it has lasted less than 3 months and chronic if it has lasted more than 3 months. It is also possible for the symptoms to be delayed. The DSM-IV notes that a diagnosis of delayed onset is given when symptoms begin to appear 6 months or more after the original trauma (APA, 1994, p. 429).

PTSD is thought to be linked to a highly traumatic experience or life-threatening event that produces intrusive thoughts related to a very disturbing aspect of the original traumatic event. Those thoughts are difficult to dislodge once they reach conscious awareness. In many cases of PTSD, the client physically and emotionally reexperiences the original traumatic event and is frequently in a highly agitated state of arousal as a result. Symptoms of PTSD usually begin within 3 months of the original trauma. In half of the cases of PTSD, complete recovery occurs within 3 months of the onset of symptoms, but many cases last more than 12 months (APA, 1994, p. 426). Ozer, Best, Lipsey, and Weiss (2003) describe the following symptoms associated with returning Vietnam veterans that led to a recognition of PTSD as a distinct diagnostic category: "Intrusive thoughts and images, nightmares, social withdrawal, numbed feelings, hypervigilance, and even frank paranoia, especially regarding the government, and vivid dissociative phenomena, such as flashbacks" (p. 54). The authors believe that the complexity of the symptoms often led to a misdiagnosis of schizophrenia.

Stein (2002) indicates that an additional symptom of PTSD is physical pain and writes, "Patients with PTSD are among the highest users of medical services in primary care settings. Ongoing chronic pain may serve as a constant reminder of the trauma that perpetuates its remembrance" (p. 922). In describing the aftermath of the 1981 Hyatt Regency disaster in Kansas City, where catwalks over a lobby used as a dance floor collapsed, killing more than 150 people and injuring many hundreds more, I (Glicken, 1986a, 1986b, 1986c) noted that many of the hotel employees who witnessed the disaster or helped in the recovery of injured victims suffered flu-like symptoms and a significant lethargy for many months after the disaster. I also reported that, while many of the employees complained of depression and lethargy, a large number felt actual physical illness and some experienced anxiety attacks that led to emergency hospital visits for perceived symptoms of heart problems, including heart palpations, severe night sweats, nausea, and arm and back pain.

Asmundson, Coons, Taylor, and Katz (2002) report that patients with PTSD present a combination of physical and mental health problems including increased alcohol consumption and depression. They also indicate that pain is one of the most commonly reported symptoms of patients with PTSD and write, "Patients who have persistent, chronic pain associated with musculoskeletal injury, serious burn injuries, and other pathologies (such as fibromyalgia, cancer, or AIDS) frequently present with symptoms of PTSD" (p. 930). In a study by White (1989), 20% of military veterans with PTSD developed chronic pain. McFarlane, Atchison, Rafalowicz, and Papay (1994) found that volunteer firemen who developed PTSD in response to acts of terrorism and violence developed a significant amount of pain, primarily back pain, as compared to 21% of those without symptoms of PTSD.

Cohen (1998) discusses the problem of using PTSD as a diagnosis for children and adolescents. Some PTSD symptoms, such as dissociation, self-injurious behaviors, substance abuse, and/or conduct problems, may obscure the original trauma and clinicians may miss the existence of PTSD. Children going through abrupt changes in development may demonstrate some of the signs of PTSD. Cohen urges clinicians to do a careful job of history taking to avoid overlooking the presence of a PTSD. To meet the criteria for a diagnosis of PTSD, the child must first have been exposed to an extremely traumatic event, which results in reexperiencing the event, avoidance and numbing, and increased arousal when memories of the event are triggered. Cohen (1998) suggests that reexperiencing the trauma may be demonstrated through repetitive play with traumatic themes, recurrent upsetting dreams about the trauma, and intense anxiety when conscious and unconscious cues remind the child of the trauma. Avoidance and numbing may be observed in children withdrawing from their usual activities and who also use techniques to avoid thinking about the trauma that may, in time, become obsessive. This may also be true of children who have a complete loss of memory about the event or seem detached and lack future thinking. Persistent symptoms of increased arousal, if they are to be considered part of the response to PTSD, must be newly observed symptoms that may include sleep problems, irritability or angry outbursts, difficulty concentrating, hypervigilance, and exaggerated startle response. Symptoms must be present for at least 1 month and cause clinically significant distress or impairment in normal functioning to be assigned a diagnosis of PTSD.

Cohen (1998) indicates that experts agree that children should be asked about the traumatic event. Clinicians often fail to ask children about the event and its impact because they fear that reminding the child of painful events may trigger anxiety, or they may not want to become involved in disturbing discussions that may change the child's memory of the event. In situations that involve litigation, a discussion of the precipitating event may confuse the child's memory and could result in liability concerns about the clinician's role in the child's confusion. Cohen believes that we often miss important evidence of the presence of PTSD. "There is a strong clinical consensus that if children are not asked, they are less likely to tell about their PTSD symptoms" (p. 998). Cohen believes that several semi-structured interviews are necessary to discover traumatic events in a child's life and suggests that clinicians pay close attention to the criteria for PTSD when they collect information from the interviews.

Gist and Devilly (2002) worry that PTSD is being predicted on such a wide scale for every tragedy that occurs that we've watered down its usefulness as a diagnostic category and write, "Progressive dilution of both stressor and duration criteria has so broadened application that it can now prove difficult to diagnostically differentiate those who have personally endured stark and prolonged threats from those who have merely heard upsetting reports of calamities striking others" (p. 741). The authors suggest that many early signs of PTSD are normal responses to stress that are often overcome with time and distance from the event. Victims often use natural healing processes to cope with traumatic events, and interference by professionals in natural healing could make the problem more severe and prolonged. In determining whether PTSD will actually develop, people must be given time to cope with the trauma on their own before clinicians diagnose and treat PTSD. To emphasize this point, Gist and Devilly (2002) report that the immediate predictions of PTSD in victims of the World Trade Center bombings turned out to be almost 70% higher than actually occurred 4 months after the event. Susser, Herman, and Aaron (2002) report that 2,001 New Yorkers were interviewed by telephone between January 15, 2002, and February 21, 2002. The interview indicated that within 4–5 months of the World Trade Center bombings, most subjects had experienced a significant decrease in stress-related symptoms initially associated with the bombings. Susser et al. write, "Many affected New Yorkers are clearly recovering naturally, a tribute to the resilience of the human psyche" (p. 76). Of course, symptoms of PTSD may develop much later than 4–5 months after a trauma. Still, the point is well taken. People often heal on their own, and a premature diagnosis of PTSD may be counterproductive.

The Potential for Developing PTSD

In describing the potential for developing PTSD, the DSM-IV (APA, 1994) reports, "The severity, duration and proximity of an individual's exposure to the traumatic event are the most important factors affecting the likelihood of this disorder" (p. 426). According to the DSM-IV, additional factors that may contribute to PTSD include the absence of social support networks, traumatic family histories or childhood experiences, and preexisting emotional problems, although people without preexisting problems can develop PTSD if the stressors of the traumatic experience are particularly severe.

There may be other factors determining whether PTSD develops following a trauma. McGaugh and Cahill (1997) found that memory formation during a traumatic event can be blocked, resulting in a reduction of the likelihood of PTSD. If this is the case, the authors wonder if we can predict who will be most likely to experience PTSD by evaluating the clarity and preciseness of the memory of the trauma. However, a review of studies determining the impact of traumatic experiences reported in the *Harvard Mental Health Letter* ("What Causes Post-Traumatic Stress Disorder: Two Views," 2002) suggests that "the people most likely to have symptoms of PTSD were those who suffered job loss, broken personal relationships, the death or illness of a family member or close friend, or financial loss as a result of the disaster itself" (p. 8). Several additional studies reported in the *Harvard Mental Health Letter* indicate that a person's current emotional state may influence the way they cope with the trauma. Environmental concerns (living in high-crime areas, for example) and health risks (disabilities that make people vulnerable, as another example) raise the likelihood of repeated traumatization that may increase the probability of developing PTSD. Stein (2002) suggests that one significant event influencing the development of PTSD is exposure to assaultive traumatic events such as serious fights, domestic violence, child abuse, muggings, sexual trauma, and other forms of traumatic violence. Stein believes that vulnerability to repetitive acts of violence greatly increases the probability of developing PTSD.

Asmundson, Coons, Taylor, and Katz (2002) observed that 70% of a sample of clients with pain who coped dysfunctionally (overly medicated themselves and/or had high numbers of doctor's visits) also met the diagnostic criteria for PTSD as compared with 35% of the sample who coped with pain in a functionally adaptive way. There is evidence to suggest that high sensitivity to anxiety in the midst of a traumatic event increases levels of fear, which may result in panic attacks and the increased likelihood of developing pain and related medical problems (Taylor, 1999, 2000). Elevated levels of anxiety during the traumatic event may be the primary factor in the development of chronic pain (Taylor, 2000), leading Asmundson et al. (2002) to conclude the following:

> When people with high anxiety sensitivity levels encounter a traumatic stressor, painful physical injury, or both, they are believed to respond with a more intense emotional reaction than do those with lower levels. In the case of PTSD, the degree of alarm caused by the stressor itself combined with alarm related to the anxiety sensations arising from the stressor amplifies the emotional reaction and thereby increases the risk of developing PTSD. (p. 933)

In studies of women who have been sexually assaulted or raped, women particularly at risk of developing PTSD are those who were injured in the assault, were threatened by the perpetrator with death or injury if they reported the rape, had a history of prior assault, or experienced negative interactions with family, peers, or law enforcement officers after the assault (Regehr, Cadell, & Jansen, 1999). In a meta-analysis of the many factors that may predict the development of PTSD after a traumatic event, Ozer et al. (2003) found the following factors to be related to the development of PTSD: (a) a history of prior trauma, (b) psychological problems before the traumatic event, (c) psychopathology in the family of origin, (d) the degree to which the client thought the traumatic event would endanger his or her life, (e) the lack of a support system to help the client cope with the trauma, (f) the degree of emotional response during and after the trauma, and (g) evidence of a dissociative state during and after the trauma. The authors found that each of these variables helped explain, to some extent, how well the client could cope with the trauma and whether PTSD would develop. When trying to use individual variables to predict PTSD, however, no single variable was predictive of the onset of PTSD. Instead of the variables noted above, the authors believe that the degree of client resilience is the best predictor of whether PTSD will develop. Highly resilient people seem to have lower incidents of PTSD following a trauma. The authors also suggest that clients who develop PTSD may be analogous to those developing the flu and write, "It is tempting to make an analogy to the flu or infectious disease: Those whose immune systems are compromised are at greater risk of contracting a subsequent illness" (Ozer et al., p. 69).

RESILIENCE AND PTSD

In considering the importance of resilience as an explanation for coping successfully with traumatic events, Henry (1999) defines resilience as "the capacity for successful adaptation, positive functioning, or competence despite high risk, chronic stress, or prolonged or severe trauma" (p. 521). Abrams (2001) indicates that resilience may be seen as the ability to readily recover from illness, depression, and adversity. Walsh (1998) defines resilience in families as the "capacity to rebound from adversity, strengthened and more resourceful" (p. 4) and continues in her definition by saying, "We cope with crisis and adversity by making meaning of our experience: linking it to our social world, to our cultural and religious beliefs, to our multigenerational past, and to our hopes and dreams for the future" (p. 45).

Werner and Smith (1982) identified protective factors that tend to counteract the risk for stress, which include (a) genetic factors such as an easygoing disposition, (b) strong self-esteem and a sense of identity, (c) intelligence, (d) physical attractiveness, and (e) supportive caregivers.

Seligman (1992) believes that resilience exists when people are optimistic, have a sense of adventure, courage, and self-understanding, use humor in their lives, have a capacity for hard work, and posses the ability to cope with and find outlets for their emotions. In their 32-year longitudinal study, Werner and Smith (1982) found strong relationships among problem-solving abilities, communication skills, and an internal locus of control in resilient children. In a review of the factors associated with resilience and stressful life events, Tiet, Bird, and Davies (1998) found that higher IQs, higher quality of parenting, positive connections to other competent adults, an internal locus of control, and well developed social skills were protective factors that allowed children to cope with stressful events. Protective factors, according to Tiet et al., are primary buffers between the traumatic event and the child's response.

The Prevalence of PTSD

The National Vietnam Veterans Readjustment Study (Kulka et al., 1990; Weiss et al., 1992) estimated that 9% of the men and 26% of the women serving in Vietnam met the diagnostic criteria for PTSD at some point after their Vietnam service. Current prevalence of PTSD among Vietnam veterans is 2% for men and 5% for women (Schlenger et al., 1992). Weiss et al. (1992) estimated that roughly 830,000 Vietnam theater veterans continued to experience significant posttraumatic distress or impairment approximately 20 years after their exposure to one or more traumatic stressors. Studies of civilian populations have found lifetime PTSD prevalence rates of between 2% and 10% (Breslau, Davis, Andreski, & Peterson, 1991). The National Comorbidity Study (Kessler, Sonnega, Bromet, Hughes, & Nelson, 1995) found that women had twice the lifetime prevalence of PTSD than that of men (10.4% for women versus 5.0% for men). Roughly 50%–60% of the U.S. population is exposed to traumatic stress, but only 5%–10% develop PTSD (Ozer et al., 2003). In studies of women who had been sexually assaulted or raped, a significant proportion of women experienced symptoms of PTSD within 2 weeks following the assault (Resnick, Acierno, Holmes, Kilpatrick, & Jager, 1999). PTSD continued to persist in survivors of rape and sexual assault at lifetime rates of between 30% and 50% (Foa, Hearst-Ikeda, & Perry, 1995; Meadows & Foa, 1998; Resnick et al., 1999).

The *Harvard Mental Health Letter* ("What Causes Post-Traumatic Stress Disorder: Two Views," 2002) reports on a study done at the University of California, San Diego, in which 132 randomly selected patients seen by family doctors completed an interview and questionnaire describing traumatic events in their lives, including combat, natural or man-made disasters, violent rape, abusive behavior, and assault. Almost 70% of the sample had experienced at least one traumatic event. Twenty percent of the sample currently had PTSD, 29% had major depressions, and 8% had both. PTSD was most likely to occur in those patients who had experienced several types of traumas, particularly those who had been assaulted. Seventy percent of the patients with current or lifetime PTSD said an assault was their worst traumatic experience.

The Impact of Recent Acts of Terrorism

Susser et al. (2002) attempted to estimate the emotional impact of the 9/11 terrorist events. The authors used three main sources: (a) current literature on disaster research, including more than 200 articles published between 1981 and 2001 concerned with the psychological consequences of 160 natural and man-made disasters affecting 60,000 people worldwide; (b) psychological reactions of the general public in the area near the Oklahoma City bombing of 1995; and (c) two quickly conducted studies in New York City examining the short-term impact of the World Trade Center attacks (Galea, 2002).

From data extrapolated by Galea (2002) in 1,008 telephone interviews with Manhattan residents, the rate of PTSD in those living close to the World Trade Center was 20%. Sprang (Galea, 2002) found that 7.8% of 145 city residents in Oklahoma City who were not near the building after the bombing had PTSD, and North (Galea, 2002) found PTSD in 34% of 182 survivors who had been in or near the building. Using statistical analysis to estimate the number of New Yorkers traumatized by the World Trade Center bombings, Susser et al. (2002) write, "The bottom line: even when making the most conservative estimates based on available data, we concluded that a minimum of approximately 422,000 New Yorkers experienced PTSD as a result of September 11" (p. 73). It should be noted that Galea (2002) only reported on PTSD and clinical depression and not on related clinical conditions including anxiety and low-level depression. Untold millions who witnessed the attacks through the media were surely shaken and experienced distress. Susser et al. (2002) go on to say, "In addition, the effects of terrorism on those already suffering from psychological conditions must be assumed to have been especially profound" (p. 74).

To add to the impact of 9/11, Hoff (2002) reports a survey of 8,266 public school students in New York City regarding their reactions to the New York City attacks. The data indicate that 10.5% of the city's 710,000 public school students experienced PTSD as a result of 9/11. Hoff also notes that the survey found high numbers of other disorders related to the bombings, including agoraphobia, the fear of open places.

Case Study: Adapting to a Terrorist Attack

Carol Schuster is a Jewish communal worker in a large Midwestern city. As the workday was ending for Carol, a man entered the Jewish agency Carol worked for and held Carol hostage for the next 2 days. He had guns and knives that he frequently pressed against Carol's body while he told her that he would kill her as retribution for an act by the Israeli Army against the village where the man's family lived, which resulted in the death of his entire family. Carol is a social worker and tried to use her skills as a therapist to calm the man down, but as the two-day siege continued, the man became increasingly agitated and violent. At one point, he beat Carol with his hands, breaking her jaw and badly cutting her face. He made her look at pictures of his family while they were alive and then at pictures of his family after their deaths. He spoke in English and another language Carol could not identify, crying and screaming at her in alternate outbursts. As the second day wore on and the police were unable to capture the man for fear that he would kill Carol, he finally gave up and Carol was released. When the man came out of the agency, the police thought he had a weapon with him, fired at him, and killed him. Carol witnessed the event.

At first, Carol seemed perfectly fine, even amazingly so given what had happened to her. She went back to work the next day and assured everyone that she was fine and happy to be back. The staff wasn't so sure and wondered if PTSD symptoms might develop, but for months Carol seemed to be asymptomatic for PTSD and no one in the agency detected any unusual signs of stress. In the privacy of her home, however, Carol was deteriorating emotionally. She was fearful of going out at night and she was afraid of falling asleep for fear that a friend of her captor would break into her house and kill her. She was also self-medicating by using Ativan she'd obtained from a friend, and she was drinking large amounts of wine, something she'd hardly ever used before the event. She was irritable and frightened. At work, her defenses began to break down and the signs of PTSD, while very slow to develop publicly, showed themselves in severe mood swings, an inability to handle many routine assignments, and a tendency to hide in her office if she saw anyone resembling the man who held her hostage.

Her supervisor told Carol that she needed to seek help, and Carol was seen over a 6-month period by a therapist who used a combination of cognitive therapy and exposure therapy in which she was asked to talk about the event so that its emotional power would begin to weaken. Carol is a strong, resilient young woman, and within 2 months of treatment, her symptoms were in remission sufficiently for her to return to full-time work at the agency. She still has frightened feelings and sometimes can't sleep. At times, she is afraid to leave the house and periodically self-medicates with liquor and tranquilizers. A year after the event, she is back to 90% of her pre-event functioning and doing better every day.

CRITIQUE

Carol had the type of life-threatening event that often leads to PTSD. The private deterioration in her functioning, unnoticed at work for many months, seems related to an inner toughness that Carol used to keep her private torment from others. This is typical of many survivors of violent acts. Some victims of violence don't develop PTSD at all, but Carol did. It's difficult to know why without more history, but one wonders if Carol had a prior traumatic event. As her therapy progressed, it was discovered that a stranger sexually molested Carol as a child, an event she kept completely to herself. The experience was responsible for her choosing to become a social worker. Carol also had family issues and grew up with two very troubled parents whom she cared for throughout her early life. Carol was the codependent child of parents who cycled from alcoholism and job loss to early institutionalization. She felt responsible for what happened to her family and vowed to learn more about people so that she could prevent something similar from happening to her. The tough and resilient outer shell was a façade for a troubled and hurt inner self that felt ill equipped to deal with life. As she had done as a child, she put all of her energies into helping others and was considered a highly sensitive and effective social worker. In her personal life, however, she lacked a support group, had no romantic involvements, had few close friends, and even before the event had begun self-medicating for sleep problems and anxiety. What she also had was a great deal of self-awareness and inner toughness that delayed the public expression of her emotional state but also helped in her recovery.

In many ways, Carol is in a much better place emotionally after the event than before. She has joined a support group for survivors of violence, has developed several good friendships, and has begun to see a young man who works at her agency with whom she feels a closeness she has never experienced before. "I'm still frightened," she says, "and I fall apart every once in a while, but in many ways, I'm better than before this happened. And I feel great empathy for the man who held me hostage. We Jews need to understand that some people have grievances against us. Rather than calling it anti-Semitism, we need to be more open to listening and understanding with our hearts. I've joined a group of Jews and Palestinians who dialogue every week about our mutual problems. I think the openness of our conversation is very healing for both sides. The group has helped diffuse some problems between the two communities, which is a hopeful and empowering sign. We're all Americans. We live in this wonderful land in harmony. Maybe our example will help resolve problems in Israel. That idea is very strong inside of me and helps on those days that aren't so good, when some of the anxiety and stress come back. And I think I had an exceptional therapist. He enlisted my help in finding out what we should do together. He asked me to look at the research literature and to help in the treatment plan. We both agreed that cognitive therapy with desensitization that allowed me to reduce my level of anxiety was the best treatment option, coupled with work on my ongoing problems with intimacy. He listened to me, consulted with me, and treated me like a professional. I felt that we were working together and that I was treated like a competent adult. I think the way he deferred to me and respected my ideas helped more than anything else. He also had a knack for reminding me about my positive behaviors, something I was all too ready to forget. I was at a point where I didn't believe I knew anything, and I was falling apart. It was really pretty scary. His encouragement and willingness to involve me was such a wonderful gift at a time when my self-esteem was very low, that I could have just hugged him for treating me so well.

"Am I cured? No. I have problems to resolve that predate those awful two days. Most of the time I'm fine, better than fine, really. I no longer think I'm responsible for everyone and I'm taking better care of myself. It's made me a much better social worker and a much healthier person. I'm optimistic about the future, but a little part of me will never be as trusting or feel as safe. I think I'll always live in a state of hypervigilance, and from the clients I work with who are survivors of terrorism, I know that you fight the feeling of being afraid all the time. So I won't say I'm cured, but I'm a lot better and I'm optimistic. And that's a long way from where I was during, after, and even before this happened to me."

Best Evidence of Effective Treatment for PTSD

EXPOSURE THERAPY

Rothbaum, Olasov, and Schwartz (2002) describe a type of treatment, based on emotional-processing theory, that believes PTSD develops as a result of memories eliciting fear that trigger escape and avoidance behaviors. Since the development of a *fear network* (the set of stimuli that activate a fear response) functions as a type of obsessive condition, the client continues to increase the number of stimuli that serve to increase his or her fear. To reduce the number of stimuli that elicit fear, the client must have his or her fear network activated so that new information can be provided that rationally contradicts the obsessive network of emotions reinforcing the PTSD symptoms. The authors believe that the following progression of treatment activities serves to reduce the client's fear network:

1. Repeated reliving of the original trauma helps to reduce anxiety and correct a belief that anxiety will necessarily continue unless avoidance and escape mechanisms are activated.

2. Discussing the traumatic event reduces negative reinforcement of the event and helps the client see it in a logical way that corrects misperceptions of the event.

3. Speaking about the trauma helps the client realize that it's not dangerous to remember the trauma.

4. The ability of the client to speak about the trauma provides the client with a sense of mastery over his or her PTSD symptoms.

The authors call this type of treatment "exposure therapy." Several types of exposure therapies show promise in the treatment of PTSD. Stress inoculation therapy is an approach that includes relaxation, cognitive restructuring, preparing for a stressor, thought stopping, covert modeling, and role playing. Cognitive-processing therapy provides traditional cognitive therapy and exposure in the form of writing and reading about the traumatic event (Resick, 1992; Resick & Schnicke, 1992, 1993). In cognitive-processing therapy, ideas and perceptions about the traumatic event are challenged and more accurate and logical perceptions are encouraged. Additionally, clients are encouraged to write about their traumas and read them aloud to therapists. The repetition of writing and reading about the trauma tends to reduce its emotional impact on the client and hopefully leads to a lessening of symptoms through an understanding of the "sticking" points that may serve to reinforce anxiety. Hensley (2002) provides an explanation of exposure therapy as it might be given to a client who has been raped:

1. Memories, people, places, and activities now associated with the rape make you highly anxious, so you avoid them.

2. Each time you avoid them you do not finish the process of digesting the painful experience, and so it returns in the form of nightmares, flashbacks, and intrusive thoughts.

3. You can begin to digest the experience by gradually exposing yourself to the rape in your imagination and by holding the memory without pushing it away.

4. You will also practice facing those activities, places, and situations that currently evoke fear.

5. Eventually, you will be able to think about the rape and resume your normal activities without experiencing intense fear. (p. 338)

In describing a typical application of exposure therapy in a number of the studies reviewed with positive results, Rothbaum et al. (2002) note the following:

1. Prolonged exposure treatment averaged about nine bi-weekly individual sessions.

2. The first two sessions were spent gathering information, explaining the rationale of treatment, and constructing a rank order of feared situations for exposure in treatment.

3. In the remaining sessions, clients were asked to relive and describe the traumatic experience as if the client was having the experience "right now."

4. Exposure went on for about 60 minutes each session.

5. Tape recordings were made of the sessions and clients were asked to listen to the taped sessions as a form of reinforcement.

6. Clients were given homework assignments that helped them safely approach situations that caused anxiety and fear.

7. Clinicians can find precise instructions for doing exposure therapy with PTSD clients in Foa and Rothbaum (1998). (p. 63)

Effectiveness studies in the current literature regarding the use of exposure therapy with symptoms of PTSD have been quite positive. In the annual review of important findings in psychology, 12 studies found positive results using exposure therapy with PTSD. Eight of these studies received special recognition for the quality of their methodologies and for the positive nature of their outcomes (Foa and Meadows, 1997). Several of the studies were done with Vietnam veterans and showed a significant reduction in the symptoms of PTSD following exposure therapy (Keane, Fairbank, Caddell, & Zimering, 1989). The same positive results were found in studies with rape victims when exposure therapy was used (Foa et al., 1999; Foa, Rothbaum, Riggs, & Murdock, 1991). Exposure therapy has been used with a variety of PTSD victims, including victims of combat traumas, sexual assaults, child abuse, and other forms of violence. Exposure therapy has the most consistently positive results in reducing symptoms of PTSD when compared to other forms of treatment (Rothbaum, Meadows, Resick, & Foy, 2000).

Exposure therapy was compared to cognitive restructuring (Deblinger, McLeer, & Henry, 1990; Foa et al., 1995). Both types of treatment were considered highly effective, but exposure therapy alone was more effective than cognitive restructuring. Better than 50% of the clients receiving exposure therapy achieved over a 70% improvement in PTSD symptoms after nine sessions, while clients receiving cognitive restructuring alone needed an additional three sessions to achieve the same results. Rothbaum et al. (2000) report that, in the past 15–20 years, exposure therapy has been used with a variety of patients experiencing a number of traumatic events leading to symptoms of PTSD. Rothbaum et al. (2002) write, "Exposure therapy has more empirical evidence for its efficacy than any other treatment developed for the treatment of trauma-related symptoms" (p. 65).

DEBRIEFING

A form of treatment with potential for use in work with PTSD victims following a tragedy such as 9/11 is a single session treatment, or what has also been called "debriefing." In this approach, clients who have experienced a trauma are seen in a group session lasting 1–3 hours within a week to a month of the original traumatic event. Risk factors are evaluated and a combination of information and opportunities are provided to discuss their experiences during and after the trauma (Bisson, McFarlane, & Rose, 2000). Most debriefing groups use crisis intervention techniques in a very abbreviated form and may provide educational information to group members about typical reactions to traumas, what to look for if group members experience any of these symptoms, and where to seek professional assistance if additional help is needed. Debriefing groups may also attempt to identify group members at risk of developing PTSD (van Emmerik, Kamphuis, Hulsbosch, & Emmelkamp, 2002).

Despite the considerable appeal of this approach, there is little evidence that debriefing works to reduce the number of people who experience PTSD following debriefing sessions, and some evidence that it may increase PTSD, compared with other forms of treatment (van Emmerik et al., 2002). Debriefing may be less effective than no treatment at all following a trauma (van Emmerik et al.). Gist and Devilly (2002) support these findings and write that "immediate debriefing has yielded null or paradoxical outcomes" (p. 742) because the approaches used in debriefing are often those "kinds of practical help learned better from grandmothers than from graduate training" (p. 742). The authors report that, while still high, the estimates of PTSD after the 9/11 attacks dropped by almost two thirds within 4 months of the tragedy and conclude, "These findings underscore the counterproductive nature of offering a prophylaxis with no demonstrable effect, but demonstrated potential to complicate natural resolution, in a population in which limited case-conversion can be anticipated, strong natural supports exist, and spontaneous resolution is prevalent" (p. 742).

There are several primary reasons for the lack of effectiveness of debriefing:

1. Debriefing interferes with natural healing processes and sometimes results in bypassing usual support systems such as family, friends, and religious groups (Horowitz, 1976).

2. Upon hearing that PTSD symptoms are normal reactions to trauma, some victims of trauma actually develop the symptoms as a result of the suggestions provided in the debriefing session, particularly when

the victim hasn't had time to process the various feelings he or she may have about the trauma (Kramer & Rosenthal, 1998).

3. Clients seen in debriefing include both those at risk and those not at risk. Better results may be obtained by screening clients at risk through a review of past exposures to traumas that may have served as catalysts for the current development of PTSD (Brewin, Andrews, & Valentine, 2000).

COMBINATIONS OF THERAPY

Resick, Nishith, Weaver, Astin, and Feuer (2002) tested two forms of cognitive therapy with women who had been sexually assaulted by using a waiting list of women as a control group. Women in the control group were told that they would need to wait at least 6 weeks for treatment, but they were contacted every 2 weeks to make certain they didn't need emergency help. Women on the waiting list were encouraged to call if they needed help and a therapist, using a nondirective approach, would provide telephone counseling. If frequent calls indicated an inability to cope with stress or suicidal thoughts, the person was terminated from the study and offered immediate help, although the researchers report that this never happened in the study. The researchers found that cognitive therapy using exposure techniques was very successful in treating PTSD in this sample and that the success of this approach would bode well for PTSD caused by traumas other than sexual assault and rape. Many of the women in the study who showed marked improvement had histories of other traumas and were considered to be chronically distressed. Therapy was equally effective for traumas as recent as 3 months ago and for prior traumas as long ago as 30 years. In contrast, the women on the waiting list did not improve at all.

Lee, Gavriel, Drummond, Richards, and Greenwald (2002) tested the effectiveness of stress inoculation training with prolonged exposure (SITPE) as compared to eye movement desensitization and reprocessing (EMDR). The authors report that 24 participants with PTSD were randomly assigned to one of the two treatment approaches. Outcome measures included self-reports by subjects, ratings by observers, and self-reported measures of depression. There was no significant difference in the improvement rate for the two therapies at the end of treatment. On the degree of intrusive symptoms, however, EMDR did much better than SITPE, and at follow-up, EMDR produced greater gain in lessening all symptoms of PTSD (Lee et al., 2002, p. 1071).

In the treatment of PTSD with children and adolescents, Cohen (1998) reports only limited evidence of the effectiveness of psychotherapy; however, she refers to three recent studies that provide empirical support for the use of cognitive-behavioral therapy in treating children with PTSD. Although there are little data to guide clinicians in their work with children and adolescents with PTSD, Cohen suggests that the primary treatment components that seem to work well with children are "direct exploration of the trauma, use of specific stress management techniques, exploration and correction of inaccurate attributions regarding the trauma, and inclusion of parents in treatment" (p. 999). Parents can benefit from education regarding the child's PTSD symptoms and by learning how they might help in managing them.

The Recovery Process

In describing the recovery process of women who had experienced sexual assaults and rape, Hensley (2002) indicates that, even though treatment research suggests good results, the recovery process can be long and difficult. "Survivors are vulnerable to victim-blame, self-blame, unwillingness to disclose the rape to others, and an overall lack of support in addition to PTSD symptoms and other significant negative psychological and physiological outcomes" (p. 342). Hensley reports that women who survive sexual assaults need validation for their experiences and positive reinforcement for their attempts to deal with the traumas they've experienced. Instead, they must often deal with limited support and even skepticism from family, friends, professionals, and from the legal system. This concern about the limited support of PTSD victims as they try to recover from the traumas they've experienced can be generalized to many other victims of traumas. Ozer et al. (2003) report that in the early and mid-1970s, Vietnam veterans with PTSD were receiving diagnoses of schizophrenia at Veterans Hospital psychiatric units, even though similar problems of PTSD had been seen in World War II and among Korean War veterans. Horowitz and Solomon (1975) predicted large-scale, stress-related problems in veterans returning home after the war, a view that was skeptically received but that turned out to be all too true. Consequently, we have begun to believe that inadequate support and validation may prolong symptoms of PTSD.

In writing about treatment and recovery myths of PTSD, Rothbaum et al. (2002) believe that many people think that clients suffering from PTSD will recover in time without help; however, prolonged suffering suggests that this may not be the case, and interventions should be introduced when client symptoms are intrusive and the client voluntarily seeks help. The authors also note that a trauma need not be current for the client to require help with recovery. Many clients who have experienced child abuse and other early life traumas benefit from therapies such as exposure therapy by focusing on their worst memory of a trauma. Reducing stress involved with that memory has carry-over benefits to other traumas. The authors report that exposure therapies are often useful in treating non-PTSD symptoms that predate the traumatic event causing PTSD, and help to provide a more complete recovery. Exposure therapies help reduce "feelings of depression, rage, sadness, and guilt [in addition] to reducing related problems, such as depression and self-blame" (Rothbaum & Schwartz, 2002, p. 71). Many of these symptoms may predate the trauma, and their removal can effectively speed up the rate of recovery.

SUMMARY

This chapter on PTSD includes the symptoms, prevalence, and best evidence of treatment effectiveness. Data from two recent terrorist attacks in the United States are also included. Assaults are one of the primary reasons for the development of symptoms of PTSD. Data from studies on a form of brief therapy known as *debriefing* suggest that its use following a trauma may actually increase the probability that PTSD symptoms will develop. A case study is provided showing the impact of a terrorist attack and an effective form of treatment. The presence of resilience is thought to be one of the primary reasons some people cope well with severe traumas. A form of therapy known as *exposure therapy* seems to provide benefit to many people suffering from PTSD.

Integrative Questions

1. Why would so many people who were not directly affected by a terrorist attack develop symptoms of PTSD? The Oklahoma City and World Trade Center attacks are examples.

2. Talking about a trauma until it no longer creates anxiety seems an inefficient way to treat PTSD. Can you think of other "common sense" approaches that may lessen symptoms of PTSD more quickly?

3. Don't you think we make too much out of stressful life experiences in the United States? Many people in other countries suffer from devastating natural disasters, hunger, and malnutrition and seem to cope well. Isn't there a point at which the culture encourages people to experience PTSD because it believes that most people are too emotionally fragile to cope with extreme stressors?

4. During 9/11, American television focused on the bravery of countless men and women. Do you think this helped reduce the impact of the tragedy on many people with potential for developing symptoms of PTSD?

5. The notion that debriefing may actually lead to an increase in PTSD seems entirely wrongheaded. Can you give some examples of the positive impact of debriefing in cases of trauma?

References

Abrams, M. S. (2001). Resilience in ambiguous loss. *American Journal of Psychotherapy, 2,* 283–291.

American Psychiatric Association. (1994). *Diagnostic and statistical manual of mental disorders* (4th ed.). Washington, DC: Author.

Asmundson, G. J. G., Coons, M. J., Taylor, S., & Katz, J. (2002). PTSD and the experience of pain: Research and clinical implications of shared vulnerability and mutual maintenance models. *Canadian Journal of Psychiatry, 47*(10), 930–938.

Bisson, J. I., McFarlane, A. C., & Rose, S. (2000). Psychological debriefing. In E. B. Foa, T. M. Keane, & M. J. Friedman (Eds.), *Effective treatments for PTSD* (pp. 39–59). New York: Guilford Press.

Breslau, N., Davis, G. C., Andreski, P., & Peterson, E. (1991). Traumatic events and posttraumatic stress disorder in an urban population of young adults. *Archives of General Psychiatry, 48,* 216–222.

Brewin, C. R., Andrews, B., & Valentine, J. D. (2000). Meta-analysis of risk factors for posttraumatic stress disorder in trauma-exposed adults. *Journal of Consulting Clinical Psychology, 68,* 748–66.

Cohen, J. A. (1998, September). Summary of the practice parameters for the assessment and treatment of children and adolescents with posttraumatic stress disorder. *Journal of the American Academy of Child and Adolescent Psychiatry, 37*(9), 997–1001.

Deblinger, E., McLeer, S. V., & Henry, D. (1990). Cognitive behavioral treatment for sexually abused children suffering from post-traumatic stress: Preliminary findings. *Journal of the American Academy of Child & Adolescent Psychiatry, 29,* 747–752.

Foa, E. B., Dancu, C. V., Hembree, E. A., Jaycox, L. H., Meadows, E. A., & Street, G. P. (1999). A comparison of exposure therapy, stress inoculation training, and their combination in reducing posttraumatic stress disorder in female assault victims. *Journal of Consulting and Clinical Psychology, 67,* 194–200.

Foa, E. B., Hearst-Ikeda, D., & Perry, K. J. (1995). Evaluation of a brief cognitive-behavioral program for the prevention of chronic PTSD in recent assault victims. *Journal of Consulting & Clinical Psychology, 63,* 948–955.

Foa, E. B., & Meadows, E. A. (1997). Psychosocial treatments for post-traumatic stress disorder: A critical review. In J. Spence, J. M. Darley, & D. J. Foss (Eds.), *Annual Review of Psychology: Vol. 48* (pp. 449–480). Palo Alto, CA: Annual Reviews.

Foa, E. B., & Rothbaum, B. O. (1998). *Treating the trauma of rape: A cognitive behavioral therapy for PTSD.* New York: Guilford.

Foa, E. B., Rothbaum, B. O., Riggs, D., & Murdock, T. (1991). Treatment of post-traumatic stress disorder in rape victims: A comparison between cognitive-behavioral procedures and counseling. *Journal of Consulting and Clinical Psychology, 59,* 715–723.

Galea, S. (2002). Psychological sequelae of the September 11 terrorist attacks in New York City. *New England Journal of Medicine, 346*(13), 982–987.

Gist, R., & Devilly, G. J. (2002). Post-trauma debriefing: The road too frequently traveled. *Lancet, 360*(9335), 741–743.

Glicken, M. D. (1986a). Work related accidents which lead to post traumatic stress reactions. *Labor Relations: Occupational Safety and Health.*

Glicken, M. D. (1986b). Post-traumatic stress syndrome and work: Treatment considerations. *EAP Journal.*

Glicken, M. D. (1986c). The after-shock of on the job accidents. *EAP Digest, September-October.*

Henry, D. L. (1999, September). Resilience in maltreated children: Implications for special needs adoptions. *Child Welfare, 78*(5), 519–540.

Hensley, L. G. (2002). Treatment for survivors of rape: Issues and interventions. *Journal of Mental Health Counseling, 24*(4), 331–348.

Hoff, D. J. (2002). A year later, the impact of 9/11 lingers. *Education Week, 22*(2), 1–3.

Horowitz, M. J. (1976). *Stress response syndromes.* New York: Aronson.

Horowitz, M. J., & Solomon, G. F. (1975). A prediction of delayed stress response syndromes in Vietnam veterans. *Journal of Social Issues, 31,* 67–80.

Keane, T. M., Fairbank, J. A., Caddell, J. M., & Zimering, R. T. (1989). Implosive (flooding) therapy reduces symptoms of PTSD in Vietnam combat veterans. *Behavior Therapy, 20,* 245–260.

Kessler, R. C., Sonnega, A., Bromet, E., Hughes, M., & Nelson, C. B. (1995). Posttraumatic stress disorder in the national comorbidity survey. *Archives of General Psychiatry, 52,* 1048–1060.

Kramer, S. H., & Rosenthal, R. (1998). Meta-analytic research synthesis. In A. S. Bellack, M. Hersen (Series Eds.), & N. R. Schooler (Vol. Ed.), *Comprehensive clinical psychology: Vol. 3. Research and methods* (pp. 351–368). Oxford, UK: Pergamon.

Kulka, R. A., Schlenger, W. E., Fairbank, J. A., Hough, R. L., Jordan, B. K., Marmar, C. R., et al. (1990). *The national Vietnam veterans readjustment study: Tables of findings and technical appendices.* New York: Brunner/Mazel.

Lee, C., Gavriel, H., Drummond, P., Richards, J., & Greenwald, R. (2002). Treatment of PTSD: Stress inoculation training with prolonged exposure compared to EMDR. *Journal of Clinical Psychology, 58*(9), 1071–1089.

McFarlane, A. C., Atchison, M., Rafalowicz, E., & Papay, P. (1994). Physical symptoms in post-traumatic stress disorder. *Journal of Psychosomatic Research, 38,* 715–7226.

McGaugh, J. L., & Cahill, L. (1997). Interaction of neuromodulatory systems in modulating memory storage. *Behavioral Brain Research, 83,* 31–38.

Meadows, E. A., & Foa, E. B. (1998). Intrusion, arousal, and avoidance: Sexual trauma survivors. In V. Follette, I. Ruzek, & F. Abueg (Eds.), *Cognitive-behavioral therapies for trauma* (pp. 100–123). New York: Guilford.

Ozer, E. J., Best, S. R., Lipsey, T. L., & Weiss, D. S. (2003). Predictors of posttraumatic stress disorder and symptoms in adults: A meta-analysis. *Psychological Bulletin, 129*(1), 52–73.

Regehr, C., Cadell, S., & Jansen, K. (1999). Perceptions of control and long-term recovery from rape. *American Journal of Orthopsychiatrty, 69,* 110–114.

Resick, P. A. (1992). Cognitive treatment of a crime-related PTSD. In R. D. Peters, R. J. McMahon, & V. L. Quinsey (Eds.), *Aggression and violence throughout the life span* (pp. 171–191). Newbury Park, CA: Sage.

Resick, P. A., & Schnicke, M. K. (1992). Cognitive processing therapy for sexual assault victims. *Journal of Consulting and Clinical Psychology, 60*, 748–756.

Resick, P. A., & Schnicke, M. K. (1993). *Cognitive processing therapy for rape victims: A treatment manual.* Newbury Park, CA: Sage.

Resnick, H., Acierno, R., Holmes, M., Kilpatrick, D., & Jager, N. (1999). Prevention of post-rape psychopathology: Preliminary findings of a controlled acute rape treatment study. *Journal of Anxiety Disorders, 13*, 359–370.

Rothbaum, B., Olasov, C., & Schwartz, A. C. (2002). *American Journal of Psychotherapy, 56*(1), 59–75.

Rothbaum, B. O., Meadows, E. A., Resick, P., & Foy, D. W. (2000). Cognitive-behavioral therapy. In E. B. Foa, M. Friedman, & T. Keane (Eds.), *Effective treatments for posttraumatic stress disorder: Practice guidelines from the International Society for Traumatic Stress Studies* (pp. 60–83). New York: Guilford.

Schlenger, W. E., Kulka, R. A., Fairbank, J. A., Hough, R. L., Jordan, B. K., Marmar, C. R., et al. (1992). The prevalence of post-traumatic stress disorder in the Vietnam generation: A multimethod, multisource assessment of psychiatric disorder. *Journal of Traumatic Stress, 5*, 333–363.

Seligman, M. (1992). *Learned optimism: How to change your mind and your life.* New York: Pocket Books.

Stein, M. B. (2002). Taking aim at posttraumatic stress disorder: Understanding its nature and shooting down myths. *Canadian Journal of Psychiatry, 47*(10), 921–923.

Susser, E. S., Herman, D. B., & Aaron, B. (2002). Combating the terror of terrorism. *Scientific American, 287*(2), 70–78.

Taylor, S. (1999). *Anxiety sensitivity: Theory, research, and treatment of the fear of anxiety.* Mahwah, NJ: Lawrence Erlbaum Associates.

Taylor, S. (2000). *Understanding and treating panic disorder: Cognitive-behavioural approaches.* Chichester, UK: Wiley.

Tiet, Q. Q., Bird, H., & Davies, M. R. (1998, November). Adverse life events and resilience. *Journal of the American Academy of Child and Adolescent Psychiatry, 37*(11), 1191–1200.

van Emmerik, A. P., Kamphuis, J. H., Hulsbosch, A. M., & Emmelkamp, P. M. (2002). Single session debriefing after psychological trauma: A meta-analysis. *Lancet, 360*(9335), 766–772.

Walsh, F. (1998). *Strengthening family resilience.* New York: Guilford Press.

Weiss, D. S., Marmar, C. R., Schlenger, W. E., Fairbank, J. A., Jordan, B. K., Hough, R. L., et al. (1992). The prevalence of lifetime and partial post-traumatic stress disorder in Vietnam theater veterans. *Journal of Traumatic Stress, 5*, 365–376.

Werner, E., & Smith, R. (1982). *Vulnerable but invincible.* New York: Adams, Bannister & Cox.

What causes post-traumatic stress disorder: Two views. (2002, October). *Harvard Mental Health Letter, 19*(4), 8.

White, P., & Faustman, W. (1989). Coexisting physical conditions among inpatients with post-traumatic stress disorder. *Military Medicine, 154*, 66–71.

Evidence-Based Practice With Substance Abusers

10

S ubstance abuse is one of the major health and mental health problems in America today. In a survey conducted by SAMSHA, an office of the U.S. Department of Health and Human Services (2000), 14.5 million Americans ages 12 or older were classified with drug and alcohol dependence or abuse, amounting to 6.5% of the total population. *Alcohol Alert,* a publication of the National Institute of Alcohol Abuse and Alcoholism (2000), reports that more than 700,000 Americans receive alcoholism treatment on any given day. Kann (2001), who uses U.S. Health and Human Services data, writes that the use of alcohol and drugs continues to be one of the country's most pervasive and serious physical and mental health problems. Kahn notes that substance abuse is a leading cause of car accidents, homicide, suicide, and HIV infection and AIDS, and it contributes to crime, poor workplace productivity, and lower educational achievements.

Diagnostic Markers of Substance Abuse

The DSM-IV uses the following diagnostic markers to determine whether substance use is abusive: A dysfunctional use of substances causing impairment or distress within a 12-month period as determined by one of the following: (a) frequent use of substances that interfere with functioning and the fulfillment of responsibilities at home, work, school, etc.; (b) use of substances that impair functioning in dangerous situations such as driving or the use of machines; (c) use of substances that may lead to arrest for unlawful behaviors; and (d) substance use that seriously interferes with relations, marriage, child rearing, and other interpersonal responsibilities (APA, 1994, p. 182). Substance abuse may also lead to slurred speech, lack of coordination, unsteady gait, memory loss, fatigue and depression, feelings of euphoria, and lack of social inhibitions (APA, 1994, p. 197).

SHORT TESTS TO DIAGNOSE SUBSTANCE ABUSE

Miller (2001) reports that two simple questions asked to substance abusers have an 80% chance of diagnosing substance abuse: (a) "In the past year, have you ever drunk or used drugs more than you meant to?" and (b) "Have you felt you wanted or needed to cut down on your drinking or drug abuse in the past year?" Miller states that this simple approach has been found to be an effective diagnostic tool in three controlled studies using random samples and laboratory tests for alcohol and drugs in the bloodstream following interviews.

Stewart and Richards (2000) and Bisson, Nadeau, and Demers (1999) suggest that four questions from the CAGE questionnaire are predictive of alcohol abuse. CAGE is an acronym for *cut, annoyed, guilty,* and *eye-opener* (see the questions following this paragraph). Since many people deny their alcoholism, asking questions in an open, direct, and nonjudgmental way may elicit the best results. The four questions are as follows:

1. Cut: Have you ever felt you should cut down on your drinking?

2. Annoyed: Have people annoyed you by criticizing your drinking?

3. Guilty: Have you ever felt guilty about your drinking?

4. Eye-Opener: Have you ever had a drink first thing in the morning (an eye-opener) to steady your nerves or get rid of a hangover? (Bisson, Nadeau, & Demers, 1999, p. 717)

Stewart and Richards (2000) write, "A patient who answers yes to two or more of these questions probably abuses alcohol; a patient who answers yes to one question should be screened further" (p. 56). Not everyone is certain that the CAGE instrument, developed in the late 1970s to distinguish heavy from moderate drinkers, is an effective diagnostic tool. Bisson, Nadeau, and Demers (1999) write: "If the CAGE had any utility as an instrument informing on the prevalence or incidence of heavy drinking within the population, it would have discriminated between heavy and nonheavy drinkers. Our results show that this is not the case" (p. 720). The authors think the instrument is less than accurate because many people have a new awareness of alcoholism and have tried to do something to limit their alcohol use. Furthermore, the instrument asks about last year's alcohol consumption. Since subjects may have changed their alcohol-related behavior, the answers may be misleading. Alcohol consumption has also decreased somewhat nationally. Consequently, a direct series of questions answered truthfully may fail to distinguish those who drink heavily from those who drink moderately, because the responses from both groups may tend to be the same. This finding supports the concern that short questions may not be accurate in diagnosing substance abuse and that diagnosis requires an in-depth social, emotional, and medical history in which the guidelines of the DSM-IV provide direction for the types of historical and medical issues one might look for. Perhaps this lack of an in-depth history is why Backer and Walton-Moss (2001) found that fully 20%–25% of all patients with alcohol-related problems were treated medically for the symptoms of alcoholism rather than for the condition itself, and that a diagnosis of alcohol abuse was never made in almost one fourth of all alcoholics seen for medical treatment.

PSYCHOSOCIAL VARIABLES

Another problem caused by the lack of a complete psychosocial history is that services are often withheld from elderly patients with substance abuse problems. Pennington, Butler, and Eagger (2000) report that older patients referred to a psychiatric service with a diagnosis of alcohol abuse failed to receive the clinical assessment recommended by the American Geriatrics Society. Rather than being treated for alcoholism as a primary problem, most elderly clients abusing alcohol (4 out of 5) were treated for depression or associated medical problems. The authors believe the reason elderly patients are not adequately screened for alcohol abuse is that "some health professionals harbor a misguided belief that older people should not be advised to give up established habits or they may be embarrassed to ask older patients personal questions about alcohol use" (Pennington et al., 2000, p. 183), even though those behaviors may be self-injurious and possibly dangerous to others.

Writing about female alcohol abuse, Backer and Walton-Moss (2001) report,

> Unlike men, women commonly seek help for alcoholism from primary care clinicians. Further, the development and progression of alcoholism is different in women than in men. Women with alcohol problems have higher rates of dual diagnoses, childhood sexual abuse, panic and phobia disorders, eating disorders, posttraumatic stress disorder, and victimization. Early diagnosis, brief interventions, and referral are critical to the treatment of alcoholism in women. (p. 13)

The authors suggest the following diagnostic markers for female alcoholics: Since women metabolize alcohol differently than men, women tend to show signs of becoming intoxicated at a later age than men (26.5 versus 22.7), experience their first signs of a recognition of alcohol abuse later (27.5 versus 25), and experience loss of control over their drinking later in life (29.8 versus 27.2). The mortality rate for female alcoholics is 50%–100% higher than it is for men. Liver damage occurs in women in a shorter period of time and with lower amounts of intake of alcohol. Backer and Walton-Moss (2001) report, "Female alcoholics have a higher mortality rate from alcoholism than men from suicide, alcohol-related accidents, circulatory disorders, and cirrhosis of the liver" (p. 15). Use of alcohol by women in adolescence is almost equal to that of male adolescents, and, although men use alcohol to socialize, women use it to cope with negative moods and are likely to use alcohol in response to specific stressors in their lives (Backer & Walton-Moss, 2001).

EARLY ABUSE OF SUBSTANCES

Kuperman et al. (2001) report several risk factors for adolescent alcoholism, including home problems, personal behavioral problems, and early use of alcohol. Home problems are considered problems with parental use and acceptance of alcohol and drugs, problems with family bonding and family conflict, ease in obtaining alcohol, a high level of peer use of alcohol, and positive peer attitudes toward alcohol and drug use. Personal behavioral problems include rebellious behavior against parents, gaining peer acceptance by drinking and other risky behaviors meant to impress peers, and self-treatment through the use of alcohol and drugs for mental health and/or academic problems. Early use of alcohol and drugs may occur in elementary school and is usually a confirmed addiction by early adolescence. Grant and Dawson (1997) report that early use of alcohol is a very strong predictor of lifelong alcoholism and indicate that 40% of young adults, aged 18–29 years, who began drinking before the age of 15 were considered to be alcohol dependent as compared to roughly 10% who began drinking after the age of 19. While Kuperman et al. (2001) suggest that early substance abuse is often predictive of alcoholism, the reasons for alcohol use offered by the authors (family and peer problems) are evident in adolescents who do not develop alcohol and drug problems and are common behaviors in a society where many adolescents are rebellious and partake in risky behaviors. Nonetheless, the wise clinician will be aware that early and frequent use of alcohol has a fairly high probability of leading to prolonged alcohol use and will understand its importance when screening clients.

RELATED MEDICAL PROBLEMS

Stewart and Richards (2000) conclude that a number of medical problems may have their origins in heavy alcohol and drug use. Head injuries and spinal separations as a result of accidents may have been caused by substance abuse. Because heavy drinkers often fail to eat, they may have nutritional deficiencies that result in psychotic-like symptoms, including abnormal eye movements, disorganization, and forgetfulness. Stomach disorders, liver damage, and severe heartburn may have their origins in heavy drinking because alcohol destroys the stomach's mucosal lining. Fifteen percent of all heavy drinkers develop cirrhosis of the liver and many develop pancreatitis. Weight loss, pneumonia, muscle loss because of malnutrition, and oral cancer have all been associated with heavy drinking. Stewart and Richards indicate that substance abusers are poor candidates for surgery. Anesthesia and pain medication can delay alcohol withdrawal for up to 5 days postoperatively. "Withdrawal symptoms can cause agitation and uncooperativeness and can mask signs and symptoms of other postoperative complications. Patients who abuse alcohol are at a higher risk for postoperative complications such as excessive bleeding, infection, heart failure, and pneumonia" (Stewart and Richards, 2000, p. 58).

Stewart and Richards (2000) provide the following blood alcohol levels as measures of the impact of alcohol in screening for abuse:

- 0.05% (equivalent to one or two drinks in an average-sized person)—impaired judgment, reduced alertness, loss of inhibitions, euphoria

- 0.10%—slower reaction times, decreased caution in risk taking behavior, impaired fine-motor control. Legal evidence of intoxication in most states starts at 0.10%.

- 0.15%—significant and consistent losses in reaction times

- 0.20%—function of entire motor area of brain measurably depressed, causing staggering. The individual may be easily angered or emotional.

- 0.25%—severe sensory and motor impairment

- 0.30%—confusion, stupor

- 0.35%—surgical anesthesia

- 0.40%—respiratory depression, lethal in about half of the population

- 0.50%—death from respiratory depression. (p. 59)

Best Evidence for the Treatment of Substance Abuse

SHORT-TERM TREATMENT

Herman (2000) believes that individual psychotherapy can be helpful in treating substance abusers and suggests five situations where therapy would be indicated:

1. as an appropriate introduction to treatment;

2. as a way of helping mildly or moderately dependent drug abusers;

3. when there are clear signs of emotional problems such as severe depression, because these problems will interfere with the substance abuse treatment;

4. when clients progressing in 12-step programs begin to experience emerging feelings of guilt, shame, and grief; and

5. when a client's disturbed interpersonal functioning continues after a long period of sustained abstinence, and therapy might help prevent a relapse.

One of the most frequently discussed treatment approaches to addiction in the literature is brief counseling. Bien, Miller, and Tonigan (1993) reviewed 32 studies of brief interventions with alcohol abusers and found that, on the average, brief counseling reduced alcohol use by 30%. In a study of brief intervention with alcohol abusers, however, Chang, Wilkins-Haug, Berman, and Goetz (1999) found that both the treatment and control groups significantly reduced their alcohol use. The difference between the two groups in the reduction of their alcohol abuse was minimal. In a study of 175 Mexican Americans who were abusing alcohol, Burge et al. (1997) report that treated and untreated groups improved significantly over time, raising questions about the efficacy of treatment versus natural recovery. In an evaluation of a larger report by *Consumer Reports* on the effectiveness of psychotherapy, Seligman (1995) notes, "Alcoholics Anonymous (AA) did especially well . . . significantly bettering mental health professionals [in the treatment of alcohol and drug-related problems]" (p. 971).

Bien et al. (1993) found that two or three 10–15 minute counseling sessions are often as effective as more extensive interventions with older alcohol abusers. The sessions include motivation-for-change strategies, education, assessment of the severity of the problem, direct feedback, contracting and goal setting, behavioral modification techniques, and the use of written materials such as self-help manuals. Brief interventions have been shown to be effective in reducing alcohol consumption, binge drinking, and the frequency of excessive drinking in problem drinkers, according to Fleming, Barry, Manwell, Johnson, and London (1997). Completion rates using brief interventions are better for elder-specific alcohol programs than for mixed-age programs (Atkinson, 1995), and late-onset alcoholics are more likely to complete treatment and have somewhat better outcomes using brief interventions (Liberto and Oslin, 1995).

Miller and Sanchez (1994) summarize the key components of brief intervention using the acronym FRAMES: *feedback, responsibility, advice, menu of strategies, empathy,* and *self-efficacy*.

1. Feedback: This includes an assessment with feedback to the client regarding the client's risk for alcohol problems, his or her reasons for drinking, the role of alcohol in the client's life, and the consequences of drinking.

2. Responsibility: This includes strategies to help clients understand the need to remain healthy, independent, and financially secure and is particularly important when working with older clients and clients with health problems and disabilities.

3. Advice: Includes direct feedback and suggestions to clients to help them cope with their drinking problems and with other life situations that may contribute to alcohol abuse.

4. Menu: Includes a list of strategies to reduce drinking and help cope with such high-risk situations as loneliness, boredom, family problems, and lack of social opportunities.

5. Empathy: Bien et al. (1993) strongly emphasize the need for a warm, empathic, and understanding style of treatment. Miller and Rollnick (1991) found that an empathetic counseling style produced a 77% reduction in client drinking as compared to a 55% reduction when a confrontational approach was used.

6. Self-Efficacy: This includes strategies to help clients rely on their inner resources to make changes in their drinking behavior. Inner resources may include positive points of view about themselves, helping others, staying busy, and good problem-solving coping skills.

Some additional aspects of brief interventions suggested by Menninger (2002) include drinking agreements in the form of drinking limits that are signed by the patient and the practitioner, ongoing follow-up and support, and appropriate timing of the intervention with the patient's readiness to change. Late-onset alcoholics are also more likely to complete treatment and have somewhat better outcomes (Liberto and Oslin, 1995). Alcoholics Anonymous (AA) may be helpful, particularly AA groups that are specifically oriented toward the elderly.

Babor and Higgins-Biddle (2000) discuss the use of brief interventions with people involved in "risky drinking" but are not as yet classified as alcohol dependent. Brief interventions are usually limited to three to five sessions of counseling and education. The intent of brief interventions is to prevent the onset of more serious alcohol-related problems. According to Babor and Higgins-Biddle (2000), "Most programs are instructional and motivational, designed to address the specific behavior of drinking with information, feedback, health education, skill-building, and practical advice, rather than with psychotherapy or other specialized treatment techniques" (p. 676). Higgins-Biddle, Babor, Mullahy, Daniels, and

McRee (1997) analyzed 14 random studies of brief interventions that included more than 20,000 risky drinkers. They report a net reduction in drinking of 21% for males and 8% for females. To improve the effectiveness of short-term interventions, Babor and Higgins-Biddle (2000) encourage the use of early identification of problem drinking, life-health monitoring by health and mental health professionals, and risk counseling that includes screening and brief intervention to inform potential alcohol abusers of the risk of serious alcohol dependence and to motivate them to change their alcohol use. This approach requires a high degree of cooperation among health and education personnel, who often are loathe to identify very young people as having "at risk" alcohol problems because they fear that doing so will exacerbate the problem through public identification, and often they believe that drinking will moderate itself as the child matures.

Fleming and Manwell (1998) report that people with alcohol-related problems often receive counseling from primary care physicians or nursing staff in five or fewer standard office visits. The counseling consists of rational information about the negative impact of alcohol use as well as practical advice regarding ways of reducing alcohol dependence and the availability of community resources. Gentilello, Donovan, Dunn, and Rivara (1995) report that 25%–40% of the trauma patients seen in emergency rooms may be alcohol dependent. The authors found that a single motivational interview, at or near the time of discharge, reduced drinking levels and readmission for trauma during 6 months of follow up. Monti et al. (1999) conducted a similar study with 18- and 19-year-olds admitted to an emergency room with alcohol-related injuries. After 6 months, all participants had decreased their alcohol consumption; however, "the group receiving brief intervention had a significantly lower incidence of drinking and driving, traffic violations, alcohol-related injuries, and alcohol-related problems" (Monti et al., 1999, p. 3).

Lu and McGuire (2002) studied the effectiveness of outpatient treatment with substance abusing clients and came to the following conclusions:

1. The more severe the drug use problem before treatment was initiated, the less likely clients were to discontinue drug use during treatment when compared to other users.

2. Clients reporting no substance abuse 3 months before admission were more likely to maintain abstinence than those who reported abstinence only in the past month.

3. Heroin users were highly unlikely to sustain abstinence during treatment, and marijuana users were less likely to sustain abstinence during treatment than alcohol users.

4. Clients with "psychiatric problems" were more likely to use drugs during treatment than clients without psychiatric problems.

5. Clients with legal problems related to their substance abuse had reduced chances of improving during the treatment.

6. Clients who had multiple prior treatments for substance abuse were less likely to remain abstinent during and after treatment.

7. Clients who were more educated were more likely to sustain abstinence after treatment.

8. Clients treated in urban agencies were less likely to maintain abstinence than those treated in rural agencies.

LONGER-TERM TREATMENTS

Walitzer and Dermen (2002) report that treatment attrition among substance abusers is such a pervasive problem in programs offering treatment services that it affects our ability to determine treatment effectiveness. Baekeland and Lundwall (1975) report dropout rates for inpatient treatment programs of 28%, and that 75% of the outpatient alcoholic patients in their study dropped out of treatment before their fourth session. Of 172 alcoholic outpatients studied, Leigh, Ogborne, and Cleland (1984) report that 15% failed to attend their initial appointment, 28% attended only a session or two, and 19% attended only three to five times. In studying 117 alcoholism clinic admissions, Rees (1986) found that 35% of the clients failed to return after their initial visit and that another 18% terminated treatment within 30 days.

To try to reduce the amount of attrition in alcohol treatment programs, Walitzer and Dermen (2002) randomly assigned 126 clients entering an alcohol treatment program to one of three groups to prepare them for the treatment program: a role induction session, a motivational interview session, or a no-preparatory session control group. They found that clients assigned to the motivational interview "attended more treatment sessions and had fewer heavy drinking days during and 12 months after treatment relative to control group" (p. 1161). Clients assigned to the motivational interview also were abstinent more days during treatment and in the first 3 months following treatment than the control group, but the difference, unfortunately, did not last for the remaining 9 months of follow-up. Clients assigned to the role induction group did no better than the control group in any of the variables studied.

In describing the motivational interview, Walitzer and Dermen (2002) indicate that it consists of the following:

(a) eliciting self-motivational statements; (b) reflective, empathic listening; (c) inquiring about the client's feelings, ideas, concerns, and plans; (d) affirming the client in a way that acknowledges the client's serious consideration of and steps toward change; (e) deflecting resistance in a manner that takes into account the link between therapist behavior and client resistance; (f) reframing client statements as appropriate; and (g) summarizing. (p. 1164)

Kirchner, Booth, Owen, Lancaster, and Smith (2000) considered the factors related to entry into alcohol treatment programs following a diagnosis of alcoholism. They found that many patients who might benefit from treatment were not referred by their medical providers because of a belief that treatment wasn't effective, even though a number of "well-designed and methodologically sound studies have repeatedly shown that treatment for alcohol related disorders can be effective not only for reducing the consumption of alcohol but also for improving the patient's overall level of functioning" (p. 339). The authors also report that improved detection of alcoholism, the first step in the provision of services, is negatively influenced by a number of factors, including younger age, non-Caucasian ethnicity, the severity of the alcohol use, lower socioeconomic status, and male gender. Drug and alcohol use to self-medicate for psychiatric disorders is also a key predictor of detection as are alcohol-related medical problems such as liver disorders, high blood pressure, and adult-onset diabetes. Herman (2000) reports that the reasons substance abusers enter treatment are usually external in nature and include legal problems with drug use (license suspension because of drunk driving), marital problems, work-related problems, medical complications caused by drug and alcohol abuse, problems with depression and anxiety that lead to self-medicating with alcohol and drugs, and referral by mental health professionals (a major reason women enter treatment programs).

TREATMENT STRATEGIES

Herman (2000) believes that the primary strategy in the treatment of substance abuse is to initially achieve abstinence. Once abstinence is achieved, the substance abuser can begin to address relationship problems that might interfere with social and emotional functioning. Herman believes that the key to treatment is to match the client with the type of treatment most likely to help. He suggests that the following phases exist in the treatment of substance abuse:

Phase 1: Abstinence.

Phase 2: Teaching the client coping skills to help prevent a relapse through cognitive-behavioral techniques that help clients manage stressful situations likely to trigger substance abuse. These techniques may include recognizing internal cues that lead to substance abuse (depression and feelings of low self-esteem); managing external cues (responses by others and interpersonal relationships); avoiding peers who are likely to continue to abuse substances and encourage the client to do the same; and alternative behaviors that help the client avoid drug use (substituting substance abuse with exercise, or attending social events where alcohol isn't available).

Phase 3: Since the underlying problems that contribute to substance abuse are often deeply internalized feelings of low self-worth, depression, and self-loathing, therapy should help the client deal with internalized pathologies that are likely to lead to relapse. The therapies that seem most effective in doing this are cognitive-behavioral therapies, the strengths approach, and affective therapies including Gestalt therapy (Herman, 2000). Herman also suggests the use of psychodynamic therapy but research evidence of the effectiveness of this form of treatment is not overly positive.

In a review of 30 years of research, the National Institute on Drug Abuse (1999) reports that the following are necessary elements of effective treatment of substance abuse:

1. correctly matching the client with the appropriate treatment approach;

2. providing treatment that is readily available and may be useful in treating other psychosocial problems experienced by the client;

3. ensuring that the treatment plan is comprehensive, the length of treatment is adequate, and the treatment plan is regularly reviewed;

4. providing medication if needed;

5. ensuring that treatment is more than help with detoxification;

6. ensuring that treatment is useful for involuntary clients;

7. monitoring the patient's drug use frequently;

8. testing for HIV/AIDS and other potential diseases; and

9. offering treatment again even after multiple relapses (as cited in Lennox and Mansfield, 2001, p. 169).

Other factors found to provide best evidence of treatment effectiveness include the following: Dahlgren and Willander (1989) compared women-only and mixed-gender treatment groups. Clients in the women-only group remained in treatment longer, had higher completion rates, and had improved biopsychosocial rates as compared to women who were in mixed-gender programs. Burtscheidt, Wolwer, Schwartz, et al. (2002) studied the treatment effects of long-term treatment by comparing nonspecific supportive therapy with two different forms of behavioral therapy (coping skills training and cognitive-behavioral therapy). One hundred twenty patents were randomly assigned to each of the three therapy approaches and were seen in treatment for 26 weeks with a follow-up period of 2 years. Patients receiving behavioral therapy showed consistently higher abstinence rates. Differences in treatment effectiveness between the two behavioral therapies could not be established. The study also established that cognitively impaired and severely personality disordered clients experienced less benefit from any of the therapies than other clients. The authors concluded that behavioral treatment had the best long-term effects and met high client acceptance, but that a great deal still needs to be done to develop even more effective behavioral therapies for clients who abuse substances.

NATURAL RECOVERY

Granfield and Cloud (1996) estimate that as many as 90% of all problem drinkers never enter treatment and that many end their abuse of alcohol without *any* form of treatment (Hingson, Scotch, Day, & Culbert, 1980; Roizen, Cahalan, Lambert, Wiebel, & Shanks, 1978; Stall & Biernacki, 1989). Sobell, Sobell, Toneatto, and Leo (1993) report that 82% of the alcoholics they studied who terminated their addictions did so by using natural recovery methods that excluded the use of professional treatment. As an example of the use of natural recovery techniques, Granfield and Cloud (1996) report that most ex-smokers discontinued their tobacco use without treatment (Peele, 1989) and many addicted substance abusers "mature-out" of a variety of addictions including heavy drinking and narcotics use (Snow, 1973; Winick, 1962). Stall and Biernacki (1989) report that people who use natural methods to end their drug addictions utilize a range of strategies including discontinuing their relationships with drug users, avoiding drug-using environments, having new goals and interests in their lives (Peele, 1989), and using friends and family to provide a support network (Biernacki, 1986). Trice and Roman (1970) indicate that self-help groups are particularly helpful with substance-abusing clients because they develop and continue a support network that assists clients in maintaining abstinence and other changed behaviors.

Granfield and Cloud (1996) studied middle-class alcoholics who used natural recovery alone without professional help or the use of self-help groups. Many of the participants in their study felt that some self-help groups were overly religious while others believed in alcoholism as a disease that suggested a lifetime struggle. The subjects in the study believed that some self-help groups encouraged dependence on the group and that associating with other alcoholics would probably complicate recovery. In summarizing their findings, Granfield and Cloud report,

Many [research subjects] expressed strong opposition to the suggestion that they were powerless over their addictions. Such an ideology, they explained, not only was counterproductive but was also extremely demeaning. These respondents saw themselves as efficacious people who often prided themselves on their past accomplishments. They viewed themselves as being individualists and strong-willed. One respondent, for instance, explained that "such programs encourage powerlessness" and that she would rather "trust her own instincts than the instincts of others." (Granfield and Cloud, 1996, p. 51)

Waldorf, Reinarman, and Murphy (1991) found that many addicted people with jobs, strong family ties, and other close emotional supports were able to "walk away" from their very heavy use of cocaine. Granfield and Cloud (1996) note that many of the respondents in their study had a great deal to lose if they continued their substance abuse and that their sample consisted of people with stable lives, good jobs, supportive families and friends, college educations, and other social supports that gave them motivation to "alter" their drug-using behaviors.

SELF-HELP GROUPS

Humphreys (1998) studied the effectiveness of self-help groups with substance abusers by comparing two groups, one receiving inpatient care for substance abuse, and the other attending self-help groups for substance abuse. At the conclusion of the study, the average participant assigned to a self-help group (AA) had used $8,840 in alcohol-related health care resources as compared to $10,040 for the inpatient treatment participants. In a follow-up study, Humphreys (1998) compared outpatient services to self-help groups for the treatment of substance abuse. The clients in the self-help group had decreased alcohol consumption by 70% over 3 years and consumed 45% less health care services (about $1,800 less per person). Humphreys (1998) argues that "From a cost-conscious point of view, self-help groups should be the first option evaluated when an addicted individual makes initial contact with professional services (e.g., in a primary care appointment or a clinical assessment at a substance abuse agency or employee assistance program)" (p. 16). Additional data on the effectiveness of self-help groups may be found in Chapter 15.

Case Study: A Brief Intervention
After an Alcohol-Related Car Accident

Jim Larson is a 17-year-old high school student who was taken to the emergency room after his car spun out of control and hit an embankment.

Three passengers in the car were slightly injured. Jim and his friends had been drinking Everclear, a 180-proof alcoholic beverage they purchased through an older friend. All four friends were highly intoxicated and had walked a block and a half from a party they were attending to their car wearing T-shirts in 40-degree-below-zero weather. Jim sustained minor injuries. After he became sober enough in the emergency room to recognize the seriousness of the accident and that his blood alcohol level was in excess of .25%, three times the allowed drinking and driving level of .08%, he became antagonistic and withdrawn. His parents rushed to the hospital and were very concerned about Jim's behavior. His drinking was unknown to them, although Jim had begun drinking at age 10 and was regularly becoming intoxicated at weekend parties by age 13. Jim thought he was doing social drinking and felt that he was no different from his other friends. The accident, however, seemed to be a wake-up call to do something about his risky behavior.

A social worker and nurse met with Jim and his parents three times over the course of a 2-day stay in the hospital. They gave out information about the health impact of drinking and did a screening test to determine Jim's level of abusive drinking. They concluded that Jim was at very high risk of becoming an alcoholic because his drinking impaired his judgment, affected his grades, and was thought to be responsible for high blood sugar readings consistent with early-onset diabetes and moderately high blood pressure. A psychosocial history taken by the social worker revealed that Jim had begun experimenting with alcohol at age 10 and was frequently using it at home and with friends from age 13 and on. He was drinking more than a quart of alcohol a week, some of it very high in alcohol content. Jim's driver's license was revoked by the court and, on the basis of the report made by the emergency room personnel, Jim was sent for mandatory alcohol counseling.

Jim is a reluctant client. He discounts his drinking problem, claiming he drinks no more than his friends. Were it not for the accident, he argues that he would not be in counseling because he was not having any serious problems in his life. That isn't altogether true, however. With an IQ of higher than 130, Jim's grades are mostly in the *D* range. He misses classes on a regular basis and often misses class in the mornings because of hangovers. His parents are having marital and financial problems and fail to supervise Jim closely. Furthermore, Jim has been fantasizing about harming his friends, who he thinks have been disloyal to him for reasons he can't validate. "Just a feeling, ya know?" he told the therapist. Was the accident really an accident? "Sure," Jim says, "what else?" His therapist isn't so sure. He has hints of Jim's antagonism toward other students and has heard Jim talk about dreams in which he harms others. Jim spends a great deal of time on the Internet and has assumed various identities, many of them harboring antisocial and violent intentions. The therapist believes that Jim is a walking time bomb of emotional distress and that his alcoholism, while robust, is just one way of self-medicating himself for feelings of isolation, low self-esteem, and rejection by his parents and classmates.

After months of treatment, during which time Jim would often sit in silence and stare at the therapist, he has begun to talk about his feelings and admits that he has continued drinking heavily. He also drives, although his license has been suspended. He is full of self-hate and thinks that he is doomed to die soon. He feels powerful when he drinks, he told the therapist, and loves the peaceful feeling that comes over him as he gets drunk. Often he can hardly wait to have his first drink of the day and sometimes drinks when he wakes up. Frequently, he substitutes alcohol for food. He is aware that this cycle of drinking to feel better about himself can only lead to serious life problems, but doesn't think he is capable of stopping.

Jim's therapist asked for Jim's assistance on an Internet search to find the best approach to help Jim with his drinking problem. It seemed like a silly request to Jim because the therapist was supposed to be the expert, but Jim was intrigued and did as he was asked. When he met next with the therapist, Jim had printed out a number of articles suggesting ways of coping with adolescent alcoholism that seemed reasonable to him and to the therapist. From the work of Kuperman et al. (2001), they agreed that Jim had a number of problems that should be dealt with, including problems at home, with friends, and with his alcohol abuse. They decided that a cognitive-behavioral approach would work best, with homework assignments and cognitive restructuring as additional aspects of the treatment. Jim was intrigued with an article he found on the strengths approach and showed the therapist an article by Moxley and Olivia (2001) that they both found quite useful. Another article on self-help groups by Humphreys (1998) convinced them that a self-help group for adolescent alcohol abusers might also be helpful. Finally, Jim brought up the issue of working with his parents and it was decided that the family would be seen together to try to resolve some of the problems they were having and to develop better communication skills.

Jim has been in treatment for more than a year. He is applying himself in school and has begun thinking about college. His drinking has modified itself somewhat. Although he still drinks too much at times, he won't drive when he is drinking or engage in risky behavior. He feels much less angry and has developed new friendships with peers who don't drink or use drugs. The changes seem very substantial, but it's too early to know if the alcoholism is likely to become problematic when he deals with additional life stressors. Jim is unsure and says, "Yeah, it's all helping me but my head isn't always on straight and sometimes I do dumb stuff. I'm more aware of it now but I still do it. I'm getting along with my folks a lot better, and my new friends are real friends, not drinking buddies. I don't know. I looked at some studies on the Internet, and it looks like I have a pretty good chance of becoming a drunk. I like booze. It makes me feel good. That's not a good sign, is it? And I'm still pretty mad about a lot of things. I spend time on the Internet in chat rooms and it's pretty bizarre, sometimes, the things I say. But yeah, I know I'm better. I just hope it keeps up."

Jim's therapist said, "Jim has a good handle on himself. I wouldn't argue with anything he said. He has lots of potential but he also has enough problems to make me unwilling to predict the future. What I *will* say is that he works hard, is cooperative, and seems to be trying to work on some long-standing issues with his family and his self-perception. I think that addictions are transitory and you never know when his desire to drink will overwhelm his desire to stay sober. The self-help group he's in keeps close tabs on his drinking, and his new friends are helpful. I'd caution anyone who works with adolescents not to expect too much from treatment. I do want to applaud the professionals he worked with in the hospital. Even though the treatment was brief, it made a lasting impact on Jim to hear that he was considered an alcoholic, and it did bring him into treatment. That's exactly what you hope for in serious alcoholics who are in denial."

Research Problems and Best Evidence

A major problem with the treatment of substance abuse is the lack of best evidence because of compelling methodological problems found in many studies. Clifford, Maisto, and Franzke (2000) write, "It is recommended that treatment outcome studies be interpreted cautiously, particularly when the research protocols involved frequent and intensive follow-up interviews conducted across extended periods of time" (p. 741). As an example of the type of errors made in substance abuse research, Ouimette, Finney, and Moos (1997) compared 12-step programs such as AA with cognitive-behavioral programs and programs that combined both approaches. One year after completion of treatment, all three types of programs had similar improvements rates when alcohol consumption was measured. Participants in the 12-step program had more "sustained abstinence" and better employment rates than the other two programs, but Ouimette et al. (1997) caution the reader not to make more of these findings than is warranted because of nonrandom assignment of patients to the different types of treatment. Clifford, Maisto, and Franzke (2000) indicate that many substance abuse studies have methodological problems that affect their validity, including infrequent follow-up, compounding effects that may suggest better results than are warranted, the lack of quality data, and research protocols that are influenced more by political correctness than science. A more in-depth discussion of research issues that affect best evidence may be found in Chapter 16.

SUMMARY

In this chapter on EBP and substance abuse, research findings are reported that suggest disagreement regarding the effectiveness of certain types of treatment, particularly very brief treatment with high-risk abusers. However, promising research on natural recovery and self-help groups suggest that treatment effectiveness may be consistently positive with these two approaches. Research issues are discussed that make the development of best evidence on the efficacy of all forms of treatment of substance abuse questionable, and the suggestion is made that before we can develop best evidence, more effective studies must be done that include adequate research designs and controls. A case study is provided that demonstrates the use of EBP with substance-abusing clients.

Integrative Questions

1. Binge drinking is epidemic on many university campuses in the United States. Do you feel that binge drinking is a sign of potential for alcoholism?

2. Brief treatment of substance abuse flies in the face of what many people believe about the long-term addictive nature of alcohol and drug dependence. What's your view about the effectiveness of brief treatment?

3. Is it fair to criticize the lack of adequate research for self-help groups treating addictions? Shouldn't we take at face value the overwhelmingly positive feedback from participants that they work very well?

4. The idea that people will walk away from their addictions when they're ready is contraindicated in studies of weight loss. In these studies, people cycle back and forth and fail to sustain weight loss. Might not the same thing be said about addictions to substances?

5. Focusing on positive behavior seems like a worthy way to treat substance abusers, but aren't there dangerous behaviors (such as unprotected sex, date rape, and automobile accidents) that need to be stopped immediately, and don't they require a type of "tough love"?

References

Atkinson, R. (1995). Treatment programs for aging alcoholics. In T. Beresford & E. Gomberg (Eds.), *Alcohol and Aging* (pp. 186–210). New York: Oxford University Press.

Babor, T. F., & Higgins-Biddle, J. C. (2000, May). Alcohol screening and brief intervention: Dissemination strategies for medical practice and public health. *Addiction, 95*(5), 677–687.

Backer, K. L., & Walton-Moss, B. (2001, October). Detecting and addressing alcohol abuse in women. *Nurse Practitioner, 26*(10), 13–22.

Baekeland, F., & Lundwall, L. (1975). Dropping out of treatment: A critical review. *Psychological Bulletin, 82,* 738–783.

Bien, T. J., Miller, W. R., & Tonigan, J. S. (1993). Brief interventions for alcohol problems: A review. *Addictions, 88*(3), 315–335.

Biernacki, P. (1986). *Pathways from heroin addiction: Recover without treatment.* Philadelphia: Temple University Press.

Bisson, J., Nadeau, L., & Demers, A. (1999, May). The validity of the CAGE scale to screen heavy drinking and drinking problems in a general population. *Addiction, 94*(5), 715–723.

Burge, S. K., Amodei, N., Elkin, B., Catala, S., Andrew, S. R., Lane, P. A., et al. (1997). An evaluation of two primary care interventions for alcohol abuse among Mexican-American patients. *Addiction, 92*(12), 1705–1716.

Burtscheidt, W., Wolwer, W., Schwartz, R., et al. (2002, September). Alcoholism, rehabilitation and comorbidity. *Acta Psychiatrica Scandinavica, 106*(3), 227–233.

Chang, G., Wilkins-Haug, L., Berman, S., & Goetz, M. A. (1999). Brief intervention for alcohol use in pregnancy: A randomized trial. *Addiction, 94*(10), 1499–1508.

Clifford, P. R., Maisto, S. A., & Franzke, L. H. (2000). Alcohol treatment research follow-up and drinking behaviors. *Journal of Studies on Alcohol, 61*(5), 736–743.

Dahlgren, L., & Willander, A. (1989). Are special treatment facilities for female alcoholics needed? *Alcoholism, Clinical and Experimental Research, 13,* 499–504.

Fleming, M., & Manwell, L. B. (1998). Brief intervention in primary care settings: A primary treatment method for at-risk, problem, and dependent drinkers. *Alcohol Research and Health, 23*(2), 128–137.

Fleming, M. F., Barry, K. L., Manwell, L. B., Johnson, K., & London, R. (1997). Brief physician advice for problem alcohol drinkers: A randomized controlled trial in community-based primary care practices. *Journal of the American Medical Association, 277*(13), 1039–1045.

Gentilello, L. M., Donovan, D. M., Dunn, C. W., & Rivara, F. P. (1995). Alcohol interventions in trauma centers: Current practice and future directions. *Journal of the American Medical Association, 274*(13), 1043–1048.

Granfield, R., & Cloud, W. (1996, Winter). The elephant that no one sees: Natural recovery among middle-class addicts. *Journal of Drug Issues, 26,* 45–61.

Grant, B. F., & Dawson, D. A. (1997). Age at onset of alcohol use and its association with DSM-IV alcohol abuse and dependence: Results from the national longitudinal alcohol epidemiologic survey. *Journal of Substance Abuse, 9,* 103–110.

Herman, M. (2000). Psychotherapy with substance abusers: Integration of psychodynamic and cognitive-behavioral approaches. *American Journal of Psychotherapy, 54*(4), 574–579.

Higgins-Biddle, J. C., Babor, T. F., Mullahy, J., Daniels, J., & McRee, B. (1997). Alcohol screening and brief interventions: Where research meets practice. *Connecticut Medicine, 61,* 565–575.

Hingson, R., Scotch, N., Day, N., & Culbert, A. (1980). Recognizing and seeking help for drinking problems. *Journal of Studies on Alcohol, 41,* 1102–1117.

Humphreys, K. (1998, Winter). Can addiction-related self-help/mutual aid groups lower demand for professional substance abuse treatment? *Social Policy, 29*(2), 13–17.

Kann, L. (2001). Commentary. *Journal of Drug Issues, 31*(3), 725–727.

Kirchner, J. E., Booth, B. M., Owen, R. R., Lancaster, A. E., & Smith, G. R. (2000, August). Predictors of patient entry into alcohol treatment after initial diagnosis. *Journal of Behavioral Health Services & Research, 27*(3), 339–347.

Kuperman, S., Schlosser, S. S., Kramer, J. R., Bucholz, K., Hesselbrock, V., Reich, T., et al. (2001, April). Risk domains associated with adolescent alcohol dependence diagnosis. *Addiction, 96*(4), 629–637.

Leigh, G., Ogborne, A. C., & Cleland, P. (1984). Factors associated with patient dropout from an outpatient alcoholism treatment service. *Journal of Studies on Alcohol, 45,* 359–362.

Lennox, R. D., & Mansfield, A. J. (2001, May). A latent variable model of evidence-based quality improvement for substance abuse treatment. *Journal of Behavioral Health Services & Research, 28*(2), 164–177.

Liberto, J. G., & Oslin, D. W. (1995). Early versus late onset of alcoholism in the elderly. *International Journal of Addiction, 30*(13–14), 1799–1818.

Lu, M., & McGuire, T. G. (2002). The productivity of outpatient treatment for substance abuse. *Journal of Human Resources, 37*(2), 309–335.

Menninger, J. A. (2002, Spring). Source assessment and treatment of alcoholism and substance-related disorders in the elderly. *Bulletin of the Menninger Clinic, 66*(2), 166–184.

Miller, K. E. (2001). Can two questions screen for alcohol and substance abuse? *American Family Physician, 64,* 1247.

Miller, W. R., & Rollnick, S. (1991). Motivational interviewing: Preparing people to change addictive behavior. New York: Guilford Press.

Miller, W. R., & Sanchez, V. C. (1994). Motivating young adults for treatment and lifestyle change. In G. S. Howard & P. E. Nathan (Eds.), *Alcohol use and misuse by young adults* (pp. 55–81). Notre Dame, IN: University of Notre Dame Press.

Monti, P. M., Colby, S. M., Barnett, N. P., Spirito, A., Rohsenow, D. J., Myers, M., et al. (1999). Brief intervention for harm reduction with alcohol-positive older adolescents in a hospital emergency department. *Journal of Consulting and Clinical Psychology, 67*(6), 989–994.

Moxley, D. P., & Olivia, G. (2001). Strengths-based recovery practice in chemical dependency: A transperson perspective. *Families in Society, 82*(3), 251–262.

National Institute of Alcohol Abuse and Alcoholism. (2000). NIAAA *Alcohol Alert* Publication No. 49. Bethesda, MD: Author.

National Institute on Drug Abuse. (1999). *Principles of drug addiction treatment: A research-based guide.* NIH publication 99–4180. Rockville, MD: Author.

Ouimette, P. C., Finney, J. W., & Moos, R. H. (1997). Twelve-step and cognitive-behavioral treatment for substance abuse: A comparison of treatment effectiveness. *Journal of Consulting and Clinical Psychology, 65*(2), 230–240.

Peele, S. (1989). *The diseasing of America: Addiction treatment out of control.* Lexington, MA: Lexington Books.

Pennington, H., Butler, R., & Eagger, S. (2000, May). The assessment of patients with alcohol disorders by an old age psychiatric service. *Aging & Mental Health, 4*(2), 182–185.

Rees, D. W. (1986). Changing patients' health beliefs to improve compliance with alcoholism treatment: A controlled trial. *Journal of Studies on Alcohol, 47,* 436–439.

Roizen, R., Cahalan, D., Lambert, E., Wiebel, W., & Shanks, P. (1978). Spontaneous remission among untreated problem drinkers. In D. Kandel (Ed.), *Longitudinal Research on Drug Use.* Washington, DC: Hemisphere Publishing.

Seligman, M. E. P. (1995). The effectiveness of psychotherapy: The *Consumer Reports* study. *American Psychologist, 50*(12), 965–974.

Snow, M. (1973). Maturing out of narcotic addiction in New York City. *International Journal of the Addictions, 8*(6), 932–938.

Sobell, L., Sobell, M., Toneatto, T., & Leo, G. (1993). What triggers the resolution of alcohol problems without treatment? *Alcoholism: Clinical and Experimental Research, 17*(2), 217–224.

Stall, R., & Biernacki, P. (1989). Spontaneous remission from the problematic use of substances. *International Journal of the Addictions, 21,* 1–23.

Stewart, K. B., & Richards, A. B. (2000). Recognizing and managing your patient's alcohol abuse. *Nursing, 30*(2), 56–60.

Trice, H., & Roman, P. (1970). Delabeling, relabeling, and Alcoholics Anonymous. *Social Problems, 17,* 538–546.

U.S. Department of Health and Human Services. (2000). *Healthy people 2010* (2nd ed., With understanding and improving health and objectives for improving health: 2 vols.). Washington, DC: U.S. Government Printing Office.

Waldorf, D., Reinarman, C., & Murphy, S. (1991). *Cocaine changes: The experience of using and quitting.* Philadelphia: Temple University Press.

Walitzer, K. S., Dermen, K. H., & Connors, G. J. (1999). Strategies for preparing clients for treatment: A review. *Behavior Modification, 23,* 129–151.

Winick, C. (1962). Maturing out of narcotic addiction. *Bulletin on Narcotics, 6,* 1.

Evidence-Based Practice With Mental Illness and Severe Mood Disorders

11

As this chapter will indicate, severe mood disorders and a range of mental illnesses have a significant impact on Americans. The prevalence of mood disorders and a range of mental illnesses in America will be noted, definitions will be provided, and best evidence of treatment effectiveness will be discussed. Although mood disorders are typically not considered to have the severity of schizophrenia, both depression and bipolar disorder may have psychotic features and are therefore included in this chapter. Best evidence of treatment effectiveness is not always in agreement because of methodological and theoretical issues that affect comparison among research studies. A case study will explore the symptoms, progression, treatment, and prognosis of a more severe form of mental illness. Questions about chronicity and the stigma attached to mental illness will also be discussed.

The Extent and Impact of Mental Illness

Data from the Centers for Disease Control (CDC, 1991) indicate that suicide, often linked to major depression, is the third leading cause of death among people ages 15–24 and the fourth leading cause of death among children ages 10–14. The incidence of suicide attempts among older adolescents is estimated at between 7% and 9% (CDC, 1991). Druss et al. (2000) report that about 3 million Americans have an emotional condition that affects their ability to work or to seek educational opportunities. Approximately 1% of the population develop schizophrenia during their lifetimes and more than

2 million Americans suffer from the illness in a given year. Although schizophrenia affects men and women with equal frequency, the disorder often appears earlier in men than in women, usually in the late teens or early twenties for men and in the twenties to early thirties for women (NIMH, 1999). NIMH (2001) estimates that more than 2 million Americans experience the symptoms of bipolar disorder each year, which include distorted views and thoughts, a lack of will to live, labile emotions that often seem out of control, and difficulties with cognition (Jamison, 1995).

A recent Canadian study using data from the National Population Health Survey indicates that the highest rates of first onset of depression (1.4%–9.1% of the population) occur among young adults (aged 12–24), and lower rates (1.3%–1.8%) occur among people 65 years of age or older (Patten, 2000). Fifteen percent of clients diagnosed with mood disorders commit suicide and fully two thirds of all suicides are preceded by episodes of depression (Bostwick & Pankratz, 2000). Clients with depressive disorders have 3 times the number of sick days in the month before the illness was diagnosed than coworkers who weren't depressed (Parikh, Wasylenki, Goerung, & Wong, 1996). Depression is the primary reason for disability and death among people ages 18–44 years (Murray & Lopez, 1997). Pratt et al. (1996) followed 1,551 study subjects without a history of heart disease for 13 years. Subjects with major depressions were 4.5 times more likely to have serious heart attacks than those without major episodes of depression.

Markowitz (1998) found that people with mental illness are "more likely to be unemployed, have less income, experience a diminished sense of self, and have fewer social supports" (p. 335). According to Markowitz, much of the reason for this finding may be a function of the stigma attached to mental illness: "Mentally ill persons may expect and experience rejection in part because they think less of themselves, have limited social opportunities and resources, and because of the severity of their illness" (p. 343). Markowitz also suggests that clients with histories of mental illness anticipate rejection and failure because they've experienced social and employment-related discrimination. Understandably, this compounds feelings of low self-worth and depression (Markowitz, 1998). Although the quality of life in America has dramatically improved over the past 50 years, Seligman (2002) reports that depression rates are 10 times higher now and life satisfaction rates are down substantially, suggesting widespread levels of unhappiness, depression, and more serious emotional disorders.

Definitions of Mental Illness and Mood Disorders

MENTAL ILLNESS

This category of serious emotional problems includes the various forms of schizophrenia and other, more nonspecific, mental disorders characterized by hallucinations, disorganized speech and thought processes, grossly disorganized behavior including catatonia, flattened affect, and other symptoms that may so impair the client that meaningful work, relationships, and self-care are seriously affected (APA, 1994, p. 285).

MOOD DISORDERS

The DSM-IV (APA, 1994) indicates that mood disorders include major depressive disorders, lasting 2 weeks or more with evidence of symptoms of depression; dysthymic disorders, in which depression has lasted more than 2 years with more depressed days than nondepressed days; bipolar disorders, where both depression and mania may be evident at a severe level and where one or both symptoms may cycle back and forth; and cyclothymic disorders, where depression and mania cycle back and forth, but not at the same levels associated with bipolar disorder (AMA, 1994, p. 317). The common bond among these various disorders is an impact on mood that suggests intermittent to long-term depression, or cycling between very high manic stages and very severe depressions. It is also possible that some mood disorders may have psychotic features, as is sometimes the case with bipolar disorder or very severe depressions. However, this is often not evident, and psychosis is only suggested for those clients demonstrating psychotic behavior and not by the DSM-IV term mood disorders.

Treatment Effectiveness Research

TREATMENT EFFECTIVENESS

In a study of treatment attrition for outpatient mental health–related problems, Edlund et al. (2002) found an attrition rate of 10% by the 5th visit, 18% by the 10th visit, and 20% by the 25th visit. Factors influencing attrition included concerns about treatment effectiveness and discomfort with the mental health treatment process. In explaining high attrition rates, Edlund et al. write, "A large proportion of respondents believed that mental health treatments are not effective. Patients who held such a belief were significantly more likely to drop out of treatment" (p. 850). The authors suggest that, to counteract negative client perceptions of treatment, clinicians should help clients understand the effectiveness of mental health treatments. One of the by-products of a negative view of mental health services is client discomfort. The authors found that clients who felt uncomfortable with mental health services because of the stigma they attached to mental illness were also more likely to drop out of treatment than patients who reported being comfortable.

Manfred-Gilham, Sales, and Koeske (2002) report that clients whose mental health workers prepared them for realistic vocational and community barriers were more likely to continue on with their treatment regimens. The authors write, "We have some evidence from Kazdin et al. (1997) that therapists' perceptions of barriers predicted client treatment continuation more strongly than did the client's own self-report" (p. 220). Manfred-Gilham et al. (2002) also point out that a strong relationship exists between the help provided by mental health workers to deal with social and vocational barriers and the client's ability to resolve those barriers.

In a computerized literature search to determine the effectiveness of social skills training with the mentally ill (also called "psychosocial interventions" in the literature), Bustillo, Lauriello, Keith, and Samuel (2001) found no evidence that it prevented rehospitalization, relapse into psychotic behavior, worsening of psychopathology, or that it improved employment status. However, employment programs that placed and trained clients appeared to help clients obtain competitive employment.

In a very negative view of treatment effectiveness with severely depressed clients, O'Connor (2001) says that most depressed people receive care that is "superficial, inadequate, and based on false information" (p. 507). He also notes that close examination of most treatments for severe depression suggests that they are inadequate (Mueller et al., 1999; Solomon et al., 2000) and that most assumptions about the treatment of depression turn out to be untrue. Those assumptions include the belief that newer antidepressants are effective, that cognitive psychotherapy helps most patients, and that most patients can recover from an episode of depression without lasting damage (O'Connor, 2001, p. 507).

Sheldon and Freemantle (1993) reviewed 12 randomized controlled trials that compared either drug treatment with no other active treatment or drug treatment with a placebo. The review found evidence that a range of drug treatments were effective in the treatment of major depressive episodes but found little evidence supporting the effectiveness of drug treatments for less severe forms of depression. The strongest predictor of a positive response to drug treatment was the severity of the depressive episode. In the majority of cases, major depression resolved itself with treatment, but 12%–15% of the patients with the condition had symptoms for 2 years or more, even while on medication (Scott, 1988; Keller et al., 1992). Relapse is also a serious problem in severe depressions, although continued treatment for several months after the symptoms have begun appears to reduce the amount and severity of relapse (Old Age Depression Interest Group, 1993; Doogan & Caillard, 1992; Prien & Kupfer, 1986).

In a more recent review of the literature, Remick (2002) found psychotherapy to be as effective as antidepressants in treating mild to moderate depressions and dysthymic disorders. The author found little support for a commonly held belief that a combination of drug treatment and psychotherapy was more effective than the use of either approach alone.

Cognitive-behavioral therapy and interpersonal therapy appeared to be the most effective psychotherapy approaches with mild to moderate depressions, requiring 8–16 weeks for maximum benefit (Remick, 2002, p. 1260).

Stark, Rouse, and Livingston (1991) compared cognitive-behavioral therapy with nondirective, supportive therapy in the treatment of highly depressed children. Following the end of treatment and 7 months post-treatment, children receiving cognitive-behavioral therapy had fewer depressive symptoms in interviews and on the Children's Depression Inventory than children receiving supportive treatment. Brent et al. (1997) obtained the same results using cognitive-behavioral therapy with adolescents. In work with depressed adults, however, the positive impact of cognitive-behavioral therapy was not observed (Elkin et al., 1989). Chambless and Ollendick (2001) found five studies showing a certain amount of improvement in depressed adults receiving cognitive-behavioral therapy. One study they report on, by Peterson and Halstead (1998), used cognitive-behavioral therapy in an abbreviated group therapy form in 6 sessions versus the typical 20 sessions. The average reduction in depressive symptoms after 6 sessions was 37%, although the degree of gain made and the length of follow-up were not described. Blatt, Zuroff, Bondi, and Sanislow (2000) compared the effectiveness of cognitive-behavioral therapy and interpersonal therapies with antidepressants and clinical management, and then with a placebo and clinical management. They found no differences among treatments at posttest, but after 18 months of follow-up, both groups receiving psychotherapy rated their life adjustment significantly better than clients receiving only medication or a placebo.

Writing about the treatment of severe depression, O'Connor (2001) believes that we often fail to recognize that what keeps people depressed is their own view of their depression as ongoing, untreatable, and hopeless. In time, these cognitive definitions of their depression become self-definitions that reinforce the depression and keep it from improving. To help his patients cope with their depressions, O'Connor provides them with "aphorisms" about depression that, he believes, serve as a way of changing long-held beliefs about their depression and about themselves. Several examples of O'Connor's aphorisms are: (a) "If I change what I do, I can change how I feel"; (b) "Change can come from anywhere"; and (c) "I am more than my depression" (p. 517). These aphorisms are "assertions about the nature of depression and recovery from it, which help patients move toward taking an active role in questioning how the condition affects them" (p. 507). O'Connor believes that "aphorisms [are] statements that perform an action simply by being spoken" (p. 512).

Powell, Yeaton, Hill, and Silk (2001) studied the effectiveness of treatment with clients experiencing long-term mood disorders. Their conclusion was that self-help groups are very important providers of positive management of mood disorders. "Social support (information, encouragement, and advocacy) provided in a self-help context may be especially effective because it is offered by people who have experienced (and may be still experiencing) the illness" (p. 9). In considering sociodemographic issues as predictors of the ability to cope with mood disorders, the researchers failed to find any specific indicator other than the level of education, which the authors believe is an important aspect of dealing with the disorder. Surprisingly, daily functioning was inversely related to the number of outpatient contacts suggesting, according to the authors, that as people improve, they see less need for professional help. Support from families and friends also failed to predict outcomes.

Writing about early detection and treatment of severe mood disorders in children and adolescents, Duffy (2000) suggests several important predictors of mood disorders:

> A family history of major affective disorder is the strongest, most reliable risk factor for a major affective illness. Other factors associated with affective disorders include female sex (risk factor for unipolar illnesses), severe life events and disappointments, family dysfunction, poor parental care, early adversity, and personality traits.
>
> Based on the current state of knowledge, emphasis on identifying and treating mood disorders as early as possible in the course and particularly early-onset (child and adolescent) cases and youngsters at high risk (given a parent with a major mood disorder) is likely to be an effective strategy for reducing the burden of illness on both the individual and society. (p. 345)

Duffy (2000) also reports that there is beginning evidence that brief, family-based psychoeducational interventions decrease the negative impact of parental mood disorders on children and improve family functioning in mood-disordered children. Individual treatment and family psychoeducational interventions in adult bipolar patients often decrease relapse rates and improve overall family functioning. Although early identification of children at risk of mood disorders is necessary, "the most effective strategy for reducing the burden of illness on individuals and society is not clear" (p. 346). However, the serious impact of mood disorders on individuals and their families and the high risk of suicide justify a need to develop new and more effective interventions. In the meantime, early interventions that utilize education, identification of family members at risk, and family interventions may decrease the seriousness of the condition and reduce fears and misconceptions among family members. Harrington and Clark (1998) indicate that early intervention through the use of appropriate medications and mood disorder therapies may actually reduce the severity and recurrence of adolescent mood disorders.

If these discrepancies in findings are confusing to the reader, it should be pointed out that in their review of effective approaches for treatment of depression and other emotional states, Chambless and Ollendick (2001) explain that studies often have different goals; that research controls vary;

that it's difficult to make certain whether the treatment group received exactly what the researchers had intended it to receive; that different psychological instruments are used to test improvement rates, which makes comparison between studies difficult; and that therapists have a different impact on clients even though they may be using the same therapeutic approach. These and other issues often make it difficult to determine treatment effectiveness when many studies are compared to one another, and may help explain discrepancies in findings.

CASEMANGEMENT

One widely accepted approach to the treatment of mental illness is the use of casemanagement, an approach that is usually associated with "case identification and outreach, assessment and service planning, service linkage, monitoring of service delivery, and advocacy" (Rubinbach, 1992, p. 139). The purpose of casemanagement is to provide a complete range of services to clients with persistent and severe mental illness and to "bind" the case-manager to the client and the community by assuring both groups that all services needed by the client will be delivered in a timely, effective, and coordinated manner. In a study of the published articles on the effectiveness of casemanagement in work with the mentally ill, Rubinbach notes a number of methodological problems that limit the validity of the findings:

> Do the foregoing studies justify current claims that case management has been shown to be effective with seriously mentally ill individuals? These studies' mixed results and the uneven quality of their research designs leave plenty of room for cognitive dissonance factors to influence different reviewers to draw different conclusions. In this reviewer's interpretation, the answer is no. (Rubinbach, 1992, p. 145)

There are many reasons for the lack of evidence for casemanagement's effectiveness, some of them methodological, and many of them organizational. To begin with, it is very difficult to find agreement on what constitutes successful treatment. As Rubinbach (1992) points out in his article, using rehospitalization as a measure of effectiveness may not be a useful indicator of success. Many programs fail to provide funding for rehospitalization and, with the advent of managed care, there is often a substantial monetary penalty for hospitalizing patients. Casemanagement agencies working with the mentally ill may have capitation limits on what will be paid for a client's treatment needs. Keeping mentally ill patients out of hospitals, even though they may badly need the services, is one of the new realities of fee-for-service delivery systems. Consequently, using rehospitalization as a measure of effectiveness is very likely to provide incorrect and misleading data. The client may be profoundly ill and dysfunctional yet still be living in a group home where his or her mental illness is dealt with by overmedication and bed rest, although social functioning may be grossly impaired. Clients attending day programs, in which casemanagement services are offered under managed care, are sometimes considered safety concerns, and police are often the only source of services following the recurrence of severe symptoms that may include harassment to others, violent behavior, substance abuse, and homelessness. Again, managed care provides a substantial monetary penalty for clients taken from group homes and placed in hospitals, and serious and dangerous symptoms may be ignored while trying to keep clients from being hospitalized.

Another measure often used to determine casemanagement's effectiveness, client well-being, is at best a vague measure of treatment effectiveness and often suffers from the rater's knowledge that a study is being done or that future funding will be based on positive change in the client's social functioning. Finally, definitions of casemangement vary greatly among researchers. A unified definition needs to be applied to further research efforts to determine treatment effectiveness and best evidence.

Organizational limitations place severe stress on the casemanagement model. Case-managers working with the mentally ill often work in agencies under extreme limitations because of budget constraints, bureaucratic inefficiencies, lack of trained personnel, high rates of worker turnover, and a lack of consistent theoretical evidence that what case-managers do actually helps clients. Coordinating services to clients often becomes clerical work rather than the sophisticated activities casemangement demands. Heavy caseloads may limit the worker's opportunity to work closely with clients. It is not unusual for clients to begin decompensating well before the case-manager is aware that this is happening. Since the client's emotional state is often judged by others (group home owners, family members, or medical staff), direct feedback about the client's condition may be inaccurate, insufficient, or not timely. Even when the client's decomposition is directly observed by the case-manager, it may be difficult to receive immediate medical care or a change in medical regimens without a costly hospital stay or frequent contact with a staff psychiatrist.

Although the evidence on the effectiveness of casemanagement is still under review and more empirical data are necessary to provide acceptable best evidence, Rubinbach (1992) notes that several treatment approaches, in conjunction with pharmacotherapy, have developed a rigorous methodological base that supports their use in practice with the mentally ill. They include family psychoeducation and management, social and vocational skills training, and psychosocial rehabilitation centers (Hogarty, 1989; Rubin, 1986, 1989). Perhaps these approaches can be used in more effective ways in conjunction with casemangement services to help clients with recurring problems of mental illness.

IS MENTAL ILLNESS A CHRONIC CONDITION?

One commonly held belief is that most clients with a diagnosis of some form of mental illness will very likely suffer throughout their life span with chronic, reoccurring episodes of mental illness. However, Carpenter (2002) reports that most people with a diagnosis of schizophrenia or other serious mental illnesses experience "either complete or significant remission of symptoms, and work, have relationships, and otherwise engage in a challenging and fulfilling life" (p. 89). In a study of more than 500 adults diagnosed with schizophrenia, Huber, Gross, and Schuttler (1975) found that greater than 20% of the sample experienced complete remission and greater than 40% experienced significant remission of symptoms. In a 40-year follow-up study, Tsuang, Woolson, and Fleming (1979) found that 46% of those diagnosed with schizophrenia had no symptoms or had only nonincapacitating symptoms. The Vermont Longitudinal Study (Harding, Brooks, Ashikaga, Strauss, & Breier, 1986a, 1986b), a 20- to 25-year follow-up study of former state hospital patients, found that 72% of the people diagnosed with schizophrenia had only slight or no psychiatric symptoms.

Despite these very optimistic findings, Carpenter (2002) believes that chronicity of mental illness is a widely accepted belief in the mental health field and that this pessimistic view of mental illness continues to be communicated to people with psychiatric disabilities and to their families (Kruger, 2000). A pessimistic view of the chronic nature of mental illness "leaves little room for a sense of hope on the part of those labeled with mental illness and, as such, may become a self-fulfilling prophecy" (Carpenter, 2002, p. 89).

THE CONSUMER-SURVIVOR RECOVERY MOVEMENT

One of the positive new approaches to the treatment of mental illness is the consumer-survivor recovery movement. Carpenter (2002) indicates that the consumer-survivor recovery movement believes that people with psychiatric disabilities can and will recover. Recovery is defined as a process of achieving self-management through increased responsibility for one's own recovery. This process is aided by a sense of hope provided by the person's professional, family, and peer support systems. Carpenter notes that "the consumer-survivor definition of the experience of psychiatric disability is as much about recovery from the societal reaction to the disability as it is about recovery from the disability itself" (p. 90). Anthony (1993) believes that recovery from mental illness is aided by what he calls "recovery triggers," which include sharing with patients, families and communities the research indicating that many people with psychiatric problems *do* recover. Another recovery trigger involves information about the availability of services and treatment options such as self-help groups and alternative treatment approaches.

In a further discussion of the consumer-survivor recovery movement, Chinman, Weingarten, Stayner, and Davidson (2001) suggest that a significant way of improving treatment results and decreasing recidivism is through the mutual support of other mentally ill clients. According to the authors, mutual support groups reduce hospitalization rates, the amount of time spent in hospitals, symptoms, and days spent in the hospital. Additionally, they improve quality of life and self-esteem, and contribute to better community reintegration of clients with severe psychiatric disorders (Davidson et al., 1999; Kyrouz & Humphreys, 1996; Reidy, 1992). Mutual support groups provide acceptance, empathy, a feeling of belonging to a community, necessary information to help with the management of social and emotional problems, new ways of coping with problems, and role models who are coping well. Chinman et al. (2001) believe, "Mutual support also operates through the 'helper-therapy' principle that suggests that by helping one another, participants increase their social status and self-esteem (Riessman, 1965)" (p. 220).

Beyond mutual support groups, Chinman et al. (2001) suggest that there is growing evidence that consumer-run services may prove to be very effective in helping clients with mental illnesses (Davidson et al., 1999) because consumer providers are often more empathic than professionals; see client strengths that professionals might miss; are tolerant, flexible, patient, and persistent; and know how to respond to client needs. These skills help create a supportive environment that serves as a catalyst for faster recovery and an earlier return to community life (Dixon, Krauss, & Lehman, 1994; Kaufman, 1995). According to the authors, studies have found that consumer-led casemanagement is as effective as conventional casemanagement. (Felton et al., 1995; Solomon & Draine, 1995).

To determine whether consumer-provided services are as effective as the prior statements would suggest, I met with administrators of consumer-provided services to the mentally ill in the Los Angeles area, whose feedback suggests the need to be cautious. The administrators noted that consumer-providers are often still dysfunctional enough that their services are sometimes provided in an unprofessional way. They also complained of consumer-provider absenteeism, erratic behavior, inability to separate personal issues from the helping roles they'd assumed, irresponsible behavior with clients and staff, arguments with staff that were often less about the need to advocate for clients and more about their own unresolved pathology, and a number of other worrisome behaviors that suggested concern about many of the consumer-providers selected to work in programs providing services to clients with mood disorders and mental illness. One administrator said a bipolar consumer-provider periodically decompensated and become highly seductive during her manic phases. Much of the administrator's time was spent keeping consumer-providers functioning rather than supervising their work with clients. Many of the grants to treat mood disorders and mental illness require consumer-providers or else grant applications are not funded. This caused many agencies to select ill-prepared people, and the supervisors cautioned that careful review and evaluation were highly necessary before someone was selected.

There were also many stories of excellent work by consumer-providers, particularly as board members, in public relations, in public speaking, and in fund raising. There were enough positive stories about beneficial work with clients to suggest that with careful screening and close supervision, consumer-providers were often excellent employees who offered a wise, practical, and empathic service to clients. Of particular note was their ability to find early signs of decompensation in other clients and their understanding of the common medications used to treat mental illness.

Case Study: Spontaneous Remission From Mental Illness

James Becker is a 23-year-old college student who suddenly began showing symptoms of schizophrenia and was diagnosed with schizophrenia, undifferentiated type (DSM-IV Code 295.90, APA, 1994, p. 289). James had no prior history of mental illness and no one in his immediate family had experienced mental illness. James was under a great deal of pressure in preparing for the oral defense of a master's thesis in oceanography. His performance in his orals would determine whether he would be accepted into a prestigious doctoral program, the key to a successful career in his field. James began to experience a feeling of gross disorganization and a strange sense of aloofness from others, described by his friends as severe withdrawal and flat affect. The symptoms grew progressively worse and his major professor sent James to the university counseling center, where the diagnosis of schizophrenia, undifferentiated type was given by a psychiatrist on staff. James was not considered a danger to himself or to others but was unable to continue with his studies. He was placed on antipsychotic medication and was seen in a day program in the community where psychoeducational treatment was offered. As his symptoms worsened, he was sent to a private inpatient facility specializing in the care of the mentally ill, where he stayed for almost 4 months. His symptoms included mild hallucinations, social withdrawal and isolation, and some delusional thinking, in which he described a presence that was about to kill him.

After 3 months in the group facility with general deterioration in his symptoms, James began to show significant signs of improvement. He was able to attend counseling sessions and contribute to the discussion. He interacted well with others and spoke about returning to school. His medication was reduced in strength, and the improvement in his condition continued. Six months after the sudden onset of symptoms, he was able to return to school with no other signs of schizophrenia a year and a half after onset.

DISCUSSION

The psychiatrist who initially treated James at the university counseling center and who followed James after he returned to school said that the original diagnosis had been amended to "single episode of schizophrenia, undifferentiated type, now in full remission" (AMA, 1994, p. 279). Like many diseases, schizophrenia may have an initial acute phase followed by a complete return to normal functioning. The cause of the single episode is difficult to determine. James was asked to comment on his experience. "I don't think I was psychotic," he said. "One day I was walking home from school and I suddenly had the most ominous feeling that I was going to die. It had never happened to me before and it was very frightening. I withdrew from people. Some days I couldn't talk. I was very certain that someone was going to kill me, but I was aware and conscious of everything taking place around me. I don't think I had any hallucinations but maybe I did. It was more that I felt a presence nearby and that it would do me great harm. Maybe I was overstressed from school pressure, but I don't think so. One minute I was fine and the next minute I was scared out of my wits. It took a long time for the fear to go away and for me to be able to talk to anyone. When I began to get better, it seemed to happen all by itself. It was like a cloud had lifted and suddenly I was well again. I doubt if the medication helped and I'm certain that therapy didn't help at all. There were some very kind professionals who were really nice to me, and many wonderful patients who sat with me when I was really frightened, but while I don't think I was psychotic, at the same time I can't tell you why this happened or why I improved. I really don't think it will ever happen to me again, but if it does, I certainly have a better handle on what to do about it."

Commenting further on James's experience, his counseling center psychiatrist said that James was one of many students he had worked with who'd had a spontaneous remission from mental illness. "We still don't know enough about brain chemistry or the reasons for the sudden onset of symptoms of schizophrenia. I'm of the opinion that a combination of life stressors and biochemical conditions interact with one another to cause symptoms that appear to be psychotic. When you talk to patients who have immediate remissions, you hear stories very similar to the one James told. I'm increasingly convinced that, like any opportunistic disease, schizophrenia attacks when the body is least capable of resisting. James was under extreme pressure to do well in his orals. His father is a professor at a prestigious university who has placed considerable pressure on James to succeed. His schoolwork took away any social life, and while he was not abusing drugs, he was using a combination of sleeping pills and Xanax to cope with anxiety. Perhaps this all contributed to his illness, and maybe it didn't. We have a lot to learn about psychosis, but optimism is something we should all have. Many people like James come out of psychotic episodes, are just fine afterward, and never have another psychotic experience. The worst part of the problem is the social stigma. I don't know how many letters I had to write on his behalf before James could return to school. He's a healthy, intelligent young man but the stigma of this one experience will very likely follow him throughout his life. He's already been turned down by a doctoral program that showed so much interest in him before his illness. The real tragedy of mental illness often takes place after the patient is cured. It's an illness full of social stigma that endlessly and needlessly harms people who have every reason to tell the world that they're just fine now."

SUMMARY

This chapter discusses the prevalence of mental illness and mood disorders in America and the often-stigmatizing effect the label of mental illness can have on patients. This stigma frequently inhibits improvement in the condition and may affect employment opportunities and further social and financial possibilities in a person's life. Several treatment approaches to mental illness noted in the chapter suggest that it should be treated as a condition affecting functioning but that the client and loved ones should not be led to think that the condition is permanent or that change isn't possible. A section on best evidence of treatment effectiveness suggests that there is considerable variance in the goals and methodologies of studies on treatment effectiveness but that best evidence is only marginally available. A case study suggested the way in which clients experiencing forms of mental illness may respond to treatment and the possibility of spontaneous remission of symptoms.

Integrative Questions

1. There are suggestions throughout this chapter that the social stigma of mental illness is a more serious long-term problem than the illness itself. Do you believe this is true?

2. Speaking of social stigma, the hospitals that treat mental illness have been portrayed as very dysfunctional places. Do you believe they are any more dysfunctional than hospitals treating patients for physical problems?

3. The initial onset of mental illness appears to differ for men and women. In your opinion, is this caused by biochemical or social and emotional differences between the genders?

4. Mood disorders and schizophrenia are very different illnesses. Do you think the inclusion of each disorder in a chapter on mental illness suggests that both are equally serious and therefore unfairly stigmatizes clients with mood disorders?

5. Do you believe that a spontaneous remission in schizophrenia may be linked to a misdiagnosis of the problem rather than a rapid change in behavior brought about for unknown reasons?

References

American Psychiatric Association. (1994). *Diagnostic and statistical manual of mental disorders* (4th ed.). Washington, DC: Author.

Anthony, W. A. (1993). Recovery from mental illness: The guiding vision of the mental health service system in the 1990's. *Psychosocial Rehabilitation Journal, 16,* 12–23.

Blatt, S. J., Zuroff, D. C., Bondi, C. M., & Sanisolow, C. A., III. (2000). Short and long-term effects of medication and psychotherapy in the brief treatment of depression: Further analyses of data from the NIMH TDCRP. *Psychotherapy Research, 10,* 215–234.

Bostwick, J. M., & Pankratz, V. S. (2000). Affective disorders and suicide risk: A re-examination. *American Journal of Psychiatry, 157,* 1925–1932.

Brent, D. A., Holder, D., Kolko, D., Birmaher, B., Baugher, M., Roth, C., et al. (1997). A clinical psychotherapy trial for adolescent depression comparing cognitive, family, and supportive therapy. *Archives of General Psychiatry, 54*(9), 877–885.

Bustillo, J. R., Lauriello, J. H., Keith, W. P., & Samuel, J. (2001). The psychosocial treatment of schizophrenia: An update. *American Journal of Psychiatry, 158*(2), 163–175.

Carpenter, J. (2002). Mental health recovery paradigm: Implications for social work. *Health & Social Work, 27*(2), 86–94.

Centers for Disease Control. (1991). Attempted suicide among high school students: United States, 1990. *Journal of the American Medical Association, 266,* 1911–1912.

Chambless, D. L., & Ollendick, T. H. (2001). Empirically supported psychological interventions: Controversies and evidence. *Annual Review of Psychology, 52,* 685–716.

Chinman, M. J., Weingarten, R., Stayner, D., & Davidson, L. (2001). Chronicity reconsidered: Improving person-environment fit through a consumer-run service. *Community Mental Health Journal, 37*(3), 215–229.

Davidson, L., Chinman, M., Moos, B., Weingarten, R., Stayner, D. A., & Tebes, J. K. (1999). Peer support among individuals with severe mental illness: A review of the evidence. *Clinical Psychology: Science and Practice, 6,* 165–187.

Dixon, L., Krauss, N., & Lehman, A. L. (1994). Consumers as service providers: The promise and challenge. *Community Mental Health Journal, 30,* 615–625.

Doogan, D. P., & Caillard, V. (1992). Sertraline in the prevention of depression. *British Journal of Psychiatry, 160,* 217–222.

Druss, B. G., Marcus, S. C., Rosenheck, R. A., Olfson, M., Tanielan, T., & Pincus, H. A. (2000). Understanding disability in mental and general medical conditions. *American Journal of Psychiatry, 157*(9), 1485–1491.

Duffy, A. (2000). Toward effective early intervention and prevention strategies for major affective disorders: A review of risk factors. *Canadian Journal of Psychiatry, 45*(4), 340–349.

Edlund, M. J., Wang, P. S., Berglund, P. A., Katz, S., Lin, E., & Kessler, R. C. (2002). Dropping out of mental health treatment: Patterns and predictors among epidemiological survey respondents in the United States and Ontario. *American Journal of Psychiatry, 159*(5), 845–851.

Elkin, I., Shea, T., Watkins, J. T., Imber, S. D., Sotsky, S. M., Collins, J. F., et al. (1989). National Institute of Mental Health Treatment of Depression Collaborative Research Program: General effectiveness of treatments. *Archives of General Psychiatry, 46,* 971–82.

Felton, C. J., Stastny, P., Shern, D., Blanch, A., Donahue, S. A., Knight, E., et al. (1995). Consumers as peer specialists on intensive case management teams: Impact on client outcomes. *Psychiatric Services, 46,* 1037–1044.

Harding, C. M., Brooks, G. W., Ashikaga, T., Strauss, J. S., & Breier, A. (1986a). The Vermont longitudinal study of persons with severe mental illness: I. Methodology, study sample, and overall status 32 years later. *American Journal of Psychiatry, 144,* 718–725.

Harding, C. M., Brooks, G. W., Ashikaga, T., Strauss, J. S., & Breier, A. (1986b). The Vermont longitudinal study of persons with severe mental illness: II. Long-term outcome of subjects who retrospectively met DSM-II criteria for schizophrenia. *American Journal of Psychiatry, 144,* 727–735.

Harrington, R., & Clark, A. (1998). Prevention and early intervention for depression in adolescence and early adult life. *European Archives of Psychiatry in Clinical Neuroscience, 248,* 32–45.

Hogarty, G. E. (1989). Metaanalysis of the effects of practice with the chronically mentally ill: A critique and reappraisal of the literature. *Social Work, 34,* 363–373.

Huber, G., Gross, G., & Schuttler, R. (1975). A long-term follow up study of schizophrenia: Psychiatric course of illness and prognosis. *Acta Psychiatrica Scandinavica, 52,* 49–57.

Jamison, K. R. (1995). *An unquiet mind.* New York: Alfred A. Knopf.

Jimenez, M. A. (1988). Chronicity in mental disorders: Evolution of a concept. *Social Casework, 69,* 627–633.

Kaufman, C. (1995). The self help employment center: Some outcomes from the first year. *Psychosocial Rehabilitation Journal, 18,* 145–162.

Kazdin, A. E., Holland, L., Crowley, M., & Breton, S. (1997). Barriers to treatment participation scale: Evaluation and validation in the context of child outpatient treatment. *Journal of Child Psychology and Psychiatry, 38*(8), 1051–1062.

Keller, M. D., Lavoir, P. W., Mueller, T. I., Endicott, J., Coryell, W., Hirshfeld, R. M., et al. (1992). Time to recovery, chronicity, and levels of psychopathology in major depression. *Archives of General Psychiatry, 49,* 809–816.

Kruger, A. (2000). Schizophrenia: Recovery and hope. *Psychiatric Rehabilitation Journal, 24,* 29–37.

Kyrouz, E., & Humphreys, K. (1996). Do psychiatrically disabled people benefit from participation in self-help/mutual aid organizations? A research review. *The Community Psychologist, 29,* 21–25.

Manfred-Gilham, J. J., Sales, E., & Koeske, G. (2002). Therapist and case manager perceptions of client barriers to treatment participation and use of engagement strategies. *Community Mental Health Journal, 38*(3), 213–221.

Markowitz, F. E. (1998). The effects of stigma on the psychological well-being and life satisfaction of persons with mental illness. *Journal of Health & Social Behavior, 39*(4), 335–347.

Mueller T. I., Leon, A. C., Keller, M. B., Solomon, D. A., Endicott, J., Coryell, W., et al. (1999). Recurrence after recovery from major depressive disorder during 15 years of observational follow-up. *American Journal of Psychiatry, 156,* 1000–1006.

Murray, C. J., & Lopez, A. D. (1997). Alternative projections of mortality and disability by cause 1990–2020: Global burden of disease study. *Lancet, 349,* 1498–1504.

National Institute of Mental Health. (1999). *Schizophrenia.* Publication 99–3517. Bethesda, MD: Author. Retrieved October 13, 2002, from www.nimh.nih.gov/publicat/schizoph.cfm

National Institute of Mental Health. (2001). *Bipolar disorder.* Publication 01–3679. Bethesda, MD: Author. Retrieved October 13, 2002, from www.nimh.nih.gov/publicat/bipolar.cfm#intro

O'Connor, R. (2001). Active treatment of depression. *American Journal of Psychotherapy, 55*(4), 507–530.

Old Age Depression Interest Group. (1993). How long should the elderly take antidepressants? A double blind placebo controlled study of continuation/prophylaxis therapy with dothiepin. *British Journal of Psychiatry, 162,* 175–182.

Parikh, S. V., Wasylenki, D., Goerung, P., & Wong, J. (1996). Mood disorders: Rural/urban differences in prevalence, health care utilization, and disability in Ontario. *Journal of Affective Disorders, 38,* 57–65.

Patten, S. B. (2000). Incidence of major depression in Canada. *Canadian Medical Association Journal, 163,* 714–715.

Peterson, A. L., & Halstead, T. S. (1998). Group cognitive behavior therapy for depression in a community setting: A clinical replication series. *Behavioral Therapy, 29,* 3–18.

Powell, T. J., Yeaton, W., Hill, E. M., & Silk, K. R. (2001). Predictors of psychosocial outcomes for patients with mood disorders. *Psychiatric Rehabilitation Journal, 25*(1), 3–12.

Pratt, L. A., Ford, D. E., Crum, R. M., Armenian, H. K., Gallo, J. J., & Eaton, W. W. (1996). Depression, psychotropic medication, and risk of myocardial infarction: Prospective data from the Baltimore ECA follow-up. *Circulation, 94,* 3123–3129.

Prien, R. F., & Kupfer, D. J. (1986). Continuation drug therapy for major depressive episodes: How long should it be maintained? *American Journal of Psychiatry, 143,* 18–23.

Reidy, A. (1992). Shattering illusions of difference. *Resources, 4,* 3–6.

Remick, R. A. (2002). Diagnosis and management of depression in primary care: A clinical update and review. *Canadian Medical Association Journal, 167*(11), 1253–1261.

Riessman, F. (1965). The helper-therapy principle. *Social Work, 10,* 27–32.

Rubin, A. (1986). Review of current research on chronic mental illness. In A. Rubin & J. Bowker (Eds.), *Studies on chronic mental illness: A new horizon for social work researchers* (pp. 5–28). New York: Council on Social Work Education.

Rubin, A. (1989). Research on the long-term care of mental illness: A challenge and opportunity for social work. In K. E. Davis, R. Harris, R. Farmer, J. Reeves, & F. Segal (Eds.), *Strengthening the scientific base of social work education for services to the long-term seriously mentally ill* (pp. 39–74). Richmond: Virginia Commonwealth University.

Rubinbach, A. (1992). Is case management effective for people with serious mental illness? A research review. *Health & Social Work, 17*(2), 138–150.

Scott, J. (1988). Chronic depression. *British Journal of Psychiatry, 153,* 287–297.

Seligman, M. E. P. (2002). *Authentic happiness: New positive psychology to realize your potential for lasting fulfillment.* New York: Free Press.

Sheldon, T. A., & Freemantle, N. (1993). Examining the effectiveness of treatments for depression. *Journal of Mental Health, 2*(2), 141–157.

Solomon, D. A., Keller, M. B., Leon, A. C., Mueller, T. I., Lavori, P. W., Shea, M. T., et al. (2000). Multiple recurrences of major depressive disorder. *American Journal of Psychiatry, 157,* 229–233.

Solomon, P., & Draine, J. (1995). The efficacy of a consumer case management team: Two year outcomes of a randomized trail. *Journal of Mental Health Administration, 22,* 135–146.

Stark, K., Rouse, L., & Livingston, R. (1991). Treatment of depression during childhood and adolescence: Cognitive-behavioral procedures for the individual and family. In P. C. Kendall (Ed.), *Child and Adolescent Therapy* (pp. 165–206). New York: Guilford.

Tsuang, M. T., Woolson, R. F., & Fleming, M. S. (1979). Long term outcome of major psychoses. *Archives of General Psychiatry, 36,* 1295–1301.

Evidence-Based Practice With Terminal Illness and Bereavement

12

Two serious health-related issues will be discussed in this chapter: terminal illness and prolonged bereavement. Significant personal growth often takes place when people cope with life-threatening illnesses and bereavement. Kubler-Ross (1969/1997) believes that terminal illness frequently leads to life-changing growth. Greenstein and Breitbart (2000) write, "Existentialist thinkers, such as Frankl, view suffering as a potential springboard, both for having a need for meaning and for finding it" (p. 486), and Frankl (1978) writes, "Even facing an ineluctable fate, e.g., an incurable disease, there is still granted to man a chance to fulfill even the deepest possible meaning. What matters, then, is the stand he takes in his predicament . . . the attitude we choose in suffering" (p. 24).

Finn (1999) believes that spirituality becomes an important aspect of terminal illness because it leads to "an unfolding consciousness about the meaning of human existence. Life crises influence this unfolding by stimulating questions about the meaning of existence" (p. 227).

Terminal Illness

Hardwig (2000) reports that terminally ill patients are often unable to deal with unfinished business in their lives because they feel abandoned by friends, family, their bodies, and God. "Many [dying patients] find that the beliefs and values they have lived by no longer seem valid or do not sustain them. These are the ingredients of a spiritual crisis, the stuff of spiritual suffering" (p. 29). Hardwig believes that the medical care system complicates the client's ability to finish unfinished business because many treatment decisions are made without actually consulting the terminally ill patient, and that the use of medication often limits the patient's ability to think clearly. Loved ones may interfere with the patient's need to find closure on important family issues, which may complicate and prolong bereavement. Because families often find it impossible to allow a loved one to die naturally, they may deny the patient's wish to die and prolong life by allowing the use of intrusive life supports and treatments.

While Caffrey (2000) believes in a role for psychotherapy with terminal illness, he thinks that the reduction of anxiety and depression in dying patients (palliative care) is narrow-minded. In comparing palliative care versus help with unfinished meaning-of-life issues, McClain, Rosenfeld, and Breitbart (2003) found that low levels of spirituality in terminally ill patients were highly related to "end-of-life despair, providing a unique contribution to the prediction of hopelessness, desire for hastened death, and suicidal ideation even after controlling for the effect of depressive symptoms and other relevant variables" (p. 1606). The authors report that high levels of spirituality in dying patients lead to hopefulness that results in a more cooperative relation with the treatment team, improved resolution of long-standing emotional problems, and the desire to live longer. As Kubler-Ross (1969/1997) wrote, "We can help them die by trying to help them live" (Caffrey, 2000, p. 519).

Lloyd-Williams (2001) found depression in 25% of the terminally ill patients he has screened and cautions that depression seriously affects the success of medical treatment to prolong life and to help the patient finish important unfinished business. Lloyd-Williams suggests the following treatment strategies with terminally ill patients to treat depression: (a) establish good rapport, (b) diagnose and treat emotional problems, (c) treat underlying organic problems that may be contributing to the depression, (d) differentiate normal sadness and grief from serious depression, (e) provide supportive therapy and reduce the patient's level of isolation from others, (f) provide family treatment and support if called for, and (g) use antidepressants in selective cases.

Blundo (2001) believes that clinicians must make a substantial shift in their work with terminally ill patients in crisis. This shift requires that clinicians engage clients in a highly collaborative dialogue that begins without any preconceived ideas of underlying pathology. Greenstein and Breitbart (2000) report that collaborative relationships with terminally ill patients often result in "patients reordering their priorities, spending more time with family, and experiencing personal growth through the very fact of having had to cope with their traumatic loss or illness" (p. 486).

Commenting on the environment in which terminally ill patients reside, Richman (2000) suggests the need for an empathic and caring approach to terminal illness. Richman reports that a study of empathy found that 40%

of the patients in the study who described their physicians as nonempathic had symptoms of depression, while 27% of the patients describing their caregivers as empathic reported depression. Patients with nonempathic physicians "were more likely to consider euthanasia or doctor-assisted suicide" (p. 485). In a finding that could have implications for the terminally ill, Finn (1999) studied the content of Internet messages sent by people with disabilities. He found that most people using the Internet wanted to discuss their health and to find out about specific issues of treatment and quality of care. Correspondents functioned as a support group by helping one another cope with emotional, medical, and social concerns that included "highly technical descriptions of medications, procedures, and equipment to subjective accounts of treatment experiences. There also was considerable discussion of interpersonal relationship issues such as marital relationships, dating, and sexuality" (p. 228). Since many terminally ill people are homebound, the Internet becomes a significant part of the communicating they do each day. This is particularly true of terminally ill people who also may have difficulty speaking or hearing.

Case Study: Evidence-Based Practice With Terminal Illness

John Pierson is a 46-year-old professor of engineering who has been diagnosed with advanced testicular cancer. John had been experiencing discomfort and pain for more than a year but failed to seek medical help until he began noticing blood in his urine. The cancer metastasized quickly and has moved into a number of organs in his body. The doctor gives him less than a year to live. He has had surgery to remove both testicles and is on chemotherapy. Neither procedure seems to be helping. John is depressed and ill from the chemotherapy treatments. He is seriously thinking of patient-assisted suicide. His personal physician has recommended that John seek help for the depression, but John has been too depressed and weak to even consider it. A hospital social worker dropped by his room during one of his chemotherapy treatments and listened to John talk about the "mess" he'd made of his life and how his early death was just another example of "what a loser I am."

Talking to the social worker seemed strangely comforting, and when she suggested that they continue talking the next day, uncharacteristically, John agreed. John hates the feminizing way helping professionals make him feel and described what it felt like going to a marital counselor when his marriage fell apart. "I felt like someone lopped off my balls, which is pretty funny because that's exactly what's happened to me now." The social worker was much more understanding than the marital counselor and John felt she wasn't going to make him feel weak or unmanly. As John continued seeing the worker on a biweekly basis, he shared his life disappointments with her. She listened and observed that he was being very hard on himself because she felt that John had done amazing things in his life. John wasn't so sure he agreed and wondered if the worker was just trying to placate him as he moved toward death. The worker assured him that she didn't believe placating ever worked, and it certainly wouldn't work with a highly intelligent man like John. As John thought about their conversations, he began to realize that he'd been successful in many small and large ways but that an inner voice, the voice of his father, kept insisting that he'd been a failure. Gradually, the inner voice changed and John felt that he was beginning to see what the worker meant. He also felt better physically, although his health was declining and death was imminent.

John decided that he would return to teaching even if he didn't make it through the semester. He felt he would be a much more considerate teacher than he had been before his illness. He also decided to talk to everyone with whom he had stopped talking because of real or imagined conflicts. This included many colleagues and family members who, he thought, had hurt him over the years. As John began to talk to old friends and members of his family, he felt elated at being able to resolve old hurts before he died. The people he spoke to felt the same way and said they'd missed John and were happy to have him back in their lives.

John made it through the semester and, with a good deal of help from his doctors, through the next semester. By the time death was only days away, John had developed a support network that consisted of formerly estranged friends, family members, former students, and the terminally ill people he'd met in the hospital during his treatment. Before he passed away, John told the worker, "You saved my life. I was full of bile before we started talking and now I feel a strange sort of happiness and contentment. I think I've made a difference in people's lives the past year. I think I lived longer because I was able to get rid of a lot of the toxic feelings I had inside. You always treated me with respect and you acknowledged my intelligence. It made me want to do as much for myself and for others as possible. I'll leave this world, but a lot of who I am will stay on. I owe a lot to you for helping me put my anger to constructive use. And sure, nobody wants to die while they're still young, but if it happens, you make the best of it and you try and touch other people in some way. Feeling so positive about myself helped me live 6 months longer and it gave me more time to make up with people I love. Thank you for the gift of life. Every day I lived beyond what the doctors said was a gift from God."

In describing her work with John, the worker said, "Like many dying patients, John was very angry. He had his mind set on suicide because of the pain he was in and because he felt so helpless. He'd always thought he had control over his life and now, for once, he had no control at all. Helping him see his strengths, respecting his anger, encouraging his need to finish unfinished business, and watching his transformation from an angry and resentful person to a loving and kind person has been a very special experience for me. I see it so often that when people search for endings that include resolving old conflicts, they live longer, happier, and more pain-free lives. While death is never pleasant, I think people like John die peacefully.

"One of the main helping approaches I used with John was behavioral charting. We found several articles in the literature about people who had dealt with serious disabilities by charting their progress each day during their physical rehabilitation and then during their jobs and personal lives. We devised goal attainment scales with realistic expectations. Given John's engineering background, he liked the idea that he could assist his treatment by maintaining good health habits and that diet and exercise might have a very positive impact on prolonging his life. He created an elaborate chart that measured a number of different variables such as calorie and fat intake, sleep, how long it took to dress and shower, fatigue at certain hours of the day, and the times when he needed to rest. He could see that, even though his condition was terminal, he actually felt better and functioned better than he had at the beginning of the charting.

"The anticipation of meeting goals had a very positive impact on him physically and emotionally. He gained weight, he enjoyed the taste of food where before he hardly noticed what he ate, and his teaching, which he evaluated after every class, was far better than it had been before his illness was diagnosed. He put time and energy into it, while before his illness was diagnosed, he had become cynical and dismissive about teaching. The charting also helped him understand how the illness was affecting him. He knew that mornings were his best time and arranged his schedule to teach in the morning. He found that he sometimes became depressed at night and decided that meeting friends and family for dinner helped lessen his depression. The end result was not only a happier and more fulfilled person, but someone who actually lived, worked, and enjoyed life a year longer than the physicians had expected. I see real value in helping terminally ill people, and I'm certain his loved ones, although saddened by his death, had a much more gentle and positive bereavement than they would have had without treatment. And I forgot to mention that he finished a book he'd been trying to write for years before he died. It's become a well-selling book; its proceeds go to his family and to several charities he supported. These are all significant achievements and they hopefully point out the benefits of psychologically treating the terminally ill. We shouldn't deny them the opportunity to grow and expand any more than we would clients with other types of problems. In John's view, he grew more in the last year of life than he had in the previous twenty."

JOHN'S BEHAVIORAL CHART

The following represent a partial list of the more than 40 goals John developed for his behavioral chart.

1. Bring his weight back to his prediagnosed state. He achieved 80% of the goal but the chemotherapy treatments made him ill and it was sometimes difficult for him to eat regularly.

2. Walk at least 1 mile a day when not hospitalized. He surpassed this goal by averaging 2 miles a day.

3. Improve his teaching from an average student rating he'd regularly received of 2.5 on a 5-point scale to 4.0. He surpassed this goal when his last set of classes was evaluated at a 4.8.

4. Improve sleeping from an average of 2 hours a night to at least 6 hours. Because the pain often kept him awake, he slept an average of 5 hours a night but napped in the afternoon for another hour.

5. Have dinner or attend a social or family event at least twice a week. He surpassed this goal by increasing social activities from less than once a week to five times a week.

6. Use biofeedback and other behavioral techniques to reduce pain and dependence on painkillers. At the start of the charting, John was averaging eight Vicodin pills a day. When he entered the hospital the final time before he died, he was taking only two pills for very intense pain.

7. Use positive feedback and supportive statements with friends, family, students and treatment staff. John went from no supportive or positive statements (most were neutral or negative) to more than 40 positive statements a day. Examples included words and phrases, such as "thanks," "that was really helpful," "well done," and "I really appreciate what you did for me." Neutral statements were silence, and negative statements included statements John typically used to make including "Stop being such an incompetent jerk," "When are you going to learn to do things right?" and "How can anyone so stupid do this kind of work?"

8. Work on his book. Although he hadn't written in 2 years, John started writing 2 hours each day. With minimal help from his students with references and editing, the book went from a very muddled half-done book to a completed and well-received book in 1 year.

9. Finish unfinished business. John made a long list of people he wanted to apologize to for past hurts and misunderstandings or simply to reconnect with them because he'd missed their company. John had been very reclusive before treatment but saw everyone on his list at least once and sometimes more before he died. He added names when it became apparent he would complete the list fairly easily.

10. Read a serious book, see a serious play or film, and/or attend plays, musicals, and lectures at least once a week. He went from doing none of these things to attending many cultural activities at least three or four times a week, often with friends and family.

11. Make an attempt to involve himself in the civic life of the community. John was selected to be an unpaid consultant to the city's engineering department. Before his illness, he had never involved himself in civic activities.

12. Try to involve himself in the religion he'd turned away from when he began to sour on life. This was a less successful activity, but he did attend most Sunday services. Although they didn't move him very much, he liked meeting friends and neighbors and joining them for meals following services.

Bereavement

Balk (1999) writes that bereavement is the loss of a significant person in one's life that can result in long-lasting physical and emotional problems, including fear and anger, sleeping disturbances, substance abuse, cognitive difficulties, and uncharacteristic risk-taking that may significantly affect relationships with others. Jacobs and Prigerson (2000) warn that bereavement sometimes develops into a complicated or prolonged grief lasting more than a year. The symptoms of complicated grief include intrusive thoughts about the deceased, numbness, disbelief that a loved one has passed away, feelings of confusion, and a diminished sense of security. Prolonged grief may be unresponsive to interpersonal therapy or to the use of antidepressants.

Stroebe (2001) points out a number of problems with the grief work usually done to treat prolonged bereavement by suggesting that there is limited empirical evidence that resolving grief is a more effective process than letting it resolve naturally. Stroebe believes that resolving prolonged bereavement is complicated by the numerous and different ways of grief resolution prescribed by cultures, religions, genders, and socioeconomic groups, and writes, "There is no convincing evidence that other cultural prescriptions are less conducive to adaptation than those of our own" (p. 854). Stroebe is also concerned that traditional treatment for grief seems to be primarily concerned about complicated grief and lacks precise definitions useful for research studies so that the researcher must ask, "What is being worked through? In what way?" (p. 855). In trying to better understand prolonged grief, Stroebe (2001) suggests the need to study the following issues in more detail:

1. What are the coping skills that allow some people to cope with loss while others don't?

2. What are the differences between normal and prolonged grief?

3. What are the primary reasons that some people resolve their grief in natural ways although others experience complicated and prolonged bereavements?

4. Is an existential approach to grief work, where meaning-of-life issues are dealt with, any more effective than focusing on removal of grief-related symptoms?

5. Do those who resolve their grief naturally and in a normal period of time experience their grief later and, if so, is it a more severe grief than that of those who experience prolonged grief?

BEST EVIDENCE FOR GRIEF WORK

Piper, Ogrodniczuk, Joyce, and McCallum (2002) studied the relationship between the expression of positive affect in group therapy and favorable treatment outcomes for complicated (long-lasting) grief. The authors found a strong positive correlation between these two variables in a number of therapy groups studied. The authors believe that positive affect (smiles, nods in agreement, sympathetic looks) conveys optimism in the person and has a positive effect on others in the group. The authors also found that positive affect correlates well with a cooperative attitude and a desire by clients to do the work necessary to resolve the complicated and traumatic grief they were experiencing. This was true regardless of the type of treatment that was offered, and no difference was seen in the effectiveness of cognitive-behavioral approaches or interpersonal approaches. Client affect rather than the approach used was the overriding factor in successful resolution of prolonged grief, according to the authors.

Kendall (1994) found cognitive-behavioral therapy to be effective with children suffering from separation anxiety after the death of a loved one. The author reports that treated children had reduced fears, less anxiety, better social skills, and lower scores on depression scales. These gains continued in follow-up a year after the end of treatment. The author is uncertain if this same finding would be applicable to adults suffering from prolonged grief.

Jacobs and Prigerson (2000) report that self-help groups have been an effective adjunct treatment to professional therapy by "offering the inculcation of hope, the development of understanding, social supports, a source of normalization or universalization, and a setting to learn and practice new coping skills" (p. 487). Raphael (1977) studied a 3-month psychodynamically oriented intervention for high-risk, acutely traumatized widows during the first stages of grief. The author defined high risk as the lack of support by a social network, the suddenness or unexpected nature of the death, high levels of anger and guilt, ambivalent feelings about the marital relationship, and the presence of other life crises related to or predating the death of a spouse. The predating life crises were often financial, work-related, and involved children, substance abuse in the spouse of the widow, or marital infidelity. When compared to the control group, the treatment group had better general health, less anxiety and depression, and fewer somatic symptoms. Marmar, Horowitz, Weiss, Wilner, and Kaltreider (1988) compared brief psychodynamic therapy to a self-help group and found that both groups experienced diminished stress and improved social functioning. However, improvement in grief-related symptoms began at the end of treatment and continued on thereafter, making the researchers wonder if the improvement was caused by the treatment or whether it would have taken place in time, with or without treatment.

Sireling, Cohen, and Marks (1988) compared "guided mourning" with a control group instructed to avoid cues that might bring about memories of their grief. The treated group had a reduction in distress and physical problems related to their grief, which was maintained for up to 9 months in follow-up studies. Kleber and Brom (1987) successfully used exposure and relaxation treatment, hypnosis, and brief psychodynamic therapy in clients experiencing prolonged grief of more than 5 years and noted sustained improvement of symptoms in follow-up studies. The authors found that low-income clients benefited more from behavioral approaches than from psychodynamic therapy.

Because they believe that traumatic grief should be considered a separate diagnostic category because of its unique set of symptoms, Jacobs and Prigerson (2000) call for the development of a specific therapy for the treatment of grief. By specific therapy they suggest one that "focuses on separation distress and relevant elements of traumatic distress and that addresses several tasks (such as educating about the nature of these types of distress), helps individuals to cope with the distress, and mitigates the distress using a variety of strategies" (p. 491).

To help provide diagnostic guidance for the assessment of prolonged grief, Jacobs and Prigerson (2000, p. 496) suggest the following symptoms lasting more than 2 months and having significant negative impact on social functioning: (a) frequent attempts not to remember the deceased; (b) feelings of hopelessness, meaningless, and futility; (c) a sense of emotional detachment and numbness; (d) feelings of shock; (e) difficulty accepting the death of a loved one; (f) difficulty imagining life without the presence of the deceased; (g) a lost sense of security; (h) assuming the physical and emotional symptoms of the deceased person including their negative behaviors; and (i) considerable signs of anger and bitterness toward the deceased.

Case Study: Evidence-Based Practice With Prolonged Grief

Edna Stern is a 47-year-old mother of three children, ages 17, 14, and 10. Edna's husband, Frank, suddenly passed away following a terminal heart attack. Frank was obsessed with good health and worked out daily, often in preference to spending time with his family. Frank thought he was experiencing chest pains in the middle of the night. As is sometimes the case with heart attack victims in extreme denial, he went to the gym at 4:00 A.M. and began vigorously working out until he lost consciousness and was pronounced dead at the scene. Edna was left with a large number of debts, no insurance, and no health benefits because Frank was self-employed and was trying to save money. She and the children get a social security survivor's pension, but it isn't enough to cover basic costs and she has had to apply for welfare to cover medical expenses.

Frank passed away more than a year ago, but Edna has traumatic grief, as indicated by severe depression, high levels of anxiety, very angry and intrusive thoughts about Frank and the condition he left them in, and obsessive thoughts about what she wished she'd said to him before he died—uncomplimentary and angry remarks that would have conveyed her depth of despair and anger over her current situation. Her physician referred Edna to a therapist when she continued to complain of the symptoms of grief more than a year after Frank's death. Edna's therapist met with her and they immediately began a discussion about what was keeping Edna from resolving her feelings of grief. Edna was stymied, so the therapist suggested that she make a list of everything that came to mind and that she also do a literature search into the typical causes of prolonged grief and the best evidence of how to treat it so that they might continue the discussion at the next session. Edna was initially angry that she was asked to do work that the therapist should be doing *for* her and complained to her refereeing physician, who encouraged Edna to give it a little more time. She half-heartedly did what the therapist had asked and came only slightly prepared for further discussion at the next meeting.

When asked why she wasn't better prepared, Edna became angry and confrontational. "You haven't even said you're sorry about my loss," she said and angrily confronted the therapist for doing what her husband always did: leaving decisions up to her. The therapist said she appreciated the feedback and *did* feel badly about Edna's loss. Still, she wondered why Edna was unprepared and explained that only by working together could they resolve Edna's painful and extended grief. Edna promised to do more work in preparation for the next session. With the help of her precocious 10-year-old daughter, she was able to find Internet articles that seemed to clearly explain why her grief wasn't going away and what she might do about it.

The next session with the therapist was very businesslike and purposeful. Edna was excited about what she'd read, described it to her therapist, and together they planned the following strategy to treat Edna's symptoms of prolonged grief:

1. Edna needed to discuss all of the reasons for her anger at Frank. The therapist urged her to write them down and to bring the list with her the next time they met. Before she could resolve her anger at Frank, she had to be clear about why she was so angry.

2. If there was anything Edna could directly do about her anger, she would do it. Examples were trying to develop a career strategy to help with finances and discussing welfare programs available to single mothers with her case-manager that might help with retraining and job placement.

3. She would begin involvement in a self-help group for clients with prolonged grief begun by a remarkable woman who had also gone through a complicated grief after the death of her 15-year-old son in a car crash.

4. Edna would be seen by a psychiatrist to evaluate the use of anti-depressant medications and to supervise the medical treatment of her depression.

5. As part of the service the self-help group offered, she would have an opportunity to take time-outs from childcare through an inexpensive childcare service run by the group. In the time she had to herself, she would reestablish old friendships and social acquaintances.

6. She would start a daily regimen of exercise and diet supervised by a nutritionist provided by her health care plan.

7. She would reestablish her spiritual and religious ties, which had been broken after Frank's death, and which she missed.

8. She would reestablish contact with Frank's family. She had distanced herself from Frank's family after his death. Although she had been close to them when Frank was alive, she felt irrationally angry and blamed them for Frank's obsessive worry about his physical condition. Frank's father began having heart attacks in his mid-forties. Edna felt they had done too little to moderate Frank's anxiety about his health and subtly encouraged his overindulgence in exercise, which may have stressed his heart and contributed to his death. Edna decided that it was important for her to reestablish her contact with the family because she and her children missed them.

9. She would continue on in individual treatment for at least 12 sessions.

Edna's prolonged grief began to moderate itself after 2 months of treatment. By the third month, she was back to her old self, although she still attended the self-help group and saw the therapist once a month to monitor the depression. She no longer takes antidepressants and has maintained her exercise regimen and diet. She sees her in-laws regularly. She's had difficulty reestablishing her religious ties and continues to blame God for taking her husband at such a young age. "Maybe I'll never feel the same way, but you never know. I keep hoping and, of course, I go to synagogue on the High Holy Days, but most of it just makes me mad and I think that maybe I'm a spiritual person but not a religious one."

In discussing Edna's grief, the therapist said, "Edna has a lot to be depressed about. I don't know that I would even call her depression prolonged. It seems to me that people experience grief in their own unique ways and Edna's quick recovery, once she began therapy, is a good example of how therapy can be so helpful. Giving people assignments to assist in their own recovery is energizing, and encouraging their own involvement in treatment can be very empowering. Edna needed a little push and then she was better. She'll have moments of sorrow and despair. When you love someone and they pass on before their time, you expect that to happen. But on every measure of social functioning, Edna is doing a great deal better. From the paucity of good sound evidence about the treatment of grief, one can't help but think that even at a professional level, we are still a death-denying society. One last thought: Grief and depression are two separate issues. Yes, people in grief feel depressed, but you have to treat the grief as a separate issue. Many people find it hard to talk about death, but you can't really help people cope with the death of a loved one without talking about that experience and the impact it's had. And you have to talk to people about their own notions of death because that's what drives their grief. In Edna's case, she had begun losing her religious faith even before her husband died. The reasons are complex, but she had a very confused relationship with her faith and yet was obligated to give her husband a religious funeral. It was very confusing to her. She says she hasn't been able to reconnect with her religious beliefs and, while I've encouraged that she try, it doesn't feel right to her. In its place, she's begun attending a group that discusses spirituality in a nonreligious context. It suits her needs now, but at some point in time, it may be important for her to have further discussions about her faith and why it's left her."

Before the chapter summary, a personal story is included in the person's own words describing a series of deaths in her family and the way she coped with her grief. This story, with an analysis, will appear in a future book I am writing on resilience (Glicken, in press).

A Personal Story: Coping With the Death of a Family

When my daughter was murdered in her bed in 1984, I went crazy. I screamed. I think, for the first and last (so far) time in my life. Later, I got drunk, so drunk I bordered on alcohol poisoning. I also did this when my dad had committed suicide the December before my daughter died in May. I have not come close to that again. From the time of the murder until the trial, life was very strange. The original trial date was in August but actually started on October 28. I finished harvesting cranberries in the morning and we drove to Seattle for the start of the trial that same day. I was the first witness. They had goofed and had not legally identified the body. I had to do this on the record or the murderer would have walked on appeal. The next several years were difficult. My daughter would get into my head. I spent many hours crying for her. I still do. I am the eldest daughter of the eldest daughter for seven generations. I have no daughter now. What do I do with the family heirlooms?

One day a Rabbi commented that there is no virtue in death, as the dead cannot worship G-d. For some reason, this struck a cord with me. I also was trying to understand the Jewish viewpoint of death. I had a Rabbi's wife tell me that my daughter died because she had strayed from the Orthodox lifestyle, and I had society telling me I should forgive the murderer. My answer was to study. The Rabbi's wife was wrong. Judaism has some very easy commonsense answers to these questions. I read and studied and learned that G-d can only forgive sins against him, not sins against people, and that we have free will. G-d didn't kill my daughter, the killer did. G-d can't interfere with the killer's free will to kill her nor can he forgive the murder. Only the victim can give forgiveness and she can't because she's dead. I find this is also the explanation for the Holocaust.

My husband died November 30, 2001 from cancer. He had beat lung cancer and was declared okay at the end of August, but there were a few other cells that had escaped and took up housekeeping in his liver. We didn't know there was a real problem until Thanksgiving Day, and he died a week later. One month later, our then 16-year-old son Jonathon was having bad headaches. The boys and I went to visit my brother for New Year's. His pain was such that he got into my purse and helped himself to some of his dad's pain pills. We didn't realize that the pillow in his room was a feather one and he had very bad allergies. His belly filled up with mucus and the pain pills kept him asleep. He vomited into his lungs and suffocated. This was December 30, 2001. Then my brother died April 28, 2002. It was not a good year.

One copes by putting one foot in front of the other. When my son died right after my husband, I basically went numb, having learned that tears don't really help. I still have "gotcha" days. Like yesterday, I received a catalog addressed to my mother, who died in 1998, and a recruiting letter for my dead son Jonathan from the Air Force.

I received a great phone call this a.m. I have signed up through a program for a telephone study buddy. They have matched me with a Rabbi's wife in Florida. I look forward to studying with her. I am currently reading Donnin's book, *To Pray as a Jew*. It is starting to make sense to me. My goal is to have a very delayed Bat Mitzvah next year. I also enrolled in a program to become a nurse. After all the

(Continued)

(Continued)

suffering I've seen, I think I'd be a natural. For now, I work in the fields harvesting cranberries. Sometimes I feel very alone. My parents are gone, my brothers are gone, two of my children are gone, and it is hell getting old. However, the alternative is not attractive. Do you think this is all crazy? Maybe it is, but it keeps me going and sometimes, when I'm feeling close to G-d as I work in the fields, I even feel at peace.

SUMMARY

This chapter discusses EBP with terminal illness and bereavement. Much of the chapter focuses on finding meaning in the crisis of illness and death. Several case studies are offered that demonstrate the use of EBP in the treatment of terminal illness and bereavement. The concept of prolonged or complicated grief is discussed, and the differences between normal grief and prolonged grief are noted. Suggestions are made regarding the treatment of prolonged grief using best evidence, and a personal story of the resolution of grief is included.

Integrative Questions

1. In some cultures and societies, prolonged grief is considered normal. Why is there an expectation in our society that we resolve our grief quickly or we fear that the grief will become debilitating?

2. Using treatments that may leave people confused, unable to communicate, or unable to resolve unfinished business is troubling. Shouldn't we allow people to die as naturally as possible?

3. Do you think grieving would be easier for most of us if terminally ill patients were allowed to die in their homes surrounded by their loved ones rather than in sterile and often uncaring hospitals?

4. The death of a parent, even a parent who is very old and infirm, often creates a serious emotional response in children. Why do you think this occurs?

5. People who never grieve at the death of loved ones are often thought to be unfeeling or emotionally disengaged. Do you think that at some

point in life this lack of grief catches up with them and shows itself in a number of emotional problems?

References

Balk, D. E. (1999). Bereavement and spiritual change. *Death Studies, 23*(6), 485–493.

Blundo, R. (2001). Learning strengths-based practice: Challenging our personal and professional frames. *Families in Society, 82*(3), 296–304.

Caffrey, T. A. (2000). The whisper of death: Psychotherapy with a dying Vietnam veteran. *American Journal of Psychotherapy, 54*(4), 519–530.

Finn, J. (1999). An exploration of helping processes in an online self-help group focusing on issues of disability. *Health & Social Work, 24*(3), 220–231.

Frankl, V. E. (1978). *Psychotherapy and existentialism: Selected papers on logotherapy.* New York: Touchstone Books.

Glicken, M. D. (in press). *Learning from resilient people: Lessons we can apply to counseling and psychotherapy.* Thousand Oaks, CA: Sage.

Greenstein, M., & Breitbart, W. (2000). Cancer and the experience of meaning: A group psychotherapy program for people with cancer. *American Journal of Psychotherapy, 54*(4), 486–500.

Hardwig, J. (2000). Spiritual issues at the end of life: A call for discussion. *The Hastings Center Report, 30*(2), 28–30.

Jacobs, S., & Prigerson, H. (2000). Psychotherapy of traumatic grief: A review of evidence for psychotherapeutic treatments. *Death Studies, 24*(6), 479–496.

Kendall, P. C. (1994). Treating anxiety disorders in children: Results of a randomized clinical trial. *Journal of Consulting and Clinical Psychology, 62,* 100–110.

Kleber, R. J., & Brom, D. (1987). Psychotherapy and pathological grief: Controlled outcome study. *Israeli Journal of Psychiatry and Related Sciences, 24,* 99–109.

Kubler-Ross, E. (1997). *On death and dying.* New York: Scribner Classics. (Original work published 1969)

Lloyd-Williams, M. (2001). Screening for depression in palliative care patients: A review. *European Journal of Cancer Care, 10*(1), 31–36.

Marmar, C. R., Horowitz, M. J., Weiss, D. S., Wilner, N. R., & Kaltreider, N. B. (1988). A controlled trial of brief psychotherapy and mutual help group treatment of conjugal bereavement. *American Journal of Psychiatry, 145,* 203–209.

McClain, C. S., Rosenfeld, B., & Breitbart, W. (2003). Effect of spiritual well-being on end-of-life despair in terminally-ill cancer patients. *Lancet, 361*(9369), 1603–1608.

Piper, W. E., Ogrodniczuk, J. S., Joyce, A. S., & McCallum, M. R. (2002). Relationships among affect, work, and outcome in group therapy for patients with complicated grief. *American Journal of Psychotherapy, 56*(3), 347–362.

Raphael, B. (1977). Preventive intervention with the recently bereaved. *Archives of General Psychiatry, 34,* 1450–1454.

Richman, J. (2000). Introduction: Psychotherapy with terminally ill patients. *American Journal of Psychotherapy, 54*(4), 482–486.

Sireling, L., Cohen, D., & Marks, I. (1988). Guided mourning for morbid grief: A replication. *Behavior Therapy, 19,* 121–132.

Stroebe, M. S. (2001). Bereavement research and theory: Retrospective and prospective. *American Behavioral Scientist, 44*(5), 854–865.

Evidence-Based Practice With Anxiety and Depression in Older Adults

13

Large numbers of anxious and depressed older adults often go undiagnosed and untreated because underlying symptoms of anxiety and depression are thought to be physical in nature, and professionals frequently believe that older adults are neither motivated for therapy nor find it an appropriate treatment. This often leaves many older adults trying to cope with serious emotional problems without adequate help. As this chapter will note, the numbers of older adults trying to cope with anxiety and depression are considerable and growing as the numbers of older adults increase in America. Health problems, loss of loved ones, financial insecurities, lack of a support group, a growing sense of isolation, and a lack of self-worth are common problems among older adults that lead to serious symptoms of anxiety and depression, problems that often coexist in many older adults. Two case studies provide added information about the cause and treatment of depression and anxiety in older adults.

Anxiety in Older Adults

The prevalence of anxiety disorders has usually been thought to decrease with age, but recent findings suggest that generalized anxiety is actually a more common problem among older adults than depression. A study reported by Beekman et al. (1998) found anxiety to affect 7.3% of an older population as compared to 2% with depression in the same population. Lang and Stein (2001) estimate that the total number of older Americans suffering from anxiety could be in excess of 10%. Since many anxious older people do not meet the criteria for anxiety found in a number of research studies, the prevalence of anxiety-related problems in older adults could be as high as 18% and constitutes the most common psychiatric symptom experienced by older people (Lang and Stein). Anxiety among older adults frequently coexists with typical physical manifestations including chest pains, heart palpitations, night sweats, shortness of breath, essential hypertension, headaches, and generalized pain. Because physicians often fail to diagnose underlying symptoms of anxiety in older patients, the emotional component of the symptoms are frequently not dealt with. Definitions and descriptions of anxiety used in diagnosing younger patients often fail to capture the unique stressors that older adults must deal with, or the fragile nature of life for older adults as they attempt to cope with limited finances, failing health, the death of loved ones, concerns about their own mortality, and a sense of uselessness and hopelessness because their roles as adults have been dramatically altered with age and retirement.

Not all studies find high levels of anxiety in older adults, however. In a large sample of older subjects, Himmelfarb and Murrell (1984) found low correlations among age, physical health, and anxiety. Wagner and Lorion (1984) found that "death anxiety" does not exist among all older adults but may be more prevalent among women, married people, African Americans, less educated older adults, and less affluent older adults. The reader is cautioned that both prior studies are older studies and may not accurately reflect the way older adults currently react to physical health and fears of death. However, Smith, Sherrill, and Celenda (1995) report symptoms of anxiety in 5%–30% of older primary care patients and believe that intense late-life anxiety results from "feelings of loneliness, worthlessness, and uselessness. Ill health, the loss of friends and loved ones, and financial problems all can contribute to the development of anxiety symptoms" (p. 5).

Lang and Stein (2001) found that women have higher rates of anxiety across all age groups, and that older adults who have experienced anxiety problems in the past are more at risk for the problem worsening as they age. Agoraphobia may also be more likely to have late-life onset as a result of physical limitations, disabilities, unsafe neighborhoods, and other factors that make some older adults fearful of leaving home. Because anxiety in older people may have a physical base or may realistically be connected to concerns about health, Kogan, Edelstein, and McKee (2000) provide some guidelines for distinguishing an anxiety disorder from anxiety related to physical problems in older adults.

A physical cause of anxiety is more likely if the onset of anxiety comes suddenly, the symptoms fluctuate in strength and duration, and fatigue was present before the symptoms of anxiety were experienced. The authors identify the following medical problems as reasons for symptoms of anxiety: (a) endocrine, cardiovascular, pulmonary, or neurological disorders and (b) the impact of certain medications, most notably stimulants, beta-blockers, certain tranquilizers, and of course alcohol and certain nonprescription medicines.

An emotional cause of anxiety is more likely if the symptoms have lasted 2 or more years with little change in severity, and if the person has other coexisting emotional symptoms. Anxiety may cycle on and off, however, or a lower level of generalized anxiety may be present that causes the older client a great deal of discomfort. Obsessive concerns about financial issues and health are realistic worries that also trouble older clients. The concerns may be situational or they may be constant, but not serious enough to lead to a diagnosis of anxiety. Nonetheless, they cause the client unhappiness and may actually lead to physical problems including high blood pressure, cardiovascular problems, sleep disorders, and an increased use of alcohol and over-the-counter medications to lessen symptoms of anxiety.

Best Evidence for the Treatment of Anxiety With an Older Adult Population

Beck and Stanley (1997) and Stanley and Novy (2000) report positive results with anxious older clients using cognitive-behavioral therapy and relaxation training. Benefits for older clients experiencing anxiety appear to be as positive as they are with younger clients. Smith et al. (1995) have found that older adults respond well to psychotherapy for anxiety, "especially if it supports their religious beliefs and encourages life review that helps to resolve both hidden and obvious conflicts associated with specific events in the patient's life history" (p. 6). The authors recommend medications only after all other options have been considered. Most anxiety problems in younger clients are treated with benzodiazepines, which have only a "marginal efficacy for chronic anxiety and are especially bad for older adults because the body accumulates the drug and may produce excess sedation, diminished sexual desire, worsening of dementing illness, and a reduction in the general level of energy" (p. 6). The authors also warn that Prozac may actually increase anxiety in older clients as a side effect and recommend pinpointing the cause of the anxiety problem before considering the use of medications.

Although the benefits of cognitive-behavioral approaches seem positive, Lang and Stein (2001) recommend that treatment of anxiety in older adults should be tailored to the individual needs and cognitive abilities of the client. Some older clients resent advice given by younger professionals, or they may find relaxation approaches inappropriate or childish. Systematic desensitization may be seen as unrelated to their situation or to the origins of their anxiety. And older adults may view changes in the way they are told to perceive life events as being dangerous to their survival because long-held beliefs and behaviors have often served them well in the past. Being asked to view a situation with clarity and rationality may suggest to older adults that workers believe they are lying about an event. Older adults may discount psychological explanations for their anxiety and prefer to think that it has a physical origin. All of these cautionary suggestions should be taken into account when working with anxious older adults or one runs the risk of having psychological treatments dismissed completely by the client.

A suggestion to achieve better acceptance of any intervention is to give clients reading materials to help them understand the origins of their anxiety and the approach most likely to help relieve their symptoms. Testimonials from other clients might be helpful as well, or suggestions made by other professionals they trust could also help the client accept treatment. Keep in mind that, even though older adults may be suffering, they may also fear that accepting new ways of approaching life might actually increase their level of anxiety. As Lang and Stein (2001) report, however, there are harmful side effects to the long-term use of many antianxiety medications. While some of the cognitive-behavioral approaches used in the treatment of anxiety may not always fit an older adult's frame of reference, it is wise to let him or her know about medical treatments and the potential for harm as one way to acknowledge that medications have risks that should be considered, just as there are associated risks in doing nothing.

Case Study: Anxiety in an Older Client

Irma Kolb is a 75-year-old resident of a condominium complex for adults 55 and older in San Diego, California. Irma's husband passed away 4 years ago, and since then, Irma has experienced generalized but manageable anxiety. She takes a mild tranquilizer to help control her anxiety. Several weeks after the condominium complex was sold to new owners, Irma discovered that the unit she and her husband had rented for almost 15 years was about to be renovated. The owners of the complex will move her, at their expense, to another unit, and when her unit is completed, they will move her back at their expense and she will continue paying the very low rent she presently enjoys.

The notification of a temporary move threw Irma into a severe anxiety state with panic attacks. Her friends have promised to help her pack, and several employees who know and like Irma have promised to pack dishes and other breakable items at no cost. Many of her friends are also experiencing anxiety because of the disruption in their lives brought on by the renovations, but Irma's level of obsessive worry and panic has become so overwhelming that she was hospitalized for a week to try to lower her anxiety level and to regulate suddenly severe chest pains and high blood pressure, neither of which have a somatic cause.

Irma's son and daughter live on the East Coast. They have spoken to her by phone and try to assure her that everything will be fine. They point out how lucky she will be to live in a nicer condominium without having to pay higher rent, but she is convinced that this is the first step in an attempt to get rid of renters who pay low rents. Many of her friends feel the same way and the level of worry is high in the complex. Irma has begun to feel that she will be forced out of her home because of the high rents she believes will be initiated over the next few years, and that she will end up on the streets as a homeless person. Her social security pension allows her little more than her rent, and she lives a very limited but satisfying lifestyle, surrounded by friends and good neighbors in a community with excellent weather and medical care she likes and uses with ease.

Since her hospitalization, she is unable to do most of the activities she did before she was hospitalized, and she sits at home obsessively worrying and unable to do the packing that needs to be done over the next week. When her friends come to help, she sits immobilized with anxiety and isn't able to give directions or instructions. The condominium complex has given her notice that if she isn't ready to move in a week, she will be evicted from her home and lose her right to return when the renovations are completed.

INTERVENTION: CASEMANAGEMENT

One of Irma's friends who volunteers at a local family service agency in San Diego contacted the head of services for older adults, who immediately sent a case-manager to Irma's home. The case-manager confirmed that Irma was immobilized with anxiety and contacted the friends and condominium complex employees who had offered to help her move and asked them to help organize the move. The agency has a fund for emergency help if anyone needs to be hired for additional help. The case-manager also called the utility companies to change Irma's service and made changes of address necessitated by the move to her bank, the social security administration, her health care provider, and others. When this was done, she and Irma walked to the temporary unit and were happily surprised to see that it was exactly like her current unit. The case-manager made a diagram of Irma's home so that she could place her furniture in exactly the same position in her new condominium. The case-manager assured the condominium company that Irma would be moved in time and had them send a letter to Irma promising her that she would be able to move back to her renovated unit at her current rent. The case-manager had several retired volunteers, who were licensed therapists, spend time with Irma to offer support and practical help with any concerns that Irma may have had.

In the course of the successful move and in the months following the move, Irma shared with the volunteer therapists that her family had been evicted many times from homes in Germany before World War II because they were Jewish and, having nowhere to go, the family often lived on the streets. Irma was just a small child then but the fear of once again living on the streets was a painful reminder of life in Germany and the hardships her family endured: starvation, dealing with extreme cold, and taunts and beatings from the German people who had so recently been their neighbors and friends. Irma's fears were enhanced when the condominium company threatened to evict her.

The president of the company personally met with Irma and her neighbors to apologize for the incident and to once again assure them that they would not have their rents raised. Irma's city councilman and representatives from the local television stations were also present. The apology and the meeting helped a great deal to ease Irma's anxiety. When her condominium unit was renovated, Irma returned to find it a lovely, modern unit. A formal letter guaranteed her current rent for a year, with the promise that yearly raises would not exceed the 4% Irma and her neighbors had experienced in the past. The letter said the company hoped Irma would stay at the complex for as long as she wished and called her a good neighbor and a great renter.

Irma continues on in therapy with several of the volunteer therapists who use a supportive and positive approach with Irma. They praise her resilience in dealing with a difficult life event and her ability to cope with life after what she endured as a child in Germany. She continues using a more substantial antianxiety medication and sees her physician frequently to monitor any health problems. Her blood pressure is lower than it was when she experienced her first anxiety attacks, but it is still too high, and a beta-blocker is being used for her hypertension and to lower her level of anxiety. Her chest pains continue at a reduced level, and although there is seemingly no physical reason for the pain, her doctor takes it seriously and wants Irma to see him often so they can be proactive if a problem arises. Irma has been encouraged by her doctor to exercise and diet. She has done this by joining a health group at her complex. She walks 2 miles every day and has lost 15 pounds. The benefit of her new health consciousness has helped lower her blood pressure and reduce her anxiety level, and has resulted in fewer episodes of chest pain.

In discussing her work with Irma, the case-manager, a licensed clinical social worker, said the following: "Older people have many realistic reasons to worry. Finances, health problems, loneliness, family loss, and little sense of contribution are common concerns for older adults. Unlike many other cultures, older adults are not revered in America and have a limited role in life, even though they've had successful lives and have made major contributions. At our agency, we view clients like Irma and her response to the move as a serious sign of difficulty. We've found that direct intervention is often necessary before clients can mobilize their own coping skills. We believe strongly in using our retired volunteers, many of whom are licensed therapists. They visit clients in their homes and provide a high level of supportive help that energizes clients and allows them to better utilize their own coping skills. We advocate directly for clients, but we only do for them what they can't do for themselves. We've found that with highly anxious older clients, managing the case requires interaction with everyone involved with the client, particularly the client's health care provider. As an agency, we often interact with other social, mental health, and health care agencies regarding the best care for older clients.

"What we've sadly discovered is that many professionals still think of older adults as somehow less cognitively able than their younger clients. Stereotypes of older people as having diminished capacities to cope with life are very common. Professionals often think that medication is the only answer and that therapy is inappropriate for older persons. However, many older clients have resilience, intelligence, and skills that haven't diminished at all over the years. What they often need is help in an emergency and some honest concern for their welfare once the emergency is resolved. We've tracked our casemanagement clients for many years. We've found that immediate help in a crisis, some homemaker care when needed, direct advocacy when the clients can't do certain things for themselves, supportive therapy, and a belief that older people have the motivation, intelligence, and ability to change when faced with problems, has resulted in few of our older clients requiring nursing care or moving into states of helplessness. We think that active people live longer, are healthier, and have happier lives. In return for our services, our clients who are able volunteer to help others. It's a quid pro quo that has resulted in extraordinary longevity and life meaning for our older adult clients."

Depression in Older Adults

While symptoms of depression are consistent across age groups, Wallis (2000) suggests that older adults may express depression through such physical complaints as insomnia, eating disorders, and digestive problems. They may also show signs of lethargy, have less incentive to do the activities they did before they became depressed, and experience symptoms of depression while denying that they are depressed. Mild and transient depression, brought on by situational events, usually resolves itself in time, but moderate depression may interfere with daily life activities and can result in social withdrawal and isolation. Severe depression may result in psychotic-like symptoms including hallucinations and loss of touch with reality (Wallis, 2000). The DSM-IV (APA, 1994) does not distinguish depression in older adults from depression in a younger population, and the subtle as well as the overt signs of depression in older adults are not discussed. This lack of differentiation of depression among age groups makes diagnosis more problematic and is one explanation of why depression is often not treated when older clients have coexisting medical problems. Whether the medical problem results in the depression or the depression contributes to the medical problem is difficult to determine and remains an area requiring more study. Clearly, however, older adults have intrusive health and mental health problems that may cause depressed feelings and may lead to changes in functioning.

In a study of older adults living in a specific community, Blazer, Hughes, and George (1987) found that 8% had symptoms of depression or other disorders serious enough to warrant treatment. Older adults in acute health care facilities had rates of depression of 5%–15%, and residents of long-care facilities had symptoms, not captured in current descriptions of major depression, of 25% (Blazer, 1993). Wallis (2000) reports a depression rate of 6% among older adults, nearly two thirds of whom are women. Wallis notes that depression is more prevalent among an older population because of loss of loved ones, health problems, and the inability to live independently. According to Wallis, 75% of older adults in long-term care have mild to moderate symptoms of depression. Casey (1994) reports a study that found rates of suicide among adults 65 and older almost double that of the general population, with completion rates for suicide among older adults 1 in 4 as compared to 1 in 100 for the general population, suggesting that older adults are much more likely to see suicide as a final solution rather than a cry for help. Older adults who commit suicide often suffer from major depression, alcoholism, severe medical problems, and social isolation (Casey, 1994). Mills and Henretta (2001) indicate that more than 2 million of the 34 million older Americans suffer from some form of depression, yet late-life depression is often undiagnosed or underdiagnosed.

To determine whether there are factors other than generalized health problems or issues of isolation that cause depression, Mills and Henretta (2001) found significant differences along racial and ethnic lines. Many more Hispanics and African Americans over the age of 65 report that their health is only fair or poor as compared to non-Hispanic white older adults. Axelson (1985) reports that Mexican Americans tend to see themselves as "old" much earlier in life than other groups (e.g., at about age 60, as compared with age 65 and 70 for black and white Americans). Axelson believes that attitudes and expectations about aging "may put the Hispanic elderly at increased risk of what has been called psychological death, meaning a giving up or disengagement from active involvement in life" (as cited in Mills and Henretta, 2001, p. 133).

While socioeconomic status has often been thought to predict life span and overall health, Robert and Li (2001) found evidence of a relationship between levels of community health and individual health. Lawton (1977) believes that older adults experience the community as their primary source of support, recreation, and stimulation rather than family or a core of friends. Lawton and Nahemow (1973) suggest that healthy community environments are particularly important for older adults who may have emotional, physical, or cognitive problems. To help in understanding the concept of healthy communities, Robert and Li (2001) define healthy communities as having (a) a physical environment with limited noise, manageable traffic, and adequate lighting; (b) a social environment with low crime rates, safe environments to walk in, and easy access to shopping; and (c) a service environment that includes easy and safe access to inexpensive transportation, senior centers, medical care, and meal sites.

Social support networks for older adults are also a factor in positive physical and mental health. Tyler and Hoyt (2000) studied the emotional impact of natural disasters on older adults who had predisaster indications of depression and found that subjects with consistent social supports had lower levels of depression before and after a natural disaster than depressed subjects without social supports. In a study of successful aging, Vaillant and Mukamal (2001) found that one can predict longer and healthier lives before the age of 50 by considering the following indicators: family cohesion, preexisting major depression, ancestral longevity, childhood temperament, and physical health at age 50. Negative variables affecting physical and emotional health that adults have control over include alcohol abuse, smoking, marital instability, lack of exercise, obesity, unsuccessful coping mechanisms, and lower levels of education.

Vaillant and Mukamal (2001) suggest that older adults have considerable control over their health after retirement. They believe that successfully aging older adults (a) see themselves as healthier than their peers, even though their physicians may not agree; (b) plan ahead and retain intellectual curiosity and involvement with their own creative abilities; (c) believe that life is meaningful; (d) use humor as a way of coping with life; (e) remain physically active and continue physical activities that were used at an earlier age including walking, tennis, and aerobic exercises; (f) have a more serene and spiritual approach to life than those who age less well; (g) continue to have friendships, positive interpersonal relationships, and satisfaction with spouses, children, and family life; and (h) are socially involved in civic and volunteer work.

Best Evidence for Treating Depression in Older Clients

Gallagher-Thompson, Hanley-Peterson, and Thompson (1990) followed older clients for 2 years after completion of treatment and found that 52% of the clients receiving cognitive treatment, 58% of the clients receiving behavioral treatment, and 70% of the clients receiving brief dynamic treatment had no return of depressed symptoms 2 years after treatment. The authors report that these rates of improvement are consistent with a younger population of depressed clients. However, Huffman (1999) reports high rates of recurrence of depression in older adults following treatment. In subjects older than 70 who received psychotherapy and a placebo as an antidepressant, the recurrence rate for depression was 63% within a 3-year period. For subjects ages 60–69, the recurrence rate was 65%. Subjects treated with just an antidepressant and scheduled office visits to check on their progress did least well, with a 90% recurrence rate for both age groups (Huffman, 1999).

Lenze et al. (2002) studied the effectiveness of interpersonal treatment in conjunction with antidepressants with depressed older clients. Not surprisingly, given the lack of awareness of late-onset depression in older clients, they report, "To our knowledge, this is the first report concerning social functioning in a controlled randomized study of elderly patients receiving maintenance treatment for late-life depression" (p. 467). The authors found improved social adjustment attributable to combined interpersonal psychotherapy and maintenance medication. While improvements in social functioning could not be related directly to therapy, maintenance of the gains made in social functioning seemed directly related to therapy. The most significant gains reported by the authors were in the areas of interpersonal conflict role transitions and abnormal grief.

Kennedy and Tannenbaum (2000) indicate that compelling evidence exists that older patients experience a variety of emotional problems including depression, anxiety, caregiver burden, and extended bereavement. The authors believe that many older clients can benefit from psychotherapeutic interventions and suggest that adjustments for clinical practice with older clients should include consideration of "sensory and cognitive" problems, the need for closer collaboration with the client's family and other care providers, and a belief by the clinician, shared with the older client and his or her family, that treatment will result in improved functioning and symptom reduction to offset stereotypes that older clients with emotional problems are untreatable or unlikely to improve. The authors suggest that work with older clients also requires skill with a variety of approaches, including work with couples, families, and groups. They also report that the use of pharmacotherapy may produce very positive results with late-onset social and emotional problems experienced by older clients.

O'Connor (2001) reports that older clients usually get better after their first episode of depression but that the relapse rate is 50%. Clients with three episodes of depression are 90% likely to have additional episodes. O'Connor suggests that we need to accept depression as a chronic disease and that therapists must be prepared to "give hope, to reduce shame, to be mentor, coach, cheerleader, idealized object, playmate, and nurturer. In doing so, inevitably, we must challenge many of our assumptions about the use of the self in psychotherapy" (p. 508). O'Connor also suggests that depressed clients seek approval from therapists and the effective therapist gives it warmly and genuinely through smiles, nods, and recognition that the client has "accomplished something difficult, an indication that you share the patient's valuation of what he/she has accomplished, an emotional mirroring of the patient's pride—these can have powerful impact on the depressed patient" (p. 522).

Denton, Walsh, and Daniel (2002) report that much of the therapy used in treating depression has no empirical base to prove its effectiveness. Before we select a treatment approach, we should consult empirically validated research studies that indicate the effectiveness of a particular therapeutic approach with a particular individual. The authors describe EBP as the use of treatments shown to be effective with a particular population. Timmermans and Angell (2001) indicate that evidence-based clinical judgment has five important features:

1. It is composed of both research evidence and clinical experience.

2. There is skill involved in reading the literature that requires an ability to synthesize the information and to make judgments about the quality of the available evidence.

3. The way in which information is used is a function of the practitioner's level of authority in an organization and his or her level of confidence in the effectiveness of the applied information.

4. Part of the use of EBP is the ability to independently evaluate the information used and to test its validity in the context of one's own practice.

5. Evidence-based clinical judgments are grounded in Western notions of professional conduct and professional roles, and are ultimately guided by a common value system.

Case Study: Depression in an Older Adult

Jake Kissman is a 77-year-old widower whose wife, Leni, passed away a year ago. Jake is emotionally adrift and feels lost without Leni's companionship and guidance. He has a troubled relationship with two adult children, who live across the country, and has been unable to turn to them for solace and support. Like many older men, Jake has no real support group or close friends. Leni's social circle became his, but after her death, her friends left Jake to fend for himself. Jake is a difficult man who is prone to being critical and insensitive. He tends to say whatever enters his mind at the moment no matter how hurtful it may be, and then is surprised that people take it so badly. "It's only words," he says. "What harm do words do? It's not like smacking somebody." Before he retired, Jake was a successful salesman, and he can be charming and witty, but sooner or later his disregard for others comes through and he ends up offending people.

Jake's depression shows itself in fatigue, feelings of hopelessness, irritability, and outbursts of anger. He doesn't believe in doctors and never sees them. "Look what the *momzers* [bastards] did to poor Leni. A healthy woman in her prime and she needed a surgery like I do. They killed her, those butchers." Jake has taken to pounding on the walls of his apartment whenever noise from his neighbors upsets him. Complaints from surrounding neighbors have resulted in the threat of an eviction. Jake can't manage a move to another apartment by himself and someone from his synagogue contacted a professional in the community who agreed to visit Jake at his apartment. Jake is happy that he has company but angry that someone thought he needed help. "Tell the bastards to stop making so much noise and I'll be fine. The one next door with the dog, shoot her. The one on the other side who bangs the cabinets, do the same. Why aren't they being kicked out?"

The therapist listens to Jake in a supportive way. He never disagrees with him, offers advice, or contradicts him. Jake is still grieving for his wife, and her loss has left him without usable coping skills to deal with the pressures of single life. He's angry and depressed. To find out more about Jake's symptoms, the therapist has gone to the literature on anger, depression, and grief. While he recognizes that Jake is a difficult client in any event, the data he collected helped him develop a working strategy with Jake. The therapist has decided to use a strengths approach (Glicken, 2004; Saleebey, 1992; Weick et al., 1989) with Jake. The strengths approach focuses on what clients have done well in their lives and uses those strengths in areas of life that are more problematic. The approach comes from studies on resilience and self-healing, and from successful work with abused and traumatized children and adults.

Jake has many positive attributes that most people have ignored. He was a warm and caring companion to Leni during her illness. He is secretly very generous and gives what he has to various charities without wanting people to know that he was the giver. He helps his children financially and has done a number of acts of kindness for neighbors and friends, but in ways that always make the recipients feel ambivalent about his help. Jake is a difficult and complex man and no one has taken the time to try to understand him. The therapist takes a good deal of time and listens closely.

Jake feels that he's been a failure at life. He feels unloved and unappreciated. He thinks the possibility of an eviction is a good example of how people "do him in" when he is least able to cope with stress. So the therapist listens and never disagrees with Jake. Gradually, Jake has begun discussing his life and the sadness he feels without his wife, who was his ballast and mate. Using a strengths approach, the therapist always focuses on what Jake does well and his generosity, while Jake uses their time to beat himself up with self-deprecating statements. The therapist listens, smiles, points out Jake's excellent qualities, and waits for Jake to start internalizing what the therapist has said about him. Slowly, it's begun to work. Jake told the therapist to go help someone who needed it when Jake's anger at the therapist became overwhelming. Jake immediately apologized. "Here you're helping me and I criticize. Why do I do that?" he asked the therapist. There are many moments when Jake corrects himself or seems to fight an impulse to say something mean-spirited or hurtful to the therapist, who recently told him, "Jake, you catch more flies with honey than you do with vinegar." To which Jake replied, "So who needs to catch flies, for crying out loud? Oh, I'm sorry. Yeah, I see what you mean. It's not about flies, it's about getting along with people."

Gradually, Jake has put aside his anger and has begun talking to people in the charming and pleasant manner he is so capable of using. The neighbors who complained about him now see him as a "doll." Jake's depression is beginning to lift and he's begun dating again, although he says he can never love anyone like his wife, "but a man gets lonely so what are you supposed to do, sit home and watch soap operas all day? Not me." The therapist continues to see Jake and they often sit and quietly talk about Jake's life. "I was a big deal once. I could sell an Eskimo an air conditioner in winter. I could charm the socks off people. But my big mouth, it always got in the way. I always said something that made people mad. Maybe it's because my dad was so mean to all of us, I got this chip on my shoulder. Leni was wonderful. She could put up with me and make me laugh. When she died, I was left with my big mouth and a lot of disappointments. You want to have friends, you want your kids to love you. I got neither, but I'm not such an *alte cocker* [old fart] that I don't learn. And I've learned a lot from you. I've learned you can teach an old dog new tricks, and that's something. So I thank you and I apologize for some things I said. It's hard to get rid of the chip on the shoulder and sometimes it tips you over, that big chip, and it makes you fall down. You're a good person. I wish you well in life."

DISCUSSION

Most of the treatment literature on work with older depressed adults suggests the use of a cognitive approach. Jake's therapist felt that the oppositional nature of Jake's personality would reject cognitive therapy. Instead, a positive and affirming approach was used that focused on Jake's strengths because "most depressed patients acutely desire the therapist's approval, and it is an effective therapist who gives it warmly and genuinely" (O'Connor, 2001, p. 522). While much of the research suggests the positive benefits of cognitive therapy, the therapist found the following description of cognitive therapy to be at odds with what might best help Jake. Rush and Giles (1982) indicate that cognitive treatment attempts to change irrational thinking through three steps: (a) identifying irrational self-sentences, ideas and thoughts; (b) developing rational thoughts, ideas, and perceptions; and (c) practicing these more rational ideas to improve self-worth and, ultimately, to reduce depression. While this approach might work with other older clients, the therapist believed that Jake would take offense and reject both the therapy and the therapist, finding them preachy and critical.

Instead, the therapist decided to let Jake talk, although the therapist made comments, asked questions to clarify, and made connections that Jake found interesting and oddly satisfying. "No one ever said that to me before," Jake would say, shaking his head and smiling. "You learn something new every day, don't you." The therapist would always bring Jake back to the positive achievements in his life, which Jake would initially toss away with comments such as "That was then when I paid taxes, this is now when I ain't gotta penny to my name." Soon, however, Jake could reflect on his positive achievements and began to use those experiences to deal with his current problems. In discussing the conflict with one of his neighbors, Jake said, "Maybe I should bring flowers to the old hag. Naw, I can't bring flowers, but she's no hag. I've seen worse. What about flowers? Yeah, flowers. Down at Vons I can buy a nice bunch for a buck. So it costs a little to be nice. Beats getting tossed out on my keester." Or he would tie something he had done when he was working to his current situation: "I had something like this happen once. A customer complained to my boss, so I go over and ask her to tell me what she's mad about so I can fix it, and she does, and it gets fixed. Sometimes you gotta eat a little crow." As Jake made connections and as he began to trust the therapist, this process of self-directed change reinforced his sense of accomplishment and led to a decrease in his depression. It also led to a good deal of soul searching about how he had to make changes in his life now that his wife was gone. "So maybe I should stop feeling sorry for myself and take better care. What do you think?"

Because the literature on the treatment of older adult depression is very limited, it is a good idea for therapists to individualize treatment by working cooperatively with the client to find an approach that feels right. It also makes sense to track client change and to set goals for treatment. Evaluating one's own practice is always important, but it's particularly important with older clients whose depressed feelings may have a strongly negative effect on health and may increase the risk of physical deterioration and even suicide.

One way to evaluate practice effectiveness is through the use of goal attainment scaling with single-subject design. In single-subject research, we are only interested in studying one subject at a time. The following discussion explains single-subject research and presents a goal attainment scale specifically developed for treating Jake's depression. A more complete discussion of single-subject research and goal attainment scaling can be found in a book I wrote on social research (Glicken, 2003).

Single-Subject Approaches to Evaluate Depression in Older Adults

SINGLE-SUBJECT RESEARCH

Single-subject research is only interested in determining how well a single client does in treatment. Unlike empirical designs that require a control group, in single-subject research, subjects act as their own control groups. The purpose of single-subject research is to measure the change made by a single client. While generalizing findings to other clients or showing a cause-effect relationship between treatment and client change as a result of a single case is not possible in single-subject research, if enough people using a similar treatment approach have similar results, it may be possible to show a link between treatment and improvement rates, but not a direct correlation.

AB DESIGNS

The most common single-subject design is the AB Design in which

1. a steady state is determined that indicates how long the condition being treated has existed,

2. a baseline measure or pretest is taken before the treatment begins,

3. the treatment approach is agreed upon with the client,

4. a time line is determined indicating how long the treatment will last,

5. a posttest is given to measure change when treatment is completed,

6. further posttests might also be given to determine how long the change may last.

If the steady state (how long the condition existed *before* treatment began) is long enough, it suggests that changes taking place once treatment is initiated are the result of the treatment and not some intervening or capricious variable(s). We can say this because change that does not occur over a long period of time before treatment (the steady state) and now occurs with treatment can logically be thought to have occurred because of the treatment. While this isn't easy to prove, there is at least strong reason to believe that the longer a depression lasts before treatment begins, the more likely it is that any improvement in the depression is the result of the treatment.

GOAL ATTAINMENT SCALING

Goal attainment scaling is used when the therapist and client agree on goals of treatment that are measurable and are then used to monitor progress in achieving those goals. Goal attainment scaling is only used for observable behaviors that are easy to measure. Goals of treatment should be based on best evidence. The amount of improvement we expect in our clients should be based on the length of time the client has experienced a problem and on its severity. The longer our treatment continues, the higher our expectation should be for change. Although goal attainment scaling is often used with single-subject designs, in which we are only interested in the improvement rate of an individual client, evaluating enough clients using a single-subject design might suggest links between treatment for a specific type of problem and its effectiveness with similar clients.

BASELINE MEASURES

A baseline measure is a pretest measuring the behaviors to be changed over the course of treatment. Baseline measures should be behavioral in nature. Some examples might be weight, blood pressure, grades, exercise regimens, and blood alcohol content. Happiness, morale, or work satisfaction would all be examples of difficult-to-measure behaviors because they are so subjective in nature. Goal attainment scaling is concerned with changes in behavior that are directly observed in the person's life and can therefore be measured. The client with a weight problem is weighed every session. The client who agrees to walk 2 miles a day must have a card signed by someone from a health facility who has observed the 2-mile walk and will verify it on paper. Independent verification is always necessary in measuring change.

POSTTESTS

The same set of goals used at the beginning of treatment must be used to determine change when treatment ends. Posttests following the end of treatment and taken several more times in an 18- to 24-month period of time will indicate whether the behavioral gains the client initially made when treatment ended were maintained and are a result of treatment.

GOALS OF TREATMENT

Goals are done conjointly with the client in the first session of treatment. The goals must be easily measured with no reliance on subjective client feedback. They must also be directly related to the new behaviors the clients must practice to change the presenting problem. For example, diet, exercise, and social activities may lead to lower rates of anxiety and depression.

A Goal Attainment Scale
Measuring Improvement in Depression

In the following goal attainment scale (Table 13.1) developed for use with Jake, we are using the CES-D instrument to measure depression (the dependent variable) and various new behaviors we think will decrease his depression as independent variables. The four independent variables are positive social interactions with his neighbors, increased contact with his children, attendance at meetings and social events in his condominium complex, and swimming as a form of exercise to decrease levels of depression. We've chosen swimming because of a nearby heated pool and because Jake likes to swim but avoids the pool because he must interact with people he dislikes. If the client exercises and improves the number of social contacts as a positive result of treatment, then it's hoped that the dependent variables (the CES-D score) will improve. All four independent variables can be verified by talking to the lifeguard at the pool, checking Jake's phone records for calls to his children, checking receipts at social events, and talking to Jake's neighbors. More examples of goal attainment scaling may be found in Glicken (2003).

DIRECTIONS FOR CREATING A
SCALE: INTERVALS AND WEIGHTINGS

On a goal attainment scale, 0% represents the client's functioning at the start of treatment. Each increment of 25% represents the "hoped for" levels of improvement. For purposes of calculating improvement rates,

Table 13.1 A Goal Attainment Scale Measuring Success in Reducing Jake's Depression

CES-D Score	Positive Interactions With Neighbors per Day	Telephone Contact With Children per Month	Swimming Laps per Day	Social Events Attended per Week
(Weighting = .5)	(Weighting = .2)	(Weighting = .1)	(Weighting = .1)	(Weighting = .1)
0% baseline score = 35 on the CES-D	0% = 0 positive interactions	0% = 0 contacts per month	0% = 0 laps per day	0% = 0 social events per week
25% improvement = 30 on the CES-D	25% improvement = 1 positive interaction per day	25% improvement = 1 contact per child per month	25% improvement = 4 laps per day	25% improvement = 1 social event per week
50% improvement = 25 on the CES-D	50% improvement = 2 positive interactions per day	50% improvement = 2 contacts per child per month	50% improvement = 8 laps per day	50% improvement = 2 social events per week
75% improvement = 20 on the CES-D	75% improvement = 3 positive interactions per day	75% improvement = 3 contacts per child per month	75% improvement = 16 laps per day	75% improvement = 3 social events per week
100% improvement = 15 on the CES-D	100% improvement = 4 positive interactions per day	100% improvement = 4 contacts per child per month	100% improvement = 24 laps per day	100% improvement = 4 social events per week

the intervals between the percent of gain made must be equal. In the following goal attainment scale, intervals on the CES-D are 5 points, and intervals of the other variables included on the scale should be consistent with what is realistic, is attainable, and will lead to a reduction in his depression. One hundred percent improvement is our agreed-on improvement rate when a goal has been fully achieved. W (weighting) is the importance of each variable. For computational purposes, total weightings cannot surpass 1.0. The CES-D is a depression instrument with good validity and reliability, which should show improvement as the other four variables improve. Social contact and exercise should increase as the depression lessens. The dependent variable (the depression scale) has a higher weighting than the independent or treatment variables (exercise, calls to his children, social events, and positive social contacts). Indications that the depression is lifting are more significant than treatment inputs but are, in themselves, suggestions that the depression may be lifting.

How to Calculate the Overall
Gain Made on a Goal Attainment Scale

To calculate the total rate of improvement as a result of our treatment with our depressed client Jake, some arbitrary improvement rates are provided for each variable on the goal attainment scale, followed by an interpretation of the meaning of the data. The following improvement rates on each variable seem possible as a result of treatment. The improvement rate on the CES-D was 75% at the end of treatment. By multiplying the actual percent of improvement on the CES-D (75%) times the weighting on the goal attainment scale (.5), we get a 37.5% improvement rate. Doing these calculations with the remaining 4 variables and adding the individual improvement rates will give us a total rate of improvement.

1. Improvement rate on the CES-D = 75%. (Multiply .075 times .5 = 37.5% gain.)

2. Improvement rate in positive social contacts with neighbors = 50%. (Multiply .050 times .2 = 10% gain.)

3. Improvement rate in contacts with his children = 50%. (Multiply .050 times .1 = 5% gain.)

4. Improvement rate in number of laps per day = 25%. (Multiply .025 times .1 = 2.5% gain.)

5. Improvement rate in social events = 75%. (Multiply .075 times .1 = 7.5% gain.)

Add all of the percentages of improvement together for a total improvement rate after 6 months of treatment for depression as follows:

$$CES\text{-}D = 37.5\%$$

$$\text{Social Contacts With Neighbors} = 10.0\%$$

$$\text{Contacts With Children} = 5.0\%$$

$$\text{Swimming Laps} = 2.5\%$$

$$\text{Social Events} = 7.5\%$$

$$\overline{\phantom{\text{Social Events}}}$$

$$\text{Total} = 62.5\%$$

In this example, 62.5% of the contracted goals were achieved after 6 months of treatment.

WHAT THE GOAL ATTAINMENT SCORES TELL US

The therapist's interpretation of the data is as follows: "Jake has achieved more than a 60% gain in the goals we jointly set. There is a 75% improvement rate on the depression scale (the CES-D), but scores on psychological tests may be prone to the halo effect and social desirability. The client has improved in all other areas. The swimming of 4 laps per day may be a realistic level for him. At the very least, he's going to the pool every day, which is certainly a good sign. He has improved in all other areas measured by the scale but, most specifically, in attending social events. This isn't surprising because he can attend an event and not interact with others. Still, all his goals show progress and, given where he was functioning at the beginning of treatment, his improvement rate is significant. Posttests at predetermined intervals will help us track whether his level of improvement is maintained or shows signs of deterioration. If deterioration is apparent, treatment should be reinitiated."

SUMMARY

This chapter discusses anxiety and depression in older adults. Both problems exist in large numbers among an older adult population and frequently coexist. Because older adults are often not thought to be amenable to therapy, underlying symptoms of anxiety and depression may be missed, ignored, or avoided, and medication or other nontherapy approaches may be used instead. Research data suggest that older clients are as positively affected by treatment as younger clients, but are more susceptible to suicide, recurrence of depression, and other serious problems resulting from untreated symptoms. An evaluation approach for measuring change in depression, known as goal attainment scaling, is described and a sample goal attainment scale is provided. This approach can also be used with anxiety and other physical and mental health problems and is just one of a number of ways of determining the link between treatment and change in a client's presenting problems.

Integrative Questions

1. Wouldn't the amount of anxiety and depression in an older population be eliminated if we had free health care, low-cost housing, and support groups for older adults?

2. How can therapy possibly help older adults deal with deteriorating health and the diminished capacity to do physical activities that were so easy for them to do when they were younger, but are now so difficult?

3. The goal attainment scaling approach fails to show a cause-effect relationship between treatment and client improvement. Can you think of some research approaches that might actually show a cause-effect relationship and would therefore be more useful in producing best evidence?

4. Evicting older people from their homes seems entirely wrong. Shouldn't we have laws prohibiting the eviction of older adults, or would there be circumstances in which an eviction might be justified? What might those circumstances be?

5. The case study describing Jake seems to suggest that we not confront older adults who have self-destructive behaviors. How else can we help them if we're unwilling to let them know that their behavior is harmful?

References

American Psychiatric Association. (1994). *Diagnostic and statistical manual of mental disorders* (4th ed.). Washington, DC: Author.

Axelson, J. A. (1985). *Counseling and development in a multicultural society.* Monterey, CA: Brooks/Cole.

Beck, J. G., & Stanley, M. A. (1997). Anxiety disorders in the elderly: The emerging role of behavior therapy. *Behavior Therapy, 28,* 83–100.

Beekman, A. T., Bremmer, M. A., Deeg, D. J. H., van Balkom, A. J., Smit, J. H., de Beurs, E., et al. (1998). Anxiety disorders in later life: A report from the

Longitudinal Aging Study Amsterdam. *International Journal of Geriatric Psychiatry, 12*(10), 717–726.

Blazer, D. G. (1993). *Depression in late life* (2nd ed.). St. Louis, MO: Mosby.

Blazer, D. G., Hughes, D. C., & George, L. K. (1987). The epidemiology of depression in an elderly community population. *Journal of the American Geriatric Society, 27,* 281–287.

Casey, D. A. (1994). Depression in the elderly. *Southern Medical Journal, 87*(5), 559–564.

Denton, W. H., Walsh, S. R., & Daniel, S. S. (2002). Evidence-based practice in family therapy: Adolescent depression as an example. *Journal of Marital and Family Therapy, 28*(1), 39–45.

Gallagher-Thompson, D., Hanley-Peterson, P., & Thompson, L. W. (1990). Maintenance of gains versus relapse following brief psychotherapy for depression. *Journal of Consulting and Clinical Psychology, 58,* 371–374.

Glicken, M. D. (2003). *A simple guide to social research.* Boston: Allyn & Bacon/Longman.

Glicken, M. D. (2004). *The strengths perspective in social work practice: A positive approach for the helping professions.* Boston: Allyn & Bacon/Longman.

Himmelfarb, S., & Murrell, S. A. (1984). Prevalence and correlates of anxiety symptoms in older adults. *Journal of Psychology, 116,* 159–167.

Huffman, G. B. (1999). Preventing recurrence of depression in the elderly. *American Family Physician, 59*(9), 2589–2591.

Kennedy, G. J., & Tannenbaum, S. (2000). Psychotherapy with older adults. *American Journal of Psychotherapy, 54*(3), 386–407.

Kogan, J. N., Edelstein, B. A., & McKee, D. R. (2000). Assessment of anxiety in older adults: Current status. *Journal of Anxiety Disorders, 14*(2), 109–132.

Lang, A. J., & Stein, M. B. (2001). Anxiety disorders. *Geriatrics, 56*(5), 24–30.

Lawton, M. P. (1977). The impact of the environment on aging and behavior. In J. E. Birren & K. W. Schaie (Eds.), *Handbook of the Psychology of Aging* (pp. 276–301). New York: Van Nostrand Reinhold.

Lawton, M. P., & Nahemow, L. (1973). Ecology and the aging process. In C. Eisdorfer and M. P. Lawton (Eds.), *The Psychology of Adult Development and Aging* (pp. 619–674). Washington, DC: American Psychological Association.

Lenze, E. J., Dew, M. A., Mazumdar, S., Begley, A. E., Cornes, C., Miller, M. D., et al. (2002). Combined pharmacotherapy and psychotherapy as maintenance treatment for late-life depression: Effects on social adjustment. *American Journal of Psychiatry, 159*(3), 466–468.

Mills, T. L., & Henretta, J. C. (2001). Racial, ethnic, and socio-demographic differences in the level of psychosocial distress among older Americans. *Research on Aging, 23*(2), 131–152.

O'Connor, R. (2001). Active treatment of depression. *American Journal of Psychotherapy, 55*(4), 507–530.

Robert, S. A., & Li, L. W. (2001). Age variation in the relationship between community socioeconomic status and adult health. *Research on Aging, 23*(2), 233–258.

Rush, A. J., & Giles, D. E. (1982). *Cognitive therapy: Theory and research in short term psychotherapies for depression* (pp. 143–181). New York: Guilford Press.

Saleebey, D. (1992). *The strengths perspective in social work practice.* White Plains, NY: Longman.

Smith, S. S., Sherrill, K. A., & Celenda, C. C. (1995). Anxious elders deserve careful diagnosing and the most appropriate interventions. *Brown University Long-Term Care Letter, 7*(10), 5–7.

Stanley, M. A., & Novy, D. M. (2000). Cognitive-behavior therapy for generalized anxiety in late life: An evaluative overview. *Journal of Anxiety Disorders, 14*(2), 191–207.

Timmermans, S., & Angell, A. (2001). Evidence-based medicine, clinical uncertainty, and learning to doctor. *Journal of Health & Social Behavior, 42*(4), 342.

Tyler, K. A., & Hoyt, D. R. (2000). The effects of an acute stressor on depressive symptoms among older adults. *Research on Aging, 22*(2), 143–164.

Vaillant, G. E., & Mukamal, K. (2001). Successful aging. *American Journal of Psychiatry, 158*(6), 839–847.

Wagner, K. D., & Lorion, R. P. (1984). Correlates of death anxiety in elderly persons. *Journal of Clinical Psychology, 40,* 1235–1241.

Wallis, M. A. (2000). Looking at depression through bifocal lenses. *Nursing, 30*(9), 58–62.

Weick, A., Rapp, C., Sullivan, W. P., & Kisthardt, W. (1989). A strengths perspective for social work practice. *Social Work, 34,* 350–354.

Part 4

Evidence-Based Practice and Alternative Approaches to Helping

Chapter 14 considers best evidence for the impact of religious and spiritual involvement in the physical health and mental health of clients. The research is fairly convincing that religion and spirituality have a very positive impact on clients, but is it good research? This chapter not only reports best evidence but also considers the research difficulties in determining best evidence.

Chapter 15 reports the compelling but somewhat subjective finding that self-help groups may be as effective and sometimes more effective than treatment provided by professionals with a number of medical and mental health problems. Research studies showing significant improvement in client functioning are provided in this chapter with common research issues identified and two case studies included that show how a self-help group is developed and the process of referring a client to a self-help group. Both cases show the way effectiveness of the groups is determined.

Evidence-Based Practice and the Significance of Religion and Spirituality

14

A number of studies provided in this chapter suggest that spirituality and religious involvement may have a positive influence on physical and mental health even though the helping professions have generally separated themselves from religious institutions and ideologies. Despite this sense that spirituality and religious involvement somehow lie outside of the orthodox notions of what mental health professionals should discuss in their practices, researchers agree that it has been a neglected area (Canda, 1988).

This chapter will consider the evidence of the impact of religion and spirituality on physical and mental health. It will also look at the role of helping professionals in dealing with issues of religious and spiritual belief. Several case studies are provided to help better understand the relationship between religion or spirituality and practice. A section at the end of the chapter considers the special research questions posed in an attempt to understand best evidence that spirituality and religion may serve a beneficial role in the lives of people.

Definitions of Spirituality and Religious Involvement

Confusion sometimes exists over the appropriate definitions of spirituality and religious belief. Fraser (Glicken, 2004) defines *spirituality* "as the means by which one finds wholeness, meaning, and purpose in life. It arises from an innate longing for fulfillment through the establishment of loving relationships with self and the community. Spirituality suggests harmony with self, others, and the world" (p. 66). Using a somewhat different definition, Manheimer (1994) says, "Spirituality, while certainly overlapping with church or synagogue affiliation, refers to a psychological and personal inward experience that may be totally independent of institutional membership" (p. 72).

Derezotes (1995) defines *religious involvement* as "a system of beliefs, rituals, and behaviors, usually shared by individuals within an institutionalized structure. It is an external expression of faith" (p. 1). George, Larson, Koenig, and McCullough (2000, p. 105) report an attempt by the National Institute of Aging, in conjunction with the Fitzer Work Group (1997), to define spirituality and religious involvement. They found the following common elements in the definitions of both:

1. Religious/Spiritual Preference or Affiliation: Membership in or affiliation with a specific religious or spiritual group.

2. Religious/Spiritual History: Religious upbringing, duration of participation in religious or spiritual groups, life-changing religious or spiritual experiences, and "turning points" in religious or spiritual participation or belief.

3. Religious/Spiritual Participation: Amount of participation in formal religious or spiritual groups or activities.

4. Religious/Spiritual Private Practices: Private behaviors or activities, including but not limited to prayer, meditation, reading sacred literature, and watching or listening to religious or spiritual radio or television programs.

5. Religious/Spiritual Support: Tangible and intangible forms of social support offered by the members of one's religious or spiritual group.

6. Religious/Spiritual Coping: The extent to which and ways in which religious or spiritual practices are used to cope with stressful experiences.

7. Religious/Spiritual Beliefs and Values: Specific religious or spiritual beliefs and values.

8. Religious/Spiritual Commitment: The importance of religion/spirituality relative to other areas of life and the extent to which religious or spiritual beliefs and practices serve to affect personal values and behavior.

9. Religious/Spiritual Motivation for Regulating and Reconciling Relationships: Most measures in this domain focus on forgiveness, but other issues may be relevant as well (e.g., confession, atonement).

10. Religious/Spiritual Experiences: Personal experience with the divine or sacred, as reflected in emotions and sensations. (p. 105)

The Impact of Spirituality and Religious Involvement on Physical and Mental Health

George et al. (2000) report a growing body of research showing the positive health benefits of religious involvement. According to the authors, religious involvement was found to reduce the likelihood of disease and disability in 78% of the studies attempting to determine the existence of a relationship between religion and health. The positive health benefits of religion were particularly noted with certain medical conditions including coronary disease and heart attacks, emphysema, cirrhosis, and other varieties of liver disease (Comstock & Partridge, 1972; Medalie, Kahn, Naufield, Riss, & Goldbourt, 1973), hypertension (Larson, Koenig, Kaplan, & Levin, 1989; Levin & Vanderpool, 1989), and disability (Idler & Kasl, 1992, 1997). In these studies, "the strongest predictor of the prevention of illness onset is attendance at religious services" (George et al., 2000, p. 108). The authors also point to a relationship between religious observance and longevity, noting that "multiple dimensions of religion are associated with longevity, but attendance at religious services is the most strongly related to longevity" (p. 108).

Although the evidence presented thus far suggests a positive relationship between church attendance and improved physical and mental health, Rauch (2003) reports that the proportion of people who say they never go to religious services has increased 33% from 1973 to 2000. To further confuse the relationship between religious attendance and physical and mental health benefits, Rauch quotes Theology Professor John G. Stackhouse, Jr. as saying: "Beginning in the 1990's, a series of sociological studies has shown that many more Americans tell pollsters they attend church regularly than can be found in church when teams actually count. In fact, actual church going may be half the professed rate" (Rauch, 2003, p. 34). This suggests that the validity of research on church attendance and positive physical and mental health benefits may be in doubt.

Ellison, Boardman, Williams, and Jackson (2001) studied the relationship between religious involvement and positive physical and mental health outcomes. Among their key findings were the following:

1. There is a positive relationship between church attendance and well-being, and an inverse association with distress.

2. The frequency of prayer is inversely related to well-being and only slightly positively related to distress.

3. A belief in eternal life is positively related to well-being but unrelated to distress.

4. Church-based support networks are unrelated to well-being.

5. "There is limited evidence of stress-buffering effects, but not stress-exacerbating effects, of religious involvement" (Ellison et al., 2001, p. 215).

Gartner, Larson, and Allen (1991) comprehensively reviewed more than 200 psychiatric and psychological studies and concluded that religious involvement has a positive impact on both physical and mental health. In another review of the literature, Ellison et al. (2001) concluded,

> There is at least some evidence of mental health benefits of religion among men and women, persons of different ages and racial and ethnic groups, and individuals from various socioeconomic classes and geographical locations. Further, these salutary effects often persist even with an array of social, demographic, and health-related statistical controls. (p. 215)

Manheimer (1994) reports that church membership plays a significant role in the physical and mental health of ethnic and racial minorities. According to Manheimer, church attendance is a strong predictor of happiness among older African Americans, and social activities in church contribute to life satisfaction and personal adjustment. As Haight (1998) notes in her study of the spirituality of African American children,

> Available empirical evidence suggests a relationship between socialization experiences emanating from the African American church and a number of positive developmental outcomes. For example, Brown and Gary (1991) found that self-reports of church involvement were positively related to educational attainment among African American adults. In an interview study of African American urban male adolescents, Zimmerman and Maton (1992) found that youths who left high school before graduation and were not employed, but who attended church, had relatively low levels of alcohol and drug abuse. In a questionnaire administered to African American adults (Seaborn-Thompson & Ensminger, 1989), 74 percent responded "very often" or "often" to the statement, "The religious beliefs I learned when I was young still help me." On the basis of data from the 1979–80 National Survey of Black Americans, Ellison (1993) argued that participation in church communities is positively related to self-esteem in African American adults. (Haight, 1998, p. 215)

Baetz, Larson, Marcoux, Bowen, and Griffin (2002) studied the level of religious interest of psychiatric inpatients to determine whether religious commitment had an impact on selected outcome variables. In the study, 88 consecutive adult patients (50% were men) admitted to an inpatient facility were interviewed about their religious beliefs and practices. Patients with a Beck Depression Inventory score of 12 or more were included for outcome analysis. The researchers report the following results:

1. Frequent worship attendees were more satisfied with their lives and had fewer symptoms of depression, shorter hospital stays, and much lower rates of current or lifetime use of alcohol when compared to subjects with less frequent or nonexistent worship attendance.

2. The authors believe that worship may protect clients against greater severity of symptoms and longer hospital stays, increase satisfaction with life, reduce the severity of symptoms, and enhance the quality of life among psychiatric patients.

Kissman and Maurer (2002) report, "People with strong faith, regardless of religious persuasion, live longer, experience less anxiety, cope better with stressful life events, have lower blood pressures and stronger immune systems" (Koening, 1998; Dossey, 1997). Krucoff and Crater (1998) found that coronary surgery patients who were prayed for by congregations had a better recovery rate when compared with patients in a control group where prayer was not used. George et al. (2000) report that religious involvement and spirituality have been shown to reduce the onset of illness. Once the illness is present, recovery is faster and longevity is greater than in those who are not involved with religion or spirituality. The authors write that healthy religious involvement may positively affect the course of an illness and lead to longer survival after heart transplants (Harris, Dew, & Lee, 1995); lower mortality rates after cardiac surgeries (Oxman, Freeman, & Manheimer, 1995); a reduced risk of repeated heart attacks, which might be fatal or nonfatal (Thoresen, 1990); reduced death rates among women with breast cancer (Spiegel, Bloom, & Kraemer, 1989); and an increased ability to cope with pain (Kaczorowski, 1989; Landis, 1996; O'Brien, 1982) and may prove to be the most significant reason for better medical recoveries and outcomes (George et al., 2000).

One of the criticisms of studies regarding evaluating the impact of religious and spiritual involvement is that methodologies are problematic; however, George et al. (2000) indicate that the studies they cite were multivariate, indicating that other factors that might affect improved health results were controlled for, and that longitudinal studies showing the long-term impact on health of religious/spiritual involvement continue to show a strong relationship. The authors also note that the evidence for the impact of religious/spiritual involvement on mental health is even stronger than it is for physical health.

Religious involvement appears to be associated with faster and more complete recovery from mental illnesses, substance abuse/dependence, and depression (George, 1992; Koenig, in press; Koenig et al., 1998). Compared to patients who report no or low levels of religious involvement, those who report stronger religious involvement are more likely to recover and to do so more quickly. Evidence indicating a relationship between religious or spiritual involvement and recovery from substance abuse is based upon studies of Alcoholics Anonymous (AA) and other

12-step programs (Emrick, 1987; Montgomery, Miller, & Tonigan, 1995; Project Match Research Group, 1997). According to George et al. (2000), "A central component of these programs is the belief that one has no personal control over the addiction, but that there is a higher power who can help the individual to control it" (p. 109). According to the authors, all of the studies they cite are again multivariate studies that control for a variety of intervening variables and that longitudinal studies following subjects over a long period of time confirm the existence of a relationship between spirituality and religious involvement and better recovery from mental illness, depression, and substance abuse.

Although the vast majority of studies indicate a positive benefit from religious and spiritual involvement, there is some evidence that certain religious beliefs may cause harm. Simpson (1989) found that a sample of Christian Scientists died at younger ages than their peers. Asser and Swan (1998) studied child deaths in families refusing medical care in favor of faith healing and found much higher rates of death. Both sets of authors believe that there are healthy and unhealthy uses of spirituality and religious involvement but have thus far been unable to determine precisely what they are and how physical and mental health are affected.

Case Study: A Client Using Religion to Cope With a Traumatic Childhood

Ellen Hanson is a 36-year-old attorney who was repeatedly sexually molested by her father between ages 6 and 17. When the molestation was finally discovered, through a complaint filed by a neighbor who overheard Ellen tell the neighbor's daughter what had been taking place in her home, Ellen went to live with her maternal grandmother, and continues to live there at present. Ellen has always been an exceptional student and won scholarships to undergraduate school and law school, where she was selected for the law review at a highly prestigious university in her hometown. Her high standing in law school led to an internship with a state supreme court justice and a partnership in one of her community's most respected law firms. Ellen is very successful at work but has become a lonely and solitary person in her personal life. She works 80–90 hours a week and has no personal life, friends, or social activities. When she returns home to her grandmother's house after work, she drinks herself to sleep.

As her grandmother has begun to experience health problems, Ellen has begun to feel panicky about her future and has sought the advice of a therapist who has done some consulting work for her law firm. The therapist suggested therapy as a first step, but Ellen was antagonistic toward the idea because her father was in treatment during the entire time she was molested. Instead of therapy, Ellen began going to a local church. At first she went on Sundays, but as the experience became increasingly positive, she began going to evening services. She found the experience warm and soothing without actually feeling any spiritual involvement. She liked the people who attended and sometimes stayed after services to chat. For the first time in her life, she felt a social connection with others. She also felt less desire to drink and began thinking about her future and where she might live if her grandmother's health continued to fail.

In describing the experience to the therapist she had initially consulted, Ellen said, "I don't believe in God and I find religion shallow and meaningless. After all, my father was a churchgoing man and look what he did to me. I think it's all hypocritical nonsense. But when I began going to services, I could feel a lot of genuine warmth and caring from the other people. I felt soothed by the experience and less angry, and I've been very angry most of my life. Who wouldn't be? I put all of my energies into succeeding, and I have, but at what a price. I have no friends. Relationships are completely out of the question. The thought of sex makes me physically ill. I find the thought of a man touching me repulsive. But going to church, I don't know, it's not very rational and I can't quite explain it, but I feel very loved there.

"Usually, I feel unclean. I mean kids who get molested, my God, what an awful thing to happen. We fight to keep our sanity and we do what needs to be done to survive, but at such a high price to our personal lives. I can't go into a crowded room and have a man accidentally bump into me without becoming sick to my stomach. I want to love and be loved, but the thought of being touched is just too repulsive for me to describe. But at church, I don't know, I feel clean. I feel loved and admired, things I never felt about myself. It's made a difference, it really has. I've joined a support group for women who were molested as kids. I mentor a young girl who was molested. I do pro bono work for women who were molested and now are being abused by their husbands and boyfriends. I feel like I've rejoined the human race. And the thing is, I've forgiven my father. What he did doesn't seethe inside me like it used to. I never see him, of course, but I don't go around thinking about him all the time or planning my revenge like I used to do. I don't think I can explain it, but being in church and watching the other people, and feeling their elation and joy, it's touched me and I don't think I'll ever be the same. I help the church with legal issues and I help the parishioners when I can. I feel like a human being and I can tell you that before going to church, that's not how I felt at all. What to make of it? I don't know, but it beats being mad all the time and it certainly beats drinking myself into a stupor. When I can figure it out for myself, maybe I'll be able to explain it better. For now, thankfully, I'm a happier and healthier person, and that's what counts, isn't it?"

DISCUSSION

Why would Ellen go to church, given the fact that her father went to church, but not enter therapy because her father was in therapy during the time he molested her? Perhaps the answer is that therapy is a more intimate and challenging experience for most people. It requires a level of engagement that church may not. Perhaps the loving and tender people in the congregation gave Ellen a level of unconditional positive regard that she hasn't experienced before. And maybe the group experience allows a certain amount of introspection and meditation that helps give her inner strength. Ellen maintains that her feelings about church and about religion remain negative. Taking her at her word, one can only assume that the social contact and the sense of community provide a needed element in Ellen's life. One can't deny the positive movement she's made, although there are still critical problems for Ellen to work through that may not be possible just by attending services. Intimacy and relationships are serious matters. Most people need both experiences in their lives to remain content and to achieve a degree of fulfillment. Can Ellen live her life without either? It would be hard to imagine her feeling complete or fulfilled when she cannot be intimate or have a loving and personal relationship with someone special. But childhood traumas often make survivors out of children and perhaps Ellen can benefit from the sense of community she's developed in church; perhaps it will lead to a journey that will include relationships and intimacy. In the meantime, Ellen seems to be headed in a positive and self-correcting direction. She is a resilient and intelligent woman, which means that almost anything may be possible.

Why Does Religious and Spiritual Involvement Impact Physical and Mental Health?

Ellison and Levin (1998) suggest three reasons for the beneficial impact of religious involvement and spirituality.

1. Controlling Health-Related Risks. Some religions have specific prohibitions against at-risk health behaviors. These prohibitions may eliminate or at least reduce the use of tobacco and alcohol, premarital sexual experiences and other risky sexual activity, use of foods that may contribute to high cholesterol and heart problems, and strong prohibitions against the use of illegal drugs. Many religions encourage good health practices. The Mormons, Seventh Day Adventists, and other religious groups with strict prohibitions concerning health-related behaviors are healthier and live longer, on average, than members of other faiths and those who are uninvolved in religion (Enstrom, 1978, 1989; Gardner &

Lyon, 1982; Lyon, Klauber, & Gardner, 1976; Phillips, Kuzma, & Beeson, 1980). However, George et al. (2000) believe that strict prohibitions on health-related behaviors only explain 10% of the reasons that religious and spiritual beliefs have a positive impact on health and mental health.

   2. Social Support. A second possible reason religion may positively affect health is the fellowship, support, and social bonds developed among people who are religiously affiliated. When compared to their nonreligious peers, people who regularly attend religious services report (a) larger social networks, (b) more contact with those social networks, (c) more help received from others, and (d) more satisfaction with their social support network (Ellison & George, 1992; Zuckerman, Kasl, & Ostfeld, 1984). Despite this, social support provides only a 5%–10% explanation of the relationship between religion and health (Idler, 1987; Zuckerman et al., 1984).

   3. Life Meaning, or the Coherence Hypothesis. A third explanation for the health benefits of religion is that people who are religious understand "their role in the universe, the purpose of life, and develop the courage to endure suffering" (George et al., 2000, p. 110). The authors call this the "coherence hypothesis" and note that the connection between a sense of coherence about the meaning of life and one's role in the universe affects 20%–30% of a client's physical and mental health, largely because it buffers clients from stress (Antonovsky, 1980; Idler, 1987).

   Other writers have noted the positive impact of spirituality and religious belief when serious illness is present. Kubler-Ross (1969/1997) suggests that coping with the possibility of death and disability often leads to life-changing growth and new and more complex behaviors that focus on the meaning of life. Greenstein and Breitbart (2000) write, "Existentialist thinkers, such as Frankl, view suffering as a potential springboard, both for having a need for meaning and for finding it" (p. 486). Frankl (1978) believed that life meaning could be found in our actions, our values, and in our suffering. Commenting on the meaning of suffering, Frankl wrote that even while facing imminent death, there is still the opportunity to find meaning in the experience. "What matters, then, is the stand he takes in his predicament . . . the attitude we choose in suffering" (Frankl, 1978, p. 24). Balk (1999), however, believes that three issues must be present for a physical or mental health crisis to create coherence: "The situation must create a psychological imbalance or disequilibrium that resists readily being stabilized; there must be time for reflection; and the person's life must forever afterwards be colored by the crisis" (p. 485).

   One further study of the coherence hypothesis is a recent longitudinal study of a Catholic order of women in the Midwest by Danner, Snowdon, & Friesen (2001). The study found that a person's positive view of life and life meaning can have a significant impact on physical and emotional health. The authors found that positive and affirming personal statements written by very young women to enter the religious order correlated with a life span as long as 10 years beyond the mean length of life for women in the religious order and as much as 20 years or longer than the general population. Many of the women in the sample of 650 lived well into their nineties, and 6 women in the order were older than 100. The authors believe that the reasons for longer life relate to good nutritional and health practices and a communal environment that focuses on spirituality and helping others.

Should Issues of Religion and Spirituality Be Included in the Work of the Helping Professions?

The prior research indicates that religious involvement and spirituality may have a positive impact on physical and mental health. However, there is a lack of agreement about whether helping professionals should learn about both issues in their training or even include either in their work with clients. In a study of 53 social work faculty members, Dudley and Helfgott (1990) found that those opposed to a course on spirituality were concerned about conflict with the mission of social work, problems stemming from the separation of church and state, and concerns that religious and spiritual material in the curriculum would conflict with the personal beliefs of faculty members and students. Sheridan, Wilmer, and Atcheson (1994) asked educators from 25 schools of social work questions regarding the inclusion of religious and spiritual content in social work programs. The majority (82.5%) supported inclusion in a specialized elective course. In another study, Sheridan, Bullis, Adcock, Berlin, and Miller (1992) surveyed 328 social work practitioners and found that 83% received little training in religion and spirituality during their graduate studies, although a third of their clients discussed religious or spiritual concerns during treatment.

Sheridan (2000) found that 73% of the social workers surveyed had generally positive attitudes about the appropriateness of discussing religion and spirituality in practice. Forty-three percent of the respondents said that religion played a positive role in the lives of their clients, and 62% said that spirituality played a positive role in the lives of clients. Spirituality was reported to play a harmful role in the lives of their clients only 12% of the time, while religion was reported to be detrimental to client functioning 21% of the time (Sheridan, 2000). A majority of the social workers responding said they had used spiritually and religiously based interventions with clients even though most (84%) reported little or no prior instruction. However, more than half of the respondents had attended workshops and conferences on religion and spirituality following completion of their professional training.

Amato-von Hemert (1994) believes we should include material on religious involvement and spirituality in graduate training, and writes, "Just as we train and evaluate how workers address issues of class, gender, and race, we must maintain our professionalism by training workers to deal with religious issues" (p. 9). Tobias, Morrison, and Gray (1995) note, "Today's multiethnic America encompasses a wide-ranging spiritual orientation that is, if anything, diverse" (p. 1), while Dudley and Helfgott (1990) suggest, "Understanding spirituality is essential to understanding the culture of numerous ethnic groups that social workers help" (p. 288).

In attempting to find a definition of practice that includes religious and spiritual content, Boorstein (2000) reports that a study by Lajoie and Shapiro (1992) found more than 200 definitions of transpersonal (spiritual) psychology. However, the authors summarized those definitions by writing, "Transpersonal psychology is concerned with the study of humanity's highest potential, and with the recognition, understanding, and realization of intuitive, spiritual, and transcendent states of consciousness" (p. 91). Boorstein (2000) indicates that the differences between traditional psychotherapy and spiritually based psychotherapy are as follows:

1. Traditional psychotherapy is pessimistic. For example, Freud said that psychoanalysis attempts to convert "neurotic misery to ordinary misery" (Boorstein, 2000, p. 413).

2. Spiritually based psychotherapy tries to help clients gain awareness of the existence of joy, love and happiness in their lives.

3. Spiritually based therapy is concerned with life meaning and not just symptom removal.

A DISSENTING VIEW

In a dissenting view of the inclusion of religious and spiritual issues in practice, Sloan and Bagiella (2001) conclude that, although interest in the impact of religious involvement and spirituality on health is great,

> the empiric support required to convert this interest into recommendations for health practice is weak and inconclusive at best, with most studies having numerous methodological shortcomings. Even if there were methodologically solid findings demonstrating associations between religious and spiritual activities and health outcomes, problems would still exist. (p. 33)

The authors point out the following methodological problems in trying to demonstrate a positive relationship between religious and spiritual involvement and improved health benefits:

First, "we have no idea, for example, whether recommending that patients attend religious services will lead to increased attendance and, if so, whether attendance under these conditions will lead to better health outcomes" (Sloan & Bagiella, 2001, p. 34). Many factors influencing health are beyond the scope of practice. While marital status is strongly associated with health effects, most practitioners would "recoil" at recommending marriage because of its positive relationship to health. Futhermore, "recommending religion to patients in this context may be coercive" (p. 34) because it creates two classes of people: those who comply and those who don't. This may lead to the implication that poor health may be linked to insufficient spiritual or religious involvement. The authors conclude that "the absence of compelling empiric evidence and the substantial ethical concerns raised suggest that, at the very least, it is premature to recommend making religious and spiritual activities adjunctive treatments" (p. 34).

In summary, there is compelling evidence that many clients have strong religious and spiritual beliefs that play an important role in the way they cope with social, emotional, and physical difficulties. While many practitioners understand and value the importance of religious and spiritual beliefs, few feel prepared to work with either issue and most feel that professional education should include content related to understanding and applying knowledge related to spirituality and religious beliefs. However, concerns were raised when faculties were asked how material would be taught, given the diverse nature of faculties and student bodies in the helping profession.

Case Study: Religious Issues Discussed in Treatment

Jack Barton is a 25-year-old man seen in treatment for problems of depression, anxiety, and substance abuse. In the course of gathering information for a psychosocial history, Jack told the therapist that an adult congregant had molested him in church when he was 10 years old, and he has been unable to attend religious services since. He used to find great meaning in his religion and realizes that a terrible event has shaken his willingness to take part in something that he thinks is important for his well-being. Jack asked the therapist if they could talk about the molestation and his subsequent absence from religious participation. The therapist agreed but told Jack that the actual reentry into the functions of the church would be a decision that he alone could make.

Jack said the congregant involved in his molestation had been spoken to by the minister but had not faced legal charges. Jack wanted to file charges against the man, who is a congregant in the same church denomination in another community. With the therapist's help, the county attorney was contacted. He investigated the case with the local authorities and found out that complaints had been filed with Jack's former church on two other occasions. The county attorney asked people with concerns about the congregant, a prominent member of his current church and president of the board of directors of the church, to come forth, and a case was made that was so compelling that the congregant resigned his position and agreed to a plea bargain sending him to jail for 5 years for child endangerment. It wasn't the severity of punishment that Jack hoped for but it helped reduce his overall feelings of powerlessness that nothing had been done in the past.

The issue of a return to the church where he had been molested was another matter. The therapist suggested that he talk to the current minister to find out if the church's theology and Jack's current religious needs were compatible, but Jack said that going back to the church would be too traumatic. Might there be other churches with similar beliefs that Jack could contact? Jack agreed to look into this and finally joined a church but had very limited involvement. When asked why, Jack just said that times were different now and what he used to believe in was no longer meaningful to him. He subsequently dropped out of the church.

Jack's progress in treatment was very limited and, believing that Jack might progress at a faster pace, the therapist began discussing Jack's religious beliefs. In the midst of an early discussion, Jack burst out crying and said that the thoughts he was having were too painful for him to manage and asked that they not talk about religion anymore. The next week, Jack came for treatment prepared to discuss the issue that had so upset him. It wasn't only the molestation that had troubled Jack, he told the therapist, it was also the excuse that Jack's parents had used with him for not reporting his molester to the police. Perhaps, they explained, Jack was partly responsible and had encouraged the molestation. Because the church Jack attended thought that people were deeply flawed and that negative things happened to sinful people, perhaps Jack had been born sinful. Jack told the therapist that he had never stopped believing that about himself and that, although the church had been important to him in childhood, he now saw the church's theology as unkind and unhealthy. He didn't think he could ever believe in any religion again, but he had nothing to take its place and felt spiritually adrift.

The therapist referred Jack to a group that discussed spirituality. Many of the people in the group had feelings about religion that were similar to Jack's. Perhaps the group could serve as a substitute for his religious needs. Jack reluctantly attended the group meetings but came away with ambivalent feelings. "I don't know what to say," he told his therapist. "It's like being in church without the sermons and the ceremonies. People in the group believe in something, but I can't be certain what it is. They say negative things about religion but they have no substitute that makes any sense to me. And most of them are very angry at religion. They think that whatever they believe now is a substitute, but I can't see that it is. I think we should talk about my other problems. Religion is a dead issue to me now."

DISCUSSION

Should the therapist have discussed religion with Jack? Certainly Jack asked her to. Why the feeling of dead-endedness then? Perhaps the issues that Jack wanted to talk about had more to do with his reasons for leaving the church. That seems like a safer and more productive avenue of discussion. And rather than offering the spirituality group as a substitute, perhaps the therapist might have asked Jack to define his religious and spiritual beliefs and to use them as a guide for finding a like-minded group of people. The need to understand his parent's behavior and a religious philosophy of human behavior that makes victims into perpetrators seems more in keeping with the therapist's area of expertise. Perhaps focusing on Jack's reaction to his parents and his relationship with them might have also proven more beneficial. Additionally, Jack's lack of progress in treatment may be completely unrelated to his religious experiences. Perhaps the issue of religion is a smoke screen to prevent discussion of other, more compelling issues such as his sexuality and his feelings of self-worth. The fact that a molester was sent to jail because of Jack's persistence, but resulted in no real improvement in Jack's functioning, is a good indication that what Jack needs to discuss only marginally has to do with theology and more probably relates to the impact of the molestation and his adaptation to it. Issues of religious and spiritual belief are important matters in people's lives, but in therapy, they may be secondary to other more pressing and current problems that, if resolved, may ultimately lead to the resolution of religious and spiritual conflict. And, finally, perhaps the therapist might have consulted the literature to find similar cases or spoken to a clergyman who might have been able to offer advice and direction. When in doubt, seeking information and advice seems the professional thing to do.

Problematic Research Issues

Many unresolved research issues still remain as we consider the relevance of religious involvement and spirituality in physical and mental health. Those issues are as follows:

1. Is there clear evidence that religion plays an important role in physical and mental health? This is still a fairly new field and do we have sufficient evidence to suggest a link? Not all of the research to date has been

positive or has found a relationship between positive health and religious involvement. In a review of the available correlational studies that attempt to link religion with positive mental health, Batson and Ventis (1982) write,

> Being more religious is not associated with greater mental health or happiness or with greater social compassion and concern. Quite the contrary, there is strong evidence that being more religious is associated with poorer mental health, with greater intolerance of people who are different from ourselves, and with no greater concern for those in need. The evidence suggests that religion is a negative force in human life, one we would be better off without. (p. 306)

2. We need clear definitions of the distinctions between religious belief and spirituality. Most people consider themselves to be spiritual. If that's the case, most people should be healthier than they really are. This raises a fundamental research problem. If you ask people whether they are healthy, most people will say yes. When you ask them if they are spiritual or religious, most people will also say yes. If this is the case, how can we determine a link between religious involvement or spirituality and well-being? Most research studies use self-reports to do this, but one wonders about their accuracy. In order to show connections with mental health, we have to prove that people are spiritual and/or religious and we need behavioral measures of well-being. How might we do this since most measures of well-being are based on self-reports or on instruments that often lack reliability and validity? These several research issues suggest great difficulty in showing links between well-being and spiritual or religious convictions, beliefs, and involvement. The wise consumer will pay great attention to a study's methodology before using the findings.

3. Do all religious groups have an equally positive impact on physical and mental health? We know that some religious groups are antagonistic toward gays and lesbians. Some groups are exclusionary and believe that nonmembers are inferior. Some religious groups have moral codes that demand such a high commitment that most people break those codes with resulting feelings of guilt. Can these religious groups have a positive impact on the physical and mental health of participants? In responding to these questions, George et al. (2000) note, "Groups of people who feel that their religion has harmed them should be studied in depth. It also would be helpful to study people who profess no religious or spiritual involvement. These patterns may have different implications for health" (p. 112).

4. Does religious affiliation and spirituality actually answer questions about life meaning, considered so important to good physical and mental health? Many people see religious attendance as primarily a social experience and not as an existential one. Rauch (2003) finds that many people have only a vague notion of the theology of their religion and are tolerant of

other people's beliefs to such a degree that Rauch has coined the term "apatheist" to describe someone "who cares little about one's own religion and has an even stronger disinclination to care about other people's" (p. 34).

5. Is it religious attendance that impacts health? That appears to be a rather vague concept. We all know people who attend religious services but who are not ethical, healthy, or spiritual. And how do we resolve the dilemma of people saying they attend religious services when they don't? These concerns have major significance for attempts to relate religious attendance to better physical and mental health.

6. Does becoming spiritual or religious late in life have any relevance for overall health? For religious affiliation and spirituality to be significant, shouldn't it occur early in life when the positive effects of either would have their most compelling impact? George et al. (2000) believe that we need to know more about a person's religious or spiritual history. Most contemporary research focuses on a person's current religious or spiritual involvement, but to really see a connection between involvement and well-being, designs must be longitudinal in nature and should consider a person's life course. George et al. write, "Does a lifetime of religious involvement have greater health benefits than a shorter, more recent history of spirituality? What about dramatic changes in one's involvement (e.g., conversion experiences, switching denominations, losses of faith)? Any or all of these might have differential effects on health" (p. 112).

7. Are men and women and diverse ethnic and racial groups equally affected by religious/spiritual involvement? Was the composition of religious groups studied in the research offered in this chapter mostly mainstream? And if so, how would marginal groups fare whose practices are sometimes cultish, disturbing, and even unlawful?

8. Is socioeconomic status a better explanation for good physical and mental health than religious and spiritual involvement? Would the evidence about the beneficial effects of healthy communities presented in the chapter on older adults be more important to physical and mental health than religious and/or spiritual involvement? A good study should factor in all the probable variables to explain well-being and test them against one another to determine which of the variables has the most positive or negative impact. Religious and spiritual involvement may be influenced by where one lives, the safety of a community, friendships, support networks, and finances, to name a few. Some congregations require very high membership dues or tithing of a certain amount of a congregant's income, requirements that may actually drive people away from religion. Might the amount one pays for dues be a stronger influence on attendance than positive associations with the religious experience? Might tithing represent a spiritual investment in the future that is more superstitious than real? If one tithes or pays higher dues, might this encourage people to believe that their experiences in life and in the afterlife will be more positive? In other

words, is the money paid a more powerful influence on well-being than the actual religious involvement?

9. Does membership in groups that give people a sense of purpose (self-help groups, therapy groups, community action groups, political groups, and charitable groups) have an equally positive impact on physical and mental health when compared to religious involvement and spirituality?

10. Although some of the writers in this chapter suggest that helping professionals should discuss issues of religion and spirituality with clients, is that a good idea and might the practitioner lose objectivity in the process? Clinicians working with clients who have a fundamentalist belief in religion may have a difficult time containing their bias. Religious discussions may also lead to proselytizing by the practitioner. These issues certainly need to be explored more fully before clinicians are encouraged to become involved in issues pertaining to religious and spiritual beliefs.

11. Are people who are inclined to become spiritually or religiously involved more likely to be physically and emotionally healthy to begin with? The study of the religious order of women in the Midwest seems to suggest this.

12. Is there a hierarchy in power between religious involvement and spirituality? Is one more significant to well-being than the other? How do we understand people who are deeply ambivalent about religion and have no real philosophy regarding life meaning, who don't think of themselves as spiritual but who are, nonetheless, very good people who are also physically and emotionally healthy?

13. A fundamental final question: Is it even possible to study the impact of religious and spiritual involvement because of the methodological problems inherent in such research? Going to church, expressing a belief in God, and finding meaning in religious observances are not easily quantifiable issues. Saying that a relationship exists between attendance and better health may be entirely spurious. Can methodologies even be constructed that avoid spurious arguments and provide meaningful answers? This is a fundamental question we need to ask when we continue research efforts to find out whether a relationship exists between well-being and religious involvement or spirituality.

SUMMARY

This chapter reports a number of positive studies showing a relationship between religious and spiritual involvement and better physical and mental health. Concerns are raised about methodological problems and whether positive findings suggest a role for mental health practitioners. The chapter notes the attempts to change curriculums in programs training helping professionals to include content on religious and spiritual beliefs and the difficult nature of the process. Even so, many professionals believe that these issues are fundamental to client well-being and that effective practitioners should know about the religious and spiritual beliefs of their clients and use them, in some fashion, in their practice.

Integrative Questions

1. Do you think religious and spiritual issues should be acknowledged and even discussed in our work with clients? Give compelling reasons why you feel or don't feel this way.

2. Much of the chapter dealt with the religious experience. Research on spirituality seems much less in evidence and was only mentioned in passing. Why do you think this is the case?

3. How would you explain people who regularly attend religious services, are observant, but are not "good" people (they're unethical, unhelpful to others, bigoted, self-centered, etc.)?

4. How can religions that have unhealthy beliefs about other people have a healthy impact on participants?

5. Would you become involved in discussions of religious and spiritual practices with clients? If so, would there be limits to the discussion? What might they be?

References

Amato-von Hemert, K. (1994). Point/counterpoint: Should social work education address religious issues? Yes! *Journal of Social Work Education, 30,* 7–11.

Antonovsky, A. (1980). *Health, stress, and coping.* San Francisco: Jossey-Bass.

Asser, S. M., & Swan, K. (1998). Child fatalities from religion-motivated medical neglect. *Pediatrics, 101,* 625–629.

Baetz, M., Larson, D. B., Marcoux, G., Bowen, R., & Griffin, R. (2002). Canadian psychiatric inpatient religious commitment: An association with mental health. *Canadian Journal of Psychiatry, 47*(2), 159–167.

Balk, D. E. (1999). Bereavement and spiritual change. *Death Studies, 23*(6), 485–493.

Batson, C. D., & Ventis, W. L. (1982). *The religious experience: A social-psychological perspective.* New York: Oxford University Press.

Boorstein, S. (2000). Transpersonal psychotherapy. *American Journal of Psychotherapy,* *54*(3), 408–423.

Brown, D. R., & Gary, L. E. (1991). Religious socialization and educational attainment among African Americans: An empirical assessment. *Journal of Negro Education, 3,* 411–426.

Canda, E. R. (1988). Spirituality, religious diversity, and social work practice. *Social Casework, 69,* 238–247.

Comstock, G. W., & Partridge, K. B. (1972). Church attendance and health. *Journal of Chronic Diseases, 25,* 665–672.

Danner, D. D., Snowdon, D. A., & Friesen, W. V. (2001). Positive emotions in early life and longevity: Findings from the nun study. *Journal of Personality and Social Psychology, 80*(5), 804–813.

Derezotes, D. S. (1995). Spirituality and religiosity: Neglected factors in social work practice. *Arête, 20*(1), 1–15.

Dossey, L. (1997). *Prayer is good medicine: How to reap the healing benefits of prayer.* San Francisco: Harper.

Dudley, J. R., & Helfgott, C. (1990). Exploring a place for spirituality in the social work curriculum. *Journal of Social Work Education, 26(3),* 287–294.

Ellison, C. G., & George, L. K. (1992). Religious involvement, social ties, and social support in a southeastern community. *Journal for the Scientific Study of Religion, 33,* 46–61.

Ellison, C. G., & Levin, J. S. (1998). The religion-health connection: Evidence theory and future directions. *Health Education and Behavior, 25,* 700–720.

Ellison, G., Boardman, J. D., Williams, D. R., & Jackson, J. S. (2001). Religious involvement, stress and mental health: Findings from the 1995 Detroit area study. *Social Forces, 80*(1), 215–235.

Emrick, C. D. (1987). Alcoholics Anonymous: Affiliative processes and effectiveness as treatment. *Alcoholism: Clinical and Experimental Research, 11*(5), 416–423.

Enstrom, J. E. (1978). Cancer and total mortality among active Mormons. *Cancer, 42,* 1913–1951.

Enstrom, J. E. (1989). Health practices and cancer mortality among active California Mormons. *Journal of the National Cancer Institute, 81,* 1807–1814.

Frankl, V. E. (1978). *Psychotherapy and existentialism: Selected papers on logotherapy.* New York: Touchstone Books.

Gardner, J. W., & Lyon, J. L. (1982). Cancer in Utah Mormon men by lay priesthood level. *American Journal of Epidemiology, 116,* 243–257.

Gartner, J., Larson, D. B., & Allen, G. D. (1991). Religious commitment and mental health: A review of the empirical literature. *Journal of Psychology and Theology, 19,* 625.

George, L. K. (1992). Social factors and the onset and outcome of depression. In K. W. Schaie, J. S. House, & D. G. Blazer (Eds.), *Aging, health behaviors, and health outcomes* (pp. 137–159). Hillsdale, NJ: Erlbaum.

George, L. K., Larson, D. B., Koenig, H. G., & McCullough, M. E. (2000). Spirituality and health: What we know, what we need to know. *Journal of Social and Clinical Psychology, 19*(1), 102–116.

Glicken, M. D. (2004). *Using the strengths perspective in social work practice: A positive approach for the helping professions.* Boston: Allyn & Bacon/Longman.

Greenstein, M., & Breitbart, W. (2000). Cancer and the experience of meaning: A group psychotherapy program for people with cancer. *American Journal of Psychotherapy, 54*(4), 486–500.

Haight, W. L. (1998, May). "Gathering the spirit" at First Baptist Church: Spirituality as a protective factor in the lives of African American children. *Social Work, 43*(3), 213–221.

Harris, R. C., Dew, M. A., & Lee, A. (1995). The association of social relationships and activities with mortality: Prospective evidence from the Tecumseh Community Health Study. *American Journal of Epidemiology, 116,* 123–140.

Idler, E. L. (1987). Religious involvement and the health of the elderly: Some hypotheses and an initial test. *Social Forces, 66,* 226–238.

Idler, E. L., & Kasl, S. V. (1992). Religion: Disability, depression, and the timing of death. *American Journal of Sociology, 97,* 1052–1079.

Idler, E. L., & Kasl, S. V. (1997). Religion among disabled elderly persons II: Attendance at religious services as a predictor of the course of disability. *Journal of Gerontology: Social Sciences,* S306–S316.

Kaczorowski, J. M. (1989). Spiritual well-being and anxiety in adults diagnosed with cancer. *Hospice Journal, 5,* 105–126.

Kissman, K., & Maurer, L. (2002). East meets west: Therapeutic aspects of spirituality in health, mental health and addiction recovery. *International Social Work, 45*(1), 35–44.

Koenig, H. G. (1998). *The Healing Power of Faith.* New York: Simon & Schuster.

Koenig, H. G. (in press). Does religiosity contribute to the remission of depression? *Harvard Mental Health Letter.*

Koenig, H. G., George, L. K., Cohen, H. J., Hays, J. C., Larson, D. B., & Blazer, D. G. (1998). The relationship between religious activities and cigarette smoking in older adults. *Journal of Gerontology: Medical Sciences, 53A,* M426–M434.

Krucoff, M., & Crater, S. (1998). Paper presented at the American Heart Association National Meeting, Dallas, TX.

Kubler-Ross, E. (1997). *On death and dying.* New York: Scribner Classics. (Original work published 1969)

Lajoie, D. H., & Shapiro, S. Y. (1992). Definitions of transpersonal psychology: The first twenty-three years. *Journal of Transpersonal Psychology, 24*(1), 79–98.

Landis, B. J. (1996). Uncertainty, spiritual well-being, and psychosocial adjustment to chronic illness. *Issues in Mental Health Nursing, 27,* 217–231.

Larson, D. B., Koenig, H. G., Kaplan, B. H., & Levin, J. S. (1989). The impact of religion on men's blood pressure. *Journal of Religion and Health, 28,* 265–278.

Levin, J. S., & Vanderpool, H. Y. (1989). Is religion therapeutically significant for hypertension? *Social Science and Medicine, 29,* 69–78.

Lyon, L., Klauber, M. R., & Gardner, J. Y. (1976). Cancer incidence in Mormons and non-Mormons in Laah, 1966–1970. *New England Journal of Medicine, 294,* 129–133.

Manheimer, R. J. (Ed.). (1994). *Older Americans almanac.* Detroit, MI: Gale Research.

Medalie, J. H., Kahn, H. A., Neufeld, H. N., Riss, E., & Goldbourt, U. (1973). Five-year myocardial infarction incidence II: Association of single variables to age and birthplace. *Journal of Chronic Disease, 26,* 329–349.

Montgomery, H. A., Miller, W. R., & Tonigan, J. S. (1995). Does Alcoholics Anonymous involvement predict treatment outcome? *Journal of Substance Abuse Treatment, 22,* 241–246.

National Institute on Aging/Fetzer Institute Working Group. (1997). *Measurement scale on religion, spirituality, health, and aging.* Bethesda, MD: National Institute on Aging.

O'Brien, M. E. (1982). Religious faith and long-term adjustment to hemodialysis. *Journal of Religion and Health, 21,* 68–80.

Oxman, T. E., Freeman, T. H., Jr., & Manheimer, E. D. (1995). Lack of social participation or religious strength and comfort as risk factors for death after cardiac surgery in the elderly. *Psychosomatic Medicine, 57*(1), 5–15.

Phillips, R. L., Kuzma, J., & Beeson, W. L. (1980). Influence of selection versus lifestyle on risk of fatal cancer and cardiovascular disease among Seventh Day Adventists. *American Journal of Epidemiology, 712,* 296–314.

Project MATCH Research Group. (1997). Matching alcoholism treatments to client heterogeneity: Project MATCH posttreatment drinking outcomes. *Journal of Studies on Alcohol, 58,* 7–29.

Rauch, J. (2003, May). Let it be. *Atlantic Monthly, 291*(4), 34.

Seaborn-Thompson, M., & Ensminger, M. E. (1989). Psychological well-being among mothers with school age children: Evolving family structures. *Social Forces, 67,* 715–730.

Sheridan, M. J. (2000, February). The use of spiritually-derived interventions in social work practice. Paper presented at the 46th Annual Program Meeting of the Council on Social Work Education, New York, NY.

Sheridan, M. J., Bullis, R. K., Adcock, C. R., Berlin, S. D., & Miller, P. C. (1992). Practitioners' personal and professional attitudes and behaviors toward religion and spirituality: Issues for social work education and practice. *Journal of Social Work Education, 28,* 190–203.

Sheridan, M. J., Wilmer, C. M., & Atcheson, L. (1994). Inclusion of content on religion and spirituality in the social work curriculum. *Journal of Social Work Education, 30*(3), 363–377.

Simpson, W. F. (1989). Comparative longevity in a college cohort of Christian Scientists. *Journal of the American Medical Association, 262,* 1657–1658.

Sloan, R. P., & Bagiella, E. (2001). Spirituality and medical practice: A look at the evidence. *American Family Physician, 63*(1), 33–34.

Spiegel, D., Bloom, J. R., & Kraemer, H. C. (1989). Effect of psychosocial treatment on survival of patients with metastatic breast cancer. *Lancet, 142,* 888–897.

Thoresen, C. E. (1990). *Long-term 8-year follow-up of recurrent coronary prevention* (Monograph). Uppsola, Sweden: International Society of Behavioral Medicine.

Tobias, M., Morrison, J., & Gray, B. (Eds.). (1995). *A parliament of souls.* San Francisco: KQED Books.

Zimmerman, M. A., & Maton, K. I. (1992). Life-style and substance use among male African American urban adolescents: A cluster analytic approach. *American Journal of Community Psychology, 20,* 121–138.

Evidence-Based Practice and the Effectiveness of Indigenous Helpers and Self-Help Groups

15

T his chapter discusses the strong presence of self-help groups in the treatment of physical and mental health problems. Because there is such passion for self-help groups in the absence of supportive data, the chapter considers the available research data on the treatment effectiveness of self-help groups and the reasons self-help groups have become so popular in America. Clearly, one reason for the popularity of self-help groups is the financial condition of the health care industry. According to Humphreys (1998),

> Professional substance abuse treatment in the United States grew extensively through the 1970s and 1980s. . . . In recent years, however, the professional treatment network has contracted due to the arrival of managed health care. . . . But there is a potential bright spot in the current gloomy addiction care picture—the possibility that self-help/mutual aid organizations can help substance abusers recover, while at the same time lowering demand for scarce formal health care resources. (p. 13)

In another article urging cooperation between self-help groups and the professional community, Humphreys and Ribisl (1999) ask, "Why should public health and medical professionals be interested in collaborating with a grassroots movement of untrained citizens?" (p. 326). Their answer is that money for health care is being reduced and that "self-help groups can provide benefits that the best health care often does not: identification with other sufferers, long-term support and companionship, and a sense of competence and empowerment" (p. 326). However, Kessler, Mickelson, and Zhao (1997) caution that self-help groups will "never be a substitute for professional care. Such groups should not be looked to as a cheap and quick fix to the health care crisis" (p. 27).

Self-Help Groups

In defining self-help groups, Wituk, Shepherd, Slavich, Warren, and Meissen (2000) write, "Self-help groups consist of individuals who share the same problem or concern. Members provide emotional support to one another, learn ways to cope, discover strategies for improving their condition, and help others while helping themselves" (p. 157). Kessler, Mickelson, et al. (1997) estimate that 25 million Americans have been involved in self-help groups at some point during their lives. Positive outcomes have been found in self-help groups treating substance abuse (Humphreys & Moos, 1996), bereavement (Caserta & Lund, 1993), care giving (McCallion & Toseland, 1995), diabetes (Gilden, Hendryx, Clar, Casia, & Singh, 1992), and depression (Kurtz, 1988). Riessman (2000) reports that "more Americans try to change their health behaviors through self-help than through all other forms of professional programs combined" (p. 47).

Kessler, Frank, et al. (1997) indicate that 40% of all therapeutic sessions for psychiatric problems reported by respondents in a national survey were in the self-help sector as compared to 35.2% receiving specialized mental health services, 8.1% receiving help from general physicians in the medical sector, and 16.5% receiving help from social service agencies. Wuthnow (1994) found that self-help groups are the most prevalent organized support groups in America today. The author estimated that 8 million–10 million Americans are members of self-help groups and that there are at least 500,000 self-help groups in America.

Fetto (2000) reports that a study done by the University of Texas at Austin found that approximately 25 million people will participate in self-help groups at some point in their lives and that 8 million–11 million people participate in self-help groups each year. Men are somewhat more likely to attend groups than women, and Caucasians are 3 times as likely to attend self-help groups as African Americans. This number is expected to be much higher with the full use of the Internet as a tool for self-help. Participants most likely to attend self-help groups are those diagnosed with alcoholism, cancer (all types), diabetes, AIDS, depression, and chronic fatigue syndrome. Those least likely to attend suffer from ulcers, emphysema, chronic pain, and migraines, in that order (Fetto, 2000).

Riessman (1997) identifies the principles defining the function and purpose of self-help groups as follows:

1. Members share a similar condition and understand each other.

2. Members determine activities and policies, which make self-help groups very democratic and self-determining.

3. Helping others is therapeutic.

4. Self-help groups build on the strengths of the individual members, the group, and the community; charge no fees; and are not commercialized.

5. Self-help groups function as social support systems that help participants cope with traumas through supportive relationships between members.

6. Values are projected that define the intrinsic meaning of the group to its members.

7. Self-help groups use the expertise of members to help one another.

8. Seeking assistance from a self-help group is not as stigmatizing as it may be when seek help from a physical or mental health provider.

9. Self-help groups focus on the use of self-determination, inner strength, self-healing, and resilience.

Wituk et al. (2000) studied the characteristics of self-help groups in a specific geographic area and report the following:

1. Groups had been in existence an average of 8 years.

2. Thirty percent of the groups studied met weekly, with an average attendance of 13 participants.

3. Twenty new members joined the group in the prior year.

4. Sixty-eight percent of the participants were female.

5. Minority participation was proportionately in keeping with the minority population of the regions studied.

6. Group outreach was usually done by word of mouth, but some groups used newspaper ads and radio and television spot ads.

7. Thirty-four percent of the groups were peer led with some professional involvement. Professionals led groups 28% of the time. Twenty-seven percent of the groups had no professional involvement, while 86% of the groups had two or more members acting in leadership capacities.

8. The primary function of the groups was to provide emotional and social support to members (in 98% of the groups reporting), while 32% of the groups provided information and education, and 58% provided advocacy services for members and their families.

9. Seventy-seven percent of the groups felt that networking with the larger community was important and did this through guest speakers, buddy systems, training seminars open to the public, and social events open to the community.

10. A large majority of the groups held meetings in very easily accessible places.

11. Many of the groups offered childcare during meetings, transportation, and bilingual meetings for non–English speaking participants.

12. More than half of the groups had national affiliations and reported a great deal of help from these organizations through brochures, newsletters, conferences and workshops but very little help with finances or information about advances in research.

13. Seventy-five percent of the groups had local affiliations with hospitals, churches, and social service agencies.

14. The self-help groups were all very well connected to the professional community.

The Indigenous Leaders of Self-Help Groups

Patterson and Marsiglia (2000) report remarkable similarities in the characteristics of two cohorts of natural (or indigenous) helpers from two very different geographic locations in the United States. The similarities included offering assistance to family and friends before it was asked for, attempting to reduce stress in those helped, and attempting to help people strengthen their coping skills. Lewis and Suarez (1995) identify the primary functions of indigenous helpers as buffers between individuals and sources of stress; providers of social support, information, and referral sources; and lay consultants. Waller and Patterson (2002) believe that indigenous helpers strengthen the social bonds holding communities together, which increases the well-being of individuals and communities.

Patterson, Holzhuter, Struble, and Quadagno (1972) found that natural helpers used one of three helping styles: (a) active listening, encouragement, emphasizing positives about the client, and suggesting alternative solutions to problems; (b) direct intervention by doing something active for the client that had an immediate impact; and (c) a combination of the first and second helping styles in a way that fit the client's needs. Memmott (1993), however, found little difference between natural helpers and professionals, although natural helpers were more inclined to advocate and intervene on behalf of clients than professionals, tended to think much less about causal reasons for a client's problems than professionals, and used direct methods of help that were atheoretical but often sound.

Bly (1985) suggests that we seek out others in the community for advice and support. He calls these natural helpers "people of wisdom" because they listen well, are empathic and sensitive, and are known for their expertise in solving certain types of problems. We gravitate to these people because they help us in unobtrusive and informal ways that are often profoundly subtle, and because the lack of formal training by natural helpers is offset by their kindness, patience, common sense, and good judgment.

Case Study: An Indigenous Helper Starts a Self-Help Group

Jack Holden is the leader of a support group for people with chronic depression. Jack has been depressed much of his life and has come to believe that it is a condition he has to live with, much as he would if he had diabetes or heart problems. Jack is a kind and empathic person, and after reading about a support group for depressed people in another community, Jack volunteered his time to organize a similar group in his own community. In preparing for this commitment, Jack met with a number of other leaders of various types of support groups in the community and attended meetings of a local volunteer organization in town to get additional ideas. He wrote to a national organization for depressed people to ask for assistance in setting up a group. They sent him a packet that explained how one might go about developing a group, which included many practical ideas about advertising, screening group members, where to hold meetings, and how to plan an agenda. Jack was able to use free ads in local newspapers and some spot ads on radio and television. Even so, the response was slow and Jack almost gave up. After 4 months, he had the names of 10 people who wanted to be part of the group and who were also willing to help in its development.

The group met over a 2-month period, and much to Jack's delight, its members were willing to work hard, entered into some very useful discussions about the mission and focus of the group, and asked Jack to be their leader under the supervision of a professional from the community who had agreed to help. The professional gave Jack some books to read on group leadership, and the national association Jack had contacted held a week-long leadership workshop for new leaders, which Jack attended. Jack found both experiences invaluable. During the first several meetings of the new self-help group, the professional observed the group, but after that she assured Jack that what he was doing was just fine. She agreed to meet with him periodically to discuss the group and to enter into a loose supervisory arrangement. She assured Jack that if there were a crisis, he could always call and they would immediately meet to discuss it. They also decided that if any member was unwilling to promise not to commit suicide, if this came up in discussion, or if group members were concerned about the possibility of a suicide by any group member, the professional would be contacted and would then make a further assessment. Fortunately, this has never happened in the 3 years the group has been actively meeting.

Gradually, the group has settled in with about 15 regular members. That's about all Jack thinks he can handle at one time. A few people have left the group because it hasn't worked for them, but others have taken their places. There are 20 people on the waiting list and Jack is trying to organize another group to be led by one of the current members with very strong leadership skills. The group meets once a week for 2 hours in the evening. All of the members have suffered from chronic depression for more than 5 years, and all the members actively see professionals in therapy and are being seen medically to monitor medication. The mission of the group is to offer support and encouragement, help with problem solving, plan social events to help group members stay socially active, and disseminate and discuss research information about depression. All of the members are responsible for sending one another new articles or research reports via the Internet at least once or twice a month. The group members have become so adept at finding new literature that many have brought information to their therapists or psychiatrists that were new even to them. The professionals have found that group members who take a very active role in their treatment also do much better in their lives, even though they continue to feel depressed some of the time. For many of the participants, depression is a struggle they have learned to live with through a combination of professional help and the self-help group.

The group believes that it should evaluate whether its work is helpful and has developed a testing instrument that measures life functioning in several key areas, including days missed at work; exercise, weight, and blood pressure; attendance at social events; social functioning, as reported weekly by spouses, mates, or friends; number of hours slept each day during the week; and depression, as evaluated by a 20-question depression inventory with good reliability and validity called the CES-D (Radloff, 1977), which can be found on pages 282 and 283. Over time, the evaluation mechanism has shown a gradual improvement in the social functioning of group members. People exercise more, maintain normal weight, miss fewer days at work, sleep less than before joining the group, and have less depression, according to reports from others and on scores from the depression instrument. Depression hasn't gone away completely for most participants, but they have learned to live with it and get on with their lives more successfully than before.

I observed this group. It is a kind, supportive, and warm group, and many people have benefited from Jack's unobtrusive and affirming leadership approach. One group member said, "Jack is so warm and kind, it filters down to the group. People come here and they're pessimistic and hopeless about their depression, but after a few weeks, Jack's optimism is contagious. We all suffer together and depression is an awful thing, but we love one another, we love Jack, and we all live with the hope that we will get better. If Jack left, we'd fall apart. Maybe that's not a good thing to admit, but Jack is the glue that holds us together. I don't mind saying that. He's a wonderful person, and that he suffers from depression like the rest of us makes us love him that much more. There are days when he's too depressed to lead the group and others fill in. We have a buddy system that gives each member another group member to talk to when things get too tough. We go out together for dinner and socialize some. It's like the extended family many of us don't have. We're lonely and isolated people and having this group is the best thing that's ever happened to me. And I'm glad that we have to maintain our contacts with professionals. It's a safety valve, in my opinion. Depressed people run a high risk of committing suicide. If it wasn't for the group and the professionals we work with, I couldn't promise not to do it if the feeling came over me really strongly. But the support network we've developed and the professional help keep us from going to extremes, and they give us hope. And for people who feel down most of the time, that's saying a lot."

Best Evidence of the
Effectiveness of Self-Help Groups

Kessler, Mickelson, et al. (1997) report that, although the research is somewhat scant on the subject of the effectiveness of self-help groups, "the little available data suggest that self-help groups are sometimes able to promote emotional recovery from life crises (Emrick, Tonigan, Montgomery, & Little, 1993; Galanter, 1984, 1988; Lieberman & Borman, 1991; Videcka-Sherman & Lieberman, 1985), [although] methodological limitations make it impossible to draw firm conclusions (Levy, 1984; Humphreys & Rappaport, 1994)" (p. 30).

Recognizing the methodological limitations of research effectiveness reports on self-help groups is important for the reader to understand because self-help groups are not under the same obligation to test for effectiveness as their professional counterparts. For that reason alone, there are a number of explanations for methodological limitations in determining best evidence of the effectiveness of nonprofessionally led self-help groups, including the following:

1. Self-help groups pride themselves on confidentiality and sometimes discourage research because it can be intrusive.

2. Most self-help groups don't think of themselves as competing with professional helpers. Trying to prove their effectiveness isn't seen as part of their mission.

3. There is no real way to force people to accept research responsibilities when services are led by volunteers, are free to the public, and make no claims to be alternatives to professional help.

4. The research process sets up barriers to the functioning of self-help groups and may subtly or overtly change the way a group operates.

5. Many people attend self-help groups to avoid the way professional treatment sometimes compromises individuality. Adding a research component may make people feel as if they have lost their uniqueness.

6. Self-help groups are loosely organized and run. People come and go as they please. It's difficult to make research effective in an atmosphere where the experimental group has only a very loose attendance pattern.

7. As Kessler, Mickelson, et al. (1997) report, more than half of the people attending self-help groups also receive professional help, making it difficult to determine whether it's the self-help or the professional help that causes improvement, or a combination of both.

With these caveats in mind, let's consider the data to date on the effectiveness of self-help groups.

SUBSTANCE ABUSE

In an evaluation of a large study by *Consumer Reports* on the effectiveness of psychotherapy, Seligman (1995) concluded that "Alcoholics Anonymous (AA) did especially well . . . significantly bettering mental health professionals [in the treatment of alcohol and drug related problems]" (p. 969). Humphreys and Moos (1996) found that, during a 3-year period of study, alcoholics who initially chose AA over professional help had a 45% ($1,826) lower average per-person health care cost than those receiving professional treatment. Even with the lower costs, AA participants had reduced alcohol consumption, had fewer numbers of days intoxicated, and achieved lower rates of depression when compared to alcoholic clients receiving professional help. In follow-up studies, these findings were consistent at 1 year and 3 years after the start of the study. Humphreys, Mavis, and Stoffelmayr (1994) report that African American participants ($n = 253$) in Narcotics

Anonymous and AA showed improvement over 12 months in six problem areas (including employment; alcohol and drug use; and legal, psychological, and family problems). African American group members had much more improvement in their medical, alcohol, and drug problems than did African American patients who were not involved in self-help groups. In a meta-analysis of more than 50 studies, Emrick et al. (1993) report that AA members who were also professionally treated alcoholic patients were somewhat more likely to reduce drinking than those who did not attend AA. Membership in AA was also found to reduce physical symptoms and to improve psychological adjustment. Alemi et al. (1996) assigned two groups of pregnant women with substance abuse histories to either a self-help group meeting biweekly or to self-help groups operated over a bulletin board accessed by telephone. Bulletin board participants made significantly fewer telephone calls and visits to health care clinics than did the group assigned to participate in the face-to-face group. Both groups had similar health status and drug use at the end of the study.

Christo and Sutton (1994) report that members of Narcotics Anonymous who stayed off drugs for 3 years or more as a result of their involvement in the group had the same level of anxiety and self-esteem as a random sample of people who had never been drug addicted. Hughes (1977) studied adolescent members of Alateen, a self-help group for children with an alcoholic parent. They report that Alateen members had significantly fewer negative moods, more positive overall moods, and higher self-esteem than adolescents who were not members and didn't have an alcoholic parent. McKay, Alterman, McLellan, and Snider (1994) report on African American participants in self-help groups for substance abuse after a 7-month follow-up. Participants with high rates of attendance at group meetings reduced their use of alcohol and drugs to half as much as the alcohol and drug use by those who had poor attendance records. Both groups were similar in their use of substances prior to the start of their group involvement. Pisani, Fawcett, Clark, and McGuire (1993) studied alcoholic patients admitted to a short hospital treatment program who were referred upon release to AA. In an 18-month follow-up study, the more days group members attended AA meetings, the longer their abstinence lasted. Interestingly, AA involvement was seen as a more powerful way to continue abstinence than the use of medication to treat the addiction. Walsh et al. (1991) report that company employees with alcohol problems who were assigned to attend AA or face the loss of their jobs lessened their drinking over a 2-year period. AA members did as well in their job-related performance as clients involved in mandatory inpatient treatment. Tattersall and Hallstrom (1992) report on a study involving a British self-help group formed to help members reduce their reliance on tranquilizers, which offered both telephone counseling and a group experience. Members had been addicted to tranquilizers for more than 12 years on average. Most members of the group reported that the symptoms for which tranquilizers had initially been prescribed had lessened and that 65% of the group members were at least moderately satisfied with their withdrawal from tranquilizers, according to self-evaluations of their quality of life.

MEDICAL PROBLEMS

Riessman (2000) reports on a project to use self-help groups with patients suffering from heart disease. Initially the project used patient-led groups to help keep patients on their diet and exercise regimens, but Reissman says it soon became apparent that "participation in the groups themselves was one of the most powerful interventions" (p. 48). Spiegel, Bloom, Kraemer, and Gottheil (1989) studied 86 women receiving treatment for metastatic breast cancer. Fifty of the 86 women were randomly chosen to supplement their oncological care with a weekly support group. The support groups were led by a psychotherapist with breast cancer in remission and a psychiatrist or a social worker. The sessions offered an opportunity to talk about living life fully, improving communication with significant others, coping with death, discussing grief, and controlling pain through self-hypnosis. Support group members lived twice as long as controls, for an average of 18 months longer. Nash and Kramer (1993) studied 57 African Americans who were involved in self-help groups for sickle-cell anemia. Those involved the longest had the fewest psychological symptoms and the fewest problems from the disease, particularly in work and relationships. Hinrichsen and Revenson (1985) compared scoliosis patients in a self-help group who had undergone bracing or surgery with patients having the same treatment who were not in a self-help group. Participants in the self-help group had a more positive outlook on life, better satisfaction with their medical care, fewer psychosomatic symptoms, better self-esteem, and fewer feelings of "shame and estrangement." Simmons (1992) evaluated members of a self-help group of diabetics for blood sugar levels and knowledge about diabetes. Members attending the group twice or more during a year had a significantly greater drop in blood sugar levels and a greater knowledge about diabetes than nonparticipants. The group emphasized education, support, knowledge sharing, and social activities.

BEREAVEMENT

Caserta and Lund (1993) found that widows and widowers participating in a bereavement group for at least 8 weeks experienced less depression and grief than nonparticipants. Lieberman and Videka-Sherman (1986) followed 36 widowers and 466 widows involved in a self-help group for bereavement. Over a period of a year, the group members experienced better social relationships, less emotional distress, and better emotional functioning than nonmembers. Marmar, Horowitz, Weiss, Wilner, and Kaltreider (1988) found that self-help groups worked as well as professional therapy in reducing symptoms of grief and in overall psychological functioning. Vachon, Lyall, Rogers, Freedman-Letofsky, and Freeman (1980) studied two groups of women whose husbands had passed away within the past month. After 6 months, the group assigned to a "widow to widow" program felt healthier and happier, and had fewer problems adjusting to single life than nonparticipants. After 12 months, the women in the support group made more friends, felt much better physically, were less anxious and depressed, were involved in more social activities, and were more open about their feelings than were nonparticipants. Videka-Sherman and Lieberman (1985) compared women in a support group with those receiving therapy because of the loss of a spouse. The authors indicate that active involvement in the support group resulted in reduced feelings of self-anger, increased ability to discuss feelings, and more social involvement with others outside of the group. Psychotherapy had none of these benefits. Group members also reported feeling happier, less anxious and depressed, and more able to discuss and resolve feelings of anger, guilt, and isolation than before the group experience began.

EMOTIONAL PROBLEMS

Edmunson and Bedell (1982) report that, after 10 months of participation in a patient-led support group, half as many former psychiatric inpatients ($n = 40$) required rehospitalization as those not participating in the support group ($n = 40$). Members of the patient-led group had average hospital stays of 7 days, compared to 25 days for nonparticipants. Kurtz (1988) reports that 82% of 129 members of the Manic Depressive and Depressive Association coped better with their illnesses after becoming members of a self-help group. Eighty-two percent of the sample required hospitalization before joining the support group, but this number fell to 33% after becoming members of the group. Kennedy (1990) studied the benefits of a self-help group for 31 participants with chronic psychiatric problems and found that members of the self-help group spent far fewer days in a psychiatric hospital over a 32-month period than did 31 former psychiatric patients matched by similar age, race, sex, marital status, number of previous hospitalizations, and other factors. Group members also experienced an increased sense of security and self-esteem and an improved ability to accept problems in their lives without blaming others. Galanter (1988) studied 356 members of a self-help group for former patients with mental illness. Although half of the members of the self-help group had been hospitalized before joining the group, only 8% of the group leaders and 7% of the recent members had been hospitalized since joining.

Q and A With the Author
About the Meaning of These Studies

The following mock question and answer exercise is offered to help the reader better understand the benefits, limitations, meaning, and practical use of reported findings on the efficacy of self-help groups.

Question (Q): Do these studies prove anything?

Answer (A): Probably not. What they *do* show is that people in self-help and support groups *report* better functioning and a higher level of life satisfaction. Whether that's the case remains to be seen. Self-reports are notoriously susceptible to social desirability. People say positive things about self-help groups when there may be no empirical evidence that change in social functioning has actually taken place. The halo effect is also likely to influence responses. People in any type of treatment often report better results than may be the case because, in the short run, they may actually feel better and because, in the case of self-help groups, they may feel a sense of loyalty to the group that encourages them to report better social functioning than may be the case. Whether better functioning has actually occurred in the studies cited in this chapter requires evidence that only an empirical study can provide. *Saying* that you feel better is not the same as actually *being* better when social functioning is considered.

Methodological problems are considerable in the measurement of self-help group effectiveness. Ouimette, Finney, and Moos (1997) compared 12-step programs such as AA with cognitive-behavioral programs and programs that combined both approaches. One year after completion of treatment, all three types of programs had similar improvement rates when alcohol consumption was measured. Participants in the 12-step program had more "sustained abstinence" and better employment rates than the other two programs, but Ouimette et al. (1997) cautioned the reader not to make more of these findings than were warranted because of the nonrandom assignment of patients to the different types of treatment. A careful look at many other substance abuse treatment studies using self-help groups suggests similar methodological concerns. Clifford, Maisto, and Franzke (2000) reinforce concerns about research methodologies used to study substance abuse programs when they point out, "It is recommended that treatment outcome studies be interpreted cautiously, particularly when the research protocols involve frequent and intensive follow-up interviews conducted across extended periods of time" (p. 741), because many external variables can confound the results and suggest improved functioning as a result of treatment when other factors may be more suggestive of the reasons the client has improved.

Q: Shouldn't we feel elated by studies that people live longer or use substances less as a result of self-help groups?

A: Not until the evidence is substantiated by empirical studies using random selection and very scientific methodology. Certainly one should not say that self-help groups are more effective than professional help, given the weakness of self-help research to date. Statements such as the following are not warranted: "The emergence of self-help groups may reflect a societal response to failures within the mental health community. Self-help groups have developed where society has fallen short in meeting the needs of its members" (Felix-Ortiz, Salazar, Gonzalez, Sorensen, & Plock, 2000, p. 339).

Q: But aren't we being too harsh? Isn't it likely that self-help groups, through support and affiliation, help people feel more accepted, appreciated, and cared for, and isn't that important for positive mental health?

A: Certainly, but it's possible that self-help groups may have short-term benefits that, in the long run, aren't likely to continue, or may actually cause harm. T-Groups and the encounter movement come to mind as examples.

Q: But what's wrong with short-term results if they're positive? Can't we say the same thing about professional treatment?

A: There's nothing wrong with short-term results, and professional treatment may have the same limited results as self-help groups, but the studies cited here don't permit us to make long-term predictions because they don't show cause-effect relationships between self-help groups and long-term improvement rates. A belief that self-help groups can replace professional help, without appropriate data, is troubling because it gives people confidence in a treatment that may not actually help and may, in some cases, do harm. During the current health care crisis, suggesting that self-help groups may replace professional help because they work better may leave a large number of clients who desperately need professional help without that option, because managed care might increasingly rely on self-help groups to treat a number of serious social, emotional, and medical problems.

Q: So what's the answer?

A: Much more research but, in the meantime, a sense of optimism that perhaps self-help groups are an alternative answer or, at least, an adjunct to professional help.

Q: Why feel optimistic in view of the weak research data to support the benefits of self-help groups?

A: A preponderance of positive results tends to suggest that something works. It may not prove that something works, but the weight of the evidence suggests that many self-help groups *do* help. This should make us optimistic without making us true believers. EBP is a conservative and cautious paradigm. It doesn't accept best evidence until it's been proven. At the same time, the evidence thus far would suggest that we cautiously use the findings. A case study is presented in this chapter that might be instructive about how best to use self-help groups when professional services are also being provided.

Q: Would you refer a client to a self-help group?

A: Yes, but only after meeting with the group leader and evaluating the group objectives to make certain that they were consistent with the needs of the client. And even then I would suggest that the client use high standards and caution before joining the group. I would also want to be involved in a discussion with the client about what was taking place in the group and the client's feelings about the effectiveness of the group. Perhaps contacting current and former group members would also help. If the group is legitimate, it wouldn't mind this happening unless, of course, confidentiality issues are involved.

Q: Aren't you being overly cautious?

A: Yes, but self-help groups, just like professional help, have the potential for doing harm. It's my responsibility to see that this doesn't happen since I'm the referring source.

Q: Really? What harm could they do?

A: Some self-help groups have been likened to cults. The tendency to make people accept a philosophy through group pressure that may be contrary to their own belief systems, or to a process that might not be right for them, may actually cause harm. Similarly, groups that are badly run may inhibit client progress. Relationships develop among group members that may be harmful. An example might be when substance abusers develop romantic or sexual attachments to one another that lead to more substance abuse. Granfield and Cloud (1996) studied middle-class alcoholics who used self-healing approaches alone with neither professional help nor self-help group intervention. Many of the participants felt that the "ideological" base of some self-help groups was in conflict with their own philosophies of life. Concerns were raised that some groups were overly religious, or that groups saw alcoholism as a lifelong struggle. The subjects in the study by Granfield and Cloud also felt that some self-help groups encouraged dependence and that associating with other alcoholics would probably make recovery more difficult. In summarizing their findings, the authors concluded:

Many [research subjects] expressed strong opposition to the suggestion that they were powerless over their addictions. Such an ideology, they explained, not only was counterproductive but was also extremely demeaning. These respondents saw themselves as efficacious people who often prided themselves on their past accomplishments. They viewed themselves as being individualists and strong-willed. (Granfield and Cloud, 1996, p. 51)

Q: But couldn't the same thing happen in a professionally led group?

A: Yes, but all professionals are bound by codes of ethics and, in a number of states, licensure laws that provide certain protections for clients against extreme behavior by professionals. Nonprofessional leaders may be less sensitive to inappropriate relationships among group members, or they may not see the harm in developing their own relationship with a group member. Professionals are also guided by a belief that they should respect the rights of clients. That would hopefully eliminate religious proselytizing or other behaviors in conflict with a client's belief system.

Q: Doesn't the fact that self-help groups are usually free of cost and non-discriminating suggest, at the very least, that they may provide a helping intervention that is an alternative to professional help?

A: Yes, but is this a financial argument or an argument about best evidence of effectiveness? Shouldn't clients in need be offered the best help available rather than the help that's cheapest?

Q: Yes, of course, but you can't argue that professional help is always excellent help or that it works, can you?

A: No, I certainly can't, and that's what makes this entire discussion so troubling. When professional help isn't effective, it means that something is fundamentally wrong with our system of treatment. An analogy would be finding that folk healers are more effective than medical doctors. If that's the case, we really would need to reexamine what we believe and whether it's worth maintaining that belief.

Q: Don't a lot of people get better on their own? Is it always necessary to compare self-help groups against professional services?

A: Good point. Waldorf, Reinarman, and Murphy (1991) found that many addicted people with supportive elements in their lives (a job, family, and other close emotional supports) were able to "walk away" from their very heavy use of cocaine. The authors suggest that the "social context" of a drug user's life may positively influence their ability to discontinue drug use. Granfield and Cloud (1996) add to the social context notion of recovery by indicating that many of the respondents in their study had fairly stable lives with social and family supports, college credentials, and a great deal to lose if they continued their substance abuse. "Having much to lose," they write, "gave our respondents incentives to transform their lives. However, when there is little to lose from heavy alcohol or drug use, there may be little to gain by quitting" (p. 55).

Q: So do you feel positively or negatively about self-help groups? You sound awfully negative.

A: Actually, I feel very positively about self-help, and I think the research makes a compelling argument that self-help groups may be very effective with a number of physical and mental health problems. And I confess that my heart is in the notion of people helping one another, but in a book on best evidence, I think the jury is still out until we have a substantial body of knowledge to show a relationship between self-help and its level of effectiveness with a range of problems experienced by a cross section of people across gender, age, ethnicity, and socioeconomic class. In other words, I hope self-help groups develop the same body of research data to show effectiveness that I expect, but often don't find, for services provided by professionals. When that happens, we'll have a basis of comparison. Until then, I'm hopeful and optimistic while still being cautious. I don't believe, however, that self-help is a substitute for professional help, and I worry that a health care system in crisis will turn to self-help as a last resort before needed services are withdrawn completely.

Case Study: Referral of a Client to a Self-Help Group for Severe Depression

Leonard is a 37-year-old client suffering from chronic depression that has lasted almost 5 years and began as his marriage started to deteriorate and finally ended in divorce. Leonard is being seen by a psychiatrist to monitor his antidepression medication and has been in therapy with a clinical psychologist for almost 5 years. The medication and therapy have a negligible impact and he still suffers from very severe depression that interferes with work, social activities, and relationships and that has, of late, begun to cause weight gain and high blood pressure. Leonard is too depressed to exercise and has become a compulsive eater, having gained almost 100 pounds since his divorce. His therapist suggested a self-help group for people with chronic depressions as an adjunct to therapy and medication, but Leonard has been unwilling to attend meetings, believing that the group would be as unsuccessful as his current treatments. The therapist arranged for Leonard to meet with the group leader, who also suffers from chronic depression but has successfully learned to cope with it.

The leader invited Leonard to attend a meeting and asked participants to stay after so they could discuss their feelings about the group and answer questions Leonard might have about the group's effectiveness. The group leader also shared effectiveness research the national chapter of the group had accumulated on the effectiveness of the self-help group across the country that, although subjective and not terribly sound methodologically, still suggested positive results. More than 2,000 former participants in group chapters around the country returned questionnaires. Five thousand questionnaires, representing a 10% sample of the 50,000 former national participants in the organization, were sent out. More than 70% of the participants who stayed in the group for more than 2 years reported fewer missed days at work, fewer doctor visits, less use of antidepressants, and fewer days of depression. The average length of depression before the respondents began their group participation was more than 5 years. Participants who stayed with the group 2 years or longer had better results than those who discontinued participation before completing a full year of group participation. Those who dropped out of the group early cited personality clashes with the group leader and differences of opinion about the purpose of the group as the major reasons for their attrition.

Since Leonard was unwilling to attend the meeting alone, the therapist met him at the group meeting and sat with him. After the group, people spoke about how the group had helped them. Following the meeting, Leonard shared his positive sense of the group with the therapist and his surprise at how strongly the members felt the experience had helped them. He decided to give it a try and began attending sessions on a regular basis while also seeing his therapist weekly and continuing to use his antidepression medication. After 6 months as a participant, Leonard summarized the experience: "It's very supportive. Everyone there is like me. They're all struggling with depression. The difference is that they get on with their lives. That's what I've begun doing. I've been assigned a young woman as a mentor whom I call when I feel so down I can hardly function. We've begun walking together and it's helped me lose weight. I feel a lot of positive acceptance from the other people, and that helps a lot. We have speakers who talk about depression and who keep us informed about the latest research. I've been assigned as a mentor to a new member and, surprisingly, he seems to find a lot of solace from our contacts. I still feel really depressed, but while it used to be every day, now I have good and bad days. Overall, I think I'm less depressed than I was before I started the group. Mainly, I think the support, the camaraderie, the loving environment, and the sense that we're all experts on depression and that we have something to say worth listening to about how to handle depression are what helps the most. I've made a couple of good friends from the group, and instead of staying home and being lonely and blue, I go out to movies or have dinner with my friends. It helps me avoid feeling lonely, which is one of the things depressed people often experience. Do I feel better than I did 6 months ago? Yes. Is it because of the group? I think some of it is but I have to admit that because of the group, I'm using therapy better. So overall, yes, I give it high marks. I'll stay with it and maybe, in time, I'll be able to get by without any help at all. That's my goal, for sure."

The CES-D: A Measure of Depression

The CES-D is a widely used and simple instrument to measure depression with good reliability and validity. Scores of 16 to 30 indicate the presence of depression requiring intervention. Scores over 30 suggest concern for suicide and would require very serious interventions. For further information on scoring, the article by Radloff (1977) in the reference section of this chapter might be an initial first source to consider.

Directions: I am going to read you some statements about the ways people act and feel. On how many of the last 7 days did the following statements apply to you?

	None	1 or 2 Days	3 or 4 Days	5 or More Days
1. I was bothered by things that usually don't bother me.	0	1	2	3
2. I did not feel like eating. My appetite was poor.	0	1	2	3
3. I felt that I could not shake off the blues even with help from friends and family.	0	1	2	3
4. I felt I was just not as good as others.	0	1	2	3
5. I had trouble keeping my mind on what I was doing.	0	1	2	3
6. I felt depressed.	0	1	2	3
7. I felt that everything I did was an effort.	0	1	2	3
8. I felt hopeful about the future.	0	1	2	3
9. I thought my life was a failure.	0	1	2	3
10. I felt fearful.	0	1	2	3
11. My sleep was restless.	0	1	2	3

12. I was happy.	0	1	2	3
13. I talked less than usual.	0	1	2	3
14. I felt lonely.	0	1	2	3
15. People were unfriendly.	0	1	2	3
16. I enjoyed life.	0	1	2	3
17. I had crying spells.	0	1	2	3
18. I felt sad.	0	1	2	3
19. I felt people disliked me.	0	1	2	3
20. I could not get going.	0	1	2	3

SUMMARY

This chapter on self-help groups offers some hopeful evidence that self-help may provide assistance to a variety of clients experiencing problems with addictions, physical health, mental health, and other social and emotional problems. A large number of Americans use self-help, but questions remain about the validity of findings indicating that self-help may be an effective alternative to professional assistance. Most of these questions relate to research issues that may be difficult to resolve, given the fact that self-help groups do not have the same need for accountability as professional help to prove effectiveness. Self-help is generally supportive in nature and usually provides an affirming and positive approach to problem solving. Some concern is raised that self-help groups may not be effective for everyone because they sometimes have an unacceptable religious ideology or encourage people to believe that recovery is a lifelong struggle. Still, the weight of findings provides a reason for optimism until empirically based research with strong methodologies provides more compelling evidence of effectiveness.

Integrative Questions

1. Do you agree that treatment provided in self-help groups can harm people? If so, under what circumstances might this happen?

2. What possible harm is there in a group of people with the same problem getting together and offering support and encouragement? Why must we think of this as treatment, and why should we even consider researching the effectiveness of this type of benign help?

3. If self-help groups turn out to be more effective than professional help, how would professionals justify their existence? What might they do to improve the effectiveness of their services?

4. Leaders of self-help groups can sometimes be officious or power hungry. Do you think either, in pursuit of honest help to people in need, would be an inhibitor to good treatment? If so, why might this be the case?

5. The research seems to suggest that the most effective self-help groups are the ones where people attend regularly and stay in the group for 2 or more years. Couldn't people get better as a result of other factors during that time? What might some of the reasons be for improvement other than the self-help received by the client?

References

Alemi, F., Mosavel, M., Stephens, R., Ghadiri, A., Krishnaswamy, J., & Thakkar, H. (1996). Electronic self-help and support groups. *Medical Care, 34*(10 Suppl.), OS32–OS44.

Bly, R. (1986, April-May). Men of wisdom. *Utne Reader,* 37–41.

Caserta, M. S., & Lund, D. A. (1993). Intrapersonal resources and the effectiveness of self-help groups for bereaved older adults. *Gerontologist, 33*(5), 619–629.

Christo, G., & Sutton, S. (1994). Anxiety and self-esteem as a function of abstinence time among recovering addicts attending Narcotics Anonymous. *British Journal of Clinical Psychology, 33,* 198–200.

Clifford, P. R., Maisto, S. A., & Franzke, L. H. (2000). Alcohol treatment research follow-up and drinking behaviors. *Journal of Studies on Alcohol, 61*(5), 736–743.

Edmundson, E. D., Bedell, J. R., Archer, R. P., & Gordon, R. E. (1982). Integrating skill building and peer support in mental health treatment: The early intervention and community network development projects. In A. M. Jeger & R. S. Slotnick (Eds.), *Community mental health and behavioral-ecology: A handbook of theory, research, and practice* (pp. 127–139). New York: Plenum Press.

Emrick, C. D., Tonigan, J. S., Montgomery, H., & Little, L. (1993). Alcoholics Anonymous: What is currently known? In B. S. McCrady & W. R. Miller (Eds.), *Research on Alcoholics Anonymous: Opportunities and alternatives* (pp. 41–75). New Brunswick, NJ: Rutgers Center of Alcohol Studies.

Felix-Ortiz, M., Salazar, M. R., Gonzalez, J. R., Sorensen, J. L., Plock, D. (2000). Addictions services: A qualitative evaluation of an assisted self-help group for drug-addicted clients in a structured outpatient treatment setting. *Community Mental Health Journal, 36*(4), 339–350.

Fetto, J. (2000). Lean on me. *American Demographics, 22*(12), 16.

Galanter, M. (1988). Zealous self-help groups as adjuncts to psychiatric treatment: A study of Recovery, Inc. *American Journal of Psychiatry, 145*(10), 1248–1253.

Gilden, J. L., Hendryx, A. S., Clar, S., Casia, C., & Singh, S. P. (1992). Diabetes support groups improve health care of older diabetic patients. *Journal of the American Geriatrics Society, 40,* 147–150.

Granfield, R., & Cloud, W. (1996, Winter). The elephant that no one sees: Natural recovery among middle-class addicts. *Journal of Drug Issues, 26,* 45–61.

Hinrichsen, G. A., & Revenson, T. A. (1985). Does self-help help? An empirical investigation of scoliosis peer support groups. *Journal of Social Issues, 41*(1), 65–87.

Hughes, J. M. (1977). Adolescent children of alcoholic parents and the relationship of Alateen to these children. *Journal of Consulting and Clinical Psychology, 45*(5), 946–947.

Humphreys, K. (1998). Can addiction-related self-help/mutual aid groups lower demand for professional substance abuse treatment? *Social Policy, 29*(2), 13–17.

Humphreys, K., Mavis, B. E., & Stoffelmayr, B. E. (1994). Are twelve step programs appropriate for disenfranchised groups? Evidence from a study of post-treatment mutual help involvement. *Prevention in Human Services, 11*(1), 165–179.

Humphreys, K., & Moos, R. H. (1996). Reduced substance-abuse-related health care costs among voluntary participants in Alcoholics Anonymous. *Psychiatric Services, 47,* 709–713.

Humphreys, K., & Rappaport, J. (1994). Researching self-help/mutual aid groups and organizations: Many roads, one journey. *Applied & Preventive Psychology, 3,* 217–231.

Humphreys, K., & Ribisl, K. M. (1999). The case for partnership with self-help groups. *Public Health Reports, 114*(4), 322–329.

Kennedy, M. (1990). Psychiatric hospitalizations of GROWers. Paper presented at the Second Biennial Conference on Community Research and Action, East Lansing, MI.

Kessler, R. C., Frank, R. G., Edlund, M., Katz, S. J., Lin, E., & Leaf, P. (1997). Differences in the use of psychiatric outpatient services between the United States and Ontario. *New England Journal of Medicine, 336,* 551–557.

Kessler, R. C., Mickelson, K. D., & Zhao, S. (1997). Patterns and correlates of self-help group membership in the United States. *Social Policy, 27,* 27–46.

Kurtz, L. F. (1988). Mutual aid for affective disorders: The manic depressive and depressive association. *American Journal of Orthopsychiatry, 58*(1), 152–155.

Levy, L. H. (1984). Issues in research and evaluation. In A. Gartner & F. Riessman (Eds.), *The self-help revolution* (pp. 155–172). New York: Human Sciences Press.

Lewis, E. A., & Suarez, Z. E. (1995). Natural helping networks. *Encyclopedia of Social Work* (19th ed., pp. 1765–1772). Silver Spring, MD: National Association of Social Workers.

Lieberman, M. A., & Borman, L. D. (1991). The impact of self-help groups on widows' mental health. *National Reporter, 4,* 2–6.

Lieberman, M. A., & Videka-Sherman, L. (1986). The impact of self-help groups on the mental health of widows and widowers. *American Journal of Orthopsychiatry, 56,* 435–449.

Marmar, C. R., Horowitz, M. J., Weiss, D. S., Wilner, N. R., & Kattreider, N. B. (1988). A controlled trial of brief psychotherapy and mutual-help group treatment of conjugal bereavement. *American Journal of Psychiatry, 145*(2), 203–209.

McCallion, P., & Toseland, R. W. (1995). Supportive group interventions with caregivers of frail older adults. *Social Work with Groups, 18*(1), 11–25.

McKay, J. R., Alterman, A. I., McLellan, A. T., & Snider, E. C. (1994). Treatment goals, continuity of care, and outcome in a day hospital substance abuse rehabilitation program. *American Journal of Psychiatry, 151*(2), 254–259.

Memmott, J. L. (1993). Models of helping and coping: A field experiment with natural and professional helpers. *Social Work Research & Abstracts, 29,* 11–22.

Nash, K. B., & Kramer, K. D. (1993). Self-help for sickle cell disease in African American communities. *Journal of Applied Behavioral Science, 29*(2), 202–215.

Ouimette, P. C., Finney, J. W., & Moos, R. H. (1997). Twelve-step and cognitive-behavioral treatment for substance abuse: A comparison of treatment effectiveness. *Journal of Consulting and Clinical Psychology, 65*(2), 230–240.

Patterson, S. L., Holzhuter, J. L., Struble, V. E., & Quadagno, J. S. (1972). *Final report, utilization of human resources for mental health* (Grant No. MH 16618). Unpublished report, National Institute of Mental Health, Washington, DC.

Patterson, S. L., & Marsiglia, F. F. (2000). Mi casa es su casa: Beginning exploration of Mexican Americans' natural helping. *Families in Society, 81*(1), 22–31.

Pisani, V. D., Fawcett, J., Clark, D. C., & McGuire, M. (1993). The relative contributions of medication adherence and AA meeting attendance to abstinent outcome for chronic alcoholics. *Journal of Studies on Alcohol, 54,* 115–119.

Radloff, L. S. (1977). The CES-D scale: A self-report depression scale for research in the general population. *Applied Psychological Measurements, 1,* 385–407.

Riessman, F. (1997). Ten self-help principles. *Social Policy, 27,* 6–11.

Riessman, F. (2000). Self-help comes of age. *Social Policy, 30*(4), 47–49.

Seligman, M. E. P. (1995). The effectiveness of psychotherapy: The *Consumer Reports* study. *American Psychologist, 50*(12), 965–974.

Simmons, D. (1992). Diabetes self help facilitated by local diabetes research: The Coventry Asian Diabetes Support Group. *Diabetic Medicine, 9,* 866–869.

Spiegel, D., Bloom, J. R., Kraemer, H. C., & Gottheil, E. (1989, October). Effect of psychosocial treatment on survival of patients with metastatic breast cancer. *Lancet, 14,* 888–891.

Tattersall, M. L., & Hallstrom, C. (1992). Self-help and benzodiazepine withdrawal. *Journal of Affective Disorders, 24*(3), 193–198.

Vachon, M. L. S., Lyall, W.A., Rogers, J., Freedman-Letofsky, K., & Freeman, S. J. (1980). A controlled study of self-help intervention for widows. *American Journal of Psychiatry, 137*(11), 1380–1384.

Videcka-Sherman, L., & Lieberman, M. A. (1985). The effects of self-help and psychotherapy intervention on child loss: The limits of recovery. *American Journal of Orthopsychiatry, 55,* 70–82.

Waldorf, D., Reinarman, C., & Murphy, S. (1991). *Cocaine changes: The experience of using and quitting.* Philadelphia: Temple University Press.

Waller, M. A., & Patterson, S. (2002). Natural helping and resilience in a Dine (Navajo) community. *Society, 81*(1), 73–84.

Walsh, D. C., Hingson, R. W., Merrigan, D. M., Levenson, S. M., Cupples, L. A., Heeren, T., et al. (1991). A randomized trial of treatment options for alcohol-abusing workers. *New England Journal of Medicine, 325*(11), 775–782.

Wituk, S., Shepherd, M. D., Slavich, S., Warren, M. L., & Meissen, G. (2000). A topography of self-help groups: An empirical analysis. *Social Work, 45*(2), 157–165.

Wuthnow, R (1994). *Sharing the journey: Support groups and America's new quest for community.* New York: Free Press.

Part 5

Evidence-Based Practice and Future Trends, Social Involvement, and Final Words

Chapter 16 discusses the future of psychotherapy and raises concerns regarding practice research. Primary among those concerns are how practice research will be used by policy makers, whether the research will result in substantial changes in treatment, and whether practice research is inaccessible to practitioners because findings are reported in ways that are sometimes difficult for practitioners to read and comprehend. Chapter 16 also provides information regarding the future of psychotherapy, suggesting that new treatment approaches will be tied to research efforts to find best evidence and that therapy, as we know it now, will be replaced by short-term treatment that is often augmented by homework assignments and self-help groups.

Chapter 17 is the concluding chapter of the book. It discusses the need for more social involvement by helping professionals in the form of volunteerism and advocacy. It also discusses concerns about overly cautious professional practices that avoid providing needed services to certain groups including men, violent children, and the elderly. While this book has often been critical of practice because of the use of treatments that have little research efficacy, the helping professionals who work on the front line with very troubled and needy clients are to be commended for their hard work and commitment. Without them, hundreds of thousands of clients in despair would lack a supportive and positive partner in the process of treating social and emotional pain.

The Future of Psychotherapy 16

In keeping with this book's theme of looking rationally at issues pertaining to psychotherapy, this chapter considers the future landscape of the helping professions and the inventions we will likely use in treating clients with social and emotional problems. At present, it seems certain that the future will be influenced by a changing mental health field, in which the amount of therapy provided will be limited, therapists will have less training, and treatment will often be superseded by the use of medications, which may offer little positive benefit for clients experiencing nonbiochemically related mental health problems. The misuse of medication, in a real sense, increases the risk of physical and emotional dependency. To provide support for the content of this chapter, predictions by practitioners and mental health providers regarding the future are included. The role that research should play in providing best evidence for more effective practice, including alternative approaches to empirically based research designs, will also be discussed.

The Need for Practice Research

Peebles (2000) writes, "In North America, policymakers have been taking an interest in the scientific evidence underlying the practice of clinical psychology. Demands for accountability have been mounting from both government agencies and managed care companies (Barlow, 1996; Parloff & Elkin, 1992)" (p. 660). When therapy was offered in private or nonprofit settings, its effectiveness was of little concern to policy makers. With the advent of huge public sector expenditures for therapeutic services, "the public gained a right and a responsibility to determine who is entitled to receive services, what conditions warrant treatment, and what treatments will be authorized (Parloff, 1979)" (Peebles, 2000, p. 659). This need for accountability, in light of increasing expenditures for therapeutic services, has been growing, and mental health providers are "scrambling," in Peebles's words, to prove the need and worth of our services to policy makers and to a skeptical public.

The challenge of proving our worth is a difficult one because, even among the helping professions, there is ambivalence about the role and the methodologies of research to measure the efficacy of therapy. Several of the following key issues define that ambivalence:

1. Are there models of research that can actually measure relationships between services provided and client change?

2. Should practice research utilize qualitative measures that may "be seen as inconsistent with the tenets (e.g., realism) and practices (objective and unbiased reporting of research results) of the scientific method" (Peebles, 2000, p. 660)?

3. Is influencing policy makers in the best interest of our clients? Managed care has certainly changed the landscape of medical practice, with its emphasis on the bottom line and on rational treatment approaches. However, the current backlash against managed care suggests that bottom lines and rational approaches often fail to result in better patient care or improved satisfaction with services, something policy makers seem to ignore, regardless of countervailing evidence.

4. Isn't psychotherapy really about the fit between what the practitioner has to offer and what the client is looking for? By its nature, psychotherapy may be too subjective and unpredictable for the use of empirical methods to evaluate efficacy.

5. Should research efforts, as Strupp (1996) recommends, "introduce modifications to experimental models and to the reporting of results from psychotherapy outcome research that include multiple-outcome indicators reflecting the perspectives of various groups of stakeholders" (as cited in Peebles, 2000, p. 661)?

6. If psychotherapy research has multiple consumers, some with political agendas rather than concerns regarding effective practice, will research be considered political rather than scientific?

Reynolds and Richardson (2000) believe that an uneasy relationship exists between practitioners and researchers because practitioners often feel that research is neither related to the problems they experience in practice nor is it helpful in making practice-related decisions. Because of heavy workloads and lack of time, practitioners are often unable to keep up with research evidence. The authors suggest that research is difficult to read and understand and that this leaves a troubling gap because "dangerous or ineffective procedures continue to be used, and effective, safe procedures are often slowly introduced into clinical practice" (p. 258). Without an understanding of the needs of clinicians, "it is possible that research activities may become disengaged from the practical needs of clinical work and thus further fuel accusations that research does not help clinicians" (Reynolds & Richardson, 2000, p. 258).

Kopta, Lueger, Saunders, and Howard (1999) suggest that, although psychotherapy is generally believed to be effective, we don't actually know why. Evidence of the effectiveness of medication to treat emotional problems continues to be uncertain, and while the relationship between theory and effectiveness is equally uncertain, new research methodologies are developing that can be used to clarify many issues for future practice. However, the authors suggest that current designs to measure treatment effectiveness are often misleading or too flawed to produce believable outcomes. As one example, using a famous study criticized for many methodological reasons, they note Seligman's use of survey material in the *Consumer Reports* study of the effectiveness of psychotherapy. Their criticisms range from low response rate, to misleading questions asked in the survey instrument, to unsupported conclusions. In response to those criticisms, Seligman (1996) writes,

> None of the criticism I have seen is about what CR [*Consumer Reports*] did but what they might have done with a great deal more money and time: a longitudinal study, using blind diagnosis, with a more representative sample of Americans, for example. But in the limits imposed by a cross-sectional survey of CR's readership, this was first-rate journalism and creditable science as well. (p. 1086)

In an earlier article, Seligman (1995) proposed an ideal survey design that would include a very large sample size, pre- and postassessment methodologies, and multiple outcome measures. However, inherent in surveys are problems related to social desirability and the halo effect. More empirical methods, such as comparing randomly selected control and treatment groups, suffer from similar difficulties. There is no way to prevent subjects in the control group from seeking help elsewhere. The help they receive may be nonprofessional (self-help groups, for example) but very effective. Additional problems with empirical methods include the following:

1. The use of control groups often suggests serious ethical concerns about the denial of services to troubled clients.

2. Instruments used to measure change in client functioning are easily manipulated by savvy clients and the instruments themselves may have questionable validity and reliability in the first place.

3. Client self-reports are often inaccurate, as are the evaluations of client progress made by clinicians, who usually find more positive change than can be reasonably supported (Chambless and Ollendick, 2001; Kopta et al., 1999).

4. Single-subject designs and other qualitative methods are inherently weak methodologically and lack objectivity.

5. Attempting to measure the effectiveness of a therapy approach with a study that uses multiple clinicians avoids the question of whether we're measuring the effectiveness of a specific therapy approach or the competence of the clinician. Workers bring with them different competencies, many of them quite separate from the theoretical approach being evaluated in a study.

6. Comparing the impact of medication to that of therapy seems unlikely to suggest a clearly superior choice. Clients may feel less depressed because of the medication, but may not learn to function better without therapy.

If it's that difficult to use current research methods to measure treatment effectiveness, what should helping professionals do?

Alternative Ideas for Research on Treatment Efficacy

The research problems just described are difficult but not unsolvable. In a positive statement about the importance of practice research for the future of psychotherapy, Reynolds and Richardson (2000) write, "There are emerging opportunities to broaden the scope of evidence-based practice. This should include neglected methods of research, for example qualitative methods, and neglected topics of research including the treatment of individuals with severe mental health problems" (p. 257). The following are additional suggestions for improving effectiveness research.

1. Only use social functioning as a measure of effectiveness. Instruments, self-reports, and the judgments of other therapists are not reliable indicators of client improvement. What helping professionals need to know is whether the client's behavior has changed. That suggests using very behaviorally oriented measurements of social functioning, which include questions about client employment, absences from work or school, consumption of substances, loss of weight, completion of homework assignments, increased exercise, and any behavior that can be independently validated and that relates directly to client problems that require change. The reader can see that using an instrument to measure levels of depression tells us nothing about social functioning, even when using an instrument with good validity. The client may seem less depressed on a depression instrument, but does the decreased level of depression coincide with improved social functioning? Very often it does not, even in very valid and reliable instruments. Until social functioning has improved, we, as practitioners, can't tell policy makers, the consumer, or the public that what we do actually improves depression. It's the same as saying that an antibiotic has removed an infection because the lab work says it has even though the client is still violently ill.

2. Question all treatment results. It is unlikely that any research study will show that change is absolutely the result of the treatment received. There are hundreds of variables that affect treatment results. While treatment may be the most significant reason, it may explain only a relatively small percentage of the total reasons for change. Another way of looking at this is to recognize that if we gather together every individual reason clients improve, we may be looking at hundreds of reasons. Many of the reasons for change are small and insignificant, but when we add up all of the reasons and discover that therapy only explains 10%–20% of the reasons for improvement, we can't say a great deal about the importance of therapy in affecting change.

3. Consider qualitative designs. While most effectiveness research is done in controlled studies, all practitioners should evaluate their own effectiveness. If enough practitioners using the same evaluative guidelines measure change with similar types of client problems and treatment inputs, we begin to get a sense of whether an approach works. Is this as good as empirical evidence? No, but it does suggest a type of consensus that, by sheer numbers, could influence treatment. It also suggests the need for practitioners to meet frequently and share their results. Describing what they did in treatment, how long they did it, and the client changes that took place as a result provides important cumulative relevance to the data.

The following is an example of what an independent practitioner might say about the evaluation of his or her own practice: "I've seen 15 clients this year with anxiety problems that seriously interfered with social functioning (work, relationships, sleep, exercise, ability to travel, and self-medication through use of alcohol). The steady state for the anxiety was an average of 2 years. Using rational emotive therapy as described by Ellis (1962), on average, clients improved in social functioning by 55% after 10 weekly sessions, 65% after 15 sessions, and reached their highest level of improvement of symptoms of 75% after 20 sessions. More than 20 sessions resulted in no added improvement at 25, 30, or 35 sessions. Clients were able to maintain a 75% improvement in symptoms for at least a year, and counting, with one monthly session of an hour of maintenance therapy."

Of course, we have to be more precise about the steady state, the therapy input, and the actual change that took place, but the reader can see that if 100 clinicians had similar results, we could, by the preponderance of evidence, know that the most gain is made in 20 sessions, that therapeutic gain is maintained with one monthly contact, and that the treatment input is the likely reason for the improvement. If some other intervening variables were responsible for the change, they would probably have affected the client's social functioning sometime prior to therapy and would, therefore, have altered the steady state. Can we say that therapy caused the change in social functioning, or that a cause-effect relationship exists? No, but we can say that a link or an association exists between what we did in treatment and client change. That may be all we need to say. As other therapists work to refine the process we've reported, we may find that 10 sessions maximizes improvement and that maintenance sessions every 2 months are sufficient to continue high rates of improvement.

Consider the problems associated with empirical research and why qualitative designs may be a good alternative approach to research in the following quote from Kopta et al. (1999):

> Researchers have repeatedly failed to find convincing evidence that different psychotherapies are differentially effective. Meta-analyses—which statistically combine and compare the effect sizes of treatment, placebo, and control groups—continually report no differences among different types of therapies (e.g. Smith & Glass 1977, Grissom 1996, Wampold et al. 1997). Occasionally, when differences are found, they disappear after methodological confounds are taken into account; for example, Robinson et al. (1990) discovered that researcher allegiance influenced the superiority of some treatment classes over others for depressed patients. (p. 467)

4. Distrust the way data are reported. Practitioners, consumers, and policy makers must be certain that the data we provide in research reports are honest and haven't been manipulated. As an example, let's consider that a hospital reports that the mortality rate for a heart procedure is 1%. The report fails to tell us that some doctors have a 10% mortality rate or that less invasive procedures may produce the same results. Because of the way the data are reported, the consumer may believe that less invasive procedures are also less effective. Reporting data in a straightforward way always results in the most useful and believable information, and the researcher who says the following is offering us something promising:

> . . . 200 clients entering a mental health clinic for complaints about depression were randomly placed on a waiting list that served as a control group. A similarly randomly selected group of 200, serving as the experimental group, were treated with cognitive therapy as described by Beck, Rush, Shaw, and Emery (1979). A third of the clients in the treatment group were seen for 10 sessions, a third for 15 sessions, and a third for 20 sessions. Using indicators of social functioning that were verified by outside sources, such as employers to verify attendance and other work-related behaviors, health club personnel to verify exercise regimens, teachers to verify attendance and grades, and laboratory workers to verify blood alcohol levels if drinking or drugs were involved, the control group surpassed the treatment group in

social functioning and in a reduction of symptoms of depression at 10 sessions by 20%, at 15 sessions by 15%, and at 20 sessions by 10%. Members of the control group were interviewed after the study was completed to determine if they sought other help for their depression. Twenty percent had sought medical help and were on antidepression medications, the same percentage as was found in the treatment group. Other reasons for the control group bettering the treatment group were explored. It was determined that the cognitive therapy in this study was not as effective at 10, 15 and 20 weeks as no therapy at all. It was also noted that differences in social functioning diminished between the treatment and control groups as the number of treatment sessions increased. This could mean that cognitive therapy requires more time to create change in the social functioning of depressed clients, or it might mean that the cognitive therapy offered in this study was ineffective with depressed clients. It might also mean that the cognitive therapy used in this study was not consistent with the description of cognitive therapy provided by Beck et al. (1979), that therapists were not skilled in cognitive therapy, or that clients placed on the waiting list experienced natural healing. Self-reports by clients in the treatment group confirmed that they were dissatisfied with the therapy, reporting that it was uncaring and overly prescriptive. These findings significantly differ from other findings in the literature that suggest treatment effectiveness with depression using cognitive therapy with similar populations of clients (Peterson & Halstead, 1998; Remick, 2002). Further evaluation of the data is in order and a replication of the study is planned to determine whether findings were influenced by variables not controlled for in this study. (An example offered by the author)

5. Consider using constructivist research designs. We researchers usually think of our research subjects as passive players in the research process. We create a questionnaire and our research subjects fill it out. We choose the various methodologies used without any involvement on the part of the subjects. But why not include the subjects in every step of the process by encouraging their involvement in determining the problem to be studied and the instrument to be used? And once the instrument is developed, why not have the same subjects fill it out? This is the essence of the constructivist paradigm: Research subjects should be our partners in the research process.

The constructivist approach is interested in a democratic relationship between the researcher and the subject. It believes that research is enhanced when subjects are involved. It also believes that findings are likely to be more accurate when subjects are very involved in the process. The idea of an equal relationship among participants and researchers is certainly worth considering, particularly if one believes that an important by-product of research is the empowerment of research subjects. Empowerment can be an elegant result of constructivist research because, once subjects are involved in the research process, they may begin to take control of the emotional problems being studied and may develop insights into their condition that could prompt changes in the way they approach their lives.

6. Use focus groups. In a focus group, a sample of clients might be brought together to discuss treatment effectiveness issues and provide feedback to researchers through consensus statements. Some researchers use videotapes to record group interactions. Linguistic techniques to analyze the interactions among the participants might also be used to factor in subjective, but meaningful, nonverbal communications. There is usually a second person present with the researcher to run the video camera and to gather information as a way of making the researcher's observations more objective. If worked with correctly, focus groups should provide a wealth of information. Writing about the use of focus groups to compensate for inaccuracies in political polls, Leman (2000) notes that political focus groups are meant to "pick up on aspects of voter unconsciousness that lie outside the questions asked in polls" (p. 107). Leman goes on to say that, under the "prodding" of the group leader, members of focus groups should be able to "free associate" and that such a process will "reveal the shadings of opinions within a single category of voters" (p. 107). In other words, focus groups permit one to define terms and to better understand feelings and thoughts that are often outside the narrow questions asked in surveys or on instruments. To a large extent, focus groups limit social desirability and capture core concerns about issues. They also narrow down opinions in a way that surveys or instruments can never do because they permit focus group members to clarify, for themselves and for others, what they really believe.

Analyzing content from focus group discussions can be complex because much of the material is subjective. The researcher must have a methodology in place for data analysis. Some researchers leave the analysis of the data to others who were not involved in the focus group. This may be done by videotaping the session and letting other researchers analyze the findings and then evaluating the objectivity of the techniques used by the focus group leader. But as a way of collecting data in a short period of time, focus groups can be very helpful to the researcher developing best evidence. Further discussion of focus group techniques may be found in Glicken (2003).

7. Use evidence-based records. One useful way to evaluate treatment effectiveness is to analyze a worker's case records describing his or her work with clients. This provides an effective way of determining the practice procedures used in certain clinical situations, the client's response to those procedures, how many sessions it took to have a positive or negative outcome, and how the worker made judgments about the effectiveness of his or her work. Although an objective protocol is necessary for the use of evidence-based records, and the content of the records is certainly open to manipulation by the workers, there are ways to check the reported results with the actual results. They include how well the client is doing based on collateral records kept by other agencies including police reports (as in the case of domestic violence); DWIs (for clients receiving substance abuse treatment); and confirmation of treatment gains using a social functioning evaluation, where people in the client's life are asked to verify gains, or losses, during and after treatment.

If used correctly, all of these alternative approaches could provide additional information on practice effectiveness that might help fill the gap left by limited effectiveness studies and might better involve clinicians in developing best evidence.

The Future of the Helping Professions

In a discussion of the future of psychotherapy, Krauth (1996) reports former American Psychological Association President Nick Cummings's predictions for psychotherapy in the next 10 years: Half of today's therapists will be out of work. Most therapists will be at the master's degree level with one third of the work following preestablished protocols for workers to follow and the remaining two thirds supervised by therapists with advanced degrees. The more advanced therapists will also do research but little therapy. Most treatment will be intermittent, with clients coming back for treatment only as needed. Treatment done over a single, long-lasting period of time will not be the norm. Most practice will consist of psychoeducational and group treatment, with only a fourth of the time spent in individual therapy. Managed care will not survive. In its place, therapists and physicians will create group practices that provide medical and emotional treatments. These group practices will contract with companies and organizations and take the financial risks involved. Utilization boards will cease to exist, and "the costly managed care utilization review administrative layer that now monitors providers will disappear as the providers police themselves with sophisticated monitoring devices, such as outcome studies" (Krauth, 1996, p. 10).

Norcross, Hedges, and Prochaska (2002) have done Delphi studies over the past several decades on the future of psychotherapy. Based on the results of their most recent study, they conclude that five trends are likely to emerge in the future:

1. The economic realities of payment for services will result in the quickest therapies, the least expensive therapist, and the least expensive therapeutic techniques.

2. Therapists will be rewarded who utilize best evidence provided by the research studies.

3. New therapy approaches will evolve, but it will be a gradual evolution.

4. New approaches will build on, rather than break with, current approaches.

5. Integration of practice theories will seek cohesion among the various approaches rather than fragmentation.

Regarding the approaches most likely to emerge in the future, the authors report that respondents to the Delphi study predicted that there will be an increased use of therapy done at home, including the use of homework assignments, computers as adjuncts to treatment, and self-help groups. The focus of help will be on short-term treatment, including problem solving, cognitive restructuring, solution-focused work, and skills training. The techniques predicted to dramatically decrease were those associated with long-term therapies and included free association, transference, and dream interpretations (Norcross et al., 2002, p. 320).

Interestingly, in the Norcross et al. (2002) study, the first round of the study predicted that managed care providers would require evidence-based psychotherapies. Although the second round found that this prediction had slipped a bit, the latest round of the study found that the majority of respondents thought that EBP would be required by health care providers and predicted that "research would generate prescriptive treatments, practice guidelines would become standard, and therapists would increasingly treat health-related behaviors" (p. 320).

Krauth (1996) believes that the next decade will be an agonizing one for the helping professions because of the continuing mental health care "revolution." She thinks that the shift to evidence-based practice might lead to transforming new approaches in the way treatment is offered but that there will be anxiety, in the meantime, as therapists find their way in the new mental health care environment. As a counterpoint to Krauth's sense that transforming new approaches will be developed, Norcross et al. (2002) report that respondents to their most recent Delphi study believed that "the second least likely scenario in the study was that revolutionary psychotherapy techniques will be discovered and will replace traditional treatments" (p. 320). It should be noted that respondents to the study by Norcross et al. were doubtful that they could predict the future, although in previous studies, their predictions seemed to coincide well with future events.

Reynolds and Richardson (2000) suggest that the future of psychotherapy will be similar to that of medicine, with more resources directed toward research efforts, ultimately leading to improved services to clients. They believe that managers will have a basis for making better judgments about the use of resources, and effectiveness research will be substantially increased. They worry, however, that without well-funded research efforts, therapy approaches with limited evidence of effectiveness will become prescribed approaches for all clients, and they give cognitive therapy as an example of an approach that works well for some clients but not well for others. Because of the concern that EBP for the helping professions will settle into a highly prescribed practice, with any evidence substituting for best evidence, they call for well-controlled studies providing research evidence that clinicians can accept and that are useful with a range of clients.

One of the repeated findings in a number of studies reviewed for this book is that master's-level practitioners will do most of the therapy in the future. This will cause a predictable decline in the use of psychiatrists and clinical psychologists, not because of issues of effectiveness, but because more highly educated practitioners are also more costly. The future of therapy seems to suggest that less highly educated practitioners will provide short-term treatment augmented by self-help groups and medication. Does this bode well for the consumer? Wallerstein (1991) reports that psychiatric residencies required an average of 600 hours of direct psychotherapeutic training in 1991 as opposed to the 3,000 hours he had received during his residency. Even more troubling are Altshuler's findings (1990) that in psychiatric residencies, less than 40% of the responding programs required any patients to be seen more than once a week within the total residency training period. According to Wallerstein, most of the time spent in residency was spent learning about medications and their most efficacious use in public-sector facilities such as Veterans Affairs medical centers and large state and county hospitals. These public facilities, with few exceptions, have not been "significant bastions of dynamic psychotherapy training" (Wallerstein, 1991, p. 442).

This same concern is raised in social work training (Council on Social Work Education, 2003), where the minimum requirement of 900 hours of supervised training for students obtaining a master's in social work (MSW) is really more a measure of the hours spent in social agencies than the hours spent in direct contact with clients. I served as a faculty liaison to field agencies for a social work department providing the MSW degree, and I kept 10 years of data ($n = 120$ students) regarding the average number of hours of direct individual and group treatment with clients, including casemanagement services requiring referral and ancillary contact, provided by students in the field. On average, a 2-year MSW student spent approximately 400 hours providing direct services to clients, or 500 hours less than the minimum hours required by the accrediting agency, the Council on Social Work Education (2003). The remaining time was spent in continuing education, staff meetings, orientation to the agency, group and individual supervisory sessions, or doing classroom assignments. Most students received about an hour of group or individual supervision a week, but the quality of the supervision was inconsistent, and supervisors seldom actually saw the students' direct work with clients. Direct observation could have been accomplished by videotaping sessions, sitting in on sessions as an observer, working as a cotherapist, or watching treatment through a one-way mirror. Instead, summary statements or process recordings were typically used to inform the supervisor of the student's work. Both methods are highly subjective and often inaccurate, in my view. It was not unusual for students to spend the majority of the first of three quarters each year in the field being oriented to the agency, and the majority of the third quarter of each year in termination. While the better average would have been 800 hours of direct practice, even that seems far too little given the important role social workers have in providing therapy in the United States.

In another area of future practice, Chambless and Ollendick (2001) note that attempts to identify and disseminate empirically supported therapies (ESTs), often in manuals or computer programs, have met with resistance from therapists and write, "Whatever the reluctance of some to embrace EST's, we expect that the economic and societal pressures on practitioners for accountability will encourage continued attention to these treatments" (p. 714). The authors caution that ESTs require good therapy skills, and that even the most complete manuals providing best evidence for practice acknowledge that "the practice of evidence-based psychotherapy is a complex one, and EST's are only one piece of the puzzle" (p. 714). Chambless and Ollendick suggest that even when treatment manuals are used, the variables that distinguish effective practice from less effective practice include the worker's ability to form a positive alliance with the client, the level of the client's initial functioning, and the overall level of the worker's skills. It remains to be seen if less well-trained workers can achieve positive results, even when training manuals are used and more advanced practitioners provide supervision.

Case Study: An Incompetent Worker Treats Chronic Depression

Julie Loren is an MSW-level social worker with 3 years of experience who recently obtained her clinical license to practice independent social work. Julie was a very good student and did well in her classes but had problems in her two field placements. Both placements were in casemangement agencies providing services to fragile elderly and disabled clients. Julie has never been supervised in a setting providing psychotherapy, and although she was able to receive her clinical license, her therapy skills are very minimal. In her field settings, two MSW supervisors raised issues about her people skills, her commitment to helping others, and her ability to form relationships. Because she did so well in her classroom work, Julie was able to complete her field experience and receive passing grades even though two field instructors and two faculty field liaisons had recommended failing grades in fieldwork. Like many university settings, grade grievances in Julie's university are litigious matters, and Julie was able to challenge her grades and receive a passing grade in both field placements. In a system using pass/fail as the grade for the field practicum, this meant that no employer could actually know how badly she had done in her fieldwork. The agency she worked for after graduation had promised to provide supervision for her license, and although her over-worked supervisor had strong concerns about Julie's abilities, she was aware that other supervisees had brought legal actions against supervisors who failed to support them at the point of licensure. She wrote a mild and innocuous letter in support of Julie's licensure application. Had the letter been read carefully, it would have confirmed the suspicion that Julie lacked the interpersonal and technical skills for clinical practice.

Upon receiving her LCSW, Julie was hired by an agency with a severe shortage of clinical workers. The agency was under review by the state for its poor level of work and had been told to increase the number of LCSWs or face loss of certification for state payments for services. Julie was given a caseload of severely depressed clients, many of them suicidal. Her over-worked supervisor, believing that Julie's license indicated the ability to work independently, provided very superficial supervision, usually on lunch breaks where the two talked about the supervisor's troubled teenaged son.

Julie recognized that she had few actual skills for work with depressed clients. She was generally superficial with clients, was nonsupportive, pro-vided innocuous clichés about what clients should do regarding their depression, was unknowledgeable about medications or the potential for suicide, and was uniformly disliked by her clients, who called her "Miss Priss" in response to her condescending and uninformed attitudes about depression. One of the clients complained to Julie's supervisor and gave her a taped interview the client had made without Julie's knowledge or consent. The supervisor refused to listen to the tape and returned it to the client, telling her that it was in violation of federal law mandating that people must consent to be taped. The client pointed out Julie's flaws as a worker, but the supervisor, thinking that the client had transference issues with Julie, refused to do anything about the complaint. Nonetheless, the supervisor began meeting with Julie for actual supervisory sessions and asked Julie to present cases. It was immediately clear that Julie knew little about depression, had a condescending attitude toward clients, and was likely to create potential for a client suicide because of her incompetent work. A complicated grievance process in Julie's unionized agency led to a number of meetings and the supervisor was cautioned to use the con-tracted grievance procedure in future work with Julie. Nothing was done to Julie and her poor quality of work, supported by numerous client com-plaints, continued.

In a highly agitated state, one of Julie's clients stabbed her after another condescending treatment session, resulting in a punctured lung and a long-term disability claim by Julie. When she was well, she returned to the agency, where she continues to provide poor-level work and has now been assigned responsibility for training MSW students. One of the students complained to the university faculty field liaison that Julie calls her clients derogatory names such as "retard, bitch, and queer." The university has decided to give up an otherwise excellent placement because Julie is too incompetent to supervise students. A meeting between the faculty field liaison and the agency director resulted in the following conversation:

Liaison (L):   We've decided not to use the agency next year because we have strong concerns about the field instructor's competence [Julie].

Director (D):   What does that mean?

L: She's an incompetent practitioner.

D: How could that be? She was one of the top students to graduate from your program and she's licensed by the state to do advanced clinical work.

L: I recognize that, but still, she's not competent and her attitude toward clients is highly negative.

D: I'm confused. How are any of those things possible if you were doing your job? How could someone you say is incompetent even get through your program, particularly the field segment of the program?

L: You have a good point, but our question is, knowing her level of incompetence, how can you allow her to work with highly disturbed clients and, more to the point, how can you assign her to train students given the terrible attitude she has toward people in difficulty?

D: We hired her on the basis of her performance in your program and on the recommendation of another LCSW who did her supervision for licensure. Once having hired her, we have a difficult time firing her just because very troubled clients complain about her work. We tried to fire her but the union interceded. It would take hundreds of hours for us to develop a case against her and, even if we did, it's doubtful she'd be fired. So we assigned her the least dangerous role we could find: training new students. We hope you'll counteract the harm she does with your students through classroom work and the field seminars you require all students to attend, but that's where we are.

L: It's a sad statement that the agency thinks training students doesn't result in harm to clients.

D: What would you do in our position?

L: Fire her.

D: We tried. Go talk to the union.

A Different Kind of Future: Workers Share Their Thoughts

I spoke to 36 clinicians representing a cross section of helping professionals providing direct psychotherapy to clients, with an equal number in public and private practice (15 MSW/PhD–level social workers; 7 PhD-level psychologists; 3 psychiatrists; and 11 MFCC-level counselors). The following summarizes their hopes for the future.

1. Clients who have suffered serious life traumas should be provided all the therapy they require at no cost to them. This is particularly true of physically abused or sexually molested children, victims of rape and domestic violence, victims of natural and man-made disasters, and clients who are troubled by long-term problems such as chronic depression, bipolar disorder, and a range of very serious problems including mental illness. Funding for long-term treatment should be provided by perpetrators and by general government sources.

2. Clinicians should be trained in research and should be required to attend frequent workshops and meetings where new evidence of best practices is shared, discussed, and evaluated in detail. This requirement should be a part of licensure renewal.

3. The standards for academic programs in the helping professions should be raised so that workers can read research, understand research, write well, and conduct their own research on the effectiveness of their practice. Required hours of direct supervised practice should be raised and students should be trained to use the most effective approaches recognized by best practice data. Student behavioral issues, such as bias against groups of people because of race, ethnicity, religious orientation, and sexual orientation, should be serious matters. Student misconduct in class and ethical violations should be grounds for dismissal from programs and should affect licensure decisions. Only students with very advanced aptitudes for the helping professions should be admitted to programs. Small, high-quality programs should be the norm and not the exception.

4. Much more funding of practice research should be a priority for our national and local funding sources, with an emphasis on finding best evidence of practice approaches that work best with specific types of problems and clients. There should also be an initiative to fund projects

that attempt to find new approaches to treatment. There appears to be promise in the research on resilience, self-help groups, the strengths perspective, and the effect of religious involvement and spirituality on the physical and mental health of clients. Perhaps these areas of inquiry will suggest new ways of treating client problems.

5. There should be more alternative training programs that provide different models of preparation for practice rather than those that closely approximate one another because of accreditation demands. An argument for accreditation in social work is that accreditation permits graduates to be very mobile because all graduate social workers from accredited schools are thought to have very similar educational experiences, and that accreditation functions to maintain standards in all programs. The counterargument is that accreditation locks schools into very conservative programs that offer curriculums that are safe and easy to accredit, but that are often disassociated from the changing needs of clients. Few social work programs offer training for work with troubled men, and very few are sufficiently clinically oriented enough because students must take a number of classes (social policy classes or generalized human behavior classes, for example) that should be prerequisites rather than required courses. Even the words *clinical practice* must often be substituted by the term *social work practice* so that accrediting teams don't think a program has forgotten its social action and advocacy roots.

This isn't a concern only among social workers but one widely held by the group. Accreditation, while necessary to maintain certain standards, has also had a very conservative impact on academic programs in the helping professions, which would sometimes rather keep accreditation status than move in more progressive directions by teaching students cutting-edge treatment approaches. The group wondered how transforming models of treatment will be developed and taught if the lead isn't taken by academic programs in the helping professions. They believed that more clinical programs with no ties to academe nor to their own licensure organizations might act to radicalize academic programs and improve clinical training.

SUMMARY

The future of psychotherapy in the United States has several distinct trends: less therapy for most clients, and that is mainly provided by master's-level practitioners in very short blocks of time and with heavy reliance on self-help groups, psychoeducational materials, and outside homework assignments. Suggestions are made for enhancing the quality of practice research, including the use of focus groups and constructivist approaches, and more reliance on all practitioners to evaluate their own practices. Concerns are raised about the difficulty of doing practice effectiveness research and what the findings actually tell us. An example of a straightforward research report is given. A case study of an incompetent worker is provided, and a group summary of a discussion about the future of psychotherapy and the changes that need to be made to ensure high quality of service are also provided.

Integrative Questions

1. If psychotherapy were highly effective, do you believe that managed care would be more responsive and positive, or do you think managed care is looking for any answer to lowering health care costs and that reducing mental health services seems the easiest one?

2. The future of psychotherapy suggests very short-term treatment using cognitive-behavioral and psychoeducational approaches. Can you think of clients who need long-term treatment and what might happen to them if they fail to receive it?

3. Subjective approaches to treatment effectiveness research were suggested as one way of improving (and increasing) practice effectiveness research. What are some of the limitations of nonempirical practice research?

4. Is it the responsibility of professional programs in the helping professions to teach practice competencies or should that come from agency work and supervision once the student is employed?

5. Private practice is often thought to be the last bastion of autonomous and creative psychotherapy practice. Do you believe this and, if so, why?

References

Altshuler, K. Z. (1990). Whatever happened to intensive psychotherapy? *American Journal of Psychiatry, 147*, 428–430.

Barlow, D. H. (1996). Health care policy, psychotherapy research, and the future of psychotherapy. *American Psychologist, 51*, 1007–1016.

Beck, A. T., Rush, A. J., Shaw, B. F., & Emery, G. (1979). *Cognitive therapy of depression.* New York: Guilford Press.

Chambless, D. L., & Ollendick, T. H. (2001). Empirically supported psychological interventions: Controversies and evidence. *Annual Review of Psychology, 52*, 685–716.

Ellis, A. (1962). *Reason and emotion in psychotherapy.* Secaucus, NJ: Citadel Press.

Glicken, M. D. (2003). *A simple guide to social research.* Boston: Allyn & Bacon/ Longman.

Grissom, R. J. (1996). The magical number .7 plus or minus .2: Meta-analysis of the probability of superior outcome in comparisons involving therapy, placebo, and control. *Journal of Consulting Clinical Psychology, 64,* 973–982.

Kopta, M. S., Lueger, R. J., Saunders, S. M., & Howard, K. I. (1999). Individual psychotherapy outcome and process research: Challenges leading to greater turmoil or a positive transition? *Annual Review of Psychology, 50,* 441–469.

Krauth, L. D. (1996, May/June). Providers confront the future. *Behavioral Health Management, 16*(3), 10–14.

Leman, N. (2000, October 16, October 23). The word lab. *New Yorker,* 100–112.

Norcross, J. C., Hedges, M., & Prochaska, J. O. (2002, June). The face of 2010: A Delphi poll on the future of psychotherapy. *Professional Psychology: Research and Practice, 33*(3), 316–322.

Parloff, M. B. (1979). Can psychotherapy research guide the policymaker? A little knowledge may be a dangerous thing. *American Psychologist, 34,* 296–306.

Parloff, M. B., & Elkin, I. (1992). The NIMH Treatment of Depression Collaborative Research Program. In D. K. Freedheim (Ed.), *History of psychotherapy: A century of change* (pp. 442–450). Washington, DC: American Psychological Association.

Peebles, J. (2000, November). The future of psychotherapy outcome research: Science or political rhetoric? *Journal of Psychology, 134*(6), 659–670.

Peterson, A. L., & Halstead, T. S. (1998). Group cognitive behavior therapy for depression in a community setting: A clinical replication series. *Behavioral Therapy, 29,* 3–18.

Remick, R. A. (2002). Diagnosis and management of depression in primary care: A clinical update and review. *Canadian Medical Association Journal, 167*(11), 1253–1261.

Reynolds, R., & Richardson, P. (2000). Evidence based practice and psychotherapy research. *Journal of Mental Health, 9*(3), 257–267.

Robinson, L. A., Berman, J. S., & Neimeyer, R. A. (1990). Psychotherapy for the treatment of depression: A comprehensive review of controlled outcome research. *Psychological Bulletin, 108,* 30–49.

Seligman, M. E. P. (1995). The effectiveness of psychotherapy: The *Consumer Reports* study. *American Psychological Journal, 50,* 965–974.

Seligman, M. E. P. (1996). A creditable beginning. *American Psychological Journal, 51,* 1086–1088.

Smith, M. L., & Glass, G. V. (1977). Meta-analysis of psychotherapy outcome studies. *American Psychologist, 32,* 752–760.

Strupp, H. H. (1996). The tripartite model and the *Consumer Reports* study. *American Psychologist, 51,* 1017–1024.

Wallerstein, R. S. (1991, Fall). The future of psychotherapy. *Bulletin of the Menninger Clinic, 55*(4), 421–444.

Wampold, B. E., Mondin, G. W., Moody, M., Stich, F., Benson, K., & Ahn, H. (1997). A meta-analysis of outcome studies comparing bona fide psychotherapies: Empirically "all must have prizes." *Psychological Bulletin, 122,* 203–215.

Some Final Words 17

Two concerns affecting practice are discussed in this final chapter:
(a) the lack of involvement by the helping professions in improving
community life through social action and volunteerism and (b) the cautious and sometimes politically correct nature of practice, with its tendency to avoid issues of great significance to our most needy people and
to our society. Both issues impact effective practice and suggest an additional direction for EBP to take in the future.

Social Involvement

No book on the effectiveness of psychotherapy should ignore the responsibility of the helping professions to actively strengthen the social, emotional,
spiritual, and economic environments of our neighborhoods, communities,
and country. However, a number of writers believe that is precisely what we
have done. Ryff and Singer (1998) argue that modern psychology has failed
to develop a view of the client beyond the absence of dysfunctional behavior. Sandage and Hill (2001) suggest that modern psychology has no model
of the civic virtues that promote healthy individual and community behaviors. In fact, the authors believe that much of psychology, and perhaps most
of the helping professions, have no model of the positive values that should
be emphasized with our clients or the necessary constructive social behaviors that will lead to an increased sense of social responsibility.

Seligman (2002) worries that Americans have become so caught up in a
personal sense of entitlement that even helping professionals have gone along
with, in fact encouraged, "the belief that we can rely on shortcuts to happiness,
joy, rapture, comfort, and ecstasy, rather than be entitled to these feelings by
the exercise of personal strengths and virtues, which results in legions of
people who, in the middle of great wealth, are starving spiritually" (ABC News,
2002, para. 18). Seligman goes on to say, "Positive emotion alienated from the

exercise of character leads to emptiness, to inauthenticity, to depression, and, as we age, to the gnawing realization that we are fidgeting until we die" (ABC News, 2002, para. 18). Seligman also believes that we have overemphasized the needs of the individual in the helping professions at the expense of healthy and flourishing community life (Sandage and Hill, 2001) and argues that we should be shifting psychology's paradigm away from its narrow focus on pathology, victimology, and mental illness and toward positive emotions, virtues, strengths, and healthy institutions that increase people's levels of happiness. Seligman believes that clinicians have ignored the importance of virtue, religion, and philosophy in people's lives and suggests the following six core virtues that define the healthy person and provide direction for helping professionals in our work with clients: (a) wisdom and knowledge, (b) courage, (c) love and humanity, (d) justice, (e) temperance, and (f) spirituality and transcendence.

Robert Putnam (Stossel, 2000) believes that this obsession with self is producing a country without a sense of social connectedness, where "supper eaten with friends or family has given way to supper gobbled in solitude, with only the glow of the television screen for companionship" (p. 1). According to Putnam,

> Americans today have retreated into isolation. Evidence shows that fewer and fewer contemporary Americans are unionizing, voting, rallying around shared causes, participating in religious services, inviting each other over, or doing much of anything collectively. In fact, when we do occasionally gather—for twelve-step support encounters and the like—it's most often only as an excuse to focus on ourselves in the presence of an audience. (Stossel, 2000, p. 1)

To support the notion of a deterioration in community life, Putnam reports that union membership has declined by more than half since the mid-1950s. PTA membership has fallen from 12 million in 1964 to 7 million. Since 1970, membership in the Boy Scouts is down by 26% and membership in the Red Cross is off by 61% (Putnam, 2000). Putnam believes that the lack of social involvement negatively affects school performance, physical health, and mental health; increases crime rates; reduces tax responsibilities and charitable work; and decreases productivity and "even simple human happiness—all are demonstrably affected by how (and whether) we connect with our family and friends and neighbors and co-workers" (Stossel, 2000, p. 1).

In further agreement with Putnam and Seligman regarding social connectedness and healthy community life, Saleebey (1996) believes, "In communities that amplify individual resilience, there is awareness, recognition, and use of the assets of most members of the community" (p. 298). In these healthy communities, informal networks of people provide "succor, instruction, support, and encouragement" (p. 298). Saleebey challenges helping professionals to work with communities because so many of the dysfunctions common to practice can be avoided. "In communities that provide protection and minimize risk," he writes, "there are many opportunities to participate, to make significant contributions to the moral and civic life of the community, and to take on the role of full-fledged citizen" (p. 298).

To demonstrate how we are all at risk when communities develop dysfunctional qualities, Putnam notes that violence exists in even the most affluent of communities and writes, "The shooting sprees that affected schools in suburban and rural communities as the twentieth century ended are a reminder that as the breakdown of communities continues in more privileged settings, affluence and education are insufficient to prevent collective tragedy" (Putnam, 2000, p. 318).

What is a healthy community? Kesler (2000) provides a model of communities that defines the social connectedness, civic virtues, and social responsibilities of its members. In healthy communities, there is "a sophisticated, integrative, and interconnected vision of flourishing of the individual and the human collective in an environmental setting" (p. 272) that involves all sectors of the community including the disenfranchised. People in healthy communities connect intimately with one another and are aware of special issues that need to be addressed. In healthy communities, a dialogue exists among people to help formulate public policy agendas that function with consensus among all community groups and political persuasions. Healthy communities are caring, mature, and aware communities that seek alliances with other community-based movements and "encourage all concerned to rise to higher integrative levels of thinking, discourse, research, policies, programs, institutions, and processes, so that they might truly begin to transform their lives, their communities, and the greater society" (Kesler, 2000, p. 271).

Putnam suggests that most Americans recognize the need to reconnect with one another and writes, "Figuring out how to reconcile the competing obligations of work and family and community is the ultimate kitchen table issue" (Stossel, 2000, p. 4). However, when we are unable to find commonality with our fellow citizens and to develop mutual helping relationships, community life often ends in what Taylor calls "entrapping niches," where membership in the community is based upon social alienation and stigma. In its place, Taylor (1993) calls for "enabling niches" where people are known for what they do and for their willingness to reach out to one another in times of need. Writing about the purest form of community outreach, the natural helpers who define the most elegant aspects of social responsibility, Waller and Patterson (2002) write that "informal helping sustains and extends resiliency in individuals and communities . . . and [is] consistent with the growing body of research suggesting that informal social support buffers the effects of stress on adaptational outcomes" (p. 80).

In their study of natural helping in a Navajo community, Waller and Patterson (2002) interviewed community members who were noted for their willingness to help others. One of the subjects they interviewed defined the sense of social responsibility one hopes would exist in most Americans. In explaining her desire to reach out to others, she said,

> Giving peace to somebody, calming somebody down. It's just something that I . . . it's just an intuition. And throughout my whole life, with my father and mother doing that . . . So I think it's just something that comes, and if I know how to do it then I will offer IT . . . out in something good and knowing that somewhere along the line you will get rewarded with something . . . and I receive the reward back in that way, but not expecting or looking for it. (p. 78)

In another example of social connectedness and reaching out, a 30-year-old female helper describes providing assistance to her 27-year-old sister-in-law.

> She had been left by her husband . . . so she had no place to go and she brought her kids here. And on top of that she had a handicapped child. She was carrying more load than we were so we accepted her in and we did our part. We would help her pull some of the load she was carrying. We spent the whole winter with her and about half of the summer. I think we did pretty good with that. And we really gave her a lot of strength to be a single parent. As of last year she graduated and she's been promoted to a higher paying job. So she got what she wanted and it makes us feel proud. A lot of times it's just like a teamwork that keeps us together, working together and understanding each other. Then we know that we have to pull together and just challenge what we're facing. (Waller & Patterson, 2002, p. 77)

To further describe the need for community outreach, Amy Glicken (2003) provides a brief description of the dynamic behind volunteerism, which seems a fitting way to end this discussion.

Volunteering as a Social Responsibility

By Amy J. Glicken (personal communication, November 14, 2003)

As the volunteer coordinator for a rural nonprofit program in Arizona, I've seen the generous nature of people when they're asked to volunteer. I think that people become volunteers as they begin to realize that someone else's tragedy can easily be their own, and while many of us feel a responsibility to give back to our communities, so often we feel powerless to make the changes that seem beyond our personal scope.

I believe we have the power to make those changes by using the skills we already have. Attorneys donate their time with legal services for the poor. Doctors provide services to the neighborhoods and communities with marginal health care. Helping professionals offer their time and expertise to the many social welfare organizations without professionals to supervise services and as board members and grant writers.

With all of the options for helping, some of us are gifted at what is sometimes called "impact work." Impact work is the attorney who chooses to represent 600 new immigrants from Mexico rather than simply representing the one immigrant who walked into her office. Impact work is going beyond providing shelter and counseling services to victims of domestic violence by looking at the causes of violence and finding new ways of preventing it. Impact work is building more low and no income housing rather than just providing temporary shelters for those without homes.

Many of us are overwhelmed with our daily workloads and feel unable to make long-term, far-reaching changes in our communities. But whether it's by peacekeeping, sculpting, growing corn, counseling, healing, or teaching children, each of us has a gift that we can use to make our communities much better than they are. The task is simply to discern what our gifts are and to utilize them. Because, in the end, we are each our own Tooth Fairies, taking what has been lost and giving gold in return.

Avoiding Serious Practice Issues

Another aspect of the lack of focus on community is how adept helping professionals have become at highly cautious and sometimes politically correct practice that keeps us from attacking challenging problems. For example, even though many men are doing more than a little badly these days, little notice is given male problems in our professional literature (Glicken, in press). In reporting data from the University of Michigan's Institute for Social Research, Gupta (2003) notes that "men outrank women in all of the 15 leading causes of death, except one: Alzheimer's. Men's death rates are at least twice as high as women's for suicide, homicide and cirrhosis of the liver" (p. 84). Slater (2003) reports that 900,000 African American males are in prison as compared to 600,000 African American males attending college, junior college, or vocational training programs, or half the number of African American females attending American colleges and universities. The discrepancy between black male and female college attendance will result in such an imbalance of college-educated men to women, that, according to Roach (2001), it will alter the "social dynamics" of the African American community.

Epidemic increases in male juvenile crime suggest another serious problem. Commenting on the significance of the increase in male-dominated juvenile crime, Osofsky and Osofsky (2001) write, "The homicide rate among males 15–24 years old in the United States is 10 times higher than in Canada, 15 times higher than in Australia, and 28 times higher than in France or Germany" (p. 287). Yet we seem to have very limited interest in antisocial and violent clients. In fact, in a book I recently published on violence in children under the age of 12, I (Glicken, 2004) noted the highly discouraging attitudes many clinicians have about our therapeutic effectiveness with violent children and, more troubling, whether there is even a role for the helping professions in work with violent children. As examples, Rae-Grant, McConville, and Fleck (1999) write, "Because exclusive individual clinical interventions for violent conduct disorders do not work, the child and adolescent psychiatrist must seek opportunities to be a leader or team member in well-organized and well-funded community prevention efforts" (p. 238). Elliott, Hamburg, and Williams (1998) believe that counseling has no positive effect on the problems of antisocial and predelinquent youth. Steiner and Stone (1999) suggest widespread pessimism among clinicians regarding effective clinical work with violent youth. And writing about why clinicians have such a poor track record with gang members, Morales (1982) believes that worker bias about the untreatability of gang members is based upon the following erroneous beliefs: (a) a belief that antisocial personality disorders and/or gang members are untreatable; (b) a fear of violent people and a belief that all gang members are violent; (c) a belief that poor or uneducated people lack the capacity for insight, a cohort usually associated with gang activity; (d) a belief that the only way people change is through treatment; (e) the opposite belief that gang members are untreatable, manipulative, and dishonest; and (f) the belief that therapists need to control the interview since they have ultimate power.

Although most clinicians are quick to point out the damage done by child abuse, in a book review of *Treatment of Child Abuse*, edited by Reece, Lukefahr (2001) writes, "Although there is a very strong effort throughout to base findings and recommendations on the available evidence, these chapters highlight the reality that this young, evolving specialty remains largely descriptive" (p. 36). Kaplan, Pelcovitz, and Labruna (1999) believe that treatment effectiveness of child abuse "has generally not been empirically evaluated. In a review of treatment research for physically abused children, Oates and Bross (1995) cite only 13 empirical studies between 1983 and 1992 meeting even minimal research standards" (p. 1218). Given the hundreds of thousands of child welfare workers in America and the billions of dollars spent on child abuse, how would any of this be possible if helping professionals were seriously involved in efforts to limit the harm done by child abuse through research-guided practice and best evidence?

And, while the number of older Americans is growing each year, many with treatable social and emotional problems, this book has examined the services offered to older adults who suffer from anxiety and depression and finds that many older adults are denied needed help because therapists often believe that older Americans cannot benefit from therapy. These perceptions come entirely from therapists and not from any objective study of the use or rejection of treatment by older adults. Since this population, when suicidal, has a very high completion rate, it seems more than a little important that we learn more about older Americans and the services we might provide to help growing numbers of depressed and anxious older adults, whose payback for years of hard work and contribution is a nonresponsive professional community.

The continuing beliefs in the chronicity of mental illness and the inevitable impact of pathology as a result of early life traumas, and the lack of recognition that many people are able to overcome social and emotional difficulties through self-righting tendencies, natural healing, and resilience are all areas of practice that beg for reappraisal by the helping professions. And any professional reading the chapter on diagnosis in this book should wonder if our diagnostic work is still too affected by a preexisting bias among therapists that demonstrates itself in misguided attitudes toward racial, ethnic, and gender groups, with social class and religious beliefs often additional factors that negatively influence diagnosis. This bias is particularly offensive and often leads to pejorative labeling and inappropriate treatment.

Finally, the professional schools in America should be at the forefront of a revolution in the development of research guided practice. Therapy is a vital and useful practice that can only prove itself worthy when provided by well-informed and prepared professionals. Toward that end, professional programs need to create learning environments that train the mind for critical thinking and the heart for loving and tender acceptance of all clients regardless of color, ethnicity, religion, gender, or social class.

Final Words

Although this book offers many examples of ineffective treatment, that doesn't diminish the fact that for many of our clients, helping professions are their last resort for badly needed help. Many helping professionals do heroic work and give well beyond the extra mile in time, effort, and energy. The errors made in treatment are the same errors that I have made as a practitioner and as a teacher. The need to correct these errors seems obvious, and this book is not written as a criticism of the helping professions, but with the hope that a more rational and research-guided practice will offer our clients the most effective, conscientious, and positive help we can humanly provide.

SUMMARY

In this chapter, two issues are discussed that require continuing recognition by the helping professions: the need for helping professionals to improve the quality of life in our communities, and treatment issues and client groups we seem to be disinclined to help. Men, older adults, and violent clients are three groups that seem underserved by the professional literature and by practice research in general. Material from work by Robert Putnam, Martin Seligman, and Dennis Saleebey is provided as evidence that our communities are often not safe and healthy places for our more needy clients. It is also suggested that our professional training programs work to improve the teaching of knowledge-guided practice and critical thinking to improve the quality of professional practice in the helping professions. Although this book is sometimes critical of professional practice, the men and women of the helping professions are commended for their diligent, energetic, and often highly effective work with clients in extreme difficulty.

Integrative Questions

1. Do you think it's fair to ask helping professional, who are already so busy and overworked, to take on yet other responsibilities, including social action and research?

2. Do you believe that America is the lonely and disconnected place Putnam portrays it to be? If not, how do you view the quality of the connections among diverse groups, family members, coworkers, and friends in America?

3. The author is very critical of the helping professions for not working with problems experienced by men. Is he implying gender bias in the helping professions and, if so, do you think it exists?

4. Not having better answers on how best to help abused children seems difficult to justify given the many people who work with abuse and the amount of money spent on treating child abuse in America. Do you think the problem has more to do with the complex nature of treating abuse or that many workers in the abuse field practice a type of treatment defined by mythology rather than fact?

5. Worker bias against certain groups, such as older adults and violent clients, is a troubling thought given the growing numbers of people who are older and the growing number of children and adolescents who exhibit violent tendencies. Why do you think workers avoid these two groups of people, or do they?

References

ABC News. (2002). Authentic happiness: Using our strengths to cultivate happiness. Retrieved October 14, 2002, from http://abcnews.go.com/sections/GMA/GoodMorningAmerica/GMA020904Authentic_happiness_excerpt.html

Elliott, D. S., Hamburg, B., & Williams, K. R. (1998). *Violence in American schools: A new perspective.* Boulder, CO: Center for the Study and Prevention of Violence.

Glicken, M. D. (in press). *The troubled lives of men.* Mahwah, NJ: Laurence Erlbaum.

Glicken, M. D. (2004). *Violent young children.* Boston: Allyn & Bacon/Longman.

Gupta, S. (2003, May 12). Why men die young. *Time, 161*(19), 84.

Kaplan, S. J., Pelcovitz, D., & Labruna, V. (1999, October). Child and adolescent abuse and neglect research: A review of the past 10 years. Part I: Physical and emotional abuse and neglect. *Journal of the American Academy of Child and Adolescent Psychiatry, 38*(10), 1214–1222.

Kesler, J. T. (2000). The healthy communities movement: Seven counterintuitive next steps. *National Civic Review, 89*(3), 271–284.

Lukefahr, J. L. (2001). Treatment of child abuse [Book review]. *Journal of the American Academy of Child and Adolescent Psychiatry, 40*(3), 383.

Morales, A. (1982). The Mexican American gang member: Evaluation and treatment. In R. Becerra, M. Karno, & J. Escolar (Eds.), *Mental health and Hispanic Americans: Clinical perspective* (pp. 144–165). New York: Grune & Stratton.

Oates, R. K., & Bross, D. C. (1995). What have we learned about treating child physical abuse? A literature review of the last decade. *Journal of Child Abuse & Neglect, 19,* 463–473.

Osofsky, H. J., & Osofsky, J. D. (2001, Winter). Violent and aggressive behaviors in youth: A mental health and prevention perspective. *Psychiatry, 64*(4), 285–295.

Putnam, R. D. (2000). *Bowling alone: The collapse and revival of American community.* New York: Simon & Schuster.

Rae-Grant, N., McConville, B. J., & Fleck, S. (1999, March). Violent behavior in children and youth: Preventive intervention from a psychiatric perspective. *Journal of the American Academy of Child and Adolescent Psychiatry, 38*(3), 235–241.

Roach, R. (2001). Where are the black men on campus? [Electronic version]. *Black Issues in Higher Education, 18*(6), 18–21.

Ryff, C. D., & Singer, B. (1998). The contours of positive human health. *Psychological Inquiry, 9,* 1–28.

Saleebey, D. (1996). The strengths perspective in social work practice: Extensions and cautions. *Social Work, 41*(3), 296–305.

Sandage, S. T., & Hill, P. C. (2001). The virtue of positive psychology: The rapprochement and challenge of an affirmative postmodern perspective. *Journal of the Theory of Social Behavior, 31*(3), 241–260.

Seligman, M. E. P. (2002). *Authentic happiness: New positive psychology to realize your potential for lasting fulfillment.* New York: Free Press.

Slater, E. (2003, June 23). Democratic candidates skewer Bush in appeal to black voters. *Los Angeles Times,* p. A13.

Steiner, H., & Stone, L. A. (1999, March). Introduction: Violence and related psychopathology. *Journal of the American Academy of Child and Adolescent Psychiatry, 38*(3), 232–234.

Stossel, S. (2000, September 21). Lonely in America [Interview with Robert Putnam]. *Atlantic Unbound.* Retrieved June 12, 2002, from www.theatlantic.com/unbound/interviews/ba2000-09-21.htm

Taylor, J. (1993). *Poverty and niches: A systems view.* Unpublished manuscript.

Waller, M. A., & Patterson, S. (2002, January/February). Natural helping and resilience in a Dine (Navajo) community. *Families in Society, 83*(1), 73–84.

About the Author

Morley D. Glicken, DSW, is the former Dean of the Worden School of Social Service in San Antonio, Texas; the founding director of the Master of Social Work Department at California State University, San Bernardino; the past Director of the Master of Social Work Program at the University of Alabama; and the former Executive Director of Jewish Family Service of Greater Tucson. He received his BA degree in social work with a minor in psychology from the University of North Dakota. He holds an MSW degree from the University of Washington and MPA and DSW degrees from the University of Utah. He is a member of Phi Kappa Phi Honorary Fraternity.

He published two books for Allyn & Bacon/Longman Publishers in 2002, *The Role of the Helping Professions in the Treatment of Victims and Perpetrators of Crime* (with Dale Sechrest) and *A Simple Guide to Social Research,* and two additional books for Allyn & Bacon/Longman in 2003, *Violent Young Children* and *Understanding and Using the Strengths Perspective.* He is currently completing two books, *Learning from Resilient People,* which will be published by Sage in 2005, and *Responding to the Troubled Lives of Men,* which will be published by Laurence Earlbaum in 2005. He has published more than 50 articles in professional journals and has written extensively for Dow Jones publications. He has held clinical social work licenses in Alabama and Kansas and is a member of the Academy of Certified Social Workers. He is currently Professor Emeritus in Social Work at California State University, San Bernardino, and the Executive Director of the Institute for Positive Growth: A Research, Treatment and Training Institute in Boise, Idaho. The institute's Web site may be found at http://www.morleyglicken.com, and the author may be reached online at mglicken@msn.com.

Index